KU-341-105

INTERNATIONAL
MIGRATION

and the

GOVERNANCE

of

RELIGIOUS
DIVERSITY

INTERNATIONAL MIGRATION

and the

GOVERNANCE

of

RELIGIOUS DIVERSITY

Edited by
Paul Bramadat and Matthias Koenig

School of Policy Studies, Queen's University
McGill-Queen's University Press
Montreal & Kingston • London • Ithaca

Copyright © 2009 School of Policy Studies, Queen's University at Kingston, Canada

SCHOOL OF
Policy Studies

Policy Studies Building
138 Union Street
Kingston, ON, Canada
K7L 3N6
www.queensu.ca/sps/

· All rights reserved. The use of any part of this publication for reproduction, transmission in any form or by any means (electronic, mechanical, photocopying, recording or otherwise), or storage in a retrieval system without the prior written consent of the publisher—or, in case of photocopying or other reprographic copying, a license from the Canadian Copyright Licensing Agency—is an infringement of the copyright law. Enquiries concerning reproduction should be sent to the School of Policy Studies at the address above.

Library and Archives Canada Cataloguing in Publication

International migration and the governance of religious diversity / edited by Paul Bramadat and Matthias Koenig.

(Migration and diversity ; 1)
Includes bibliographical references and index.
ISBN 978-1-55339-266-8 (pbk.).—ISBN 978-1-55339-267-5 (bound)

1. Religious pluralism—Political aspects—Western countries. 2. Religious pluralism—Social aspects—Western countries. 3. Religion and politics—Western countries. 4. Religion and sociology—Western countries. 5. Western countries—Emigration and immigration—Religious aspects. 6. Western countries—Emigration and immigration—Social aspects. 7. Religious minorities—Western countries. I. Bramadat, Paul, 1967- II. Koenig, Matthias III. Queen's University. School of Policy Studies IV. Series: Migration and diversity ; 1

JV6035.I58 2009   322'.1   C2008-908120-X

In partnership with

Cover photograph, "Sunday Walk," courtesy of Mareike Ahner.

Dedicated to our friends and colleagues in the Metropolis Project, and especially to John Biles, who has done so much to advance research and policy development on religion and migration.

Contents

Preface

Religious diversity is receiving growing attention among scholars and practitioners working in the field of migration. While a decade ago religion was almost absent in academic and policy debates about international migration and integration, there is now a steadily increasing stream of symposia and workshops, papers, journals, and books devoted to this topic. Religion certainly figured prominently in the program for the International Metropolis Conference in Vienna (2003). Among the events and publications, there was a session at the conference on religion and diversity in the international context that not only provided the occasion for the editors of this volume to meet, but became the starting point for a long-term engagement in deepening the transatlantic understanding of the significant role of religious factors in the phenomena associated with migration and integration. In our discussions, we quickly realized that despite growing awareness of the importance of religion in these areas of research and policy-making, there was a lack of comparative and policy-oriented research about the governance of religious diversity. While the questions of how nation-states regulate migration and integrate ethnic minorities have already received considerable attention in the literature, policy responses to religious diversity are still relatively understudied. When Jim Frideres (University of Calgary) and Paul Spoonley (Massey University), the editors of the new Metropolis book series, Migration and Diversity: Comparative Issues and International Comparisons, asked us to edit a volume related to international migration and the governance of religious diversity, it was with immediate and great enthusiasm that we embarked on this project.

The publication of our book would not have been possible without support from the International Metropolis Project, which provided much of the infrastructure for our research. As a platform for interaction among academics, policy-makers, and representatives of non-governmental agencies, the Metropolis network always kept the policy implications of our comparative analyses in the foreground of our work. In addition to our initial meeting in Vienna, we organized sessions at other Metropolis Conferences in Lisbon (2006) and Bonn (2008) where draft papers were presented and critiqued at large workshops attended by the editors, contributors, other scholars, and policy-makers.

This brings us to the debts and gratitude that always accumulate during a project of this kind. Next to our series editors, we are grateful to John Biles who has not only supported a great deal of research on the connection between religion, diversity, and migration but has also directly contributed to this research through his own keen insights. We would furthermore like to thank Nelly Joppich, Kerstin Rosenow, and Sabine Trittler at the University of Göttingen who at various stages helped us to bring all of these chapters and the index into a consistent format. Particular thanks go to Ellie Barton, certainly one of the most careful and sensitive editors with whom we have ever worked, as well as to Valerie Jarus from McGill-Queen's University Press who with great patience and prudence brought the book to its ultimate conclusion. We hope that this book will be of use to colleagues, students, and others interested in the dialectical relationship between migration and religion in a world in which our basic thinking about both phenomena is in great need of critical re-evaluation.

Paul Bramadat
University of Victoria, Canada

Matthias Koenig
University of Göttingen, Germany

March 2009

Chapter 1

Religious Diversity and International Migration: National and Global Dimensions

PAUL BRAMADAT

While human populations have always moved around the world in response to a wide variety of "push" and "pull" forces, it is arguably the case that the world's political and intellectual elites have never been as focused as they are now on the challenges associated with migration. These economic, political, and cultural challenges may transform not merely particular local contexts, but entire states. Migration is therefore, in many Western liberal democracies, rather predictably perceived as a threat that needs to be contained. The anxieties now more and more openly articulated in the West about the effects of migration are not new. However, what is fairly new is the prominence of religion in the recent debates about the changing nature of migrant-receiving societies and migrant cohorts.

This book explores the governance of religious diversity in Western societies. Our approach to the complex processes associated with this issue is decidedly interdisciplinary: we employ methods and insights from sociology, anthropology, ethnic studies, cultural studies, public policy studies, and religious studies. Other books focus on the relations between religion and politics from a cross-cultural and international perspective.[1] However, the present book approaches these questions in a uniquely focused and yet interdisciplinary manner by concentrating exclusively on the governance of religious diversity in the context of migration.

Given the enormous scope of the issues we address, the diverse backgrounds of the authors, and the unique national settings they examine, a thorough discussion in this introduction of all the themes and debates related to the governance of religious diversity is clearly impossible. It

International Migration and the Governance of Religious Diversity, eds. P. Bramadat and M. Koenig.
Montreal and Kingston: McGill-Queen's University Press, Queen's Policy Studies Series.
© 2009 The School of Policy Studies, Queen's University at Kingston. All rights reserved.

is necessary and possible, however, to introduce some of the broader political and academic concerns that animate this book and to discuss some of the common pitfalls in the study of religion within an international perspective. After these comments, I introduce the chapters and the structure of the book as a whole.

Migration and Religion: Emerging Issues

In the international arena, and especially in the North American, European, and Australian national contexts, it has become quite clear that religion is powerfully related to many of the most complex features of contemporary migration. After all, religions are often intimately involved in conflicts that lead people to flee from one country to another; they are involved in the forms of resistance people employ to articulate political views both in the "homeland" and in the "diaspora"; they are typically foundational features of the social structures of the minority communities in the host societies; they (especially different forms of Christianity) are often the recipients of historic state privileges that are emblematic of entrenched power disparities in immigrant-receiving societies; they help to create institutions that facilitate the transfer of money to family members in sending countries; and, of course, they inform the moral standards, aesthetic sensibilities, and social institutions that provide migrants with a sense of meaning and purpose both during migration and in their new settings.[2]

Although these aspects of religion have only recently become apparent to contemporary academic and government commentators, religion has always been intimately linked to migration and cultural diversity. For example, the ratio of Protestants, Roman Catholics, and Jews has historically been the cause of significant anxieties in the dominant North American (Protestant) population.

It is interesting, if also troubling, to note that in North America, popular nineteenth- and early twentieth-century views of Roman Catholic migrants and citizens—who were widely perceived by the dominant white Anglo-Protestant elite to be essentially unassimilable and unpatriotic (Casanova 2005; McGowan 2008)—presaged the contemporary anxieties in Europe and North America over Muslims. Similarly, concerns about the place of Jews in twentieth-century North American society reflected the hegemony of a particular Christian caricature of Jews that took on sinister forms in Europe in the 1930s and 1940s and resulted in anti-Semitic immigration and education policies in Canada and the United States that lasted until well after the Second World War.

Nonetheless, while Western societies have always had to respond in some way to changing religious demographics and to perceived outsiders, and while these responses have ranged from the xenophobic to the multicultural, the recent discussions around religion and migration are distinctive for several reasons.

First, the religions at the centre of these debates in the West are no longer mainly Christianity and Judaism, but now include Islam, Hinduism, Sikhism, Buddhism, and the cluster of traditions one might call Chinese religion (Paper and Thompson 1998). (As the chapters in this book demonstrate, it is clearly Islam that fosters the greatest anxieties among so many in the West; I shall return to this shortly.) Inasmuch as Christianity is relevant in these discussions, it is largely because it is still the dominant religion in European and North American societies, and thus it forms part of the backdrop against which contemporary debates must be understood. As well, debates sometimes surround Christianity because it is the common object of two related processes: the differentiation of some of our societies (and their concomitant official de-Christianization) on the one hand, and the de-Europeanization of many of the major Christian communities in the United States, Canada, the United Kingdom, and Australia (Bramadat and Seljak 2008; Ebaugh and Chafetz 2002; Weller 2005) on the other hand. The increasingly non-Christian (and non-European Christian) religious affiliations of the migrants now settling in Western societies have left policy-makers with significant challenges and opportunities. Moreover, as Permoser and Rosenberger explain in their chapter on the Austrian context, today's immigrants are also far more likely than previous generations to make use of the human rights laws, codes, and discourses at the heart of the Western societies to which they migrate (Koenig 2005; Soysal 1994).

Second, the salience of religion has become most obvious to scholars and policy-makers in the last 15 to 20 years, and especially since 2001. The role of the events of September 11th in the shifts we have seen in migration patterns and policies is extremely important, although it is imprudent to focus solely on these phenomena. While these events naturally attract the attention of many people interested in the various forces at work in contemporary migration and the current state of religion in the world, this book's authors remind us that global migration patterns and policies have also been profoundly influenced by the end of the colonial era in Africa and elsewhere, the end of the Cold War, the emergence of a single American superpower, the rapid modernization of the Chinese economy, and globalization.

Nonetheless, it is true that in the fall of 2001, those who expected that after the Cold War we would witness a period of historical denouement—or perhaps even an "end of history" (Fukuyama 1989, 1992)—that would lead to the final global triumph of liberal democracy were suddenly forced to face the perplexing power of religion in the world.[3] Many people began to seek ways of explaining and responding to the role of religion in the way people around the world addressed a number of issues: the centuries-old resentments and humiliations related to the legacy of colonialism and orientalism; the excesses of certain forms of corporate globalization; the reverberations or "blowback" of Western foreign policy adventures in the Middle East, Africa, and Central and South Asia; and the rise within the Muslim world of a relatively new and rigid form of Islam.[4] As the following chapters demonstrate, the religious and political maelstroms that followed September 11th certainly led to new approaches to both religion and migration in many of the countries the authors consider.[5] However, these new policies and attitudes must be interpreted in terms of the broader global environment and the individual societies articulating these approaches.

Third, the connection between religion and migration can only now be fully appreciated because unidirectional and simplistic versions of the secularization hypothesis have begun to break down to reveal the far more complicated realities this hypothesis previously obscured (Swatos 1999). As I discuss below, the beginning of the decline of this hypothesis as a reliable explanatory tool in the social sciences predates 2001 by roughly two decades.

While the increase in non-Christian populations in the West, the aftershocks of September 11th, and the decline of the vulgar version of the secularization hypothesis have made it obvious that scholars and policy-makers should pay close attention to the relationship between migration and religion, very little systematic and comparative work exists that might illuminate this connection and help policy-makers respond meaningfully to the world in which we live. The paucity of this kind of research is a significant political and intellectual problem; after all, religion is now at, or very near, the centre of so many of the world's most pressing and complicated issues. This book seeks to address this rather sizable gap in the academic and policy literatures and to guide future work on this topic.

Islam, Christianity, and Secularism

The meta-narrative of the "separation of church and state"—as either a de jure institutional reality or as a de facto cultural project unfolding under conditions of structural differentiation and pluralism—is certainly popular in Western states, even though it does not really describe the current formal relations between religions and the states in which they exist. As Veit Bader (2007a, 2007b) explains, such relations have always been characterized by heterogeneity. In fact, where the state does support or give preference to Christianity (as it does in England, Germany, Sweden, and Canada, just to name a few examples), one could argue that this privilege is increasingly symbolic in nature, and the church is likely to lose the political clout it once wielded. Later in this chapter, I contend (following Casanova 1994) that this does not necessarily mean that religious organizations, beliefs, and sensibilities will cease to exist or will no longer exert influence over a given society's public arena and political machinery. However, the differentiation evident within liberal democracies, and the tendency within these societies to reframe the relationship between religion and the state according to emerging pluralistic human rights norms are just two of the forces working against the continuation of the historically conferred privileges of establishment.

However, for many in the West, the debate over the accommodation of newcomer religions and religious individuals in established state and cultural structures seems regressive. After all, according to many Westerners, the place of Christianity in their societies was settled decades if not centuries ago. (We should always remember that while we are now grappling with the accommodation of a variety of religious claims and communities in the public realm, for centuries in the West, the real debate involved the negotiations between the two major forms of Christianity.) Since these new arrangements required Western Christian communities to accept, among other things, the differentiation of secular and religious spheres of activity and suasion (Casanova 1994), perhaps secular Westerners—and liberal Christians and Jews—resent, even if only on a subconscious level, being asked to participate in the debate about religion in the West. In the face of the currently heated debates around whether and how European and North American societies might integrate Islam and Muslims, the Christians, Jews, agnostics, and atheists who comprise the vast majority in these societies might well ask: Have we not solved this problem already? Have we not already accepted that Christianity—that religion as such—is neither the main protagonist in most liberal democratic institutions, nor diffused throughout our body politic as it once was? Even in the United States, where many people claim religion and politics are officially separated (but in practice are intricately enmeshed, as the Levitt and Hejtmanek chapter in this book demonstrates), new debates about religion—though they are mostly about Islam and fundamentalist Protestantism—disturb the liberal "consensus" around the privatization of religion. Regrettably, these debates sometimes evoke resentment and irrational prejudices in the face of even the most modest demands of religious groups.

It must be said that this debate is not merely a matter of Islam versus the West; in fact, the fundamental issue at stake is the place of religion in modern liberal democracies. Obviously, the carnage of September 11th is most immediately responsible for the public and political focus on Islam, but a slight change in political realities might have thrust another religion into the centre of the international spotlight.[6] It is not particularly difficult to explain historically or politically why a particular form of Islam—rather than Sikhism or Buddhism—has emerged as, or is imagined to be, the quintessential contemporary challenge to Western liberal democracy (Etzioni 2007; MacMillan 2002; Rashidi 2004; cf. Arat 2005). Nonetheless, even while one might agree that religion (rather than Islam) is the core issue in these debates, it is now impossible to deny that to many Europeans and North Americans, Islam has become a symbol of religious and cultural otherness, illiberalism, and pre-modernism,[7] and that therefore the existence of large Muslim populations throughout European and North American societies has become problematic for many people in the West. While the authors in this book situate the governance of religious diversity within the broadest possible context in the countries and theoretical debates they have been assigned, most of the chapters in this volume also reflect the virtually exclusive focus on Islam in contemporary national and international public discourse on religion and migration.

Multiple Modernities: Multiple Patterns of Secularism

One rationale behind this book is the emerging consensus among scholars, policy-makers, and members of non-governmental organizations that we need to compare and contrast the various ways states interact with or regulate religion (cf. Bader 2007a, 2007b). After all, an effective model of state governance must now, in addition to pursuing other supposedly secular objectives, seek to create the context in which members of ethnoreligious minority communities can negotiate identities for themselves in relation to the dominant national cultures. Such integration is easier said than done, and in each of the jurisdictions explored in this book, quite distinct challenges emerge. The contrast between these settings cannot be overstated. Indeed, in contrast to earlier theories of modernization, recent research on the relations between politics and religion, drawing on the literature on "multiple modernities" (Eisenstadt 2000), has aimed to identify distinctive patterns of secularism (Casanova 2006; cf. Milot's chapter in this book). It is important for us to pay attention to the profound differences between, for example, the post-1905 *laïcité*[8] in France and the older American tradition of non-establishment (i.e., the "tall wall of separation" between religion and the state), not to mention the situation in the United Kingdom in which the Queen is the Supreme Governor of the Church of England and Head of State. Although all three of these states are mature liberal democracies and all of them are related historically and geopolitically, the challenges created by religious diversity in each context are quite distinct.[9] If there is a multiplicity of ways that religious diversity is problematized (and sometimes resolved) in the United Kingdom, France, and the United States, one can anticipate the differences to be found, say, between Germany and Canada, or Australia and Denmark.

There are several reasons for these divergences. First, the individual historical paths followed by each of these states as they entered the contemporary era have set up distinctive social, political, and economic conditions that have, in turn, strongly influenced the way religious diversity is interpreted and governed by policy-makers in each state (Casanova 2007; Martin 1979; Rokkan 1970). Of course, the relationship between such seemingly secular historical conditions and the religious realities they are supposedly governing is dialectical, as we can see most explicitly in Canada, where the post-1763 awkward balance between English Protestant and French Roman Catholic interests that defined and to some extent still defines the religious landscape is perhaps as much a cause of the way Canadian social history has unfolded as it is an effect of this development (Bramadat and Seljak 2008).[10]

Second, each of the states we discuss in this book has its own history of contemporary migration, determined largely by post–World War II policies related to the resettlement of refugees, the needs for guest workers, population replenishment, economic development, and nation-building (Brubaker 1992; Casanova 2007; Favell 2001a, 2001b; Joppke 2005; Koenig 2005; Pauly 2004). As well, of course, the post-colonial reorganization of states once bound by colonial links (say, the United Kingdom and India/Pakistan on the one hand, and France and Algeria on the other hand) has greatly influenced the current state of ethnic and religious diversity in places such as London and Paris. As a result of these twentieth-century changes, these societies are characterized by unique demographic profiles regarding religious diversity. Such diversity should not discourage scholars from engaging in comparative analyses; rather, a familiarity with the historical path dependencies that characterize each setting should make such research more fruitful.

Third, the diversity within each of the states we consider is not a mathematical product of the historical religion-state relations or of twentieth-century immigration policies. Actually, it is increasingly obvious that the governance of religious diversity in each of these contexts is influenced not just by national forces but also by powerful global or transnational forces (Beyer 2006; Ebaugh and Chafetz 2002; Van der Veer 2001). Although this book's authors—especially Bader, Juergensmeyer, and Koenig—will discuss this relatively new feature of religious diversity in greater depth in the following chapters, I offer two examples that capture some of the forces at work in the new post-colonial world of globalized religious movements.

Consider the Danish cartoon scandal of 2006 that became symbolic for so many Muslims (and some non-Muslims) of the West's disdain toward Islam. It seems clear now that a full consideration of the solidarity of many Muslims in opposition to the publication (and then republication and broad circulation) of these intentionally provocative cartoons would need to go beyond merely the outrage about the cartoons themselves and take into account, among other factors, the level of frustration in the international *ummah* (Muslim community) regarding the miserable political situations in Iraq, Afghanistan, and Palestine/Israel; the putative incommensurability of Islam and Western secular democracies;[11] and the narrative or experience of frustration one finds among some orthodox or Islamist citizens in largely Muslim countries with regard to their own "westernized" Muslim leaders.[12] After all, the cartoon scandal was often framed among Muslims as one more humiliation suffered by Islam at the hands of the secularist West.[13]

If the cartoon debacle reflects the way communities separated by vast distances can now almost immediately mobilize themselves around real or perceived threats from the outside, another closely related phenomenon is what we might call the "internationalization of religious conflict" exemplified by the strife between the Indian government and Sikh separatists in the Punjab. The separatist movement in question is just one expression of the so-called communal tensions within the northernmost regions of South Asia that were exacerbated when some Sikhs felt excluded from the state-building and independence decisions preceding the British withdrawal from India in 1947. Much to the surprise of many Canadians (Sikhs and non-Sikhs), Canadian multiculturalism (as a policy, a tradition, and a reality) did not neutralize these conflicts once Sikhs came to Canada, even though the roots of the imbroglio are thousands of kilometres away. In fact, since the 1980s (and especially since the Indian government's Operation Bluestar in 1984), southern British Columbia has been marked by violence (even murder) and dissension directly related to political conflicts in the Punjab. These events culminated in June 1985 when Air India flight 182 exploded off the west coast of Ireland; on the same day in Narita, Japan, another bomb exploded and killed two baggage handlers as they loaded baggage onto another Air India flight bound for Bangkok. The destruction of flight 182[14] has inspired a deeper appreciation of the fact that understanding such events requires observers to move beyond finite national contexts (India and Canada, for example) to transnational spheres of action (i.e., to the Internet, to communities of displaced and disaffected Punjabis living in any number of states, and to the welter of post-colonial identity formation that can be observed in India, Britain, Pakistan, Canada, and elsewhere; see Vertovec 2000, 2001).

These examples illustrate that when seeking to understand and respond to a given local phenomenon, we need to remember that each event is embedded in a web of global movements and loyalties (cf. Beyer 1994). This methodological truism is more relevant today than ever before now that revolutions in air travel and communications have greatly accelerated the flow of people and information as well as the development of groups and movements. When analyzing local-yet-global events, the commentator has three possible foci to consider. One can focus on the immediate sphere, meaning the obvious local context in which the phenomenon in question occurs; one can delve into the virtual sphere, meaning the a-spatial, a-historical, and perhaps what semioticians might call the hyper-real context of the Internet; or one can explore the projected sphere, meaning the ethnic, political, and religious imaginary in which the phenomenon in question, which is "actually" happening in France or Australia, is simultaneously and perhaps principally a reflection of events in, say, India, Saudi Arabia, or Syria.

Religious Illiteracy and the Secularization Hypothesis

As important as it is to note the extent to which the integration of minority religions in each specific national setting is a function of both national and global forces, equally crucial is the recognition that many of the people ostensibly in charge of shaping public policies are as a whole woefully unprepared to factor religion into their deliberations. There is, within the elite levels of public discourse in Western societies, a pervasive "religious illiteracy" (Sweet 1997). In several Western contexts (e.g., Canada, the United States, the Netherlands), this illiteracy reflects the inadequate or non-existent public funding of dispassionate education about religion;[15] in other national contexts (such as in Austria) in which the state does fund religious education, this education is often delivered by and directed at religious insiders, and is therefore not necessarily conducive to fostering a broad familiarity with the world's (or that nation's) religious diversity. What is rare is strong political support for balanced and objective education about religion (although Micheline Milot's chapter in this book indicates that in the province of Quebec, culturally critical multifaith courses have been initiated; similar courses exist in the United Kingdom).

While there are as many reasons for religious illiteracy as there are Western contexts in which this particular problem is evident, it is worthwhile to reflect on the connection between the dearth of political interest in dispassionate education in so many liberal democratic states and the emergence in the last century of a near-consensus among so many Western intellectuals, journalists, lawyers, pundits, politicians, and activists with regard to religion. What undergirds this intellectual conformity with respect to religion is, of course, the enormous confidence that many in the educated elite shared and still share that religion, if it is not actually en route to extinction, is at least best suited to the private realm (cf. Casanova 2007).

The choice in so many Western societies to marginalize knowledge about religion bespeaks a value system with its own genealogy. The

Enlightenment and the Industrial Revolution combined to create intellectual and societal conditions that construed a technocratic knowledge as the *summum bonum* of any developed and enlightened society. Since Kant's *Religion within the Limits of Reason Alone* appeared in 1753, elite members of civil society and the scholarly world have increasingly framed religion, religious knowledge and, more recently, knowledge about religion, as peripheral, or at least as suitable for a realm of discourse and practice not reliant (as philosophy and science supposedly are) on reason, objectivity, and certainty. Lincoln (2003, 58) explains that, after Kant, "religion is thus not overthrown altogether, but given a privileged, if marginal sphere of activity. Insofar as educated European elites were persuaded by these arguments, a new regime of truth took shape, which gave rise to a new type of culture" (cf. Casanova 2007).

There is no doubt that the emphasis on a technical, rationalist, and humanist mode of knowledge and the concomitant marginalization of most forms of knowledge related to religion has had significant and often salutary consequences for European and North American intellectual, scientific, and commercial development. However, in many cases, this historic shift has had the unintended consequence of virtually guaranteeing that many of us are now unable to understand the religious dimensions of a great many of the major political events that have so deeply etched our societies for the last several decades.

Of course, within this post-Kantian elite community of consensus regarding religion, one finds agnostic, atheistic, and deeply religious people, all of whom might disagree vehemently on what Paul Tillich called matters of ultimate concern but who generally share what Lincoln describes as a "minimalist" vision of the place of religion in social life (2003, 59). According to minimalists, however important religion might be to oneself, one's family or one's religious community, the eventual hegemony of the Enlightenment vision of reality within elite sectors of Western societies has meant that religious institutions in these countries have agreed to behave as though "religion" and "the state" named two incommensurable spheres of activity and horizons of meaning. Each of these spheres of activity should be governed by different people, rules, and principles, and each of them must leave the other alone, except on ceremonial occasions when the latter wishes to borrow the supernatural aura of the former (as when officials use a prayer to solemnize an event), or in political situations in which the former seeks cooperation, privileges, and concessions from the latter (as when religious groups wish to benefit from tax relief, zoning regulations, and constitutional protection).

Closely associated with this minimalist sensibility is one of the most widely familiar of all sociological theories: the secularization hypothesis.

This hypothesis is rooted in the nineteenth century and can be traced through the work of Auguste Comte, Emile Durkheim, Max Weber, Karl Marx, Sigmund Freud, and others. Each of these intellectuals in different ways reflected his society's (or at least his social stratum's) belief that religion—especially in its maximalist (Lincoln 2003, 59) form in which it pervaded the whole society, including the state—would not only eventually shrink in the face of the development of complex, rationalized, and increasingly differentiated democracies, but ought to do so.

Most readers will know that the simple version of this theory has been challenged over the past 15 or 20 years by some of its earlier advocates (Berger 2000), by stalwart critics who never succumbed to the theory's gilded promises (Baum 1975), by a paucity of unequivocal evidence, and by people such as José Casanova (1994) who have helped to disentangle the various social processes that have become conflated in our discussions about this concept. The debate over the secularization hypothesis continues to rage among sociologists of religion, and this is clearly not the place to engage or enumerate the various schools of thought on this matter.[16]

However, it is worth noting that most social scientists would agree that in most liberal democracies, religion has become or is becoming disentangled from education, health care, social services, the law, and government such that if in a public arena one wants to persuade another of the validity of one's argument about health care or a legal claim, one knows that one cannot easily rely on an explicitly religious argument (Habermas 2005).[17] In fact, if one makes use of such logic, one is very likely to be viewed with suspicion as an apostate from rationality. The expectation among liberal minimalists was that erecting barriers to the use of explicitly religious arguments in the public arena would make the public spaces in liberal democratic societies more inclusive of non-Christians, minority Christians, agnostics, and atheists.

The forces described in the preceding paragraph need not necessarily lead to an extensive or permanent "privatization of religion," or even to a diminishment of the overall influence of religion in a given society. After all, as Casanova observes, religion has not disappeared from the lives of individuals or from societies. As evidence of this, in his *Public Religions in the Modern World* (1994), he discusses four sites—Spain, Poland, Brazil, and the United States—in which religion has emerged as a vehicle of decidedly contemporary social change. His examples are Western, but all over the world, religion continues to be of personal and political salience. This is not to deny the massive changes we can see throughout the Western world in the nature and influence of religion, nor the kinds of losses (in terms of membership, attendance, identification, and financial contributions) mainstream Christians in the West have been reporting over the past several decades. Yet Casanova's work reminds us not to be surprised by the persistence of public religion in the modern world (cf. Taylor 2007).

It may well be true, as Asad (1993, 2003) contends, that the ideas associated with secularism as an ideology and secularization as a theory or hypothesis need to be understood as contingent products of the often orientalist, ethnocentric, and capitalist sensibilities embedded in the Western societies in which this cluster of ideologies and ideas was born in the first place.[18] It may also be the case that the notion that religion might play a constructive public role in liberal democratic and secularist regimes of knowledge and power presupposes both a certain variety of religion (one that supports the supposedly self-evident and worthwhile objectives of a form of liberal democracy deeply associated with capitalism) and a certain definition of "the secular"; this reminds us that when we discuss issues associated with both "religion" and "the secular," we need to be extremely cognizant of the incursion of unintended ideological or theoretical presuppositions.

So, the grand narratives of secularization, progress, rationalization, and so forth may not reflect any Hegelian teleological spirit at work in Western civilization. Nonetheless, these stories are still potent and ubiquitous quite apart from the fact that they may not accurately reflect what is really developing on the proverbial "ground" or what has shaped our societies until now. As such, we need to acknowledge these stories—here one might invoke the term *myths* in both its senses as a false belief and a story that provides meaning and purpose—as stubbornly real and yet as realities we can (with some effort) problematize in order to enable a more nuanced reading of social reality.[19]

In fact, I would surmise that even after so many studies and political realities have cast aspersions on this hypothesis, and even after most sociologists who study religion seriously have abandoned the simple version of this hypothesis, the assumptions emanating from it are probably as influential as they have ever been in international and national elite discourses. While most social scientists and humanists would reject the rigid positivism associated with the most basic ideological and prescriptive form of the secularization hypothesis, when our academic colleagues are forced to think, speak, and write about religion, one can still often observe a deep positivistic disposition toward the issue.

To return to a claim I made at the beginning of this section, because of the enduring popularity of this particular meta-narrative, the elite classes out of which scholars, policy-makers, journalists, lawyers, business people, and other leaders are drawn in the West have been rendered quite incapable of responding meaningfully to some of the most complicated, troubling, and dynamic events in the world today. The failure to take religion seriously and to think creatively as we imagine the shape the world will take in the next several decades has serious ramifications.

After Essentialism

Two habits of mind bedevil efforts to resolve the challenges posed by religious diversity and new patterns of migration in liberal democracies, and both are evident in the common ways religion is constructed in both elite and popular discourses. It is increasingly common within elite academic and policy-making circles for conversants to be vigilant about a crude ethnocentric form of essentialism with regard to religion. Although the public awareness of the evils of racism and other forms of discrimination grew after the Second World War and the broad promulgation of the discourse of human rights, discrimination has continued to plague Western societies. More recently, after September 11th, acts of anti-Semitism and Islamophobia increased; furthermore, discrimination appears to be on the rise especially in certain parts of Europe with regard to Muslims (Casanova 2007; Seljak 2007; Weller 2005).[20] This variety of essentialism—in which a particular religion (in the West, the religion in question is usually Islam) is identified in popular and sometimes in elite discourse with violence, ignorance, and evil—is the attitude that "multiculturalist" or even "assimilationist" public policies related to religious diversity seek to diminish or at least contain. Arguably, in political contexts informed by human rights norms, codes, and laws—and the liberal democracies featured in this book are arguably so informed—blanket condemnation of entire religious groups on the basis of some usually malignant essential quality the group is supposed to embody is considered socially as well as legally inappropriate. Western states have in the past decade or so sought ways to study and combat such views through laws, advertising campaigns, and public education (cf. Koenig 2007; Koenig and de Guchteneire 2007; Seljak 2007; Weller 2005).[21] Since this form of ethnocentric essentialism is dealt with by several authors in this book, I would like now to turn my attention briefly to the opposite tendency to be found in public discourse about religion and diversity in national as well as in international discourse.

Political and public discourse about religion at the local, national, and international levels typically relies on a highly formalized mode of communication, as though participants have all agreed to communicate in a language that is not native to anyone so as to avoid offending anyone. This style of communication about religion may be well-intended, and it may at times help to avert fissures between individuals, religious communities, and nations, but it makes it rather difficult for people to understand one another in a meaningful way. For example, so many interpretations of the role of religion in a given social movement or political event begin with the claim or the assumption that a "problematic" person's or a "problematic" group's stated religious motivations are in fact merely smokescreens for their true political motivations. Such claims reflect the hegemony of a distinctly modern Western narrative in which religion is understood to be, in essence, a benevolent personal force relating one to the universe and perhaps to one's "higher self." In this modern narrative, autonomy and authenticity (Taylor 1991)—rather than, say, obedience to a text, familial loyalty, or attachment to an ethnic, class, or religious group—are assumed to be the definitive features of full humanity (cf. Asad 2003) and authentic religiosity.[22]

In the style of communication we can witness in public conversations about religion, religious conversants often transform themselves into rather jolly caricatures of themselves or of their religious communities. When social movements articulated "in the name of [insert religion here]" turn to violence, the caricatured representative is expected to—and almost invariably will—contend the following: [insert religion here] is actually essentially peaceful and altruistic but has regrettably been "hijacked" by a minuscule number of evil, insane, or resentful people whose "real" motives are economic and political. Such claims are themselves products of a particular liberal approach to religion that sees it as essentially private, benevolent, and instrumental. Such an approach would strike many of the world's religious people (today and throughout most of human history) as completely absurd and divorced from a far more heterogeneous reality.

It is probably not an accident that this particular understanding of religion that is so common within the elite, cosmopolitan sectors of liberal democratic societies fits quite well into consumerist and individualist cultures in which religion is often framed as—or is only allowed to be—a matter of private choice. Thus essentialized as individualistic, apolitical, and perhaps finally a commodity subject to the vagaries of other individual choices, religion becomes a sweet but sometimes hapless hand-servant to the true master-forces of our society: the economy, politics, and culture.

Once a state agency or an academic commentator—acting on the basis of this very limited, liberal understanding of religion—defines a religious group or movement in these terms, the problematic group is in effect tamed and made knowable by the dominant group. Any stated religious motivations of the group or movement in question can be bracketed as expressions of "real"—that is, economic, political, or cultural—dissent. So, to take a hypothetical example, once loud street demonstrations by hijab-wearing (or green-bandana-wearing) anti-war activists holding the Qur'an and placards aloft can be attributed simply to poverty or to a petulant refusal to integrate into the host society, the group seems, momentarily, to be more assimilable, less other, if only because Westerners can identify with their ostensibly secular political motivations and perhaps sympathize with their material deprivation. This naïve reductionism, at the very least, brings into the spotlight of public discourse the material conditions linked to (but not necessarily determinative of) a given religious movement or migrant community. As such, one might consider this a positive side-effect of this discourse.

However, it is rather problematic to treat the religious claims of a group as though they in fact represent political, economic, or idiosyncratic objectives (rooted nonetheless in the supposedly common well of human values and motivations) that are secreted into public discourse in the Trojan horse of religion. Indeed, for many of the fundamentalist or maximalist-oriented religious traditions now problematized by Western elites, religion is not merely a private or idiosyncratic sphere of consciousness but rather the overarching canopy under which all of human life takes place and has meaning (Bramadat 2000; Juergensmeyer 2002; Lincoln 2003).

There is no reason to believe that "such people" are immature subjects incapable of seeing and employing distinctions between religious, economic, and political categories of thought and behaviour when they engage in matters of concern. Rather, in general and in practice, religion functions quite naturally in their lives as the dominant orienting force, and all other forces (politics, culture, economics) are understood as epiphenomena of this reality-grounding Archimedean point, in much the same way that a highly secular European or North American might experience the world to be an expression of natural forces, socio-economic shifts, *realpolitik*, and his or her own will to power. There is no need in either case for subjects to try to look at the world as if it might be (in the first case) God's creation and the battleground between Satan and God, or (in the second case) a consequence of natural forces and the will to power. For people firmly ensconced in these subcultures, these basic orientations are the most important a priori foundations of their perceptions.

As Taylor (2007) observes, the exclusively humanistic perspective is certainly the newer of these two orientations and the one most closely tied to the modern liberal project, but both are now at home in the contemporary world. Moreover, while both an exclusive humanism and an exclusive theism may be totalizing systems of meaning and purpose, they are not nearly as impenetrable as their most zealous proponents may make them seem: after all, many avowedly secular/atheist students also espouse "new age" views about fate and illiberal views about women and minorities, and many of the avowedly fundamentalist Christians I have studied also embrace many features of liberal scientific culture (Bramadat 2000). An openness to exploring both the ways each perspective can become naturalized for members of the same society and the ways each perspective can prompt a high degree of engagement with putatively antagonistic worldviews is a prerequisite to understanding (and creating policies to address) the religious and ethnic pluralism that characterizes the contemporary West.

The philosophical perspective that makes it difficult to see oneself— but rather easy to see another—as a product of a contingent set of historical forces represents a significant obstacle to productive interactions between religious communities and the ostensibly secular, liberal democratic states in which they sometimes find themselves. In the cases in which a state (or an ostensibly secular representative of the liberal minimalism described above) faces a religious individual or group, experience tells us that we are likely to see an enactment of one of two equally erroneous fallacies: (a) that all people are at root motivated by the same things (a desire for liberty, romantic love, wealth, human rights, and the pursuit of happiness, for example); and the ultimate corollary (b) that liberals cannot communicate meaningfully with people who appear not to be motivated by these supposedly common values.

What emerges as important here is the need for us to develop the capacity among policy-makers, journalists, scholars, and other elite members of society to enter into—or even just to imagine—conversations with people who might frame the world in a manner that is utterly different from those more closely identified with that group's norms. In fact, more important than merely entering into such conversations is the manner in which one operates within these discussions: we can make no progress toward understanding the religious diversity that current migration patterns have produced until we jettison the polite caricatures that we have been accustomed to using when discussing religion. Arguably, it is not only "we" liberal democrats or secularists who might wish to abandon one-dimensional portraits of the religious others we hope to engage; international public discourse would also be enriched if the main subjects of this book—the maximalists, the "illiberal moderates" (Etzioni 2007), the migrants and minorities—allowed their own self-presentations to reflect more accurately the heterogeneity evident within their religious and ethnic communities.

Book Outline

The book is divided into three sections. In the first section, the authors examine some of the theoretical and practical matters associated with the study of religion and migration in liberal democratic societies.

The second section consists of in-depth case studies of the way particular countries have responded to religious diversity. The countries we have selected—France, the United States, the United Kingdom,

Australia, Canada, Austria, and Switzerland—were chosen because they have been the sites of many of the most complex and difficult challenges in the past decade. These, together with Germany and the Netherlands, are also the countries in which we are likely to see some of the most complex responses to religious diversity in the future. We asked the authors in this second section to consider their chosen subjects within the broad parameters of a common template. Accordingly, all authors give background information on the religious composition of the country in question as well as on the institutional arrangements of "church and state" (though in some cases "mosque and state" and "synagogue and state" relations are also formally articulated). As well, the authors introduce the country's immigration patterns and the religious background of migrants, including the most important and most current statistical/demographic data available. Furthermore, the authors focus on selected policy problems and controversies that they deem to be of greatest significance in the country they are discussing. In some cases, for example, the authors examine the national and international public debates associated with well-known events (such as the debates over the hijab in France), but in other cases, authors may choose to focus on incidents that will be unfamiliar to readers but which might more adequately exemplify a state's approach to religious diversity. The final task for these authors is to situate their analyses within larger international debates on changing integration policies, political challenges, and demographic changes.

The third section of this book includes chapters in which the authors reflect comparatively on some of the themes evident throughout the other chapters, some of the implications of these themes, and some possible avenues for future research that might extend the analyses provided in this book. Thus, Matthias Koenig disentangles some causal complexities that account for how different nation-states respond to religious diversity and discusses the inherently dynamic character that characterizes such responses. Will Kymlicka discusses, in normative perspective, the contrast between old immigration countries with a tradition of denominationalism and new immigration countries with more corporatist religious cultures—warning us against easy transfer of "best practices" across national contexts.

Conclusion: The Theatre of Politics

The development of political and intellectual discourses at the national and global levels is perhaps more influenced by the compelling performance of moral and ideological claims than by the cut and thrust of rational debate regarding moral and political problems (Juergensmeyer 2002; cf. Goffmann 1959; Turner 1969). The current vilification of "the West" (read "the United States") by Vladimir Putin's supporters, George

W. Bush's "mission accomplished" speech and photo opportunity aboard the USS Abraham Lincoln in 2003, and passionate American and British claims at the United Nations Security Council about "weapons of mass destruction" in Iraq powerfully exemplify political theatre in the sense that each of these performances leans on caricatures of putative adversaries, "cosmic war" discourses (Juergensmeyer 2002), and perverse distortions of the realities in question. As well, of course, these events illustrate political theatre in the more descriptive sense that they attracted massive audiences, influenced public opinion, and created discursive sea changes at both the elite and popular levels of the societies involved.

Similarly, the events of September 11th were immensely powerful and were later used as the backdrop for dramatic performances of patriotism, sacrifice, and the threat of pathological "evil-doers" to "freedom-loving" members of liberal democratic societies. So powerful were these kinds of relatively opportunistic performances that the proverbial actors, directors, and producers involved were able to justify two wars, invade two countries, reorient the world's largest economy, alter the securitization regimes of many states, and ignore several other human rights atrocities around the world.[23]

It is, of course, deeply problematic to find some benefit in the maelstrom and aftermath of September 11th (here I refer not just to events in the United States but also to those related events in the United Kingdom, Spain, Iraq, the Philippines, Bali, Pakistan, India, and Afghanistan). Nonetheless, it does strike me that this traumatic episode offers us an opportunity to reconsider common views of the development of Western civilization and the role of religion therein. Certainly the events of the past decade have reminded those of us in the West that religion continues to be a profound source of motivation for people throughout the world and, moreover, that the "occidental rationalism" described by Weber demonstrably lacks universal appeal well over a century after it was identified. The intractable bonds between the economic, political, cultural, and religious spheres have never been as apparent as they are now, and one can no longer look at any of these forces in isolation. The media and other contributors to public discourse have often not clearly articulated the extent to which we are observing clashes between "minimalist" and "maximalist" models for the relationship of religion and societies—that is, clashes within civilizations, not clashes of civilizations. It is the conviction of this book's authors that those observers who are able to appreciate this facet of the conflict in national societies as well as at the global level will be in a better position to comprehend and respond to the increasingly complex and dynamic world in which we all live.

Notes

1. For a review of these issues, see Jelen and Wilcox (2002); cf. Asad (2003); Beyer (1994); Byrnes and Katzenstein (2006); Casanova (1994); Cesari (2004); Esposito and Watson (2000); Haar and Busuttil (2003); Juergensmeyer (2005); Metcalf (1996); Norris and Inglehart (2004); Pauly (2004); Robert (1995); Rudolph and Piscatori (1997); Vertovec and Peach (1997); Warner and Wittner (1998).
2. See Bramadat and Seljak (2005, 2008); Chong (1998); Ebaugh and Chafetz (2002); Eck (2002, 2003); Foley and Hoge (2007); Menjivar (2003); Van Tubergen (2006); Warner and Wittner (1998).
3. Terry Eagleton writes: "Those who complacently proclaim the End of History, or at least were in the habit of doing so until the demolition of the World Trade Centre, mean to announce the permanent triumph of capitalism; but it is exactly this crass triumphalism which has stirred' the revolt of the masses in the Muslim world, thus launching a whole new historical epoch. The closing down of history has only succeeded in opening it up again" (2005, 106).
4. On these forces, see Ali (2002); Esposito (2002); Juergensmeyer (2002); Klein (2002, 2007); MacMillan (2002); Rashidi (2004); Said (1979); and Shiva (2005).
5. See, for example, Zolberg's (n.d.) "Guarding the Gates in a World on the Move."
6. Of course, the power of Christianity in recent American political life and the role of Hinduism in Indian nationalism are the subjects of intense national and international debate and study, but it is probably the case that it is Islam that is understood in the West as the most basic and most internationally salient of these instances; it is certainly the case that in the West it is framed as such.
7. See the European Monitoring Centre on Racism and Xenophobia (2006); Panagopoulos (2006); and Pew Research Center (2006, 2007).
8. The famous "Loi du 9 décembre 1905 concernant la séparation des Églises et de l'État" formally articulated the separation of church and state in France. For example, the second article of this famous law reads: "La République ne reconnaît, ne salarie, ne subventionne aucun culte."
9. Asad (2003, 6) writes: "Thus, although the secularism of these three countries has much in common, the mediating character of the modern imaginary in each of them differs significantly. The notion of toleration between religiously defined groups is differently inflected in each. There is a different sense of participation in the nation and access to the state among religious minorities in the three countries."
10. For European examples of similar linkages, consider Bermeo and Nord (2000); Casanova (1994); Ertman (2000); Pauly (2004); and Rokkan (1970).
11. Among others, Ayaan Hirsi Ali, Daniel Pipes, David Bukay, Bernard Lewis, and Samuel Huntington have argued that the current conflict indicates a

"clash of civilizations" (Huntington 1993). Conversely, leaders such as Ayatollah Mohammad Taghi Mesbah Yazdi, Sheikh Ahmed Yasin, Osama bin Laden, Mahmoud Ahmadinejad, Saalih bin Al Fawzan, and other Salafists and Islamists have argued that on September 11th, we witnessed the consequences of the West's debauched, narcissistic, imperialistic ways. See Appleby (1997), Bukay (2007), Rippin (2005), and Said (1979) on this notion of fundamental antipathy.

12. Commenting on some of the unintended complications associated with the colonial European effort to export the nation-state formation, Lincoln (2003, 64) writes: "Most volatile of all is the situation created when Europeans bequeathed a state committed to the project of minimalizing the role of religion in culture to post-colonial elites. Having internalized Euroamerican models and ideals as part of the self-fashioning that prepares them for power, such people may embrace a liberal understanding of 'secularization' as a key element of modernity. That notwithstanding, they rule over and are accountable to largely religious nations."

13. Similarly, the riots that broke out in parts of France in 2005 must be interpreted not merely in terms of the history of French secularism, or in terms of protests against French policies on employment, crime, immigration, and naturalization. These are important factors, of course, but these troubling events must also be understood in light of struggles within postcolonial Algeria regarding the role of Islam within that state's society, and a sense within the global *ummah* that France is a kind of test case for the way a modern secularist liberal state might (or might not) integrate Muslim citizens.

14. Until the September 11th attacks in the United States, these Air India bombings were the worst terrorist attacks involving an airplane, with a total of 329 dead, 280 of whom were Canadian citizens.

15. On this topic, see Bramadat and Seljak (2005, 178-200), the journal *Religion and Education*, the Religion and Public Education Resource Centre website (http://www.csuchico.edu/rs/rperc/), and the American Academy of Religion's Publications on Religion and Public Education website (http://www.aarweb.org/profession/ris/publications.asp).

16. cf. Asad 2003; Baum 1975; Berger 2000; Bruce 2002; Casanova 1994; Martin 1979; Norris and Inglehart (2004); Swatos 1999.

17. For a critique of this assertion, see Asad (2003, 181-201) and Casanova (2006).

18. Asad writes: "I am arguing that 'the secular' should not be thought of as the space in which *real* human life gradually emancipates itself from the controlling power of religion and thus achieves the latter's relocation. It is this assumption that allows us to think of religion as 'infecting' the secular domain or as replicating within it the structure of theological concepts. The concept of 'the secular' today is part of a doctrine called secularism. Secularism doesn't simply insist that religious practice and belief be

confined to a space where they cannot threaten political stability or the liberties of the 'free-thinking' citizens. Secularism builds on a particular conception of the world ('natural' and 'social') and of the problems generated by that world" (Asad 2003, 191; cf. Taylor 2007).

19. An anecdote reflects this challenge: I recently had a conversation with a highly educated Nigerian-Canadian civil servant, in which he told the story of how he was a Pentecostal when he was in Africa, "with all the hand-waving eee-oooh, eee-oooh, aaahs." His faith lasted until he met a Dutch colleague at a Canadian graduate school. The colleague repeatedly argued against the Nigerian's religious sensibilities, saying, according to my friend, "Come on, you have to stop believing in this nonsense. It's totally backwards." The civil servant noted that his Dutch friend's strong arguments helped him to see how his religious sensibilities were really "the views of peasants and illiterates." In order to problematize his unidirectional notion of secularization, I pointed out that rates of religious observance, identification, and orthodoxy in the United States were quite consistently high. To this he replied: "Well, those high numbers don't really reflect what people actually believe." Similarly, for most of my own students, even large, relatively nuanced surveys of their own country's religious life-ways, evidence from abroad, and their own lived experience of the combination of vitality and decline that characterize contemporary religion cannot dispel this particular theory's common-sense appeal. So, here we have a blind faith in what we can call the "vulgar" secularization hypothesis, an unassailable secularism in which religion is aligned with ignorance and underdevelopment and will inexorably recede in the face of knowledge and modernization.

20. See also Joppke's (2005) and Brubaker's (2001) claims that the non-discriminatory immigration practices adopted in the past several decades by many liberal democracies may be subject to abrogation.

21. Casanova (2007, 64) writes: "Liberal secular Europeans tend to look askance at such blatant expressions of racist bigotry and religious intolerance coming from nationalists and religious conservatives. But when it comes to Islam, secular Europeans also tend to reveal the limits and prejudices of modern secularist toleration. One is not likely to hear among liberal politicians and secular intellectuals explicitly xenophobic or anti-religious statements.... The controversies over the Muslim veil in so many European societies ... may be an extreme example of illiberal secularism. But in fact one sees similar trends of restrictive legislation directed at immigrant Muslims in liberal Holland."

22. Inherent to most modern liberal democracies is a mythology centred on the ineluctable drive to individual autonomy and reason that supposedly characterizes human nature. Habermas (2005, 5) writes: "The assumption of common human reason is the epistemic base for the justification of a secular state which no longer depends on religious legitimation." See Delanty (1997) and Casanova (2004) for comments on the "teleological

philosophy of history" (Casanova 2004, 13) still evident in Habermas's comments on a post-secular Europe.

23. Part of this drama required the principal players to universalize the shock and changes to Western societies. That is, they were required to exclaim that this was the day "the world changed" (Bramadat 2005). Indeed, something powerful and horrendous did occur that day, and certainly it had reverberations throughout the world, but of course randomness, violence, terror, and the death of loved ones are, for some people, all too familiar experiences. No doubt many people felt that Chomsky (2001) ought not to have mentioned so soon after September 11th that strictly in terms of the number of victims, this event represented far less of a loss than many others (such as the roughly 25,000 people who die of hunger each day). Nevertheless, his comments highlighted the problems associated with the claim—or the cliché—that not just Western but indeed world history had utterly changed that day.

References

Ali, T. 2002. *The Clash of Fundamentalisms: Crusades, Jihads, and Modernity*. London: Verso.

Appleby, R.S., ed. 1997. *Spokesmen for the Despised: Fundamentalist Leaders of the Middle East*. Chicago: University of Chicago Press.

Arat, Y. 2005. *Rethinking Islam and Liberal Democracy*. Albany, NY: SUNY Press.

Asad, T. 1993. *Genealogies of Religion: Discipline and Reasons of Power in Christianity and Islam*. Baltimore: Johns Hopkins University Press.

— 2003. *Formations of the Secular: Christianity, Islam, and Modernity*. Stanford, CA: Stanford University Press.

Bader, V. 2007a. "The Governance of Islam in Europe: The Perils of Modelling." *Journal of Ethnic and Migration Studies* 33(6):871-86.

— 2007b. *Secularism or Democracy? Associational Governance of Religious Diversity*. Amsterdam: Amsterdam University Press.

Baum, G. 1975. *Religion and Alienation*. New York: Paulist Press.

Berger, P. 2000. *The Desecularization of the World*. Grand Rapids, MI: Eerdmans and the Ethics and Public Policy Centre.

Bermeo, N. and P. Nord, eds. 2000. *Civil Society Before Democracy: Lessons from Nineteenth-Century Europe*. Lanham, MD: Rowman and Littlefield.

Beyer, P. 1994. *Religion and Globalization*. London: Sage Publications.

— 2006. *Religions in Global Society*. New York: Routledge.

Bramadat, P. 2000. *The Church on the World's Turf: An Evangelical Christian Group at a Secular University*. New York: Oxford University Press.

— 2005. "Religion, Social Capital and 'the Day that Changed the World.'" *Journal of International Migration and Integration* 6:201-18.

Bramadat, P. and D. Seljak, eds. 2005. *Religion and Ethnicity in Canada*. Toronto: Pearson Longman.

— 2008. *Christianity and Ethnicity in Canada.* Toronto: University of Toronto Press.

Brubaker, R. 1992. *Citizenship and Nationhood in France and Germany.* Cambridge, MA: Harvard University Press.

— 2001. "The Return of Assimilation? Changing Perspectives on Immigration and Its Sequels in France, Germany, and the United States." *Ethnic and Racial Studies* 24:531-48.

Bruce, S. 2002. *God Is Dead: Secularization in the West.* Oxford: Blackwell.

Bukay, D. 2007. "Can There Be an Islamic Democracy?" *Middle East Quarterly* 14(2): 71-79.

Byrnes, T.A. and P.J. Katzenstein, eds. 2006. *Religion in an Expanding Europe.* Cambridge: Cambridge University Press.

Casanova, J. 1994. *Public Religions in the Modern World.* Chicago: University of Chicago Press.

— 2004. "Religion, European Secular Identities, and European Integration." *Eurozine.* Accessed 14 October 2008 at http://www.eurozine.com/articles/2004-07-29-casanova-en.html

— 2005. "Catholic and Muslim Politics in Comparative Perspective." *Taiwan Journal of Democracy* 1:89-108.

— 2006. "Rethinking Secularization: A Global Comparative Perspective." *The Hedgehog Review* 8:7-22.

— 2007. "Immigration and the New Religious Pluralism: A EU/US Comparison." In *Democracy and the New Religious Pluralism,* ed. T. Banchoff. New York: Oxford University Press.

Cesari, J. 2004. *When Islam and Democracy Meet: Muslims in Europe and in the United States.* New York: Palgrave.

Chomsky, N. 2001. *9-11.* New York: Seven Stories.

Chong, K.H. 1998. "What It Means To Be Christian: The Role of Religion in the Construction of Ethnic Identity and Boundary among Second-Generation Korean Americans." *Sociology of Religion* 59:259-86.

Delanty, G. 1997. "Habermas and Occidental Rationalism: The Politics of Identity, Social Learning, and the Cultural Limits of Moral Universalism." *Sociological Theory* 15(1):30-59.

Eagleton, T. 2005. *Holy Terror.* Oxford: Oxford University Press.

Ebaugh, H.R. and J. Chafetz. 2002. *Religion Across Borders: Transnational Religious Networks.* Walnut Creek, CA: AltaMira Press.

Eck, D.L. 2002. *A New Religious America: How a "Christian Country" Has Become the World's Most Religiously Diverse Nation.* San Francisco, CA: Harper.

— 2003. *Encountering God: A Spiritual Journey from Bozeman to Banaras.* Boston: Beacon Press.

Eisenstadt, S.N. 2000. "Multiple Modernities." *Daedalus* 129(1):1-29.

Ertman, T. 2000. "Liberalization, Democratization and the Origins of a 'Pillarized' Civil Society in Nineteenth-Century Belgium and the Netherlands." In *Civil Society Before Democracy: Lessons from Nineteenth-Century Europe,* ed. N. Bermeo and P. Nord. Lanham, MD: Rowman and Littlefield.

Esposito, J.L. 2002. *Unholy War: Terror in the Name of Islam.* New York: Oxford University Press.

Esposito, J. and M. Watson, eds. 2000. *Religion and Global Order.* Cardiff: University of Wales.

Etzioni, A. 2007. *Security First: For a Muscular, Moral Foreign Policy.* New Haven, CT: Yale University Press.

European Monitoring Centre on Racism and Xenophobia. 2006. "Muslims in the European Union: Discrimination and Islamophobia." Accessed 10 September 2008 at http://fra.europa.eu/fra/material/pub/muslim/Manifestations_EN.pdf

Favell, A. 2001a. *Philosophies of Integration: Immigration and the Idea of Citizenship in France and Britain,* 2nd edition. Basingstoke, UK: Palgrave.

— 2001b. "Integration Policy and Integration Research in Europe: A Review and Critique." In *Citizenship Today: Global Perspectives and Practices,* ed. T.A. Aleinikoff and D. Klusmeyer. Washington, DC: Brookings Institute/Carnegie Endowment for International Peace.

Foley, M. and D. Hoge. 2007. *Religion and the New Immigrants: How Faith Communities Form Our Newest Citizens.* New York: Oxford University Press.

Fukuyama, F. 1989. "The End of History." *The National Interest* 16 (Summer): 3-18.

— 1992. *The End of History and the Last Man.* New York: Free Press.

Goffman, E. 1959. *The Presentation of Self in Everyday Life.* New York: Doubleday.

Haar, G. and J. Busuttil, eds. 2003. *The Freedom To Do God's Will: Religious Fundamentalism and Social Change.* London: Routledge.

Habermas, J. 2005. "Religion in the Public Sphere." Lecture presented at the Holberg Prize Seminar, Norway, 29 November.

Huntington, S. 1993. "The Clash of Civilizations?" *Foreign Affairs* 72 (Summer): 22-49.

Jelen, T.G. and C. Wilcox, eds. 2002. *Religion and Politics in Comparative Perspective. The One, the Few, and the Many.* Cambridge: Cambridge University Press.

Joppke, C. 2005. "Are 'Nondiscriminatory' Immigration Policies Reversible?" *Comparative Political Studies* 38(1):3-25.

Juergensmeyer, M. 2002. *Terror in the Mind of God: The Global Rise of Religious Violence.* Berkeley, CA: University of California Press.

— 2005. *Religion in Global Civil Society.* New York: Oxford University Press.

Klein, N. 2002. *No Logo: Taking Aim at the Brand Bullies.* New York: Picador.

— 2007. *Shock Doctrine: The Rise of Disaster Capitalism.* New York: Henry Holt.

Koenig, M. 2005. "Incorporating Muslim Migrants in Western Nation States: A Comparison of the United Kingdom, France, and Germany." *Journal of International Migration and Integration* 6:219-34.

— 2007. "Europeanizing the Governance of Religious Diversity – Islam and the Transnationalization of Law, Politics and Identity." *Journal of Ethnic and Migration Studies* 33(6):911-32.

Koenig, M. and P. de Guchteneire, eds. 2007. *Democracy and Human Rights in Multicultural Societies.* Aldershot, UK: Ashgate Publishing.

Lincoln, B. 2003. *Holy Terrors: Thinking about Religion after September 11*. Chicago: University of Chicago Press.

MacMillan, M. 2002. *Paris 1919: Six Months That Changed the World*. New York: Random House.

Martin, D. 1979. *A General Theory of Secularization*. New York: Harper and Row.

McGowan, M. 2008. "Roman Catholics: Anglophone and Allophone." In *Christianity and Ethnicity in Canada*, ed. P. Bramadat and D. Seljak. Toronto: University of Toronto Press.

Menjivar, C. 2003. "Religion and Immigration in Comparative Perspective: Catholic and Evangelical Salvadorans in San Francisco, Washington, DC, and Phoenix." *Sociology of Religion* 64:21-45.

Metcalf, B., ed. 1996. *Making Muslim Space in North America and Europe*. Berkeley and Los Angeles: University of California Press.

Norris, P. and R. Inglehart. 2004. *Sacred and Secular: Religion and Politics Worldwide*. Cambridge: Cambridge University Press.

Panagopoulos, C. 2006. "The Polls-Trends: Arab and Muslim Americans and Islam in the Aftermath of 9/11." *Public Opinion Quarterly* 70:608-24.

Paper, J. and L.G. Thompson, eds. 1998. *Chinese Way in Religion*, 2nd edition. (1st edition by L.G. Thompson.) Belmont, CA: Wadsworth.

Pauly, R. 2004. *Islam in Europe: Integration or Marginalization*. Aldershot, UK: Ashgate Publishing.

Pew Research Center. 2006. "Prospects for Inter-Religious Understanding: Will Views Towards Muslims and Islam Follow Historical Trends?" Paper prepared for the Pew Forum on Religion and Public Life. Accessed 10 September 2008 on the Pew Forum website at http://pewforum.org/publications/surveys/Inter-Religious-Understanding.pdf

— 2007. "American Muslims: Middle Class and Mostly Mainstream." Accessed 10 September 2008 on the Pew Research Centre website at http://pewresearch.org/assets/pdf/muslim-americans.pdf

Rashidi, K. 2004. *Resurrecting Empire: Western Footprints and America's Perilous Path in the Middle East*. Boston: Beacon.

Rippin, A. 2005. *Muslims: Their Religious Beliefs and Practices*. London: Routledge.

Robert, R., ed. 1995. *Religion and the Transformations of Capitalism*. Abingdon, VA: Routledge.

Rokkan, S. 1970. *Citizens, Elections, Parties*. New York: David McKay.

Rudolph, S.H. and J. Piscatori, eds. 1997. *Transnational Religion and Fading States*. Boulder, CO: Westview Press.

Said, E. 1979. *Orientalism*. New York: Vintage Books.

Seljak, D. 2007. "Religion and Multiculturalism in Canada: The Challenge of Religious Discrimination and Intolerance." Report submitted to the Multiculturalism and Human Rights Program at the Department of Canadian Heritage, Gatineau, Quebec.

Shiva, V. 2005. *India Divided: Diversity and Democracy Under Attack*. New York: Seven Stories.

Soysal, Y.N. 1994. *Limits of Citizenship. Migrants and Postnational Membership in Europe.* Chicago: Chicago University Press.

Swatos, W., ed. 1999. "The Secularization Debate." Special issue, *Sociology of Religion: A Quarterly Review* 60(3).

Sweet, L. 1997. *God in the Classroom: The Controversial Issue of Religion in Canada's Schools.* Toronto: McLelland and Stewart.

Taylor, C. 1991. *The Malaise of Modernity.* Concord, ON: House of Anansi Press.

— 2007. *A Secular Age.* Cambridge, MA: Belknap Press of Harvard University Press.

Turner, V. 1969. *The Ritual Process: Structure and Anti-Structure.* Chicago: Aldine.

Van der Veer, P. 2001. *Transnational Religion.* Princeton, NJ: Princeton University Migration Working Papers.

Van Tubergen, F. 2006. "Religious Affiliation and Attendance among Immigrants in Eight Western Countries: Individual and Contextual Effects." *Journal for the Scientific Study of Religion* 45:1-22.

Vertovec, S. 2000. *The Hindu Diaspora: Comparative Patterns.* London: Routledge.

— 2001. "Transnationalism and Identity." *Journal of Ethnic and Migration Studies* 27(4):573-82.

Vertovec, S. and C. Peach. 1997. *Islam in Europe: The Politics of Religion and Communiy.* London: Macmillan Press.

Warner, R.S. and J.G. Wittner. 1998. *Gatherings in Diaspora.* Philadelphia, PA: Temple University Press.

Weller, P. 2005. "Religions and Social Capital: Theses on Religion(s), State(s), and Society(ies): With Particular Reference to the United Kingdom and the European Union." *Journal of International Migration and Integration* 6:271-90.

Zolberg, A. n.d. "Guarding the Gates in a World on the Move." Accessed 18 July 2007 on the Social Sciences Research Council website at http://www.ssrc.org/sept11/essays/zolberg.htm

Part I
Theoretical
Perspectives

Chapter 2

Global Migration and Religious Rebellion

MARK JUERGENSMEYER

Religion plays a role in immigrant communities in two ways, and both may lead to violence. It is often a part of the fabric of an established ethnic identity that is defended—sometimes violently—in the face of an assault on its character or a threat to its existence. And religion may also be part of a new identity created in response to social dislocation and the emergence of multicultural societies in which both newcomers and previous residents may feel out of place. Strident religious radicalism can erupt on either side.

Religious conflict in the contemporary world is seldom about religion, at least not if one defines that term simply by its beliefs and practices (see also the Introduction to this volume). Rather, the conditions of conflict that lead to tension are usually matters of social and political identity—issues regarding who a people are, and what makes them cohere as a moral community. Often these questions are associated with social dislocation related to the range of experiences associated with migration—including a loss of identity by immigrant groups and, on the side of the host community, a perceived assault on a previously homogeneous culture. This social dislocation is sometimes manifested as a defence of the homeland or, as Robert Pape describes it, a protection of a specific territory or culture that is perceived to be challenged by outside powers (Pape 2005). At some point in the conflict, however, usually at a time of frustration and desperation, the political and ideological contest can become "religionized." Then what was initially a worldly struggle takes on the aura of sacred conflict. This creates a new set of problems.

In this chapter, I will explore these problems in a global perspective by examining the similarities and differences among the religious responses to the social and existential dislocations caused by

International Migration and the Governance of Religious Diversity, eds. P. Bramadat and M. Koenig.
Montreal and Kingston: McGill-Queen's University Press, Queen's Policy Studies Series.
© 2009 The School of Policy Studies, Queen's University at Kingston. All rights reserved.

globalization. Movements of religious rebellion—including Sikh militants in the Punjab, Muslim separatists in Kashmir, Buddhist anti-government protesters in Sri Lanka, the Aum Shinrikyo movement in Japan, the Shi'ite revolution in Iran, Sunni insurgents in Palestine and Iraq, Messianic Jewish movements in Israel, Christian militia in the United States, and the transnational movement of jihadi activists around the world—share some common similarities. All are affected in some way by social mobility and migration: communities pushed out, as in Kashmir and Palestine; new communities moving in, as in Sri Lanka, Israel, and multicultural America; internal migration and modernization, as in Japan, Iraq, and Iran; expatriate communities of support, as in the case of Sikhs and Sri Lankan Tamils and Sinhalese; and transnational networks of peoples uprooted from their homelands, as in the jihadi movements of radical Islam. All of these cases are examples of social identities in turmoil, expressions of communities whose members perceive themselves to be fragile, vulnerable, and under siege.

These cases also share a common ideological component: the perception that the modern idea of secular nationalism has let them down. The European Enlightenment notion of the nation-state assumes that national cultures are homogeneous, immobile, and clearly defined, assumptions that are challenged by the global character of twenty-first-century society. For this reason, there has been a rising sense that nationalism is in flux, and a deep suspicion that the secular state is insufficient to protect either traditional or transitional communities, or to provide the moral, political, economic, and social strength to nurture them. Increasingly, community activists around the world have lost faith in secular nationalism.[1] In many cases, the effects of globalization have been in the background as global economic and communications systems undercut the distinctiveness of nation-state identities. In some cases, the hatred of the global system has been overt, as in the American Christian militia's disdain of the "new world order" and the jihadis' targeting of the World Trade Center. Thus, underlying their political activism was a motivating "cause"—if such a term can be used—that was not a yearning for a specific political goal but a gnawing sense of loss of identity and control in the modern world.

This social malaise is not necessarily a religious problem, but it is one for which religion provides a solution. Hence, in each of the cases mentioned above, religion became the ideology of identity and protest. Particular religious images and themes were marshalled to resist what were imagined to be the enemies of traditional culture: global secular systems and the secular nation-state supporters of those systems.[2] There are other similarities: in each of these cases, those who embraced radical anti-state religious ideologies felt personally upset with what they regarded as the oppression of the secular state. They experienced this oppression as an assault on their pride and felt insulted and shamed as a result. The failures of the state—though economic, political, and cultural—were often experienced in personal ways as humiliation and alienation, as a loss of selfhood.

It is understandable then, that the men (and they were usually men) who experienced this assault on their identity and pride would lash out in violence—the way that men often do when they feel frustrated and humiliated. Such expressions of power are meant, at least symbolically, to affirm their manhood.[3] In each case, however, the activists channelled their feelings of humiliation into narratives and images borrowed from their religious traditions.

The idea of cosmic war was a remarkably consistent feature of all of these cases. It is a powerfully restorative image for social malaise. Those people whom we might think of as terrorists often see themselves as soldiers. They are engaged in attempts to restore their sense of power and control through what they imagine to be sacred battles. Acts of religious terror serve not only as tactics in a political strategy but as symbolically empowering sacred deeds. These are performances of violence, enacted to create a moment of spiritual encounter and personal redemption. As I have argued elsewhere (Juergensmeyer 2002), religious violence is especially savage and relentless since its perpetrators see it not just as part of a worldly political battle but as part of a scenario of divine conflict.

So, although religion may not be the problem, the religious response to the problem of identity and control in the modern world is often problematic. When anti-modernism, anti-Americanism, and anti-globalization are expressed in the idiom of religious struggle, a whole new set of powerful social forces emerges. For one thing, religion personalizes the conflict. It provides personal rewards—religious merit, redemption, the promise of heavenly luxuries—to those who struggle in conflicts that otherwise would have only social benefits. It also provides vehicles of social mobilization that embrace vast numbers of supporters who otherwise would not be mobilized around social or political issues. In many cases, it provides an organizational network of local churches, mosques, temples, and religious associations into which patterns of leadership and support may be tapped. It gives the legitimacy of moral justification for political encounters. Even more important, it provides a justification for violence that challenges the state's monopoly on morally sanctioned killing. Using Max Weber's dictum that the state's authority is always rooted in the social approval of the state to enforce its power through the use of bloodshed—in police authority, punishment, and armed defence—religion is the only other entity that can give moral sanction for violence, and it is therefore inherently at least potentially revolutionary (see Weber 1964).

Religion's images of cosmic war add further complications to a conflict that has become baptized with religious authority. The notion of cosmic war gives an all-encompassing world view to those who embrace it. Supporters of Christian militia movements, for instance, have described their "aha" experience when they discovered the totalizing ideology of Christian Identity that helped them make sense of the modern world and their increasingly peripheral role in it. They saw themselves as religious soldiers who could literally fight back against the forces of evil and set the world right. When the template of spiritual battle is implanted onto a worldly opposition, it dramatically changes the perception of the conflict by those engaged in it and vastly alters the way that the struggle is waged. It absolutizes the conflict into extreme opposing positions and demonizes opponents by imagining them to be satanic powers. This absolutism makes compromise difficult to fathom, and holds out the promise of total victory through divine intervention. A sacred war that is waged in a godly span of time need not be won immediately, however. The timeline of sacred struggle is vast, perhaps even eternal.

I once had the occasion to point out the futility—in secular military terms—of the Islamic struggle in Palestine to Dr. Abdul Aziz Rantisi, the late leader of the political wing of the Hamas movement. It seemed to me that Israel's military force was such that a Palestinian military effort could never succeed. Dr. Rantisi assured me that "Palestine was occupied before, for two hundred years," perhaps referring to the time the Holy Land was held by Crusaders.[4] He explained that he and his Palestinian comrades "can wait again—at least that long." In his calculation, the struggles of God can endure for eons. Ultimately, however, they knew they would succeed; in the religious frame of reference, a defeat is never really a defeat since in the vast timeline of sacred warfare the righteous will be victorious.

So religion can be a problematic aspect of contemporary social conflict even if it is not *the* problem, in the sense of being the root cause of discontent. Much of the violence in contemporary life that is perceived as terrorism around the world is directly related to the absolutism of the conflict. The demonization of enemies allows those who regard themselves as soldiers for God to kill with moral impunity. In many cases, they feel that their acts will reap spiritual rewards.

Curiously, the same kind of thinking has crept into some of the responses to terrorism. The "war on terrorism" that was launched by the United States government after September 11th is a case in point. To the degree that the reference to war is metaphorical, and meant to imply an all-out effort in the manner of previous administrations' "war on drugs" and "war on poverty," this rhetoric is an understandable attempt to marshal public support for security measures and police surveillance.

The September 11th attacks were, after all, hideous acts that deeply scarred the American consciousness, and one could certainly understand that a responsible government would want to wage an all-out effort to hunt down those culpable and bring them to justice.

But for some public commentators and politicians who espoused a war on terrorism, the militant language was more than metaphor. God's blessing was imagined to be bestowed on a view of confrontation that was, like all images of cosmic war, all-encompassing and absolutizing and demonizing. This conviction led to the invasion and occupation of two Muslim countries, and justified an amendment of civil rights for the purpose of surveillance and exacting information from prisoners of war. What was problematic about this view was that it brought an impatience with solutions that required the slow procedures of liberal democratic systems of justice—even if these were ultimately more effective in locating terrorists and less provocative in creating more acts of violence. Instead, the rhetoric associated with the "war on terrorism" demanded the quick and violent responses that lent simplicity to the confrontation and a sense of divine certainty to its resolution. Alas, as the escalating violence in Iraq has borne testimony, such a position could fuel the fires of retaliation, leading to more terrorism instead of less (Falk 2002).

The role of religion in this literal war on terrorism has, in a curious way, been similar to the role of religion in the cosmic war imagined by those perpetrating the terrorism that it was attempting to counter. In both cases, religion has been a problematic partner of political confrontation. Religion brought more to the conflict than simply a repository of symbols and the aura of divine support. Religion problematized the conflict through its abiding absolutism, its justification of violence, and its ultimate images of warfare that demonize opponents and cast the conflict in transhistorical terms.

The religiously related political movements that have entered the public arena since the late 1970s have had diverse careers. Several religious revolutions have been attempted—including the Taliban's harsh regime in Afghanistan and the Islamic Courts Council's brief rise to power in Somalia—but Iran remains the only continuing contemporary example of a successful religious revolution and the creation of a radical religious state. It has founded a political order based on religious ideology, fanned the fires of nationalism with religious zeal, enacted laws that privilege particular religious ideas and practices, and brought into the sphere of political influence clerics whose principal credentials were their theological acumen (see Arjomand 1988). Even in Iran, though, the main business of government has been the same as anywhere else—providing a stable and just political order, and supporting economic development. These mundane aspects of politics have no particular religious claim. Moreover, the influence of the clergy and religious ideology in Iran has waxed and waned since the 1979 revolution.

In other countries, religious movements have assimilated into the political process in a non-revolutionary way. They have become political parties or have used their political support to back particular candidates. The Hindu religious nationalist movement that supports the Bharatiya Janata Party in India has scored huge electoral successes in both state and national parliaments. In Palestine, the Hamas movement transformed itself into a political party and gained victory in the 2006 parliamentary elections. In Algeria, the Islamic Salvation Front (or FIS, for the French phrase, *Front Islamique du Salut*) continued to be politically influential even after it was outlawed following the military crackdown that terminated its electoral success in 1991. In Egypt, the Muslim Brotherhood has also often been outlawed though it sometimes fielded de facto candidates by supporting those contestants sympathetic to its cause, as it did in the 2005 elections in Egypt. The candidates it supported formed the largest opposition bloc in the parliament. The Egypt case shows that as a general rule, when religious movements turn to electoral politics they abandon violent tactics, but if the movements are banned, the level of violence rises again. Compromise with the secular political order, however, may lead to divisions within the movement and the formation of extremist splinter groups that are even more violent than the mainstream movement.

In other cases, religious rebellions have been brutally suppressed before they have had a chance to take the reins of power. The Sinhalese arm of the radical JVP movement in Sri Lanka was essentially killed off in the 1990 military action against the movement, but it then resurfaced in later years. In India, rebellious Sikhs were killed in the thousands along with large numbers of armed police in a protracted ten-year war that ended, in the early 1990s, as much from exhaustion and in-fighting as from the government's militancy. Eventually, many villagers who were weary of all the violence refused to give the Sikh militants safe shelter.

Elsewhere, factionalism weakened a good number of other movements, including the Christian militia in the United States, opposition nationalist churches in the Ukraine, Shi'a factions in Lebanon, and rival Muslim groups in the resistance movement in Palestine. In Iraq, extremist groups of Shi'a and Sunni Muslims have set about killing one another, shifting the pattern of militancy in the post-Saddam era from anti-occupation insurgency to civil war. These developments give rise to the possibility that some movements might end up turning against themselves as in-fighting essentially destroys them from within.

In other cases, the violence of rebellious religious movements was curtailed through legal means. In Japan, after the 1995 nerve gas attacks in the Tokyo subways, the Aum Shinrikyo was placed under extensive government surveillance. All of the major participants were arrested and, after lengthy trials, were sentenced to long prison terms and more. The leader of the movement, Master Shoko Asahara, was sentenced to death by hanging in 2004. Though the movement resurfaced under a new name, Aleph, it was non-violent. In China, the government outlawed religious movements it regarded as potentially dangerous, including Falun Gong (also known as Falun Dafa). Though the group protested that it was being persecuted by the Chinese, there has been little bloodshed on either side.

Perhaps the most successful conclusion to movements of terrorism through non-violent means was the Good Friday Agreement in 1998 that set Northern Ireland on a path of peace. The Northern Ireland solution brought an end to the violence that for decades had terrified the residents of London, Belfast, and other cities. It showed the value of not responding in kind to provocative terrorist attacks and letting the patient process of negotiation and compromise work out a solution of accommodation. The agreement called for both Protestant and Catholic communities in the region to have guaranteed representation through a commission supported by both the state of Ireland and the United Kingdom.

Could other violent situations be settled in a manner similar to Northern Ireland's Good Friday Agreement? It would not take a huge stretch of imagination to think that the agreement could serve as a model, especially when the issue is largely over contested land, including those conflicts created by the presence of large immigrant communities. The Kashmir situation is remarkably similar to Northern Ireland, in that two religious communities occupy and lay claim to the same territory. India and Pakistan could join in a settlement similar to the Good Friday Agreement. The Israeli-Palestinian conflict is more complex, but like Northern Ireland it is essentially a squabble over territory to which both sides have a moral and political claim. Since the Oslo Agreement in 1993, a negotiated settlement in the region has seemed a realistic though still elusive possibility.

In yet other cases, moderate members of the movements were assimilated into the public arena after the extremists were isolated. In Northern Ireland, the radical positions of activists such as the Protestant Rev. Ian Paisley were largely ignored and negotiations were conducted with more moderate members of the Protestant and Catholic communities. Similarly, in Sri Lanka, the most radical of the Sinhalese Buddhist supporters of the anti-government movement could be partially destroyed because moderate religious nationalists had been appeased by the government's policies.

Some movements have abandoned political activism altogether as the futility of their efforts encouraged their leaders to turn toward other ventures. In the case of the Christian militia in the United States, there is some indication that the enormity of the violence perpetrated by Timothy McVeigh in bombing the Oklahoma City Federal Building in 1995 had a sobering effect on the right-wing Christian movement in the rest of the country. Yet another factor in diminishing the role of the violent religious right after the Oklahoma City bombing was the fact that this movement was largely ignored by the public authorities and the news media. Neither the prosecution nor the defence side of Timothy McVeigh's much-publicized trial made any effort to link McVeigh with the larger underworld of the Christian militant movement in the United States. The absence of media attention served to further marginalize Christian militants in the public sphere.

By contrast, when a similar sort of terrorist attack resulted in the catastrophic collapse of the World Trade Center and damage to the Pentagon on 11 September 2001, the connections to radical Islam became the central issue. Within days, the al-Qaeda network became identified as America's most vicious foe and Osama bin Laden the Hitler of the new world war. When American leaders adopted bin Laden's rhetoric of religious war and vaunted him to the level of the nation's global foe, they inadvertently promoted his image and ideas throughout the Muslim world. It is possible that this emboldened al-Qaeda even more. The paradoxical effect of the "war on terror" might well have been to encourage the proliferation of terrorism. The popularization of jihadi ideology as an anti-American posture of protest may have been due in no small part to US policy, which elevated such groups into the role of the quintessential enemy of the West.

To a large degree, the future of religious rebellions against the secular state depends not only on the religious movements themselves but also on the way in which government authorities respond, especially in Europe and the United States. It is important to recall that much of the passion behind the religious rebels' positions has come as a response to what they have perceived as the West's attitude of arrogance and intolerance toward immigrant communities and non-Western regions of the world. If they could perceive the West as changing its attitude—respecting at least some aspects of their position—perhaps their response would be less virulent. In fact, a recent sensitivity in Europe and the United States to the perceptions of outsiders has moderated Western responses to acts of terrorism. In Spain, for instance, one response to the Madrid bombings was an attempt by the Spanish government to be more hospitable to the Muslim immigrant minority living in the country (see, for example, Arigita 2006).

Attitudes are difficult to sway, however, and the frequency of acts of terrorism associated with the radical jihadi movement has led to a certain Islamophobia in Europe and the United States.[5] In Europe, tensions between immigrant Muslim groups and xenophobic nationalists have led to stereotyping on both sides. Many in the West feel now as they did in the Cold War: that Western civilization is under siege, attacked by a hostile and alien force. This, in turn, has led to the notion that all Muslim activists—or even all Muslims—are the same. Policies based on this perception widen the gulf between the two sides, just as they did during the Cold War, and even more violence is the result. As one US state department official put it, "We have to be smarter in dealing with Islam than we were in dealing with communism thirty or forty years ago."[6]

For Americans and Europeans who are comfortable with the tenets of secular society, the difficulty is a matter of accepting not only a non-Christian or non-Jewish religion but also a form of political religion. In other words, all forms of religious activism are suspect. Most Westerners are not used to the notion that religion has a role to play in defining public order and in articulating its basic values. Although religion is historically part of the background of Western secular nationalism, that heritage is largely neglected. If religion were a more vital force in Western societies in ways that could be seen as facilitating public life and promoting the common welfare, perhaps it would be easier to accept the public presence of religion in other parts of the world.

From time to time, there are calls for a more active role for religion in American public life.[7] One of the reasons that figures such as Bishop Desmond Tutu, Mother Theresa, and Mohandas Gandhi appeal to so many people in the West is that, without being aggressively religious, these individuals brought a moral and spiritual consciousness into the public sphere. Just as poet T. S. Eliot lamented the "wasteland" of empty spirituality in the West, Gandhi once described the absence of spirituality in Western civilization as a "sickness." In a treatise entitled *Hind Swaraj, or Indian Home Rule*—arguably his only sustained writing on political theory—Gandhi wrote that the West's materialism separated it from its spiritual soul (Gandhi 1938, 33-4). Many Westerners have agreed. Among them is Reinhold Niebuhr, the American Protestant theologian who influenced the Roosevelt government in the 1940s and who has been respectfully quoted by such diverse American politicians as former president Jimmy Carter and Jeane Kirkpatrick, US ambassador to the United Nations from 1981 to 1985. One of Niebuhr's central theses had to do with the limited moral ability of nations. States could not be selfless, Niebuhr claimed, because they are by nature nothing more than a collection of the self-interests of all the individuals contained within them. He added, however, that religion can help to transform political organizations and make them more like communities: it can ameliorate some of the harsher characteristics of self-interest and draw people together through a common recognition of "profound and ultimate unities" (Niebuhr 1932, 255).[8]

Yet both Gandhi and Niebuhr can be faulted for failing to provide adequate models for the fusion of religion and public responsibility. In Gandhi's case, it is said that he went too far: as Ainslie Embree suggests, "Gandhi's use of a religious vocabulary— inevitably Hindu in origin"—may have exacerbated relations between Hindus and Muslims, and in any event his form of cultural politics cannot be transposed easily to the West (Embree 1990, 45). In Niebuhr's case, he may not have gone far enough: despite his appreciation of the values that religion provides, when it came to politics he was a consummate secular liberal. His greatest fear was that nations would become too religious, absorbed with their own illusions of power and grandeur. Niebuhr was deeply concerned about the destructive role that illusion—in religion or moral ideals—could play. "Illusion is dangerous," Niebuhr wrote, because it "encourages terrible fanaticisms." It must, therefore, "be brought under the control of reason" (1932, 277). Even so, Niebuhr cautioned against overreacting: keeping religion too far from political life could obscure the positive images of a perfected society that the religious imagination is capable of producing. "One can only hope," he added, "that reason will not destroy it [religion] before its work is done" (277).

Over 70 years after Niebuhr wrote these words, religion is not on the brink of being destroyed by reason, yet it is possible that Niebuhr's dark vision has come to pass, and reason and religion have begun to war with one another on a global plane. Because there is ultimately no satisfactory compromise on an ideological level between religious and secular views of the grounds for legitimizing public authority, the current situation of religious rebellion against the secular state has moved from mutual suspicion and sporadic violence to a level of widespread hostility approaching the dismal climate of the old Cold War. One can foresee the emergence of a united bloc of Muslim radicalism stretching from Southeast and Central Asia through the Middle East to Northern Africa. In this worst-case scenario of the future, it is possible to envision popular movements of jihadi rebellions toppling fragile governments (as one saw in Somalia). Saudi Arabia and Egypt seem particularly vulnerable to such changes. One could imagine a wave of Islamic revolutions from Morocco to Indonesia, creating an arc of anti-American power that could come to dominate global politics. With an arsenal of nuclear weapons at its disposal and a youthful populace fuelled by a hatred of the West, this emergent bloc of Islamic radicalism might well replace the old Soviet Union as a united global enemy of the secular West.

Such a conflict might be compounded by the rise of new religious radicals in Europe and the United States, including members of recent immigrant communities whose religious pride is stoked by the experience of social marginalization (see notably the contributions on Europe in this volume). The Internet offers a whole new arena of global networking and the illusion of involvement in an imagined war (see Knorr-Cetina 2005). Such cyber connections can promote decentralized bands of activists engaged in acts of sabotage and terrorism in almost anywhere in the world. The new Cold War between secular and religious politics could truly be a global confrontation.

Barring the emergence of this apocalyptic vision of a worldwide conflict between religious and secular nationalism, there is reason to be hopeful. It is equally likely that most religious activists—even those who share the same religious tradition—are incapable of uniting easily with one another. It is also clear that when they have positions of real political influence, they seek some kind of economic and political accommodation with the secular world. In this event, a grudging tolerance might develop between religious activists and secular nationalists. In optimal conditions, each might be able to admire what the other provides: communitarian values and moral vision on the one hand, individual latitude and rational rules of justice on the other. After all, both are responses to, and products of, the modern age.

In Sri Lanka, India, Iran, Egypt, Algeria, Afghanistan, Indonesia, Central Asia, China, Japan, the United States, Eastern and Western Europe, and all other places where groups of religious activists have experimented with forms of politics related in some way with religion, they have done far more than resuscitate archaic ideas of religious rule. They have created something new: a synthesis between religion and modern politics. In places like Iran, this has led to a merger between the cultural identity and legitimacy of old religiously sanctioned monarchies and the democratic spirit and organizational unity of modern industrial society.

This combination can be incendiary, for it blends the absolutism of religion with the potency of modern politics. Yet it may also be necessary, for without the legitimacy conferred by religion, the authority of political order cannot easily be established in some parts of the world. In some of these places, even the essential elements of democracy have been conveyed in the vessels of new religious politics. In a curious way, at the same time that political actors have embraced religious ideologies, religious groups have embraced some of the ideals of the modern state. The revival of tolerant forms of moderate religion may therefore be a part of the cure for the excesses of its rebellious and intolerant extremes.

Notes

1. The loss of confidence in secular nationalism is explored more fully in my book (Juergensmeyer 2008), from which portions of this essay have been taken.

2. The rise of public religion as a response to the changing perceptions of secularism in the present period of later modernity is a theme also explored by Asad (2003); the essays in Berger (1999); Casanova (1994); and Madsen et al. (2001).

3. I explore the topic of male empowerment as a factor in violence in Juergensmeyer (2002, 198-209).

4. Interview with Dr. Abdul Aziz Rantisi, cofounder and political leader of Hamas, in Khan Yunis, Gaza, 1 March 1998.

5. For further information see, for instance, the European Monitoring Centre on Racism and Xenophobia report entitled "Muslims in the European Union: Discrimination and Islamophobia," available at http://fra.europa.eu/fra/material/pub/muslim/Manifestations_EN.pdf; and the Pew Forum study "Prospects for Inter-Religious Understanding: Will Views towards Muslims and Islam Follow Historical Trends?" available at http://pewforum.org/publications/surveys/Inter-Religious-Understanding.pdf.

6. A "senior Administration official" quoted in Wright (1992, A1).

7. The appeals to religion come from both ends of the political spectrum. The conservative political theorist Eric Voegelin, for instance, has called for a greater influence of Christianity in American political thinking in order to counter what he regards as a Gnostic tendency toward utopianism that corrupts the "civil theology" of the modern West (Voegelin 1987, 162). Interestingly, Islamic activists have also encouraged the United States to take biblical religion more seriously. Alann Steen reports that while he was held hostage in Lebanon, his Islamic captors, loyal followers of the Ayatollah Khomeini, gave the hostages Bibles and encouraged them to read them (Interview with Alann Steen, in Honolulu, 11 March 1992).

8. Schlesinger, who served in the administrations of Franklin D. Roosevelt and John F. Kennedy, said that Niebuhr "cast an intellectual spell" on him and his generation of political thinkers (Schlesinger 1992, A13; 1984, 189-222). Niebuhr was highly critical of Gandhi's "sentimental" view of human nature and its implications for politics.

References

Arigita, E. 2006. "Representing Islam in Spain: Muslim Identities and the Contestation of Leadership." *The Muslim World* 96:563-84.

Arjomand, S.A. 1988. *The Turban for the Crown: The Islamic Revolution in Iran.* New York/Oxford: Oxford University Press.

Asad, T. 2003. *Formations of the Secular: Christianity, Islam, Modernity.* Stanford, CA: Stanford University Press.

Berger, P., ed. 1999. *The Desacralization of the World: Resurgent Religion and World Politics.* Grand Rapids, MI: Eerdman's.

Casanova, J. 1994. *Public Religions in the Modern World*. Chicago: University of Chicago Press.

Embree, A.T. 1990. *Utopias in Conflict: Religion and Nationalism in Modern India*. Berkeley: University of California Press.

Falk, R. 2002. *The Great Terror War*. Northhampton, MA: Interlink Publishing Group.

Gandhi, M. 1938. *Hind Swaraj, or Indian Home Rule*. Ahmedabad, India: Navajivan Press.

Juergensmeyer, M. 2002. *Terror in the Mind of God: The Global Rise of Religious Violence*. San Francisco: University of California Press.

— 2008. *Global Rebellion: Religious Challenges to the Secular State*. Berkeley: University of California Press.

Knorr-Cetina, K. 2005. "Complex Global Microstructures: The New Terrorist Societies." *Theory, Culture and Society* 22:213-34.

Madsen, R., W.M. Sullivan, A. Swidler, and S.M. Tipton. 2001. *Meaning and Modernity: Religion, Polity, and Self*. Berkeley: University of California Press.

Niebuhr, R. 1932. *Moral Man and Immoral Society*. New York: Scribner's.

Pape, R. 2005. *Dying to Win: The Strategic Logic of Suicide Terrorism*. New York: Random House.

Schlesinger, A. Jr. 1984. "Reinhold Niebuhr's Role in American Political Thought." In *Reinhold Niebuhr: His Religious, Social and Political Thought*, rev. edition, ed. C.W. Kegley. New York: Pilgrim Press.

— 1992. "Reinhold Niebuhr's Long Shadow." *New York Times*, 22 June 1992.

Voegelin, E. 1987. *The New Science of Politics: An Introduction*, 2nd edition. Chicago: University of Chicago Press.

Weber, M. 1964 [1921]. "Politics as Vocation." In *From Max Weber*, ed. C. Wright Mills and H. Gerth. New York: Oxford University Press.

Wright, R. 1992. "U.S. Struggles to Deal with Global Islamic Resurgence." *Los Angeles Times*, 26 January 1992.

Chapter 3

The Governance of Religious Diversity: Theory, Research, and Practice

VEIT BADER

Immigration represents a significant challenge to the governance of religious diversity. With immigrants often come "strange" religious beliefs and practices that may force "us" to reconceptualize religion, to find more adequate policies of accommodation, and to change established institutional arrangements of state / politics and (organized) religions. Newcomers also pose challenges for the social sciences and political theory. It therefore does not come as a surprise that in the last decades we have found a veritable explosion of social scientific studies of religion and migration (see Bader 2007b; Maussen 2007a).

Anthropologists of religion have explored changes of religiosity in sending and receiving countries (regions, cities) under the conditions of migration, transnationalism, globalization, and post-colonialism. Sociologists of religion have addressed the effects on religion of class, sex, age, generation, citizenship status and, obviously, of divergent religious traditions and interpretations. Political scientists, who have recently become more attuned to issues of religion, have investigated the effect of external societal or "opportunity" structures in receiving societies on newcomer religions (claims making, organization, mobilization, and religiosity). And comparative analysts have studied what immigrant religions do to receiving polities, including reinterpretation, renegotiation, and more or less drastic changes in institutionalized patterns of relationships between organized religions and society, politics, national identity, or statehood.

In this article, I argue that we need a broader theoretical perspective on the governance of religious diversity from an actor-centred, institutionalist approach that combines what institutions do to actors and,

International Migration and the Governance of Religious Diversity, eds. P. Bramadat and M. Koenig.
Montreal and Kingston: McGill-Queen's University Press, Queen's Policy Studies Series.
© 2009 The School of Policy Studies, Queen's University at Kingston. All rights reserved.

vice versa, what actors do to institutions. I shall firstly introduce this perspective. Then, in a second step, I focus on theoretical and empirical problems for the social sciences in dealing with the governance and government of religious diversity against the background of the huge institutional diversity of governing religion in states with liberal democratic constitutions. Against this background, I turn, thirdly, to explicitly normative issues in dealing with the governance of religious diversity from a perspective of empirically grounded normativity. And finally, I briefly summarize my policy recommendations: maximum accommodation of religious diversity constrained by minimal morality and associative democratic institutions—a policy that I consider as a real utopian alternative to strict separation and to neo-corporatist, selective cooperation.

Governance and Government of Religious Diversity

Governance is an increasingly fashionable concept among theorists and policy-makers, but it has not yet been widely applied to the incorporation of ethnic and national minorities in studies of multiculturalism in general and of religious minorities in particular. The governance of religious diversity also has been neglected in the sociology of religion, which traditionally focuses on describing and explaining the diversity of religious beliefs and practices.

While governance may be a fashionable concept, it is certainly often used in a vague and unspecified way (Héritier 2002; Pierre and Peters 2000; Treib, Bähr, and Falkner 2006). Therefore, I wish to clarify the conceptual distinctions between societal structures, governance, and government as used in comparative institutional studies in the social sciences. *Societal structures* (or patterns, formations, configurations, *Ordnungen*) contain all relevant interactions between economic, social, cultural (including ethno-national), political, legal, judicial, administrative, and religious domains in all their diversity. Studies of patterns of society and religion thus have to analyze all mechanisms of action coordination—markets, networks, associations, communities, and private and public hierarchies (Hollingsworth and Boyer 1997)—as well as all relevant actors and coalitions of actors, including governments and government departments at all levels, and their organizations, mobilization, and strategies.

The concept of *governance* is narrower as it focuses on regulation.[1] Governance includes only those mechanisms of action coordination that provide active intentional capacities to regulate, including co-regulation and self-regulation. Thus, while markets are important mechanisms for coordinating actions, they do so by an invisible hand; they have no regulatory capacity and therefore should not count as modes of governance. The concept of governance is, however, much broader than that of *government*, which focuses on one specific (internally highly diversified) actor—the state—and on action coordination by the public hierarchy and by rules, particularly law and law-like regulations. The fact that the concept of governance includes more actors and more modes of coordination explains recent shifts in the field of regulation from government to governance.[2] Yet governance also excludes some broader issues: not all coordination is governance, but only coordination by "policies" in a very broad sense.

Governance, in general, can best be understood by distinguishing two axes of regulation: internal and external governance, and democratic (bottom-up) and hierarchical (top-down) governance. Both internal and external governance can be top down or bottom-up. Let me apply these distinctions to explain three points about religious governance. First, while the relatively free competition of all types of religions in "God's Biggest Supermarkets" may be crucial for the chances of divergent religions and also for overall religiosity as maintained by proponents of the "new religious economics," this competition is not in itself a mode of governance. Rather, it is an invisible-hand mechanism that, in turn, is regulated at least implicitly by other forms of religious governance (e.g., by rights to religious freedom; by all kinds of customs, conventions, or laws; by self-regulation within and among competing religions; by co-regulation; and by public bodies).

Second, religious governance refers to the internal and external regulation of religious diversity and to their dynamic interaction. Internal governance by the respective religious communities—here understood as those groups that share certain religious beliefs and practices, however contested the boundaries and the beliefs and practices may be—includes self-regulation by religious laws and customs (ecclesiastical law and *nomos)* of many aspects of life from the cradle to the grave. The rules and their interpretations and applications can be either more autocratic and hierarchical (e.g., ordained by formally organized, autocratic church hierarchy and religious elites) or more democratic and bottom-up (e.g., interpreted by religious congregations and democratically elected religious organizations / leaders or, indeed, by more informal networks and associations of believers; by religious counter-elites like dissenting theologians; by religious movements in opposition to church hierarchy; by leaders of religious political parties; and by communal business elites).[3] Internal governance of religious diversity should not be called "management" (Bouma 1999) because management refers to hierarchy and top-down competencies usually confined either to private hierarchies (e.g., church hierarchy or corporate governance) or to public hierarchies. Internal governance of religious communities clearly varies widely between religions, and this variation is also obvious in the historical development of specific religions. For example, Islam, Roman Catholicism, and radical Protestantism reflect distinctive internal governance traditions, with Islam characterized by decentralization, Catholicism by a tendency toward centralized authority, and Protestantism by relatively democratic congregationalism.

Third, external governance of religious diversity includes more *voluntary* and democratic forms of self-regulation by interfaith networks, movements, associations, and ecumenical organizations—an oft-neglected field of study. The governance perspective enables and stimulates analysis of the regulations of religious diversity within so-called semi-public and private organizations—within private hierarchies of all kinds, whether the organizations are for-profit or non-profit—by more or less autocratic or democratic forms of corporate governance; this perspective also facilitates analysis of the impact of these regulations on the ways in which religious practices, particularly the practices of religious minorities, are accommodated. Most scholarly attention has been focused on the external governance of religious diversity by *governments* or *public hierarchies*—in other words, on what polities (from local to supra-state), legislations, administrations, jurisdictions, and the different departments of government *do to religions*, particularly by law or law-like rules. Comparative studies of the divergent ways in which religions, particularly Islam, are governed in Europe have been initiated by legal scholars (e.g., Ferrari 1996; Ferrari and Bradney 2000; Robbers 1995; Shahid and Koningsveld 2002). Much less research has been done on what states (e.g., courts, administrations) actually do, on how these diverse and changing practices relate to the country-specific, predominant legal models or to ideological policy models (Fetzer and Soper 2005; Monsma and Soper 1997; Soper and Fetzer 2007), and on how different religious minorities respond to those policies (Maussen 2007b), which include not only legal opportunities and threats but a broad spectrum of other resources (money, expertise, networks) and policy options (incentives and persuasions).

Compared with the traditional focus on the government of religious diversity, the perspective of governance has two important advantages. First, if governments follow policies of deregulation and "privatization" vis-à-vis the religious field, the governance perspective will enable analysis of the huge variety of public but non-state and non-market actors and of the semi-public and private actors who play a major role in regulating religious diversity and who are gaining in importance through the shift from government to governance (Minow 2000; Monsma and Soper 2006).[4] Second, the concept of governance is a more appropriate tool for undertaking the study of religious regimes such as

American denominationalism that are characterized by fairly thin legal regulations and little "official" cooperation between the state and religions.

Variations in the Governance of Religious Diversity

A governance approach is typically oriented toward the following questions:

- How do legal regimes of government, state authorities, and non-state actors affect (organized) religions—the external opportunity structure, broadly speaking?
- How do religious organizations affect actual religiosity?
- How do religious practitioners and their organizations actually affect states and non-state actors?

Actor-centred institutionalism (Scharpf 1997) invites us to start our analysis with institutionalized regimes of governance ("what institutions do to actors") that provide the setting in which all kinds of actors talk, negotiate, and contest each other in trying to realize their claims and by doing so ultimately also change or reproduce predominant regimes of government and governance ("what actors do to institutions"). The ways in which immigrants define themselves, raise their claims, organize, and mobilize mainly depend on the external opportunity structure; this helps explain why immigrants with the "same" background behave so differently in various countries. A traditional, well-established approach for mapping the empirical diversity of "what states do to religions" is to focus on legal/constitutional regimes, or on legal regulations of organized religions in a broad variety of dimensions (the focus of the next subsection). Next, one has to analyze what states actually do and how continuing diversity can be *explained* (e.g., as the result of path-dependent, entrenched, or nested institutional structures). For both historical and synchronic comparisons, "models" are implicitly or explicitly used. In the subsection Explaining State Variation, I discuss some perils of modelling and explain the advantages of a fairly disaggregated approach.

Country-Specific Legal Regulations of Organized Religions

Legal regulations of religious diversity within liberal states have been amply studied in recent literature. I briefly summarize some of the main results by distinguishing between several dimensions of regulations.[5]

When it comes to the legal status of (organized) religions, states can choose to treat them exactly the same as other associations or to grant them some special status. The first approach is evident in Ireland (after 1871), in the United Kingdom and, albeit in a more contradictory fashion, in France. Religious communities normally can become legal entities—the legal forms vary according to different traditions of national private law—and can perform some basic economic and legal transactions. The second option, granting religious communities some special status, is expressed in different ways and degrees in all other European states. There are various options on a scale from minimal to maximal legal recognition. Religions then are either "regulated by special laws enacted for religious associations, different from (and more favourable than) the laws applying to associations in general" (Ferrari 2002, 10) or they are granted specific legal exemptions in tax law, labour law, and military conscription as well as legal privileges. Legal rights and privileges include religious instruction in public schools, public money for the building or maintenance of houses of worship and religious schools, religious cemeteries, faith-based care and social services, and entitlements of access for chaplains to military forces, prisons, and hospitals. Legal exemptions and privileges normally are not granted indiscriminately to all religious communities but require at least some kind of state registration and control.

Some established churches (e.g., in Sweden until 2001, and in Denmark and Finland more so than in England) are near the *maximum* pole of legal and financial privileges; however, even without constitutional establishment, some religions—culturally and politically "established" majority religions but also important minority religions—may enjoy a high degree of exemptions and privileges. It is important to note that all Western states, in spite of the prevailing strict separationist ideology in some countries like France and during some periods of history in the United States, not only have to recognize religions in the actual (local) administrative practice but also must guarantee at least a minimum of special legal treatment (whether by special and general laws or by jurisdiction and case law). Even the laïcist systems are clearly less laïcist than normative (predominantly French and American) ideologists assume. Depending on national legal traditions, this regulation may take the form of, for example, *Körperschaften öffentlichen Rechts* (corporations of public law)—as in Germany, Belgium, Luxemburg, and Austria—or even bilateral special treatises or concordats (as in Italy).

State recognition and regulation of religious communities requires some minimal thresholds in terms of numbers of adherents, duration, and stability of religious groups or organizations even without any explicit intent to discriminate against minority religions. The selective recognition and cooperation may thus be ranked according to how open regimes are to religions: "open-universalist," "pluralist," "hegemonial," or "closed" (Messner 1999). All countries that guarantee religions some special status or public recognition are characterized by a pyramidal pattern of privileges and corresponding regulations or controls, with possibly harsh normative dilemmas (Bader 2007a; Ferrari 2005).

A second dimension of legal regulation pertains to the autonomy of churches and religious communities—liberal states have to guarantee at least a minimum. I propose to distinguish between non-intervention regulations that are central to church autonomy and positive privileges that enable legal and financial state actions. In the latter case, an increase in substantive autonomy is normally paid for by a loss in formal autonomy due to an increase in state interference. With regard to the inner domain of faith, doctrine, and core ministry, all Western states recognize the religious incompetence of the state, no matter what legal status is granted to churches or religious communities. The relevant legal restrictions imposed by the state on religions concern generally recognized, though divergently interpreted, limits to freedom of speech (such as preaching violence or libel) and to religious practices that seriously infringe on the basic human rights of members.

In matters of organization, polity, and administration, the different legal statuses formally and actually matter. Formal autonomy seems highest in cases of non-registered, non-recognized, and non-established religions. Legal registration, recognition, and establishment presuppose some conditions and controls. State churches that enjoy the most privileges and powers have been traditionally subjected to strong state intervention and control in matters of faith and doctrine, organization, policy, and administration. Even today, the autonomy of established churches is limited to doctrinal affairs, although state authorities are less and less willing to interfere with the internal organization of religious groups and refrain from making full use of their legal powers in this field. Generally speaking, the doctrinal and organizational autonomy of religious groups is on the rise. All Western states respect church autonomy in matters of organization, polity, and administration and treat religious groups favourably compared with most non-religious organizations by exempting them from requirements of internal democratic structure, from the application of labour law and collective agreements, and from equal treatment and non-discrimination laws.

A third dimension of regulation concerns the *public financing of religions*. In this context, there are three options: (a) churches and religious communities receive no public money, directly or indirectly; (b) some or all of them receive public money indirectly by means of tax exemptions, general subsidies, or vouchers; (c) in addition to indirect funding, some receive public money directly through payment of salaries or other costs, religion-specific subsidies, or "church taxes." Interestingly, there is actually no system of governance in which religions depend exclusively on the voluntary contributions of members (without any direct or indirect assistance by state administrations) or on donations (without any specific tax exemptions). This is so even in the most separationist systems in the United States and France, where some general and some religion-specific tax exemptions are granted. Hence, in all Western states, some churches or religious communities receive public money at least indirectly, through various tax exemptions or favours, or through general subsidies. For example, we find subsidies for the restoration of churches within the framework of heritage programs, city development, or social and cultural activities. Indirect financing of specific churches and religious communities is often combined with the direct payment of salaries, pensions, or other costs by the state (as in Belgium, Luxemburg, and Denmark); with direct subsidies for specific religious communities; with considerable administrative help by state administrations in collecting contributions (as in Germany, Austria, Sweden, and Finland); and with modernized versions of church taxes (as in Spain, Italy, and Hungary). The latter are involuntary taxes on every resident taxpayer. However, together with their income tax declarations, taxpayers can decide whether the money goes to a church or to other social or cultural ends.

The relevant options in financing faith-based organizations in education, which constitutes the fourth dimension, range from full through partial to no public financing. Public money is normally coupled with some public regulation and control: full financing means the least autonomy, partial financing increases autonomy, and no financing may mean full autonomy with no state regulation and control. Only Bulgaria, Greece, Italy, most Swiss cantons and, until 2002, the United States reject nearly all public financing of private faith-based educational institutions. In Europe, Australia, and some Canadian provinces, we find a wide variety of systems of full public financing (Austria, Belgium, the Netherlands, England, Wales, and some Canadian provinces) or partial financing (Scandinavian states, Australia, Germany, Hungary, France, Spain), and direct or indirect public financing of various faith-based educational institutions (see Glenn and Groof 2002a, 2002b). In addition, in faith-based education one finds a considerable variety of public regulation and control in the selection of staff and students, organizational form, the content of the curriculum and even of classes and lessons, selection of teaching materials, didactics, examination, recognition of diplomas, and public inspection. Most states also acknowledge that some affinity with—or at least no public opposition to—the core of the respective religion is a relevant criterion for the hiring and firing of teaching personnel (not of other administrative personnel), although the area of exemptions from anti-discrimination articles in constitutions and labour law is increasingly circumscribed by law.

When it comes, fifth, to the regulation and financing of religious instruction in public schools, the question is whether or not religious instruction is part of the curriculum. In the context of strict separation such as in the United States and in France, extracurricular religious instruction may still take place in school buildings, free or for rent. In other contexts, the following issues have arisen: Is religious instruction—that is, instruction in religion and not just about religion—obligatory for all (as in Denmark, Germany, Spain, Ireland until 1970, Austria, Italy, and the United Kingdom), or are there alternatives such as non-religious "ethics" courses (as in Quebec, Finland, some German *Länder*, and Alsace-Moselle)? At which educational level is instruction provided? Is it provided in separate lessons (in most countries) or integrated into the general curriculum? By which religions and confessions? (Established religions would obviously have a head start.) Who selects the instructors? Who decides on the curriculum and organizes the lessons? (Things get muddy if states presume competence in "non-confessional" Christian instruction—as in England, Norway, and Denmark—or introduce "neutral" courses in religious or interfaith education, or in the history and sociology of world religions). Is there state supervision of the curriculum and the actual lessons in religious instruction (see Willaime 2005)? All these questions testify to the complexity of institutional governance of religious diversity.

Sixth, all Western countries finance faith-based care and social service organizations either indirectly (through vouchers and tax exemptions of all kinds) or directly (through subsidies). These services include care for children, youngsters, and the elderly; people with physical or mental illness and disability; drug addicts; people in criminal rehabilitation; the homeless; and poor and low-income people. Religious organizations also offer "welfare-to-work" programs (Monsma and Soper 2006) at community centres and, at times, even other cultural and leisure activities. The importance of and the need for such organizations differ: both the importance and the need are relatively low in social-democratic welfare systems, higher in liberal systems like the United Kingdom and the United States, and highest in conservative-corporatist systems like Germany, Austria, and the Netherlands. As with schools, public money is normally conditional upon statewide standards of quality and professionalism, but organization and provision, including hiring and firing, are internal concerns of the religious communities responsible for the institutions. Their personnel are normally covered by collective and individual labour law, social security and pensions, and sector-specific collective agreements.

In order to illustrate the way liberal states deal with religious diversity, it is useful to compare their various constitutional regimes. Written constitutions of liberal democratic states regulate the relations between (organized) religions and the state. From a constitutional perspective, the choice is between the constitutional establishment of one church, or non-establishment. Legal establishment can be further subdivided into strong and weak establishment. Close to approaching strong establishment regimes are Greece, Serbia, and Israel. Historically speaking, strong establishment has been the point of departure for disestablishment, plural establishment, and non-establishment. Weak establishment means constitutional or legal establishment of one State-Church, and de jure and de facto religious freedom and pluralism. It is compatible with some administrative recognition of religious pluralism and with different degrees of de facto institutionalization of other religions. Weak establishment may recognize a certain religious pluralization of the cultural nation; England, Scotland, Norway, and Denmark approximate this ideal type. An intermediate option is plural establishment. Constitutional pluralism exists nowadays only in Finland with two state churches (the large Lutheran Church of Finland and the small Orthodox Church of Finland) in a non-denominational state.

Non-establishment characterizes all of the other Western states—though often only recently through constitutional disestablishments: in the Netherlands (1983) and Sweden (2001) but also in Turkey, Mexico, and India. Obviously, non-establishment or the "constitutional separation of state and (organized) religions" may be expressed very differently in reality.

An exclusive focus on legal-constitutional regulation clouds the divergent constitutional realities that we find. States such as Germany, the Netherlands, Sweden, Italy, and Spain on the one hand, and France and the United States on the other, are lumped together as non-establishment countries. A first step in capturing the relevant differences is to distinguish between three patterns commonly used by legal (Ferrari 2002; Robbers 1995, 2001) and political theorists (Fetzer and Soper 2005; Monsma and Soper 1997): countries with a state or national church, separatist countries, and selective cooperation countries. We find selective cooperation in Italy, Germany, Austria, Spain, and Portugal. Separatist and selective cooperation countries share constitutional non-establishment yet differ with regard to the legal status of religious organizations and related aspects (for example, the regulation and financing of faith-based education, care, and welfare organizations). It is possible to broaden the relevant dimensions and include a wider latitude in the respective scales of strict separation versus *Verflechtung* or linkage (Minkenberg 2003a), or deregulation versus regulation (Chaves and Cann 1992) of state and organized religions.[6] We also find combinations with welfare state typologies or degrees of "stateness" and other modes of governance.

Hence, constitutional and legal non-establishment is definitely not the same as the separation of state from religion (let alone of nation from religion), either historically or structurally. And it is not the same as a separation of political or civil society from churches and religions. To illustrate this, we need only remember that the constitutional non-establishment or disestablishment in the United States proved compatible with the political and cultural hegemony of one church and one religion and with coalitions of churches and religions.

What States Actually Do

If we want to describe what states actually do when they govern religions, the description of legal rules and regulations is obviously only a first step. We need thick sociological and anthropological descriptions of actual practices that might be guided by legal rules, might make use of extensive margins of discretion, or might actually contravene or undermine official laws related to the governance of religion. Moreover, we have to disaggregate government. Actual state policies with regard to religions have to be analyzed along four different axes:

- the interplay between constitutional, legal, and administrative regulation, and political and cultural interference;
- the wide variation in the aims of states and in the strategies to achieve those aims;
- the different approaches of various departments of state and levels of government; and
- the complexity of the actual government, in contrast to the legal regulation, of religious diversity.

Interplay between Regulation and Interference. Constitutional regulation (if any) articulates religious freedoms and the specific forms of establishment or disestablishment of churches or religions. Legal regulation, here understood as the traditional combination of legislation and jurisdiction, most often is a multilevel system (Galanter 1966, 269-70); it may also imply normative legal pluralism (e.g., recognizing private religious law and jurisdiction). Legislative regulation may be fairly general and limited, or very specified and extensive as in Austria or Spain, depending on the legal traditions of the countries and on the actual degree of state regulatory and policing powers—which have increased dramatically with modern welfare states (Ferrari 2002; Monsma and Soper 1997).

Under conditions of religious diversity in modern welfare states, the administrative interference of the state is inevitably extensive and varied, and the degree of administrative discretion is fairly high (guided by general norms like "public order" and "equity"), particularly if legislation is general or laws are supplemented by general executive orders. Even if guided by the idea of strict or formal neutrality, legislation and administration under such conditions cannot be neutral in their effects

(Laycock 1987). Jurisdiction by administrative or constitutional courts, if guided by such a meta-legal principle, would inevitably unfairly restrict freedom of religious exercise (Monsma and Soper 1997).

Legislation, administration, and jurisdiction interfere politically in public debates regarding state-religion relationships and may explicitly attempt to exert some *cultural* influence. A consequence of a differentiation along such lines is that legal recognition should not be confused with political recognition and administrative recognition. Formal legal recognition of newly organized religions is not a necessary precondition of actual recognition; it may even impede de facto administrative recognition, as the cases of Germany or Belgium clearly show. Another consequence is that legal guarantees of individual or collective religious freedoms do not imply actual protection, as the predicament of Catholics in nineteenth-century United States or of Muslims and many "new religious movements" today (Richardson 2004) clearly show.

Aims and Strategies of States. The aims of states vary widely. States may attempt to (a) suppress and prosecute all individual or collective religious beliefs and practices of specific (e.g., new and "strange" minority) religions; (b) adopt a stance of tolerant negligence; (c) ensure formal or actual protection of religious freedoms for all religions or for specific religions; (d) offer formal or substantive relational neutrality; or (e) provide privileges for all or some (established) religions. States can choose a mix of different strategies in order to achieve their aims to suppress or protect all or specific religions, treat them equally, or positively facilitate and privilege them (Rath et al. 1996, 245). They may control, concede, separate; they may persuade, reward, punish. States may apply direct or indirect strategies, reactive or proactive strategies (Bader 1991, 291-92). In addition, states can use a variety of means to realize their aims and strategies. The specific means of states are laws and jurisdiction (monopolies of legislation and jurisdiction) and the threat of enforcement (monopoly of legal violence). States, however, can use many other resources in order to influence religions: provision or promise of material resources (e.g., land, buildings), money, information, political legitimacy, and qualification of state personnel.

Diversity of Approaches within States. The state is not a homogeneous, monolithic actor: its different branches (legislative, judicative, executive) as well as its different executive departments do not always follow the same aims, strategies, and policies. Justice and Home-Office departments differ significantly from departments of taxation, education, health and child care, housing and urban planning, cultural and social affairs, and so on, particularly in situations of declared security threats. The same holds true, obviously, for the different levels of state organization: federal, state, and local. Local administrations are facing urgent and legitimate demands from religious immigrants more directly and are generally more accommodationist than the central government.

Complexity of Government. Finally, state laws and policies do not only directly or indirectly regulate highly sensitive religious issues like family, sexuality, abortion (Minkenberg 2003b), euthanasia, genetic engineering, and education but also many other policy issues such as taxation, employment, enterprise, housing, health, and social services that may be crucially important for religious minorities. As a consequence, legal regulation is not the same as actual government. Actual government is a far messier matter. Therefore, the first imperative of all research on what states are actually doing in governing religious diversity is to establish what is happening "on the ground."

Explaining State Variation: The Perils of Modelling

Getting it right in this regard is also a first step when we start to explain why states do the things they do. As for all explanatory strategies, we have to ask relevant and specific explanatory questions: Why did states do it now and not then? Why do states follow a certain course of action in a particular neighbourhood, municipality, or region but not in another? What is the specific and changing relationship between governing religions (what the state on all levels is doing) and governance (what non-state actors are doing)? Specific regimes of governance may help explain what states actually are doing.

In all these regards, researchers who want to explain variations in the accommodation or non-accommodation of the demands of new immigrant religions should seek the guidance of sociologists of religion who study societal patterns and regimes of religious governance. The main reason for this is that historical and comparative research is in need of explicitly constructed, theoretically guided typologies; even single case studies use such models at least implicitly. It is therefore important to turn our attention to the perils of modelling but also to remind ourselves that we cannot do without such models.[7]

Path-Dependency and Historical Change. Societal patterns may help explain the continuing diversity of state reactions to new religious diversity. Area patterns (e.g., the American, English, Scandinavian, Mixed, Latin, Right Statist, Left Statist, and Nationalist patterns distinguished by Martin 1978, 59-60), in spite of the contingency of their origins, require some degree of stability in a diachronic, historical perspective. Nested structures exclude other institutional options, and path-dependency, in spite of its critical edge against "necessitarian" evolution, excludes other paths (Crouch and Farrell 2004; Deeg 2005; Pierson 2000b, 2004; Streeck and Thelen 2005). Yet, path-dependency has to allow for modifications and even breaks in patterns: history is not destiny. In constructing patterns, one has to avoid the temptation to present them as more stable over time than they actually are.

Synchronic Comparisons of National Societies. Cross-national comparisons of societies often construct fairly comprehensive, internally more or less coherent or consistent patterns in order to spell out differences (Why here and not there?) more clearly and markedly. If one starts with such homogeneous models, one should be aware of the danger inherent in comparative methods of neglecting important internal heterogeneity: states in the same area-cluster differ from each other, regions within states differ from each other, and so on. Generally speaking, societies may be better described as patchworks or bricolages than as orders with a very high degree of systemic integration.

Inductive and Deductive Models: Sensitivity versus Consistency. Informative models should be more than historical, singular, one-case narratives focused on nation-states (Minkenberg 2003a, 120). Two methods to construct comparative models are available: inductive generalization and deductive theoretical construction. Inductive generalizations usually are more sensitive to the complexity of (overlapping) dimensions but often lead to a proliferation of more and more patterns. Deductive theoretical constructions are more parsimonious, using only one or two dimensions that result in fewer—usually two or by cross-tabulation four—patterns. There seems to be a clear trade-off in this regard between the parsimony and consistency associated with deductive constructions on the one hand, and the historical and comparative sensitivity associated with inductive generalizations on the other hand. The more patterns or types, the higher the historical sensitivity and the empirical "fit" with cases but the more complex and eventually useless these models become for comparative research.[8] Parsimonious, consistent models, however, seem to lack minimally required historical sensitivity and empirical fit. Patterns, after all, have to capture, condense, and articulate crucial structures and traits that really characterize areas, polities, or historical epochs.

Overly Complex Models. Models containing many dimensions (e.g., constitutional, legal, administrative, and judicial; social, political, and cultural) are historically and empirically more informative than models focusing on only one dimension—usually the constitutional/legal relationship between "state and church." However, these models are also usually less consistent because all of these dimensions, though interacting, do not change simultaneously or in the same direction. The operationalization of the respective dimensions in indicators and criteria may lead to models that are overly complex, making testing even more difficult and contested.[9]

Clarifying the Purpose of Models. Finally, models can be analytically constructed for descriptive and/or explanatory purposes or for normative purposes (both evaluative and prescriptive ones). Obviously, the line between these two purposes is often blurry, as evidenced by notorious debates about the "model" of French *laïcité*. It therefore helps if implicit normative assumptions in modelling are made explicit.

Moreover, one should distinguish as clearly as possible among explanations of the emergence, stabilization, and reproduction of distinct patterns (here patterns are dependent variables); explanations of changes in patterns (we should not expect that the same cluster of causes that might explain the emergence and stabilization of patterns could also explain the change and demise of patterns); explanations of diversity in religious politics in general (Minkenberg 2003a, 2004); and explanations of the incorporation of new religious minorities in particular (e.g., Fetzer and Soper 2005; Koenig 2003, 2005). In the incorporation of religious minorities, patterns may serve as independent variables—obviously in combination with other causes because historical explanations by definition require multicausal approaches (Humphreys 1989).[10]

In my view, then, we need disaggregated models of the relationship between (organized) religions, societies, politics, nations, and polities/states that contain all relevant dimensions or "variables" both for descriptive and for explanatory purposes.[11] These disaggregated, conceptual, pre-theoretical frames could be used in a direct way for the rich descriptions of cases, for informed synchronic comparisons, and for the analysis of diachronic changes.

However, if the construction of models is saddled with such difficulties why, one may ask, should we construct models of more aggregated patterns at all?

First and foremost, the complexity of the dimensions, relationships, and indicators is overwhelming and the modelling and theorizing are meant to reduce this complexity in a controlled and reflective way. Second, even if societies and, more specifically, the religions-states-politics relationships are not fully systemically integrated, they show some minimal internal coherence. The construction of patterns has to demonstrate these linkages, mechanisms, and tendencies. Understanding these dynamics is more urgent for researchers who are not content with multivariate statistical analyses but aim at some causal, structural, or functional explanations (Bhaskar 1975; Humphreys 1989).

Third, fairly aggregated models of the religions-states-policies relationship are actually constructed and used by states and policy-makers to design and legitimize institutions and policies as well as by political philosophers, political theorists, legal theorists, judges, administrators, political parties, journalists, and non-governmental organizations. These institutional and policy models of the desirable or acceptable relationship between states, policies, and religions are explicitly normative. In spite of the variety of policies across fields and levels, state policies are guided, or at least legitimized, by very general and rough models of desirable end-states (e.g., the three models of constitutional regimes referred to earlier) and by acceptable ways to achieve these aims. Competing models are important for critics and opponents. In my view, it is reasonable to assume that the highest degree of aggregation and also the highest degree of consistency and coherence of policies will be found in *ex ante* legitimations and designs. Consistency will decrease when it comes to more detailed laws, policy documents, and actual policies in different fields and on lower levels.

Within this context, the task of the *social sciences* is to describe and explain the emergence and reproduction of these predominant and oppositional normative institutional and policy models, their actual impact on policies, and their effects. This task includes the analysis of the actual power relations between the different coalitions of actors who construct and use such models or discursive frames—politicians, judges, philosophers, social scientists as public intellectuals, journalists, and so on—and their impact on public discourse. In policy-evaluation studies, the sharp line between descriptive and prescriptive analysis gets blurred even though these studies are usually guided by the stated aims of policy-makers (Bader and Engelen 2003, 382-88). All those who design alternative institutions and policies, or who want to defend or modify existing ones, have to spell out their own normative principles (and political philosophers and theorists are considered to be normative specialists in this regard).

Fourth, the gap between these predominant normative models of appropriate institutions and policies and "what is going on on the ground" is significant, particularly in countries such as France or the United States where ideal models of the strict separation of state and religions are paramount. It should be evident that normative models do not determine institutions and policies, but the same is also true for institutionalized empirical patterns of state/politics and religions. In explaining differences in the state accommodation of religious practices by Muslim immigrants in Germany, the United Kingdom, and France, Fetzer and Soper (2005) convincingly demonstrate that "church-state theory" is more powerful than competing paradigms associated with social movement theories such as resource mobilization, political opportunity structure, and political ideology. In a recent article (Soper and Fetzer 2007), however, they make it clear that state-church relations do not "determine" but rather "shape" accommodation policies. Indeed, established or institutionalized patterns, like principles and rights (e.g., religious freedoms), have been and have to be continuously reinterpreted and reframed, and framing depends on competing discourses of incorporation, on discourse coalitions and power relations, and on crucial events (Koenig 2007). For instance, the predominant interpretation of state-church relations in France is historically changing and, at any given time, is not sufficient to explain local variations (Bowen 2007; Maussen 2007a).

Minimal Morality, Maximum Accommodation, and Associative Democracy

So far I have presented a broad variety of constitutional models of state-religion relationships and some attempts to reduce this complexity: weak establishment of one or more "churches," and non-establishment in a separatist and in a selective cooperation version. Because weak and plural establishment are defended mainly for prudential and strategic reasons, the morally promising options seem to be strict separation and neo-corporatist, European selective cooperation (Bader 2007a, 201-10). We have also seen that, contrary to prevalent mythologies, all countries—France and the United States included—recognize organized religions either legally or administratively, finance religions either directly or indirectly, finance faith-based organizations in caregiving and education directly or indirectly, and privilege freedoms of religion by granting adherents and not others many exemptions.

Associative democracy, the alternative that I would defend, is embedded in a more empirically grounded normativity based on a critique of abstract, universalist, monist, and theoreticist moral theories. Associative democracy favours moderate universalism as opposed to moral relativism and a view from nowhere; conflicting, equally important moral principles and basic rights (moral pluralism) as opposed to clear, context-independent lexical hierarchies; underdeterminacy of principles and rights; and a broad conception of practical reason acknowledging that there is at least some "reason" in practical or tacit knowledge, in practices and in institutions (Bader 2007a, chap. 2). Only an explicitly contextualized morality brings this criticism home without falling prey to a simple defence of the status quo. Empirically grounded normativity promotes comparisons of practices, policies, and institutions in order to determine preferable ones (this perspective is now predominant in comparative social science evaluation studies).

Contextualized morality also allows for more radical criticism of all existing institutions and policies but insists on "democratic experimentalism" instead of theoretical "blueprinting" and elitist "institutional design" (Bader and Engelen 2003).

This approach is elaborated and tested in my recent book (Bader 2007a). Here I present the briefest summary of the main normative recommendations. I criticize all varieties of the secularization thesis in sociology and reject the predominant knowledge regime of secularism in normative theory, for three reasons. First, liberal democratic states are not secular states but constitutional states, guaranteeing minimal morality (including the two autonomies of states from religions and vice versa) and, in addition, standards of liberal democratic morality, minimally understood. A contextualizing criticism of secularism shows that the use of secularism terminology is historically, structurally, and strategically understandable but misleading. The important thing is not whether states are secular but whether they are minimally decent or liberal-democratic. Second, I argue that first-order ethical secularism and second-order political secularism—both insisting on "secular" reasons—should be rejected. Third, I show why both (a) an independent political and secular ethics as a foundation of liberal democracy and (b) the exclusion of religious reasons (exclusivist secularism) or of all comprehensive reasons (Rawlsian "reason-restraints") from public debate are unfair, implausible, and at odds with antipaternalism and the freedoms of political communication—the two cornerstones of modern democracies. In short, I argue that secularism of all sorts has to be replaced by a *priority for liberal democracy.*

A moderately universalist morality has to be, in my view, a fairly *minimalist morality* guaranteeing the basic needs and rights to security (life, liberty, bodily integrity, due process, and protection against violence), to subsistence, and to collective and individual toleration. This minimalist morality can be complemented by stepwise more demanding moralities—by liberal democratic morality (adding equal civic and political rights), by more egalitarian morality (adding equal socioeconomic and fair cultural rights and opportunities), or by very demanding moralities of comprehensive liberalism or even pluralism—if, and only if, these standards and policies do not infringe upon or endanger the moral minimum. My claim is that this approach helps to clarify and resolve the thorny issues of possibilities and limits to accommodate religious practices in liberal democracies. The limits of accommodation are clearly defined by the moral minimum that has to be guaranteed in all polities by legal sanctions (core of criminal law) and by other prudent forms of external intervention against those religious minorities (and majorities) whose practices violate the basic needs and rights of others.

I distinguish two distinct clusters of cases of accommodation circumscribed by these crucial moral and legal constraints. In hard cases in which the practices of illiberal and non-democratic religions—isolationist or retiring, "totalistic," ultra-orthodox or fundamentalist but internally and externally peaceful minorities—conflict with the minimally interpreted standards of liberal democratic morality (equal civil and political rights, particularly non-discrimination rights), I argue for maximum accommodation if they do not vie for public money. If their faith-based organizations do, however, it is legitimate to use minimal standards of liberal democratic morality. Then, one has to balance the "associational freedoms" and "non-discrimination and equal opportunity" that we expect from moral pluralism and which reflects the normal concern of constitutional courts. Compared with most other approaches, my approach is characterized by an explicit attempt to resist liberal democratic congruence, by clearly spelling out that differences among conflicts, issues, and groups are important, and by acknowledging the wide spectrum of policy repertoires.

Different kinds of claims to pragmatic and symbolic accommodation by new religious minorities that clearly do not conflict with liberal democratic morality present softer cases. Even if they may require considerable legal and practical accommodation, they should be much easier to resolve, particularly if liberal democratic states and politics are committed, as they should be, to the principles of relational religious neutrality and fairness as expressed in even-handedness in cultural matters (my reconceptualizations of the standards of neutrality and equality). Contrary to republican claims, minimal liberal democratic morality does not, for instance, require a governmental monopoly over the school sector. However, in systems that realize a near monopoly of governmental schools, the demand to pluralize curricula, pedagogy, and the culture of governmental schools is even more pressing than in educational systems that allow for publicly funded non-governmental religious schools and for pluralized religious instruction in governmental schools. Resistance to fair accommodation in all these cases is as typical of actual educational policies in all countries as it is morally impermissible, and the same holds for claims to fair exemptions from, and fair accommodations of, existing rules and practices in public administrations and private organizations. Resistance to fair pluralization of public cultures and symbols of national identity is as widespread and even fiercer, and demands for fair representation of new religious minorities in the political process—as defended by associative democracy—that would empower them to raise these morally legitimate claims more effectively are rejected outright by republican and liberal assimilationists.

Associative democracy is a moderately agonistic variety of democratic institutional pluralism that differs from libertarian, liberal, deliberative, republican, and strong or empowered democracy mainly because it allows for a much wider range of institutional pluralism—combining territorial pluralism (multilayered polities associated with federalism) with social pluralism (organized interest representation of classes, professions, clients, consumers), and with autonomy and representation of territorially less concentrated or non-concentrated minorities such as gendered minorities and many ethnic and religious minorities. Associative democracy is also much more in tune with recent shifts from government to governance. In turn, it is more flexible and open than the existing corporatist, neo-corporatist, or consociational forms of democratic institutional pluralism—power-sharing systems that guarantee divergent units in the political process in addition to meaningful autonomy or self-determination to decide specific issues.

Associative democracy introduces into political and public discourse a realist model of religious governance that is in contrast with the exclusive alternative and the ritualized opposition between American denominationalism and (neo-)corporatist varieties of selective cooperation still dominating policy discourses and blocking institutional imagination and practical experiment. Associative democracy, like all existing varieties of religious institutional pluralism, empowers religions but—as a moderately libertarian version—is more conducive to old and new religious minorities and, particularly, to vulnerable minorities within minorities in the following ways. First, in addition to guaranteeing exit rights from religions, it provides meaningful exit options. Second, it tries to encourage debate and discussion inside religious organizations, particularly if they accept public money and want to be represented in the political process, without overriding meaningful associational autonomy. Third, recognition and institutionalization of religions enlarge the possibilities and the means of minimal, legitimate state supervision and control. And, last but not least, associative democracy makes productive use of the idea of differentiated morality; that is, standards of minimal morality have to protect the basic needs, interests, and rights of all, including vulnerable minorities within minorities such as minors and women. The basic interests of vulnerable minorities require external supervision, control, and sanctions (by the liberal state) without overriding meaningful associational autonomy, as evangelists of liberal autonomy and liberal democratic congruence propose. Contrary to liberal and republican assimilationism, associative democracy recognizes the tensions between individual and associational autonomy. Instead of heroically propagating tragic choices or big trade-offs between "your (individual) rights" and "your (collective) culture," its institutions enable better and more sensible balances.

Two advantages of associative democracy are particularly important for religions. First, associative democracy allows religions a wide range of service provision on their own terms—limited by negotiated quality standards—instead of "one model fits all" public service delivery by states presented (inaccurately, as I have demonstrated above) as culturally neutral. Such a polycentric model of service provision is also clearly more in tune with recent conditions of a "reasonable pluralism of the good life." Second, it empowers religious majorities and minorities not only in terms of accommodation and service provision but also by providing various forms of engagement for organized religions in the political process. In this way, associative democracy helps to make the state and public policies more relationally neutral and even-handed.

Although many theoretical approaches include dilemmas of recognition, organization, and mobilization for religions and for liberal democratic states and policies, my claim is that associative democracy is better able to productively deal with these dilemmas of institutionalization compared with European corporatist selective cooperation and American denominationalism. As we have seen, at least some degree of recognition by political bodies is inevitable. Instead of allowing, for instance, tax administrations or urban planning departments nearly unlimited discretion, according to associative democracy the rule of law demands that judicial control and legislative regulations bring the tricky judicial decisions of inclusion/exclusion more into the open and make them democratically more legitimate.

Moreover, it is obvious that the demand for representative spokespersons and organizations of religions very much depends on the differential opportunity structure. If states grant direct or indirect funding to faith-based organizations in social services, care, and education—as all liberal democratic states actually do—the contested thresholds for recognition in terms of numbers, territorial concentration, organization, credibility, and duration are usually and inevitably much higher. If states provide institutional opportunities for religions in setting standards, implementation, and control of provisions and also some formal representation of organized religions in the political process—as institutionally pluralist regimes of selective cooperation do—the thresholds are again higher.

Formal recognition of organized religions inevitably creates dilemmas for religious groups and the state. For example, some religious adherents may feel that church autonomy is in conflict with any increased degree of public control or involvement, and some state actors may feel that state-guaranteed basic rights are threatened by the autonomy allowed to religious organizations. Fairness requires us to acknowledge that these dilemmas exist in all possible regimes of governance but also that they are sharpened by regimes of official selective cooperation (as in Canada) and, particularly, by existing neo-corporatist regimes that work systematically in favour of old, established religious majorities (rigid, closed, over-exclusive) as one finds in many European countries.

An extremely brief comparison of the development of representative Muslim organizations in Europe and the United States may demonstrate this. In some European countries, Islam was recognized by law fairly early on: in the Russian and Austro-Hungarian Empire (1912), Poland (1936), and Austria (1979). In some countries recognition came later (Belgium, Spain, France), while in other countries Islam has not been recognized at all (United Kingdom, Italy, Germany). The situation in Germany and Italy is particularly pressing because the lack of legal recognition denies Muslims many important privileges granted to officially recognized religions in these corporatist regimes. In general, we see the emergence of three different patterns of central Muslim representation: a more "church"-like central, unitary organization (mainly as a result of state-crafting from above, as in Belgium and France); a confederal association that represents the common interests of independent Muslim organizations in a coordinated and legally recognized way (the Spanish *Comisión Islamica de España*); and several independent, loosely coordinated, publicly recognized organizations (as in Sweden and Norway).

The situation in the United States is quite different (Casanova 2007) in three important regards. First, the weakness or absence of establishment and of caesaro-papist "ethnicized" or "territorialized" religions, together with the highly competitive religious market, eventually turns all religions into denominations. These denominations are characterized by a congregational structure, by the importance of lay people in the internal governance, and by the development of community centres with different kinds of educational and social services, fellowship, and recreational activities. Second, the absence of an elaborate system of selective cooperation, particularly at the federal level, means that religions are not encouraged by positive incentives to develop national organizations and that federal administrations are not in need of interlocutors representing religions. This also implies, third, that the state does not attempt to impose a uniform organizational and representational pattern or its favourite "liberal" or "civilized" version on Islam or on any other religion. How Muslims will develop an appropriate organizational and representational structure is fairly open. They might fall prey to the Protestant evil of denominationalism (endless splits grounded in socioeconomic and ethno-racial divisions); they might organize themselves into a national, Catholic church-like *ummah*, able to bridge their internal ethno-linguistic and juridical-doctrinal divisions; they might develop a Jewish-like board of deputies representing common interest; or, more likely, they might find their own distinct pattern.

In contrast with the situation of Muslims in Europe, in the United States this choice is not massively crafted by state administrations. This fact considerably alleviates the related problems of church autonomy, the equal treatment of religions, and relational state neutrality. Islam is less forced into an imposed "American Islam." The Americanization of Islam from below is more the unintended but welcome by-product of the American system of religious governance than the result of intentional state policies, in contrast with attempts to create a French Islam from above (see Jocelyne Cesari's chapter in this volume).

Associative democracy shares with American denominationalism its outspoken voluntarism (exit rights, self-definition, and self-organization guaranteed by freedoms of political communication and association)[12] and its insistence that the self-organization of religious minorities should develop more or less spontaneously from below. American denominationalism is much friendlier toward new, small religious minorities and shows a much higher degree of religious diversity (and both are no small achievements!). In all these regards, American denominationalism is clearly preferable to the existing European regimes of corporatist selective cooperation. Yet, American denominationalism also has its well-known downsides.

First, the guarantee of exit rights is not accompanied by the provision of meaningful exit options, particularly for vulnerable minorities within totalistic minorities where social ostracism results not only in inevitable identity costs and the loss of social relations and networks but also in high material costs (loss of care, shelter, social security, and employment; Warren 2001, 99-103). The absence in the United States of a comprehensive welfare system contrasts starkly with most European systems and, particularly, with associative democracy's proposal of a basic income.

Second, American denominationalism is known for the huge but informal impact on politics of socially and culturally established religions, still mainly Protestant; it is also well known that it took quite a while and protracted contest and organization[13] before the American state could be made de facto more relationally neutral and before American civil religion inconclusively shifted from Protestantism to include Catholicism and Judaism. Islam is still largely an outsider, and even a possibly emerging Abrahamic (i.e., Jewish/Christian/Muslim) civil religion would be monotheistic. Systems that restrict interest representation to informal ways of influencing governments through network building, lobbying, and so on de facto privilege old, big, established religions because they have huge and unchecked advantages in terms of power, resources, and strategies.

Third, this public/private split is also counterproductive when it comes to all kinds of welfare and social services (Minow 2000) that crucially depend on charities and faith-based organizations. Moreover, the predominant educational ideology rather hinders innovative experiments of cooperation in education (Liebman and Sabel 2003).

Associative democracy promises clear advantages in all these regards that would also benefit the governance of religious diversity in contexts of migration. But can it avoid the downside of corporatist European systems that privilege the old, established majority religion(s)? Can it avoid unfair privileges, selectivity, closure, and rigidity? Although associative democracy cannot avoid providing *selective* recognition and cooperation, it insists that the differentiated criteria have to be applied equally and indiscriminately to all religions, old or new, big or small. Associative democracy acknowledges that all systems of selective cooperation inevitably involve distinctive thresholds. For registration and for administrative and judicial recognition of religions, thresholds in terms of time and numbers can and should be minimal (e.g., ten practitioners for, say, a year). Thresholds increase when systems of official cooperation between administrations and publicly recognized religions and faith-based organizations emerge or are proposed; when faith-based organizations participate in standard setting, implementation, and control; and when organized religions gain rights and opportunities of representation in the political process. Reasons of history, number of adherents, social roots, and so on clearly matter, and they do so legitimately, at least according to a contextualized theory of morality. Hence, newcomers are, inevitably, disadvantaged. Elsewhere, I have proposed how one might deal with the tricky problem of functionally required exclusion and how one might also guarantee the inclusion of relevant stakeholders and make systems more open, flexible, transparent, and accountable (Bader 2008, 15-16). If such proposals can withstand the expected resistance of established insiders, associative democracy's system of selective cooperation promises to combine the advantages of American denominationalism and European selective cooperation regimes.

Associative democracy, then, would be a realist framework that, in principle, could build on existing regimes of governance in various countries. Institutionally pluralist regimes (e.g., in the Netherlands) may provide better opportunities and mechanisms for institutional learning compared with countries such as France or the United States (although Liebman and Sabel [2003] have demonstrated that quite similar experiments can be found in the United States in certain regions and municipalities). Above all, associative democracy has to deal with real dilemmas that do not allow for one optimal solution independent of contexts. Instead of institutional blueprints or elitist design, trust is put in democratic experimentalism.

Notes

1. Richardson (2004) uses the term "regulating religion," which is much narrower because he focuses on social control, specifically state control from above (neglecting governance from within and below), and on legal and judicial control. The relation with other forms of regulation is only touched upon in discussing "discretion" more broadly, including executive and administrative discretion. Moreover, the substantial focus in Richardson (2004) is on cults and sects or "New Religious Movements," which form only a small, albeit radical, part of new religious minorities.

2. In a broader sense, governance as an umbrella concept includes government and governance in the narrower sense.

3. See Kalyvas (1996) for a discussion of democratic governance within Christianity, and Mazower (2005, chap. 3, 8) for the internal governance of the Jewish community in Salonica.

4. See the concise summary of recent developments in Schmitter (2000) and Kersbergen and Waarden (2001).

5. I first present the two extreme options on a scale (dichotomous modelling) before adding intermediate options (gradualist modelling). The following is based on Bader (2007a, chap. 1 and 3). For more extensive documentation, see Bader (2006, chap. 2), Robbers (1995, 2001), and the case studies in this volume.

6. Ferrari (2002) elaborates the forms of cooperation between states and religious groups by detecting a pyramidal pattern of selective cooperation with three levels (10–12 for European countries). Monsma and Soper (1997) and Fetzer and Soper (2005) distinguish between three basic types: the strict church-state separation model, the established church model, and the pluralist or structuralist model. Fox (2006, 546-55) tries to operationalize the extent of separation of religion and state and of government involvement in religion by using five variables and a huge number of indicators or codes. Full separation of religion and state is called separationism, whereas accommodation means "official separation of religion and state and a benevolent or neutral attitude toward religion" or selective cooperation.

7. See Bader (2007a, chap. 2; 2007b, 875-80) for a more extensive discussion of different approaches. All these problems are more or less extensively discussed as attempts to model the variety of institutions and policies in other areas. For the variety of types or models of the capitalism debate, see Amable (2003); Crouch and Streeck (1997); Hollingsworth and Boyer (1997); Kitchelt et al. (1999); and Whitley (2000). For the varieties of welfare states see Esping-Andersen (1990) and Pierson (2000a); for types of democracies see Lijphart (1984); and for regimes of incorporation of minorities see Bader (1997, 5). See also for a short criticism Crouch and Farrell (2004).

8. The refinement of types and subtypes eventually tends to produce models presenting each country as a separate type. In addition, one would still have to answer the question: Why states and not subnational regions?

9. For each relevant dimension and indicator, one can choose between a *dichotomous* strategy (allowing two poles or extremes only) and a *gradualist* strategy (allowing for several important options on a scale between the extremes). Again, there seems to be a trade-off: dichotomous modelling is consistent and parsimonious at the price of neglecting important options, whereas gradualist modelling is more murky but open to relevant—descriptive and prescriptive (normative and practical-political)—distinctions.

10. As always, it is crucial for the construction of theoretically guided models to get the explanatory "why" questions right. Regarding the religions-states-policies relationship, one should distinguish much more clearly among (a) their *origin* (Why did they emerge at all?), (b) their existence and *reproduction* (Why and how do they continue to exist?), and (c) their *change and demise*. From Max Weber (see Bader and Benschop 1989, 265-74), we can learn that answers to these questions are not the same; there are different variables and constellations. Simplistically speaking, religio-cultural pluralism (civilizations) and political pluralism (polities) are the crucial "independent variables" explaining the emergence of different patterns. They clearly existed long before the development of modern capitalism, industrialization, urbanization, cultural secularization, and modernization, which may help to explain the reproduction or demise of patterns. Clearly different from these explanatory questions are questions regarding (d) the *impact on policies* (direct and indirect influence) of such existing and institutionalized patterns—their *political and legal impact* on legislation and jurisdiction in all relevant areas (not only in private law, particularly family, marriage, and divorce law), as well as on administration, implementation, and control and, obviously, their direct or indirect *socioeconomic and cultural* impact.

11. See my general arguments for such conceptual and pre-theoretical disaggregation (Bader and Benschop 1989; Bader 1992).

12. Charges of essentialist categorization are rejected in my criticism of Baumann (see Bader 2001). The insistence on self-definition is crucial, but it should also be stressed that redistributive claims have to be checked more objectively and that identity claims should not pay (see Bader 2003, 146-48; and Bader 2007c; cf. the criticism of Barry 2000).

13. In the case of Islam, this is underestimated even by Casanova (2007).

References

Amable, B. 2003. *The Diversity of Modern Capitalism*. Oxford: Oxford University Press.

Bader, V. 1991. *Kollektives Handeln.* Opladen, Germany: Leske and Budrich.

— 1992. "'Grand Theories,' Empirismus oder Pro-Theorie; Bewegungsforschung am Scheideweg." *Forschungsjournal Neue Soziale Bewegungen* 5(2):9-21.

— 1997. "Incorporation of Ethnic or National Minorities. Concepts, Dimensions, Fields, and Types." Unpublished manuscript. Available at http://home.hum.uva.nl/oz/baderv/1997_incorporation.doc

— 2001. "Culture and Identity: Contesting Constructivism." *Ethnicities* 1(2):251-73.

— 2003. "Democratic Institutional Pluralism." In *The Social Construction of Diversity*, ed. C. Harzig and D. Juteau. New York: Berghahn.

— 2006. "Secularism or Democracy." Unpublished version. University of Amsterdam, Department of Philosophy, Amsterdam.

— 2007a. *Secularism or Democracy? Associational Governance of Religious Diversity.* Amsterdam: Amsterdam University Press.

— 2007b. "The Governance of Islam in Europe: The Perils of Modeling." *Journal of Ethnic and Migration Studies* 33(6):871-86.

— 2007c. "Defending Differentiated Policies of Multiculturalism." *National Identities* 9(3): 197-215.

— 2008. *Complex Citizenship and Legitimacy in Compound Polities (MLPs and MLG): The EU as Example.* Eurosphere Working Paper No. 5. Accessed 19 November 2008 at http://www.eurosphere.uib.no/knowledgebase/workingpapers.htm

Bader, V. and A. Benschop. 1989. *Ungleichheiten.* Opladen, Germany: Leske and Budrich.

Bader, V. and E.R. Engelen. 2003. "Taking Pluralism Seriously: Arguing for an Institutional Turn in Political Philosophy." *Philosophy and Social Criticism* 29(4):375-406.

Barry, B. 2000. *Culture and Equality.* Cambridge: Polity Press.

Bhaskar, R. 1975. *A Realist Theory of Science.* Leeds, UK: Leeds Books.

Bouma, G.D. 1999. "From Hegemony to Pluralism: Managing Religious Diversity in Modernity and Post-Modernity." *Australian Religion Studies Review* 12(2):7-27.

Bowen, J.R. 2007. "A View from France on the Internal Complexity of National Models." *Journal of Ethnic and Migration Studies* 33(6):1003-16.

Casanova, J. 2007. "Immigration and the New Religious Pluralism: A European Union/United States Comparison." In *Democracy and the New Religious Pluralism*, ed. T. Banchoff. New York: Oxford University Press.

Chaves, M. and D. Cann. 1992. "Regulation, Pluralism, and Religious Market Structure." *Rationality and Society* 4:272-90.

Crouch, C. and H. Farrell. 2004. "Breaking the Path of Institutional Development?" *Rationality and Society* 16(1):5-43.

Crouch, C. and W. Streeck. 1997. *Political Economy of Modern Capitalism.* London: Sage.

Deeg, R. 2005. "Change from Within." In *Beyond Continuity*, ed. W. Streeck and K. Thelen. Oxford: Oxford University Press.

Esping-Andersen, G. 1990. *The Three Worlds of Welfare Capitalism*. Cambridge: Polity Press.

Ferrari, S. 1996. *L'Islam in Europa*. Bologna, Italy: Il Mulino.

— 2002. "Islam and the Western European Model of Church and State Relations." In *Religious Freedom and the Neutrality of the State: The Position of Islam in the European Union*, ed. S. Koningsveld and W.A.R. Shadid. Leuven, Belgium: Peeters.

— 2005. "The Secular State and the Shaping of Muslim Representative Organizations in Western Europe." In *European Muslims and the Secular State*, ed. S. McLoughlin and J. Cesari. Aldershot, UK: Ashgate.

Ferrari, S. and A. Bradney, eds. 2000. *Islam and European Legal Systems*. Aldershot, UK: Ashgate.

Fetzer, J. and J.C. Soper. 2005. *Muslims and the State in Britain, France and Germany*. Cambridge: Cambridge University Press.

Fox, J. 2006. "World Separation of Religion and State into the 21st Century." *Comparative Political Studies* 39(5):537-69.

Galanter, M. 1966. "Religious Freedoms in the United States: A Turning Point." *Wisconsin Law Review* 2:217-96.

Glenn, C. and J. de Groof. 2002a. *Finding the Right Balance: Freedom, Autonomy and Accountability in Education*, vol. 1. Utrecht, Netherlands: Lemma Publishers.

— 2002b. *Finding the Right Balance: Freedom, Autonomy and Accountability in Education*, vol. 2. Utrecht, Netherlands: Lemma Publishers.

Héritier, A. 2002. "Introduction" and "New Modes of Governance in Europe." In *Common Goods*, ed. A. Héritier. Oxford: Rowman and Littlefield.

Hollingsworth, J.R. and R. Boyer, eds. 1997. *Contemporary Capitalism: The Embeddedness of Institutions*. Cambridge: Cambridge University Press.

Humphreys, P. 1989. *The Chances of Explanation: Causal Explanation in the Social, Medical and Physical Sciences*. Princeton, NJ: Princeton University Press.

Kalyvas, S.N. 1996. *The Rise of Christian Democracy in Europe*. Ithaca, New York: Cornell University Press.

Kitchelt, H., P. Lange, G. Marks, and J.D. Stephens, eds. 1999. *Continuity and Change in Contemporary Capitalism*. Cambridge: Cambridge University Press.

Koenig, M. 2003. *Staatsbürgerschaft und religiöse Pluralität in post-nationalen Konstellationen*. PhD dissertation, Marburg University, Germany.

— 2005. "Incorporating Muslim Migrants in Western Nation States." *Journal for International Migration and Integration* 6:219-34.

— 2007. "Europeanizing the Governance of Religious Diversity." *Journal of Ethnic and Migration Studies* 33(6):911-32.

Laycock, D.H. 1987. *Cooperative Government Relations in Canada: Lobbying, Public Policy Development and the Changing Cooperative System*. Saskatoon, SK: Centre for the Study of Cooperatives, University of Saskatchewan.

Liebman, J. and C. Sabel. 2003. "A Public Laboratory Dewey Barely Imagined: The Emerging Model of School Governance and Legal Reform." *Journal of Law and Social Change* 23(2):183-304.

Lijphart, A. 1984. *Democracies*. Berkeley, CA: University of California Press.

Martin, D. 1978. *A General Theory of Secularization*. New York: Harper and Row.

Maussen, M. 2007a. "Islamic Presence and Mosque Establishment in France." *Journal of Ethnic and Migration Studies* 33(6):981-1002.

— 2007b. *The Governance of Islam in Western Europe. A State of the Art*. International Migration, Integration and Social Cohesion (IMISCOE) working paper No. 16. Accessed 24 September 2008 at http://www.imiscoe.org/publications/workingpapers/documents/GovernanceofIslam.pdf

Mazower, M. 2005. *Salonica*. London: Harper.

Messner, F. 1999. "La Législation Culturelle des Pays de l'Union Européenne." In *Sectes et Démocratie*, ed. F. Champion and M. Cohen. Paris: Seuil.

Minkenberg, M. 2003a. "Staat und Kirche in westlichen Demokratien." Special issue, *Politik und Religion – Politische Vierteljahresschrift* Sonderheft 33:115-38.

— 2003b. "Religion and Policy Effects." In *The Policy Impact of Church-State Relations: Family Policy and Abortion in Britain, France and Germany*, ed. J. Madeley and Z. Enyedi. London: Frank Cass.

— 2004. "Religious Effects on the Shaping of Immigration Policy in Western Democracies." Paper presented at the European Consortium for Political Research (ECPR) 32nd Joint Session, Uppsala University, Sweden, 13–18 April.

Minow, M. 2000. "Partners, Not Rivals?" *Boston University Law Review* 80:1060-94.

Monsma, S.V. and J.C. Soper. 1997. *The Challenge of Pluralism: Church and State in Five Democracies*. Lanham, MD: Rowman and Littlefield.

— 2006. *Faith, Hope and Jobs*. Washington, DC: Georgetown University Press.

Pierre, J. and B.G. Peters. 2000. *Governance, Politics and the State*. Basingstoke, UK: Macmillan.

Pierson, P. 2000a. "Three Worlds of Welfare State Research." *Comparative Political Studies* 33(6):791-821.

— 2000b. "Increasing Returns, Path Dependence, and the Study of Politics." *American Political Science Review* 94(2):251-67.

— 2004. *Politics in Time*. Princeton, NJ: Princeton University Press.

Rath, J., R. Penninx, K. Groenendijk, and A. Meyer. 1996. *Nederland en zijn Islam*. Amsterdam: Spinhuis.

Richardson, J.T., ed. 2004. *Regulating Religion: Case Studies from Around the Globe*. New York: Kluwer Academic/Plenum Publishers.

Robbers, G., ed. 1995. *Staat und Kirche in der Europäischen Union* [State and Church in the European Union]. Baden-Baden, Germany: Nomos.

— ed. 2001. *Church Autonomy*. Frankfurt am Main: Peter Lang.

Scharpf, F.W. 1997. *Games Real Actors Play: Actor-Centered Institutionalism in Policy Research*. Boulder, CO: Westview Press.

Schmitter, P.C. 2000. *How to Democratize the European Union?* Oxford: Rowman and Littlefield.

Shahid, W.A.R. and P.S. van Koningsveld, eds. 2002. *Religious Freedom and the Neutrality of the State: The Position of Islam in the European Union*. Leuven, Belgium: Peeters.

Soper, J.C. and J. Fetzer. 2007. "Religious Institutions, Church-State History and Muslim Mobilization in Britain, France and Germany." *Journal of Ethnic and Migration Studies* 33(6):933-44.

Streeck, W. and K. Thelen. 2005. "Introduction." In *Beyond Continuity*, ed. W. Streeck and K. Thelen. Oxford: Oxford University Press.

Treib, O., H. Bähr, and G. Falkner. 2006. "Modes of Governance: A Note Towards Conceptual Clarification." European Governance Paper No. N-05-02. Accessed 24 September 2008 at http://www.connex-network.org/eurogov/pdf/egp-newgov-N-05-02.pdf

Van Kersbergen, K. and F. van Waarden. 2001. *Shifts in Governance: Problems of Legitimacy and Accountability.* The Hague: Netherlands Organization for Scientific Research (NWO).

Warren, M.E. 2001. *Democracy and Association.* Princeton and Oxford: Princeton University Press.

Whitley, R. 2000. *Divergent Capitalisms.* Oxford: Oxford University Press.

Willaime, J.-P., ed. 2005. *Des Maîtres et des Dieux.* Paris: Belin.

Part II
National Case
Studies

Chapter 4

Constructing Religious Pluralism Transnationally: Reflections from the United States

Peggy Levitt and Jessica Hejtmanek

As we write this chapter, the United States is in the throes of the 2008 presidential campaign. Every Monday, Democrats and Republicans appear on the front pages of newspapers across the country walking down the steps after Sunday morning church services. From Obama to Huckabee, they are quoted citing scripture to congregation members. Their stump speeches conclude with the requisite "God Bless You." How can this be in a country where the line between church and state is allegedly drawn indelibly? Why is it that so much religious discourse and imagery seep into politics when these realms are supposedly so separate?

In this paper, we offer three responses. First, we argue that while church and state may be legally separate, there is no such thing as a cultural separation of church and state. The cultural mixing of religion and politics in the United States has deep roots. Second, and because of this, faith has always been a powerful catalyst for immigrant integration. Recent immigrants who introduce new faith traditions or ethnicize old ones only enhance faith's role in public discourse: they are changed by their interaction with US religious and political institutions and, at the same time, transform those institutions. And third, we argue that the disconnect between expectations about religion and politics and the actual interaction between them stems, in part, from misguided assumptions about what religion is and how it works. Whether we like it or not, faith does not simply pack itself up and disappear after eleven

International Migration and the Governance of Religious Diversity, eds. P. Bramadat and M. Koenig.
Montreal and Kingston: McGill-Queen's University Press, Queen's Policy Studies Series.
© 2009 The School of Policy Studies, Queen's University at Kingston. All rights reserved.

o'clock on Sunday mornings. Rather, it is, or at least can be, a comprehensive worldview influencing all aspects of daily experience. Nor does religion stop at the borders of the nation-state. Religious dynamics in the United States, as elsewhere, have always been shaped by forces inside and outside national boundaries. Even if it were possible to draw an indelible line between church and state, it would not stop at the US border.

In the following sections, we offer a brief history of the relationship between church and state in the United States, a broad brush-stroke panorama of the ways in which religion affects immigrants and immigrants influence religion, and a discussion of contemporary challenges to religious pluralism given this changing landscape.

The Formal Management of Church and State

America's founding fathers proposed two views of religion's normative function in democracy. The first, as articulated by George Washington in his inaugural address and later elaborated by de Tocqueville in *Democracy in America*, sees religion as the moral and cultural anchor of democracy. In liberal democracies, which are based on private freedoms, private morality is the key source of public morality. Private religion exerts a strong influence over private morality and therefore becomes an important source of public and political standards of conduct. From this perspective, religious communities are natural training grounds for political community spirit and engagement.

The rival thesis, as articulated by James Madison in *Federalist*, number 10, denies that religion has a political function. Instead, religious communities are seen as factions or interest groups that act in their own self-interest and often work against the interests of others and the common good. Religious communities cannot be relied upon or trusted to support or sustain universal standards of public morality. Rather, religious diversity, and checks and balances between different sects, ensure religious liberty.

America's founding fathers were concerned about religious conflict, and hence the Establishment Clause in the First Amendment of the Constitution prohibits naming an official national religion. Here again, disagreements abound over what this clause actually means. Accommodationists understand it as allowing the state to adopt policies that are equally supportive of religion across faiths. In public schools, for example, allowing prayers that are associated with a particular denomination would not be acceptable but allowing generic prayers that speak to all faiths would be. Separationists, in the tradition of Thomas Jefferson's "high wall between church and state," interpret this clause to mean that the state should not support religion in general or privilege any particular faith over another.

Proponents on both sides differ over what the appropriate public role of religion should be. Because accommodationists believe that the nation is generally united over moral and religious issues, they see strong church–state relations as a positive thing. Separationists see religion as a source of tension and therefore advocate for a much more restrictive, less visible role for faith in the public square.

These debates are often decided by the Supreme Court, but its rulings have swung back and forth in response to shifting social trends. Until the late 1940s, backed by strong public opinion, the Court often ruled with the accommodationists. From the end of World War II until recently, though, reflecting America's increasingly diverse, secular society, the Court adopted a more separatist stance. For example, the Court ruled in favour of bans on displaying religious symbols on public property, and also ruled against collective prayer or moments of silence in public schools. Recent rulings, however, suggest a swing in the other direction. The Establishment Clause has been reinterpreted to allow taxpayer financing of evangelical student newspapers and the construction of buildings at sectarian (mostly Christian) schools. Court observers claim that this happened because the debate has shifted from traditional clause questions—Does this constitute government funding of religious activities? to concerns about freedom of religion—Would denying religious institutions this benefit constitute discrimination?

There is also disagreement about the Free Exercise Clause and about the types of religious behaviour it safeguards. Some scholars interpret this clause in a communitarian manner, arguing that prevailing community standards can limit religious behaviours that offend the moral sensibilities of the broader public. Others adopt a more libertarian stance, arguing that all religious behaviour should be protected unless there is a compelling state interest for limiting it. In general, communitarians see religion as a source of social cohesion and state legitimacy. The government can forbid certain practices permitted or required by particular religions, provided such restrictions apply neutrally to religious and secular behaviour alike. Libertarians see religious values as empowering individuals and, therefore, as limiting the power of government and public opinion. In general, the Supreme Court has taken a more libertarian stance, although in recent years it has handed down several rulings that seemingly limit free exercise among religious minorities, including prohibiting the Native American practice of using peyote in religious ceremonies (Sink 2004) and the right of Orthodox Jews to wear headgear under helmets.

What Do Americans Believe?

The vast majority of Americans (over 85 percent) claim that religion matters to them, no matter what their faith (Dillon 2003). According to the World Values Survey (see Swanbrow 1997), people in the United States attend church more frequently than do those in any other nation at a "comparable level of development."[1] While it is not the most religious country—90 percent of the populations of Pakistan, India, Indonesia, and several countries in Africa agree that "religion plays a very important role in their lives"—the US stands alone among "wealthy" countries for the number of residents who agree with that statement (59 percent, nearly double that of Canada, Great Britain, Eastern Europe, and Western Europe; Pew Research Center 2002). Citing the profound secularity of even traditionally Catholic Italy (at just 27 percent), the Pew Global Attitudes Project confirms that America's religiosity is closer to that of developing nations. While a high percentage of people in some industrialized nations believe in God (56 percent in the UK and 65 percent in Russia), the United States still surpasses them, with 86 percent of the population saying they believe in a higher power (BBC 2005).

Church attendance in the United States has dropped slightly from its peak of about 50 percent in the 1950s and 1960s to the 40–44 percent that is generally the norm today (Carroll 1999). However, the number of Americans who consider themselves members of a religious group has remained steady at 65–70 percent during the same period (Carroll 2004; Gallup Organization 1976–2006). In his 1998 National Congregations Survey, Chaves (2004, 3, 18-19) reported that there were 300,000 religious congregations in the United States but that membership was unevenly distributed. Most people were associated with large congregations, but the majority of congregations were small (a median of 75 persons) and struggling financially (with a median budget of $56,000). Protestant groups, in general, were experiencing significant declines in membership. Catholic membership vacillated up and down but, on average, remained fairly stable. The Jewish population was declining slightly. The most significant growth was among non-Christian groups and non-Protestant Christians (Kosmin, Mayer, and Keysar 2001; Lyons 2005).

Most scholars agree, however, that the importance of religion to Americans cannot be measured by church attendance alone. The meaning of religion has become much more malleable—it is "spiritual," "experiential," or "expressive." Stark, Hamberg, and Miller (2005) argue that although as many as one-third of Americans are "unchurched," they are far from irreligious. The majority pray (only 4 percent never pray) and believe in God or in a higher power. Roof (1999) also found that among the 14 percent of Americans who were "not religious," two-thirds claimed to be "spiritual." It is the "failure to define religion with sufficient breadth and nuance" (Stark, Hamberg, and Miller 2005, 20; see also Wuthnow 1998) that blinds us to what Grace Davie (2007) has called "believing non-belongers."

America's deep religiosity carries with it a profound ambivalence and often outright contradictions. At a Pew forum in Washington, religious historian Dionne (2003) observed, "It isn't simply that we Americans are divided into opposing camps . . . secular and religious . . . [it's] a great ambivalence within ourselves." He cited a 2002 Pew Research Center survey on religion in public life that asked Americans, on the one hand, whether they wanted a president with strong religious beliefs (70 percent) and, on the other, whether they disliked politicians who talked too much about how religious they are (50 percent). Dionne used the term *flexidoxy*, coined by David Brooks (2000) in his book *Bobos in Paradise*, as an apt metaphor. "Many Americans want the moral and spiritual certainty of orthodoxy," Dionne told the forum, "but being Americans of their age, they also want their orthodoxy to be flexible."

According to Alan Wolfe (2003), although Americans define themselves by their religion, many "shape and reshape" the traditions and identities to suit their own sense of egalitarianism and personal identity. Americans want fellowship and community but are often suspicious of the religious institutions that provide them. People in the United States find their faith highly valuable and important to their lives but are "reluctant to shove anything down anyone else's throat" (246). Yet despite the importance of faith in the lives of Americans, Wolfe finds that believers actually know very little about the details of their religion: "58 percent of Americans cannot name five of the Ten Commandments, just under half know that Genesis is the first book of the Bible . . . and 10 percent believe that Joan of Arc was Noah's wife" (247).

The predominant religious cultural template in the United States is Protestantism. Martin Marty calls it "the wallpaper in the mental furnishing department in which America lives, always in the room but barely noticed."[2] Many ideological debates as well as governance strategies and organizational forms reflect the country's Protestant roots. Seymour Martin Lipset (1996), for example, attributed America's weak welfare state and anti-statist disposition to its unique religious character which fostered radical individualism. America's Protestant roots have also given rise to highly individualistic notions of freedom of conscience. As Peter Dobkin Hall (1998, 101) writes: "Far from being a 'second-order phenomenon,' religion (in particular, liberal Protestant values) was integral to the development of American corporate technology. The rationales and methods of bureaucratic and corporate organization actually emerged from the domain of religion and spread from there to the economic, political and social institutions."[3]

The seemingly ubiquitous presence of faith in the United States is sometimes described as a product of America's civil religion in which the national political creed assumes many of the communal and symbolic functions associated with traditional religion. Civil religious principles unite what can be a fractious democratic society around common political ideas legitimated by divine inspiration. Because faith is linked to nationalism, civil obligations assume a sacred character. Civil religion infuses politics with a religious dimension and institutionalizes the worship of democratic principles by imbuing them with a sort of semi-religious character. A belief in a generic Judaeo-Christian monotheism unites the nation because the contours of that faith remain largely indistinct. Thus, it is not particularly surprising that US coins are imprinted with "In God We Trust," that school children pledge allegiance to "One Nation Under God," or that the US Congress begins each day with a prayer. According to a 2004 survey, only 18 percent of Americans would remove the Ten Commandments from public buildings, a solid majority (59 percent) favour teaching creationism in schools, and nearly one-third support making *Christianity the official religion of the United States* (Barna Research Group 2004).

Several unique traits of the American political system also make it easier for interest groups and social movements to mobilize and influence politics in the United States than in other countries. First, American political parties are relatively porous and undisciplined. There is no binding party platform. Second, candidates for office are not appointed by party leaders but are chosen through primaries, caucuses, and conventions. Third, parties do not function like membership organizations. In fact, in some states, any citizen can vote for any party during the primary campaign. These dynamics make the Democratic and Republican parties particularly vulnerable to the influence of social movements. The relationship between political parties and religious groups is in some ways symbiotic. Political organizations rely on such groups to reach prospective voters and to lend their infrastructure and resources in support of political campaigns. Democratic candidates, for example, have often looked to African American churches to bring out the African American vote, just as Republican candidates have relied on the Christian right to reach out to conservative white Protestants. Religiously motivated activists have played major roles in the abolitionist movements, the early women's rights movement, the temperance movement, and the civil rights movement. And because national, state, and local elections operate separately, there are many entry points at which interest groups can intervene and exert their influence.

This is a two-way street, however. As many aspects of national life grew more secular, that modern, secular culture incited new religious reactions. Religious denominations have become more numerous and diverse. "The growth of the new American democratic republic meant not only the democratization of religion, but also the growing self-assertion and self-defense of separate religious groups directed against each other" (Mewes 2002, 17).

Immigrants' religious lives take shape against this backdrop. Their everyday lived religious experiences further challenge the cultural feasibility of a separation of church and state. Levitt (2007) found that for many migrants, religion and culture were inextricably linked. They found it difficult to separate their ethnicity from their religion—the Irish and Catholic, the Pakistani and Muslim components of their identity, for example. Even among people who said they were not religious, faith guided how they lived their everyday lives, those with whom they associated, and the kinds of communities to which they belonged.

As a result, many immigrants bring a distinctive understanding of what religion is and where they might find it in their lives. When they adorn their refrigerator doors with "saint magnets," hang cross-stitched samplers with religious teachings on their walls, light candles in honour of the Virgin, or decorate their rearview mirrors and dashboards with photos of their *gurujis*, they imbue the quotidian with the sacred. The religious and the spiritual often spill over into the workplace, the schoolyard, the health clinic, and the law office. When Latino parents celebrate their daughter's 15th birthday or a Hindu son invites his elderly father to come live with him in the United States, they are performing religious as well as "cultural" acts. For some people, American values are, in part, religious values, not just made in the USA but in countries around the world.

Many immigrants also understand membership in religious congregations differently than do native-born Americans. While some immigrants belong to official congregations with leaders who espouse a codified version of faith, many others do not. They have no ongoing relationship with a leader who tells them what to think and feel, nor do they belong to one religious community with whom they pray on a regular basis. For these people, there is no one right way to practice their faith, no creed or ritual to which they must subscribe. Faith for them is an individual affair, not a collective experience. They are comfortable worshipping at any church, temple, or mosque. They can practice their faith just as well at home or in a park as in an official sanctuary. As one respondent told Cadge et al. (forthcoming) in their study of religion and integration among immigrants in Portland, Maine:

> The mosque is just a place or the church is just a physical place. . . . You don't actually need a building to be a Catholic or a Muslim. . . . It's each individual acting in certain ways spiritual . . . so that building's just a

symbol for me. You know, I'm not a big mosque-goer. But I meditate at home a lot, and like I think of myself [as] very spiritual. But it doesn't matter to me whether I go to the mosque every week, you know, but there are people who swear by it and don't think that they're praying unless they're in there and then you see people who don't think they're Catholics unless they go to Sunday mass. You know. So to each his own.

And, just as the walls of religious buildings are permeable, so are the boundaries between faiths. According to Tweed (2002), many scholars of religious studies still tend to assume that identity is singular and fixed, characterized by a core essence. But when we characterize people as adherents or non-adherents based on their adoption of particular beliefs or behaviours, we miss those who call themselves followers without adopting the entire package. When we look through the lens of fixed categories, we fail to see how traditions change when they interact with each other, and the hybrid forms that result. Religious identity is complex because (a) religions can be functionally compartmentalized, (b) people mix and match when there are no negative consequences, and (c) people mix and match even when there are negative consequences (cf. McGuire 2003).

The American context, with its wide array of religious choices, strongly encourages this kind of mixing and matching. And immigrants bring different understandings of religion, adding to this diversity. Thus the legal separation of church and state stands in stark contrast to the ways in which culture and religion interact in the daily lives of many Americans.

A Brief History of Religious Pluralism

Together, race and religion underlie the US social hierarchy, though each according to its own logic. Racial stratification contributed to inequality and discrimination while religious denominationalism, at least as defined by the Constitution, was egalitarian and positively promoted (Casanova 2006). According to Will Herberg (1955), whose book *Protestant, Catholic, Jew* is still a classic on immigrant religious life, while immigrants were expected to abandon their nationality and language, they were not expected to abandon their religion. In fact, through religion, immigrants and their children carved out a space for themselves in America, and religious institutions have always played an important role in facilitating immigrant incorporation. To be American was to be religious. Asserting a religious identity was an acceptable way to be different and to be American at the same time.

Thus the American story has always been a religious story with a diverse cast of characters. It is also a story about successive waves of religious accommodation that have had global dimensions. Many religious institutions were founded on universal claims—on values that were envisioned as worldwide in scope. Although these claims may have taken root in particular countries and legal systems, in the current period of globalization the universality of religion often takes precedence over its national forms. Religion, like capitalism or politics, is not bounded by the nation-state.

The first encounter between immigrants of different faiths in the United States occurred between people professing distinct forms of Protestantism. Seventeenth-century New Amsterdam, where 18 different languages were spoken, is often cited as an early example of modern American "pluralism." Although the Dutch West India Trading Company gave the Dutch Reformed Church official responsibility for the colony, after a few short years religious diversity expanded to include Jesuits, Anabaptists, Mennonites, Presbyterians, Puritans, and Lutherans. In fact, in spite of Governor Stuyvesant's reservations, Trading Company directors insisted on a policy of tolerance and prevented him from banishing Quakers and Jews. They wanted to ensure the successful conduct of trade and commerce without interference from cultural or religious conflict (Gaustad and Schmidt 2002). Ahlstrom (2004, 67) offers a glimpse of this religiously diverse society:

> A traveler in 1700 making his way from Boston to the Carolinas would encounter Congregationalists of varying intensity, Baptists of several varieties, Presbyterians, Quakers, and several other forms of Puritan radicalism; Dutch German and French Reformed; Swedish, Finnish and German Lutherans; Mennonites and radical pietist Anglicans, Roman Catholics; here and there a Jewish congregation; a few Rosicrucians; and of course, a vast number of the unchurched—some of them powerfully alienated from any form of institutional religion.

The Christianity that early immigrants brought with them was neither simply transplanted nor completely homegrown. Their faith was inherently "transnational," influenced by people and ideas crisscrossing the Atlantic. For example, the Puritan heritage so strongly associated with New England, and considered seminal to the awakening and development of a distinctly "American" religious identity, underwent continual interactions with Catholicism in France and Spain. It was fertilized by and itself nourished religious thought, belief, and practice all over the world. As a result, we must see religious development in America, urges historian David D. Hall, with a "double vision," as being dependent on but independent of its European counterparts, cosmopolitan and provincial in the same breath (Hall 2004, xiii-xiv).

Protestant denominations constantly changed in response to newly arriving members and transnational influences. The Lutheran Church, for example, experienced continual schisms and bouts of Americanizing and de-Americanizing. Thus the official language of the Lutheran Church in early eighteenth-century New York changed from German to English and then, following a pre–Civil War influx of immigrants, back to German (Ahlstrom 2004, 518-22).

D'Agostino (2004) offers another example of a transnational perspective on American religious history. In his discussion of American Catholics' involvement in the "Roman Question," he dismantles a "trope" of American Catholicism which depicts it as "a quirky Protestantism, divorced from its international matrix" (3-4). Catholics throughout the world, he argues, took up the cause of a Papal State, which was seen as a "prisoner" within the kingdom of "Liberal Italy" rather than as a sovereign territory of its own: "Rome, not Jerusalem, Washington, Baltimore, or Dublin, was the center of the American Catholic world from 1848 to 1940" (3). Thus the bitter struggles, especially between colonizers France and England, were more than "competition for empire"—they were a conflict of cultures, beneath which lay two contrasting interpretations of the Christian faith (Ahlstrom 2004, 67). The cultural creation of a "Popish menace" remained a symbol that continued to underwrite Protestant anti-Catholicism in the United States for the better part of two centuries.

While religious adherents imported ideas, they also exported ideas of their own. What has been analyzed separately as the American Great Awakening, the English Evangelical Revival, and the Scottish Cambuslang Wark was perceived by many participants to be a single, God-inspired phenomenon. Historians have generally attributed the "cross-fertilization" that occurred in the mid-eighteenth century to George Whitefield, a minister from Gloucester, England, who made numerous transatlantic journeys. But Susan O'Brien (1986, 815) suggests that eighteenth-century revivalism, led in the US by Jonathan Edwards and his compatriots, was not an isolated event but part of a continuum of Protestant evangelical development beginning with the Puritans' transatlantic networks of the seventeenth century and extending to contemporary global movements. Edwards and other key players such as Whitefield, Isaac Watts, and John Guyse were part of an established network of evangelists who encompassed the Colonies, England, Scotland, Wales, and Holland. The ten ministers at the centre of this revival wrote thousands of letters offering reflections and pastoral advice, and received testimonials and letters of thanks from lay people on both sides of the Altlantic. Missives organizing Prayer Days were transnationally disseminated. Lay people, including financial backers and printers, not only copied and distributed these messages but also founded newspapers and journals and gave public readings. When Jonathan Edwards wrote to Boston's core member Benjamin Colman of the Northampton awakening, the letter "took on a life of its own." It was sent overseas and published in London (Marsden 2003, 171-73).

The transnational face of the Catholic Church in America, beginning with the massive influx of southern Europeans in the nineteenth century, represents the second wave of religious accommodation in the United States. During this time, Catholics and Jews were included, to varying degrees, in the Protestant mix. Again, transnational flows moved in both directions. On the one hand, immigrants brought with them an array of ethnically particular traditions and maintained those practices in the United States. In 1892, for example, Antonin Dvorak had no trouble following the prayers at St. Wenceslaus' parish in Spillville, Iowa, which he visited on his vacation (Noll 2002, 2-3). Similarly, people visiting from Brazil today feel perfectly comfortable worshipping at St. Tarcisius in Framingham, Massachusetts, where there is a large Brazilian immigrant congregation (Levitt 2007). At the same time, the structure of the Catholic Church in America has changed from one which tolerated a range of ethnic traditions into what some have called a "national" church. Somewhat reluctantly, the Vatican has accepted American Catholic positions on authority, procedures, and church order that reflect the unique democratic, individualistic, and liberal culture of the United States (Noll 2002).

Many European churches remained strongly connected to their expatriate members, feeling responsible for them but also seeking their political and financial support. Some, fearing that migrants would convert in the United States, contributed money, clergy, and resources to create ethnic congregations (Nardi and Simpson 1916). These financial incentives were intended to reinforce emigrants' loyalty to their sending church. In some cases, these incentives also helped maintain emigrants' support of the sending government. The Hungarian government, for example, directly subsidized loyal churches, priests, schools, and newspapers, regardless of their members' ethnicity, to dampen opposition among those living abroad (Bodner 1985).

Other European and Asian churches and governments feared migrants and returnees, anxious that converts would stir things up by proselytizing or challenging their authority. Such fears were not unfounded. During the first two decades of the 1900s, Chinese Protestants successfully persuaded Chinese Americans to support a republican government in China. Drawing upon evangelical teachings, Chinese Protestants criticized China as a backward, pagan land that would become modern and democratic only if it became Christian. They wanted to redeem China by converting young men who would ultimately return to their homeland (Tseng 1999). In Europe, returnees normally did not treat priests as deferentially as they had before they left. Thousands used the political organizing skills they had learned abroad to create village organizations, labour unions, and even political parties, which challenged the power of the church (Wyman 1993).

What we are witnessing today, then, is the logical next step along an expanding continuum of religious diversity that has always been driven by forces inside and outside US borders. America's sacred texts, particularly the Constitution, laid the groundwork for religious diversity to flourish. In the 1960s and 1970s, the civil rights and anti-war movements simply transformed this "culture of pluralism" into something mainstream.

The Contemporary Panorama

Statistically speaking, the United States remains overwhelmingly Christian. Of the 82 percent who call themselves Christians, the majority (52 percent) are Protestant, followed by Catholics (24 percent). Those who claim "no religious preference" comprise about 10 percent of the population (Pew Research Center 2002). Although the numbers of Muslims and Buddhists have doubled in the past decade, and the number of Hindus has tripled, non-Christians still represent a fairly small portion of America (Kosmin, Mayer, and Keysar 2001). Jews and Muslims represent only 2 and 1.5 percent of the population respectively, and "Eastern" religions, such as Buddhism and Hinduism, weigh in at less than 1 percent each (World Christian Database 2004). The most remarkable change in American religion has been the increasing number of individuals who say they have no religion, up from just over 8 percent in 1990 to between 9 and 14 percent a decade later (Kosmin, Mayer, and Keysar 2001).

Embedded in these categories, though, is much more diversity than broad labels like "Christian" or "Catholic" reveal. Jasso and her colleagues (forthcoming), using data from the New Immigrant Survey and the General Social Survey, find significant differences in the distribution of religious preferences between the foreign and native-born (see Table 1). Only two-thirds of the immigrant population identified themselves as Christian compared with 82 percent of the native-born population. The Christian immigrant population is largely Catholic (42 percent), while native-born Christians are largely Protestant (55 percent). The immigrant population is more religiously diverse, with a larger percentage belonging to the "Eastern" religions of Islam, Hinduism, and Buddhism. The only non-Christian religion in which native-born Americans outnumber immigrants is Judaism.

Table 1: Religious Preferences of Immigrants and Native-Born Americans

Religion	Immigrants	Native-Born
Catholic	42.0	23.4
Protestant	9.3	55.0
General Christian	n/a	29.1
Orthodox Christian	10.5	0.4
Muslim	7.9	0.1
Hindu	7.8	negligible
Buddhist	3.9	0.4
Jewish	1.3	1.8

Source: Jasso et al. (forthcoming).

Jasso et al. (forthcoming) also find that new immigrants attend religious services more frequently. Catholic immigrants have the highest rate of church attendance, with 45 percent reporting that they attend services at least once a week, followed by Protestants (34 percent), Jews (30 percent), and Orthodox Christians (24.4 percent). Among native-born Americans, the highest frequency of attendance is reported by Protestants (31 percent), Catholics (27.9 percent), and general Christians (30 percent). Adherents of these groups reported that they attend religious services once a week or more.

New immigrants are "Latinoizing" and "Asianizing" well-established denominations, particularly the Catholic Church. By some estimates, Mexican and other Latin American foreign-born individuals account for nearly 40 percent of the country's Roman Catholics. According to the US Conference of Catholic Bishops' Information Project (2006, 3-4), approximately 39 percent—or 26 million of the nation's 69 million Catholics—are Hispanic. They report that Latinos account for 71 percent of the growth in the US Catholic population since 1960. Based on these figures, Latinos will make up more than half of all US Catholics by the second decade of the twenty-first century (2006, 5).

Moreover, the religious diversity of the immigrant population is increasing, perhaps because the make-up of Asian immigrants to the United States has changed in recent decades. Between 1990 and 2001, the proportion of newly arriving Asian Christians fell from 63 to 43 percent while those professing Asian religions increased from 15 to 28 percent (Kosmin, Mayer, and Keysar 2001). Jasso et al. (forthcoming) have found that the proportion of foreign-born professing faiths other than Judaeo-Christianity is more than four times greater than that of the native-born—nearly 17 percent versus 4 percent. Surveys conducted in 2003–2004 indicate a continued rise in non-Christian religious preferences, although the researchers carrying out this work differ as to how much (Barna Research Group 2004; Gallop 2004).

Incorporating newcomers is an age-old story for Catholics, who have had lots of practice turning Irish and Italian immigrants into American Catholics and are using many of the same techniques to incorporate contemporary Brazilians and Vietnamese. But mainline and evangelical Protestant faiths are not as experienced at integrating newcomers, although they face great incentives to do so, given their declining native-born populations. The religious affinities of many of these newcomers are the legacy of missionary work done in Latin America and Asia during the 1900s. The descendents of those who converted are now bringing their own version of Christianity back to the United States and asking to practice their faith alongside their denominational brothers and sisters. New and old members have to invent ways to pray, learn, and pursue social change together. Their views about how to do this are often quite different and there is no obvious referee. The ultimate compromise will be a major source of religious change.

The Challenge of Pluralism in Action

Religious historian William Hutchinson (2003) explains that pluralism as it is currently defined in the United States has only been conceptualized as such since the 1920s. Prior to that, he writes, there had been moments of acceptance (tolerance) or occasionally even of welcome (inclusion), but these instances did not add up to actual engagement. Hutchinson makes an important distinction—that diversity *happened* to American religion at the beginning of the nineteenth century but that pluralism was a *conscious* choice that did not take root until the second half of the twentieth century. And though we now recognize that religious pluralism is more than just tolerance and inclusion, Hutchinson argues that it is still a work in progress. Diana Eck (1993, 10) agrees:

> *Pluralism* is not the sheer fact of *plurality* alone, but active engagement with plurality. Pluralism and plurality are sometimes used as if they were synonymous. But plurality is just diversity, plain and simple—splendid, colorful, maybe even threatening. Such diversity does not, however, have to affect me. I can observe diversity. I can even celebrate diversity, as the cliché goes. But I have to participate in pluralism. . . . Pluralism requires the cultivation of public space where we all encounter one another.

Some scholars argue that our understanding of pluralism demands even further revisiting. As Courtney Bender (2007) cautions, religions do not encompass discrete and recognizable communities and traditions with explicit boundaries across which interchange and conflict occur in a neat and controlled fashion. Pluralistic encounters are likely to be much messier than such descriptions imply. Indeed, Bender (2007) and her colleague Pamela Klassen (2007) have found the boundaries between religious traditions to be porous, which encourages the lending and borrowing of elements from different faiths so much so that the original origins and owners are not clear. Moreover, the structures and institutions in which these encounters occur shape the nature of the interactions and the kinds of translations and vernacularizations that emerge. While pluralism has been an important prescriptive model for recognizing and respecting religious difference in multicultural societies, it is not necessarily an apt descriptive or analytical model. Because this construct focuses on mainstream, formal, and familiar religious institutions, it obscures the range of diversity within religions and between religions.

In the remainder of this paper, we explore the points of intersection between religion and politics outside of their formal structures. We look specifically at religious institutions as shapers of new forms of citizenship, as providers of social services, as sites of political and civic engagement, and as advocates for immigrant rights.

Religion as a Basis for Citizenship

Religion is a consummate boundary crosser. "God needs no passport" because faith traditions give their followers symbols, rituals, and stories with which to create alternative sacred landscapes, marked by holy sites, shrines, and places of worship (Levitt 2007; Tweed 2002; Vásquez and Marquardt 2003). For some people, these spaces take a back seat to the actual political geography. Although they may think of themselves as living in the "kingdom of God," they recognize that political boundaries and authorities reign supreme. Other people see themselves as living in religious landscapes that coexist with and even complement the political geography. They code switch, moving back and forth between a world bounded by spiritual landmarks and one bounded by national borders, using religious tools to solve some problems and political tools to address others.

For another group, though, the religious landscape takes precedence over its secular counterpart. These individuals imagine themselves living in a "Hindu" or "Muslim" country that encompasses sites around the world where fellow believers live. Minarets, crosses, and sanctuaries, not national monuments, flags, and historic structures, are the salient landmarks. What is more, religion for these believers transcends the boundaries of time. Followers feel that they are part of a chain of memory and promise, connected to a past, a present, and a future (Hervieu-Léger 2000; Tweed 2002). That is why Cuban immigrants living in Miami bring their newborns to be baptized at a shrine they built in honour of their national patron saint. When they worship there, they induct their children into an imagined Cuban nation with a past in their ancestral land, a present in Miami, and a future they hope to reclaim once again in Cuba. Even believers who identify more with the physical landscape than with a sacred reality sometimes see themselves as religious global citizens. They do not privilege their nationality or think of themselves as cosmopolitans—as citizens of the world understood in secular terms, but as members of a community of faith. Religious global citizenship entails rights and responsibilities that may complement or contradict other forms of belonging. But for this group, the religious imperative matters most.

Levitt (2007) found religious global citizens among the Hindu, Muslim, Protestant, and Catholic immigrants she studied in the United States. They understood religious citizenship to mimic the logic of its political counterpart, using similar words and analogies to describe both membership categories. Like political citizenship, religious global citizenship comes with benefits and obligations. Adherents pay taxes (by tithing) and obey the leader and the rules of the faith, and in return they are protected and represented. Some felt that their ties to co-religionists outweighed their ties to co-ethnics or co-nationals, although these relationships sometimes overlapped. Those who saw themselves exclusively as religious citizens felt responsible, above all, to other members of their religious group regardless of their street address. Others acted more like religious cosmopolitans; they entered the world community through a religious door, but their faith inspired them to care for all humankind.

Religious Institutions as Social Service Providers

Historically, religious institutions played a major role in providing social services and supports to immigrants. Catholic parishes in the mid-nineteenth century, for example, became neighbourhood centres of charity, serving the sick, the unemployed, and people with disabilities (Dolan 1985). Protestant and Jewish congregations formed local chapters of nationally organized charitable societies to aid those in need (Cnaan 1997).

Today, this tradition of charitable service continues. Indeed, changes in the welfare system, initiated during the Clinton administration and consolidated under George W. Bush's so-called compassionate conservatism, have enhanced the capacity of religious groups to provide social services by allowing them to compete for government funds. When the *Personal Responsibility and Work Opportunity Reconciliation Act* of 1996 eliminated federal spending on public assistance, instituted work requirements for benefit recipients, and limited immigrants' eligibility for services, other providers stepped in. The Charitable Choice provision, Section 104 of the Act, attempted to shore up the social safety net in the wake of the government's retreat by permitting religious organizations to apply for government funding for service provision. In fact, supporters of the Act argued that religious groups would provide social services more effectively than their secular counterparts because they were motivated by faith. State agencies responsible for allocating funds were required to treat religious group applicants in the same way as other organizations. In turn, religious providers were not allowed to discriminate between clients on the basis of religion, nor could they require clients to participate in religious activities in exchange for goods and services. If a prospective client did not want to receive services in a faith-based setting, another service provider had to be found. Religious groups, however, could use religion as a criterion for hiring staff. Supporters saw these developments as a positive step forward, while critics raised real concerns about the ability of faith-based communities to provide social services in a neutral fashion.

It is not yet clear how well this arrangement is working. Ebaugh and Pipes (2001) studied faith-based organizations in Houston, Texas, and found that more services were provided by faith-based coalitions than by individual congregations. Yet they also found that many prospective providers were confused about the Charitable Choice program and worried that the acceptance of government funds would compromise their religious principles. The kinds of services provided and the structures used to deliver them varied considerably. Ebaugh and Pipes (2001) attributed these variations to differences in congregational involvement, client demographics, local resources, leadership, and theological orientation.

In a follow-up study of 656 faith-based providers nationwide, Ebaugh, Chafetz, and Pipes (2005) found that it was much easier for large, well-established organizations to compete for government grants. Smaller, informal religious groups were at a disadvantage because they did not have professional grant writers or data demonstrating their competence in service delivery. This study also revealed that faith-based coalitions were more likely to form between less expressively religious congregations. More religiously expressive groups did not seek government funding because they believed it would thwart their religious mission.

Religious Institutions as Sites of Political Socialization and Mobilization

Commitments to religious identities and organizations facilitate the acquisition of an American cultural toolkit: a new language, new loyalties, and a new political and civic culture that can be harnessed toward home- or host-country activism. Religious networks, celebrations, rituals, and organizations serve as forums in which many first- and second-generation citizens receive an American political education and lay claim to public recognition for their communities, which cover the full political spectrum (Ebaugh and Chafetz 2002; Levitt 2004; Menjívar 1999; Vásquez and Marquardt 2003; Yang 1999; Yang and Ebaugh 2001). Religious affiliation also influences conceptions of citizenship and socioeconomic outcomes (DeSipio 2007; Levitt 2007; Martes and Rodriguez 2002; Ong 2003).

The political attitudes and behaviours of post-1965 immigrants in the United States have been the focus of much research. Early studies charted general patterns of political activity among first-generation immigrants including voting, working on campaigns, donating to political parties, signing petitions, and participating in demonstrations. Ramakrishnan's (2005) comprehensive overview of first-generation political participation reveals that the straight-line assimilation model does not hold for many post-1965 immigrant groups. His research suggests that only Asians show a "linear" increase in political participation from first to third generation. Second and third generation whites, blacks, and Latinos exhibit "bumpier" patterns of political activism.

Numerous social scientists have explored the connection between religious institutions and political participation in the United States (Calhoun-Brown 1996; Jones-Correa and Leal 2001; Verba, Lehman Schlozman, and Brady 1995; Wuthnow 1999). Some religious institutions mobilize adherents indirectly by imparting leadership, fundraising, and public speaking skills or by promoting a shared group identity and consciousness (Calhoun-Brown 1996; Verba, Lehman Schlozman, and Brady 1995). Other religious groups directly organize members for political purposes, as recent pro-immigrant rallies in Los Angeles have demonstrated (Reiff 2006). However, much of this research has focused on Latinos and recent immigrants, overlooking the experience of Mexican Americans who have been living on US soil for generations (DeSipio 2007).

Furthermore, when people interact with each other in their neighbourhoods, at work, or during coffee hour after worship, they create "social capital"—the various enabling and empowering resources generated by human relations including trust, shared norms, and reciprocity (Putnam 2000). Connections forged by faith are by far the most powerful generators of social capital, Putnam argues. His research reveals that nearly half of the associational memberships in America are church related, half of all personal philanthropy is religious in character, and half of all volunteering occurs in religious contexts. Not all social capital is equal, however. Putnam and others distinguish between social capital that is "bonding"—that reinforces homogeneous identities and positions—and social capital that is "bridging," arising from networks that encompass people from a wide spectrum of social strata and political ideologies.

There are significant debates about how the relationship between religious and political participation actually works. Churches clearly played a key role in motivating Irish and Italian immigrants to become active in politics in the early 1900s, but whether this still holds for contemporary migrants is not clear. Verba, Lehman Schlozman, and Brady (1995) found that involvement in churches enhanced the resource base for African Americans, but not for Latinos. Latinos went to church less often than African Americans, though more often than Anglos, and yet they were the least likely to participate in non-religious activities at church. Verba and his colleagues suggest that membership in Protestant and Catholic congregations results in different kinds of "civic" education. They attribute the low political participation rates among Latinos to their high level of involvement in Catholicism.

While Jones-Correa and Leal (2001) agree that religion influences political activism, they do not attribute differences in participation to denominational affiliation. They found no association between Catholicism and lower levels of electoral and non-electoral participation for Latinos or Anglos. In fact, controlling for demographic predictors of Latino participation revealed that Latino Catholics were more likely to participate in politics than Latino non-Catholics. They argue that it is church attendance, not belonging to a particular denomination, that explains these differences. Members of religious groups learn to participate in associations and then transfer these skills to other organizational arenas.

Lee, Pachon, and Barreto (2002) found very limited differences in voting, contacting government, or protesting based on religious affiliation or practice. Where they did find differences, it was with respect to voting, where evangelical Christians voted less than their Catholic counterparts. DeSipio (2007) found that even controlling for education, age, and nativity status, religious practice had a statistically significant impact on voting. Compared to Catholics, Latinos who practice other faiths are less likely to vote by a margin of about 30 percent. There was no statistically significant difference between Catholics and those Latinos who did not practice an organized religion. While Latinos do participate less than other racial and ethnic groups, DeSipio concludes that this gap cannot be attributed to the large numbers who are Catholic in this community. Finally, Jamal (2005) found that the effect of religious participation on political engagement varied by ethnicity. Going to a mosque was a significant predictor of political activity among Arab Muslims but not among African American or South Asian Muslims, suggesting that religious participation and political activity can mean different things and manifest in different ways in the same ethnically divided religious group. Religious participation and political activity undoubtedly differ across immigrant generations as well.

And what about the children of immigrants who ultimately will reinvent what it means to be a Muslim or a Hindu in the United States today? Much recent work on the new second generation largely ignores the role of religion in shaping immigrant incorporation, reinforcing ethnic community connections, and maintaining homeland ties. We are still guided by Hansen's (1937) classic notion of "third generation return": what the children of immigrants reject, the grandchildren will re-embrace. But religion is clearly alive and well among the second generation. A visit to any college campus website reveals a panoply of religious organizations in which students are active. Kim (2004) observes an "astonishing" growth in the number of ethnic Christian campus fellowships at major American universities, attracting large numbers of second-generation Asian Americans (Kurien 2007). Similar campus religious organizations exist for Hindu, Muslim, and Buddhist students although less is known about their membership numbers and demographics.

Young people attending institutions of higher education are confronted with multicultural environments, often for the first time. The experience propels many students to rethink their own ethnic and religious selves. Campus religious organizations offer personal and educational resources for students seeking to answer what it means to be Buddhist, Hindu, Muslim, or even Christian in the United States. These organizations help to reaffirm religious values and priorities, instill new ones, and guide young people's choices about how to act, on what kinds of issues, and with what kinds of partners. The "politics of multiculturalism" (Kurien 2004a), combined with the integration of students from a wide array of subtraditions within their religions, means that the discussions taking place within these student organizations often yield novel formulations of religious practice and action.

The nationalistic, fundamentalist, and extremist discourses that sometimes arise from these negotiations have been a recurring theme in the small body of literature on student religious groups (Cainkar 2004; Eade 1997; Kurien 2004b, 2005; Raj 2000). Second-generation immigrants clearly use religion to distinguish themselves from other groups. They embrace Hinduness, for example, to avoid other racial or ethnic labels. In some cases, the version of faith they articulate is inclusive, tolerant, and responsive to the surrounding sociocultural context. In others, their faith in its form and content rejects outright what they see as the moral laxity and individualism pervading the United States. Moreover, what fundamentalist expressions mean in the homeland often differs from what they signify abroad. For example, while *Hindutva* signifies superiority, truth, and anti-Muslimness in India, Kamat and Mathew (2003) argue that Hindus in the United States adopt *Hindutva* within the American liberal discourse (and paradoxically because of it) because it gives them an ethnoreligious door through which to enter US racial politics. The multiculturalist discourse that prevails in the United States, which calls favourable attention to "neglected" minorities, justifies a certain kind of Hindu-Americanness. Multiculturalism tolerates a certain level of fundamentalism as well (Kamat and Mathew 2003).

Religious Institutions as Mobilizers for and against Immigrant Rights

Some religious communities energetically mobilize to protect immigrant rights. In 2008, the New Sanctuary Movement, which builds on efforts begun in the 1980s to help Central American refugees, included representatives from 18 cities, 12 religious traditions, and 7 denominational and interdenominational organizations. In its current interfaith campaign, religious congregations are offering long-term refuge to undocumented immigrants facing deportation from the United States (Barron 2007).

Advocating for the rights of the poor and the marginalized has many historical antecedents among religious congregations, particularly in the Latino community. In the 1960s, Cesar Chavez appealed to the Catholicism of Mexican and Filipino farmworkers when he organized the United Farmworkers. The Industrial Areas Foundation, which originated in Texas, has created small community groups based on parish structures that are composed primarily of Mexican American constituents (Warren 2001). More recently, in March 2006 Cardinal Roger Mahony of the Archdiocese of Los Angeles instructed his lay and religious staff to disregard the provisions of House Bill HR4437 that made it a crime to provide humanitarian aid to people without checking their legal status. Latino representation among church leadership, though, falls far short of their numbers among the rank and file.

Catholics alone do not have a lock on these activities. And religious activists often act in tandem with people of other faiths. Interfaith Worker Justice, for example, is a network of people who feel compelled by their religious values to organize and mobilize the religious community to improve wages, benefits, and conditions for workers (Land 2006). Hondagneu-Sotelo (2007) found that religious activists use their faith to make claims and to pursue immigrant rights in four different ways: moral justification and motivation for action, religious resources, religious legitimacy, and religious ritual and cultural symbols.

However, religious activism in support of immigrant rights is not without controversy. The New Sanctuary Movement has been criticized for taking religious texts out of context to justify its activities and for exaggerating the obligations these verses place on believers. Richard Land, head of the Ethics and Religious Liberty Commission for the theologically and politically conservative Southern Baptist Convention, acknowledges that Christians must love their neighbours and "do unto others as we would have them do unto us." He supported the comprehensive immigration reforms proposed in 2007. But he also argues that the New Sanctuary Movement goes farther than the Bible mandates.

> I think that's an awfully drastic step, to say that we are going to disobey the law. I would never turn someone away. If they showed up, you should help them. But that's different from me saying, "If you're illegal, then we will protect you from the government." I don't think the Bible requires that. (Land 2006)

To back his position, Land and almost every other Sanctuary opponent cite Romans 13: 1–7: "Let every person be subject to the governing authorities. For there is no authority except from God, and those that exist have been instituted by God."

Conclusion

In the United States, religion leaves a major cultural footprint in the broader society. One way to demonstrate Americanness is to belong to a religious community. That is why, says José Casanova (2006), the same Italians who migrated to Argentina and became anarchists migrated to the United States and became ardent Catholics. As Herberg (1955) predicted, it was Irishness and Italianness that would wane in the United States, not Catholicism. It was felt that as long as newcomers believed in something, and their belief fell within the broad parameters of Judaeo-Christianity, the details of that belief need not concern the rest of us.

The challenge now is to expand that vision. This means learning not only how to think outside the nation-state box by recognizing that American religion is not just made in the USA but also how to think outside the Christian box. For many people, religious belonging is not about worshipping collectively, whether with the same group or with different groups. Religious belonging is based not on a bounded set of practices but rather on a collection of beliefs and rituals that shift and combine in formal and informal settings.

Across the ocean, the boundaries of belonging are also expanding, although many European scholars do not view religions as vehicles of inclusiveness. They cite indicators such as declining church attendance to justify the claim that Europe is secular; however, these studies tend to overlook the long shadow cast by a history of organizing social life around established religious structures and sensibilities. It is true that Americans think of the United States as a country of immigrants, and widespread acceptance of multiculturalism makes it easier to be a hyphenated-American than to be, say, a Moroccan-Frenchman or a Turkish-German. Nevertheless, the use of religion to express belonging and to make claims in the European context is not as far-fetched as many would believe.

In closing, we want to stress the difference between tolerance and pluralism, as Bender (2007) and Klassen (2007) messily conceive these concepts. True religious pluralism requires making room for all varieties of religious experience and understanding what these different expressions mean for the role of religion in public life. It means taking a hard look at taken-for-granted national assumptions and acknowledging honestly who is thereby welcomed and who is rendered invisible. Tolerant people acknowledge difference and are willing to live side by side with people who are not like them, but they are unwilling to be changed by these encounters. Pluralists go beyond "separate but equal"; they are willing to engage with and be changed by others, creating something new in the process. Pluralists believe that no single religion has absolute authority over truth. Pluralism means not just letting individuals speak but letting them shape the collective narrative so that they recognize their voice within it. As Charles Taylor (1992) argues, in a multicultural world people are ethically obligated to extend a "moral cognizance" to those whose worldviews differ sharply from their own. Intercultural understanding is an obligation, not an option. This obligation extends to religious understanding as well.

Notes

1. World Values Survey researchers, along with Presser and Stinson (1998) and Chaves and Stephens (2003), offer the same caveat, however, that people are inclined to say they go to church far more often than they actually do. But even so, if only 20 percent attend services weekly, instead of the self-professed 44 percent, the closest country in the Westernized cohort, Canada, has much lower church attendance figures—10 percent (Inglehart 1997).

2. Quoted from an interview with Bob Abernathy, 3 May 2002, *Religion & Ethics Newsweekly*, Episode 535, produced by Thirteen/WNET New York. Transcript available at http://www.pbs.org/wnet/religionandethics/transcripts/535.html

3. Norris and Inglehart (2004) make a similar argument with respect to Europe. They observe that religion's role remains strong even as societies

grow more secular in other ways: "The distinctive worldviews that were originally linked with religious traditions have shaped the cultures of each nation in an enduring fashion; today, these distinctive values are transmitted to the citizens even if they never set foot in a church, temple or mosque" (17). Although less than 5 percent of people in Sweden attend church weekly, there is "a distinctive Protestant value system that they hold in common with the citizens of other historically Protestant societies such as Norway, Denmark, Iceland, Finland, Germany, and the Netherlands. . . . Even in highly secular societies, the historical legacy of given religions continues to shape worldviews and to define cultural zones" (17). In other words, people who do not believe in God acknowledge that religion still influences them: "'We are all atheists; but I am a Lutheran atheist and they are Orthodox atheists'" (Norris and Inglehart 2004, 17, citing an Estonian colleague describing the differences between Estonians and Russians).

References

Ahlstrom, S.E. 2004. *A Religious History of the American People*. New Haven and London: Yale University Press.

Barna Research Group. 2004. "How Christianized Do Americans Want Their Country To Be?" 26 July. Accessed 19 January 2009 at http://www.barna.org/FlexPage.aspx?Page=BarnaUpdate

Barron, J. 2007. "Congregations to Give Haven to Immigrants." *New York Times*. Available at http://www.nytimes.com/2007/05/09/nyregion/09sanctuary.html

Bender, C. 2007. "Opening Remarks." In *After Pluralism: Rethinking Models of Inter-religious Engagement Workshop*. Columbia, NY: Columbia University Press.

Bodner, J. 1985. *The Transplanted*. Bloomington: Indiana University Press.

British Broadcasting Corporation (BBC). 2005. "What the World Thinks of God: A Survey." ICM Research Limited. Accessed 14 January 2009 at http://news.bbc.co.uk/2/hi/programmes/wtwtgod/default.stm

Brooks, D. 2000. *Bobos in Paradise: The New Upper Class and How They Got There*. New York: Simon and Schuster.

Cadge, W., S. Curran, B.N. Jaworsky, P. Levitt, and J. Hejtmanek. forthcoming. "The City as Context: Spaces of Reception in New Immigrant Destinations." Under review at *City and Community*.

Cainkar, L. 2004. "Islamic Revival among Second Generation Arab-American Muslims." *Bulletin of the Royal Institute for Inter-Faith Studies* 6:99-120.

Calhoun-Brown, A. 1996. "African American Churches and Political Mobilization: The Psychological Impact of Organizational Resources." *Journal of Politics* 4:935-53.

Carroll, J. 2004. "Religion is 'Very Important' to 6 in 10 Americans." *Gallup News Service*, 24 June. Accessed 14 January 2009 at http://www.gallup.com/poll/12115/Religion-Very-Important-Americans.aspx

Carroll, M.P. 1999. *Irish Pilgrimage: Holy Wells and Popular Catholic Devotion.* Baltimore, MD: Johns Hopkins University Press.

Casanova, J. 2006. "Religion, European Secular Identities, and European Integration." In *Religion in an Expanding Europe*, ed. T.A. Byrnes and P.J. Katzenstein. Cambridge: Cambridge University Press.

Chaves, M. 2004. *Congregations in America.* Cambridge, MA: Harvard University Press.

Chaves, M. and L. Stephens. 2003. "Church Attendance in the United States." In *Handbook of the Sociology of Religion*, ed. M. Dillon. Cambridge, MA: Cambridge University Press.

Cnaan, R.A. 1997. *Social and Community Involvement of Religious Congregations Housed in Historic Religious Properties: Findings from a Six-City Study (A Report).* Philadelphia: University of Pennsylvania Press.

D'Agostino, P.R. 2004. *Rome in America: Transnational Catholic Ideology from the Risorgimento to Fascism.* Chapel Hill: University of North Carolina Press.

Davie, G. 2007. "Pluralism, Tolerance and Democracy: Theory and Practice in Europe." In *Democracy and the New Religious Pluralism*, ed. T.F. Banchoff. Oxford: Oxford University Press.

DeSipio, L. 2007. "Power in the Pews?" In *From Pews to Polling Places: Faith and Politics in the American Religious Mosaic*, ed. J.M. Wilson. Washington: Georgetown University Press.

Dillon, M. 2003. *Handbook of the Sociology of Religion.* Cambridge: Cambridge University Press.

Dionne, E.J., Jr. 2003. "Religion Returns to the Public Square: Faith and Policy in America." Event transcript, Pew Forum on Religion and Public Life, 28 February. Accessed 19 January 2008 at http://Pewforum.org/events/index.php?EventID=44

Dolan, J.P. 1985. *The American Catholic Experience: A History from Colonial Times to the Present.* Garden City, NY: Doubleday.

Eade, J. 1997. "Identity, Nation and Religion: Educated Young Bangladeshis in London's East End." In *Living the Global City. Globalization as a Local Process*, ed. J. Eade. London: Routledge.

Ebaugh, H.R.F. and J. Chafetz. 2002. *Religion Across Borders: Transnational Immigrant Networks.* Walnut Creek, CA: AltaMira Press.

Ebaugh, H.R.F., J. Chafetz, and P.F. Pipes. 2005. "Faith-Based Social Service Organizations and Government Funding: Data from a National Survey." *Social Science Quarterly* 86(2):273-92.

Ebaugh, H.R.F. and P.F. Pipes. 2001. "Immigrant Congregations as Social Service Providers: Are They Safety Nets for Welfare Reform?" In *Religion and Social Policy for the 21st Century*, ed. P. Nesbitt. Walnut Creek, CA: AltaMira Press.

Eck, D.L. 1993. "Challenge to Pluralism (God in the Newsroom)." *Nieman Reports* 47:9-15.

Gallop, J., ed. 2004. *Critical or Uncritical*. New York: Routledge.

Gallup Organization. 1976–2006. Religion section. "Do You Happen to Be a Member of a Church or Synagogue?" Available at http://www.gallup.com/poll/1690/Religion.aspx

Gaustad, E.S. and L.E. Schmidt. 2002. *The Religious History of America*, rev. edition. San Francisco, CA: Harper.

Hall, D.D. 2004. "Introduction." In *A Religious History of the American People*, by S.E. Ahlstrom. New Haven, CT: Yale University Press.

Hall, P.D. 1998. "Religion and the Organizational Revolution in the United States." In *Sacred Companies: Organizational Aspects of Religion and Religious Aspects of Organizations*, ed. N.J. Demerath III, P.D. Hall, T. Schmitt, and R.H. Williams. New York: Oxford University Press.

Hansen, M.L. 1937. *The Problem of the Third Generation Immigrant*. Rock Island, IL: Augustana Historical Society.

Herberg, W. 1955. *Protestant, Catholic, Jew*. Garden City, NY: Doubleday.

Hervieu-Léger, D. 2000. *Religion as a Chain of Memory*. Cambridge: Polity Press.

Hondagneu-Sotelo, P. 2007. *Religion and Social Justice for Immigrants*. New Brunswick, NJ: Rutgers University Press.

Hutchinson, W.R. 2003. *Religious Pluralism in America: The Contentious History of a Founding Ideal*. New Haven, CT: Yale University Press.

Inglehart, R. 1997. *Modernization and Postmodernization: Cultural, Economic, and Political Change in 43 Societies*. Princeton, NJ: Princeton University Press.

Jamal, A. 2005. "The Political Participation and Engagement of Muslim Americans: Mosque Involvement and Group Consciousness." *American Politics Research* 33:521-44.

Jasso, G., D.S. Massey, M.R. Rosenzweig, and J.P. Smith. forthcoming. "The U.S. New Immigrant Survey: Overview and Preliminary Results Based on the New-Immigrant Cohorts of 1996 and 2003." In *Immigration Research and Statistics Service Workshop on Longitudinal Surveys and Cross-Cultural Survey Design: Workshop Proceedings*, ed. B. Morgan and B. Nicholson. London, UK: Crown Publishing.

Jones-Correa, M. and D.L. Leal. 2001. "Political Participation: Does Religion Matter?" *Political Research Quarterly* 54:751-70.

Kamat, S. and B. Mathew. 2003. "Mapping Political Violence in a Globalized World: The Case of Hindu Nationalism." *Social Justice* 30:4-17.

Kim, C. 2004. *Korean-American Experience in the United States: Initial Thoughts*. Cheltenham, UK: Hermit Kingdom Press.

Klassen, P. 2007. "Opening Remarks." In *After Pluralism: Rethinking Models of Inter-religious Engagement Workshop*. Columbia, NY: Columbia University Press.

Kosmin, B.A., E. Mayer, and A. Keysar. 2001. *American Religious Identification Survey 2001*. Accessed 19 January 2009 at http://www.gc.cuny.edu/faculty/research_studies/aris.pdf

Kurien, P. 2004a. "Christian by Birth or Rebirth? Generation and Difference in an Indian American Christian Church." In *Asian American Religions: The Making and Remaking of Borders and Boundaries*, ed. T. Carnes and F. Yang. New York: New York University Press.

— 2004b. "Multiculturalism, Immigrant Religion, and Diasporic Nationalism: The Development of an American Hinduism." *Social Problems* 51:362-85.

— 2005. "Being Young, Brown, and Hindu: The Identity Struggles of Second-Generation Indian Americans." *Journal of Contemporary Ethnography* 34:434-69.

— 2007. *A Place at the Table: Multiculturalism and the Development of an American Hinduism*. New Brunswick, NJ: Rutgers University Press.

Land, R. 2006. "Immigration Crisis Requires Biblical Response." Accessed 14 January 2009 on the Ethics and Religious Liberty Commission website at http://erlc.com/article/immigration-crisis-requires-biblical-response/

Lee, J., H. Pachon, and M. Barreto. 2002. "Guiding the Flock: Church as Vehicle of Latino Political Participation." Paper presented at the annual meeting of the American Political Science Association, Boston, Massachusetts.

Levitt, P. 2004. "I Feel I Am a Citizen of the World and of a Church without Borders: The Latino Religious Experience." Paper presented at the Latinos: Past Influence, Future Power Conference of the Tomas Rivera Policy Institute, Newport Beach, California, 31 January– 1 February.

— 2007. *God Needs No Passport: How Immigrants are Changing the American Religious Landscape*. New York: The New Press.

Lipset, S.M. 1996. *American Exceptionalism: A Double-Edged Sword*. New York: Norton.

Lyons, L. 2005. "Tracking Religious Preferences over the Decades." *Gallup News Service*, 24 May. Available at http://www.gallup.com

Marsden, G.M. 2003. *Jonathan Edwards: A Life*. New Haven, CT: Yale University Press.

Martes, A.M. and C. Rodriguez. 2002. "Church Membership, Social Capital, and Entrepreneurship in Brazilian Communities in the U.S." In *Ethnic Entrepreneurship: Structure and Process*, ed. C.H. Stiles and C.S. Galbraith. Oxford, UK: Elsevier Science.

McGuire, M.B. 2003. "Contested Meanings and Definitional Boundaries: Historicizing the Sociology of Religion." In *Defining Religion: Investigating the Boundaries between the Sacred and Secular*, ed. A.L. Greil and D.G. Bromley. Amsterdam and London: JAI Press.

Menjívar, C. 1999. "Religious Institutions and Transnationalism: A Case Study of Catholic and Evangelical Salvadoran Immigrants." *International Journal of Politics, Culture, and Society* 12:589-612.

Mewes, H. 2002. "Religion and Politics in American Democracy." In *The Secular and the Sacred: Nation, Religion and Politics*, ed. W. Safran. London: Routledge.

Nardi, B.P. and A.B. Simpson. 1916. *Michele Nardi, the Italian Evangelist: His Life and Work*. New York: Mrs. Blanche P. Nardi.

Noll, M.A. 2002. *The Old Religion in a New World: The History of North American Christianity.* Grand Rapids, MI: Eerdmans.

Norris, P. and R. Inglehart. 2004. *Sacred and Secular: Religion and Politics Worldwide.* Cambridge: Cambridge University Press.

O'Brien, S. 1986. "A Transatlantic Community of Saints: The Great Awakening and the First Evangelical Network, 1735–1755." *The American Historical Review* 91(4):811-32.

Ong, A. 2003. *Buddha Is Hiding: Refugees, Citizenship, the New America.* Berkeley: University of California Press.

Pew Research Center. 2002. "What the World Thinks in 2002: First Major Report of the Pew Global Attitudes Project." Washington: Pew Research Center for the People and the Press.

Presser, S. and L. Stinson. 1998. "Data Collection Mode and Social Desirability Bias in Self-Reported Religious Attendance: Church Attendance in the United States." *American Sociological Review* 63:137-45.

Putnam, R.D. 2000. *Bowling Alone: The Collapse and Revival of American Community.* New York: Simon and Schuster.

Raj, D.S. 2000. "'Who the Hell Do You Think You Are?' Promoting Religious Identity Among Young Hindus in Britian." *Ethnic and Racial Studies* 23(3):535-58.

Ramakrishnan, S.K. 2005. *Democracy in Immigrant America: Changing Demographics and Political Participation.* Stanford, CA: Stanford University Press.

Reiff, D. 2006. "Nuevo Catholics." *New York Times Magazine*, 24 December, 40-87.

Roof, W.C. 1999. *Spiritual Marketplace: Baby Boomers and the Remaking of American Religion.* Princeton, NJ: Princeton University Press.

Sink, M. 2004. "Religion Journal; Peyote, Indian Religion and the Issue of Exclusivity." *New York Times*, 14 August. Accessed 19 January 2009 at http://query.nytimes.com/gst/fullpage.html?res=9C01EFD8153FF937A2575BC0A9629C8B63

Stark, R., E. Hamberg, and A.S. Miller. 2005. "Exploring Spirituality and Unchurched Religions in America, Sweden, and Japan." *Journal of Contemporary Religion* 20:3-23.

Swanbrow, D. 1997. "Study of Worldwide Rates of Religiosity, Church Attendance." *University of Michigan News Service*, 10 December. Available at http://www.ns.umich.edu/htdocs/releases/story.php?id=1835

Taylor, C. 1992. *Multiculturalism and 'The Politics of Recognition': An Essay.* Princeton, NJ: Princeton University Press.

Tseng, T. 1999. "Filipino Folk Spirituality and Immigration: From Mutual Aid to Religion." In *New Spiritual Homes: Religion and Asian Americans*, ed. D.K Yoo. Honolulu: University of Hawaii Press, in association with UCLA Asian American Studies Center, Los Angeles.

Tweed, T.A. 2002. "Who Is a Buddhist? Night-stand Buddhists and Other Creatures." In *Westward Dharma: Buddhism Beyond Asia*, ed. C.S. Prebish and M. Baumann. Berkeley: University of California Press.

US Conference of Catholic Bishops. Department of Communications. 2006. *The Catholic Church in America – Meeting Real Needs in Your Neighborhood*. A report from the Catholic Information Project, Washington. Available at http://www.usccb.org/comm/2006CIPFinal.pdf

Vásquez, M.A. and M.F. Marquardt. 2003. *Globalizing the Sacred: Religion Across the Americas*. New Brunswick, NJ: Rutgers University Press.

Verba, S., K. Lehman Schlozman, and H.E. Brady. 1995. *Voice and Equality: Civic Voluntarism in American Politics*. Cambridge, MA: Harvard University Press.

Warren, M.R. 2001. *Dry Bones Rattling: Community Building to Revitalize American Democracy*. Princeton, NJ: Princeton University Press.

Wolfe, A. 2003. *The Transformation of American Religion*. Chicago: University of Chicago Press.

World Christian Database. 2004. Available at http://worldchristiandatabase.org/wcd

Wuthnow, R. 1998. *After Heaven: Spirituality in America Since the 1950s*. Berkeley/London: University of California Press.

— 1999. "Mobilizing Civic Engagement: The Changing Impact of Religious Involvement." In *Civic Engagement in American Democracy*, ed. T. Skocpol and M.P. Fiorina. Washington: Brookings Institute Press.

Wyman, M. 1993. *Round-trip to America: The Immigrants Return to Europe, 1880–1930*. Ithaca, NY: Cornell University Press.

Yang, F. 1999. *Chinese Christians in America: Conversion, Assimilation, and Adhesive Identities*. University Park: The Pennsylvania State University Press.

Yang, F. and H.R.F. Ebaugh. 2001. "Transformations in New Immigrant Religions and Their Global Implications." *American Sociological Review* 66:269-88.

Chapter 5

Modus Co-vivendi: Religious Diversity in Canada

MICHELINE MILOT

Three major components of political life have a decisive influence on the expression and governance of religious diversity in Canada: multiculturalism as official policy of the state; the Charter of Rights and Freedoms, which is embedded in the Constitution; and the bi-national history of the country. In this chapter, I will examine the way these three aspects come into play in terms of the new challenges that growing religious diversity represents for the Canadian state. This growth is, in large part, the result of immigration. To start, I provide data on immigration and religious diversity in Canada. Next, I introduce normative aspects of multiculturalism and fundamental rights by targeting the principal aspects of diversity and religious rights. In the main body of the chapter, I discuss certain controversies and debates associated with religious diversity in the public sphere. These episodes involve (a) the compatibility between assertions of religious identity and social integration, (b) the equality between men and women, and (c) the laicity[1] of the state. As we will see, the reaction one is likely to observe to these three phenomena depends largely on whether they are expressed in French Canada (Quebec) or in English Canada. I will attempt to elucidate the reasons for these different responses.

Multicultural policy and the Charter of Rights and Freedoms are positive vehicles for incorporating diversity and social integration that are consistent with the fundamental norms of justice and liberal democracy. Both multiculturalism and the Charter represent contexts in which the state seeks to establish a balance between respect for

International Migration and the Governance of Religious Diversity, eds. P. Bramadat and M. Koenig.
Montreal and Kingston: McGill-Queen's University Press, Queen's Policy Studies Series.
© 2009 The School of Policy Studies, Queen's University at Kingston. All rights reserved.

individual identity and respect for citizen identity; both policies form part of the dynamic of recognition.[2] In liberal democracies, we can observe the emergence during recent decades of what might be called a democracy of identities. Political theories have been greatly transformed, especially regarding the issue of recognition. In the United States, philosopher John Rawls opened up the issue of justice as a fundamental prerequisite for the equality of citizens in a pluralistic society. His theory undoubtedly improved the prospects for recognition, even though the latter concept is not central to his political philosophy. Canadian philosopher Charles Taylor (1992) made a more direct contribution by giving the "politics of recognition" an important role in his social theory. Nancy Fraser (2005) later formalized a new way of thinking about recognition, asserting the need to stop thinking only in terms of redistribution (of economic and social goods) and emphasizing the recognition of personal dignity. In a quite different approach, Axel Honneth (2000) maintains that the idea of recognition, together with its opposite (humiliation, lack of respect), constitutes an excellent litmus test for attitudes toward justice in a multicultural society. According to Honneth, the normative premises of social interaction are based on the reciprocal principles of mutual recognition that help form a positive self-image. There is a connection between this thesis and that found in the work of Taylor, who stresses the dialogue through which identity is formed:

> The thesis is that our identity is partly shaped by recognition or its absence, often by the *mis*recognition of others, and so a person or group of people can suffer real damage, real distortion, if the people or society around them mirror back to them a confining or demeaning or contemptible picture of themselves. (Taylor 1992, 25)

In that vein, I consider recognition to be a central value of the paradigm of multiculturalism.

Religious Characteristics of Canadian Immigration and Religious Diversity

Institutional Arrangements of Church and State

The Canadian model of the relationship between religions and the state has never been defined constitutionally—neither as a system in which one or another Christian denomination is formally established, nor as a system in which the state and the church are separate. This constitutional silence is even more surprising given the historical context: since the British defeat of the French near Quebec City in 1759 and the subsequent Treaty of Paris (1763), the state has evolved under the guidance of Great Britain and has always assumed the virtue and catholicity of an established Anglican Church tradition.[3] Furthermore, France and the United States, where the separation of political and religious powers was proclaimed during periods of upheaval, were generally regarded as counter-models for Canada, which had never experienced any major conflict involving an adjustment in the relationship between the religious and political spheres.

In fact, laicity and neutrality are constructions that have arisen during the course of the historical development of Canadian jurisprudence (Milot 2002; 2005, 13-27). This fact is noteworthy here; it is what one might call a *downstream* laicity, rather than an abstract principle already set out in formal law. Since the mid-twentieth century, legal judgments have explicitly reiterated a principle articulated clearly in 1955 by the Supreme Court: "In our country, there is no state religion."[4] This orientation is based on a tradition that goes back to the eighteenth century.

The only two references to religion in the Constitution are found in Article 93 and in the Preamble. Article 93 was formulated during the constitutional agreements of 1867. At that time, based on the principles of the division of jurisdictions between the federal parliament and the provinces, education was assigned to the provinces. Protestants, who found themselves in a minority in the province of Quebec, asked for full administrative authority over their schools, as did Ontario's Roman Catholics. To resolve the turbulent debates unleashed by this request, the parties agreed to insert an article to protect Catholic and Protestant school boards in regions where they were in a minority (and in Montreal and Quebec City). In 1997, Quebec requested and obtained an amendment to eliminate this constitutional protection.

The other reference is found in the Preamble to the 1982 Constitution, which begins, "Whereas Canada is founded upon principles that recognize the supremacy of God and the rule of law...." This comment about the supremacy of God was inserted at the urging of Jake Epp, a Mennonite tory member of parliament, in the 1980s. In other words, this reference is not a relic of the past (as many people would assume) but a puzzling recent insertion. This reference might lead one to believe that the Canadian system is not neutral. What is the real impact of asserting the supremacy of God? Once again, we need to refer to judicial precedents (Milot 2005, 23-24). Two judgments rendered by the Federal Court of Canada provided the following interpretation: this principle prevents Canada from becoming an atheistic state but does not prevent it from being a secular (lay) state, that is, a state that does not concern itself with religion.[5] Notably, in *O'Sullivan c. M.R.N.*, Judge Muldoon states the following (my emphasis):

By including recognition of God's supremacy in the Constitution of Canada, were they seeking to turn Canada into a theocracy? Certainly not. If this phrase had been included a century ago or more, we might have concluded from this that Canada was a Christian state or kingdom. . . . So what does the preamble mean? . . . By guaranteeing this protection to believers, recognition of God's supremacy means that unless and until the Constitution is modified, *Canada cannot become an officially atheist state*, as was the Union of Soviet Socialist Republics.

The court considers that Canada as a secular state quite simply does not concern itself with matters of conscience and religion, with one exception based on sheer reason. This exception obliges the state to intervene to prevent the application or expression of conscience and religion from doing physical or mental harm to others, or infringing upon the rights guaranteed to others by the Constitution. . . . In fact, it is the inclusion in the Constitution of these widely disparate freedoms that establishes *the intrinsically secular character of the Canadian state.*

In other words, the comment in the Preamble about God's supremacy has no real legal efficacy. Moreover, it has never motivated the courts to interpret the right to freedom of conscience and religion found in the Charter of Rights and Freedoms (paragraph 2a) restrictively—a clause that protects both atheism and religious affiliation. Thus, it is the freedoms included in the Constitution that establish the secular character of the state and that allow jurists and judges to state that the Preamble is of no use in modifying its character, which is associated with the interpretive tradition in law. *A fortiori*, religious affiliation is not considered a necessary condition for citizenship, either directly or indirectly.

Religious Diversity and Immigration

The majority of the Canadian population is Christian, although regular attendance at church services has declined significantly over the last several decades. According to the 2001 Canadian census, 6.3 percent of the population stated that they were non-Christian while 16 percent indicated that they had "no religion." Of the former category, Muslims constituted the largest group (1.9 percent of the population), followed by Jews (1.1 percent). Buddhists, Hindus, and Sikhs each accounted for about 1 percent of the population. Among immigrants specifically, almost 52 percent of those admitted to Canada between 1991 and 2001 stated that they belonged to a non-Christian tradition. During that decade, the Muslim, Buddhist, Sikh, and Hindu populations roughly doubled.[6]

The distribution of newcomers and non-Christian groups is highly uneven; these groups are not well represented throughout Canada but are heavily concentrated in the major cities. Of the 579,640 Canadians who described themselves as Muslim in 2001—and this number is growing—the majority (352,500) live in Ontario, primarily in Toronto, and 108,600 live in Quebec (nearly all of them in Montreal). Most of the 278,400 Sikhs in Canada have settled in English-speaking cities: 90,590 are in the Toronto area and the 135,310 in British Columbia are mostly in the greater Vancouver area. There are 297,200 Hindus in Canada. Like Sikhs, the vast majority of Hindus live in Toronto and Vancouver, although the demand for workers in Alberta's oil industry is probably responsible for attracting some of the 15,965 Hindus who have settled in that province. These figures were current in 2001 and had nearly doubled or (in the case of Muslims) more than doubled during the ten years prior to that census; as such, it is reasonable to expect similar increases the next time religious identity is measured in the national census (in 2011).

It should be noted that Christians—from Asia, Africa, and Latin America, for example—account for a large proportion of the immigrant population (see Bramadat and Seljak 2008). However, the Muslim, Sikh, and Hindu communities are growing the most rapidly; this expansion has been obvious to observers in Canadian urban settings because the rituals, places of worship, and clothing styles associated with these communities are more conspicuous.[7]

The Impact of Religious Diversity

The concentration of non-Christian religious diversity in Canada's three major cities (Montreal, Toronto, and Vancouver) suggests that both the non-immigrant population and state governance must come to terms with the new demands for recognition in public institutions. In certain cases, demands for recognition and accommodation come into conflict with democratic values considered non-negotiable by the dominant group in that society. Sometimes adjustments are made naturally (such as adjustments regarding food requirements) and, at other times, with greater difficulty (such as accepting Sikhs' wearing of a kirpan at school, especially in Quebec, where the Sikh population is small). Sometimes, clumsy attempts to adjust are blown out of proportion by the media, which literally creates a social problem where none existed. For example, the media drew attention to a decision of an Ontario judge to not allow a Christmas tree to be erected in front of the courthouse, even though no non-Christian minority had lodged a complaint about this tradition.

Adapting to religious diversity and recognizing new signs of affiliation raises inevitable questions about policy, identity, and recognition. The answers to these questions may be found in the political and legal traditions of nations. What can we say about the Canadian model?

Multiculturalism and the Recognition of Diversity

The roots of the concept of multiculturalism can be found in Anglo-Saxon countries such as Australia, Canada, the United Kingdom, and the United States. There are several types of multiculturalism, and each has followed its own trajectory within a specific social and political context. In fact, multiculturalism is not limited to Anglo-Saxon societies. It is also linked to the historical development of other national and ethnic communities (such as France, Germany, and Spain) in which one can witness "an historical collection of political agendas, intellectual debates and practical experiences founded on the idea that modern democracies must ensure recognition of different cultures by reforming their institutions and giving individuals effective ways to cultivate and transmit their differences" (Doytcheva 2005, 16, translation). This "historical collection" constitutes the framework within which a diversity-based model of governance takes shape, though there may be a gap between the official position and the population's reaction to this type of governance. I will return to this point later.

Political and Legal Aspects of Canadian Multiculturalism

In 1971, Canada became the first country to adopt an official policy of multiculturalism. This policy was launched by the Liberal prime minister of the time, Pierre Trudeau, although the official *Multiculturalism Act* was not passed until 1988 under the leadership of Conservative prime minister Brian Mulroney. The multiculturalism policy is accompanied by two guarantees, one constitutional and the other legal.[8]

Political Aspects. The policy of multiculturalism in Canada has its roots in the rising tensions between Francophones and Anglophones that marked the 1960s. In 1963, the Royal Commission on Bilingualism and Biculturalism was set up to find a solution to the long-standing conflict between what many people call Canada's "two solitudes." However, something unexpected occurred in the process: the discussions and debates went beyond the polarization between the two dominant groups. For, in reaction to the assimilationist model—which until then had been dominant in countries of immigration—representatives of various ethnic groups informed the commissioners that the model was not only a failure but was also unjust. Many immigrants belonged to communities that had lived in Canada for several generations, and they pointed with pride to their involvement in the war effort and the construction of the country's major institutions and infrastructure. Members of these communities (such as Ukrainians) argued that an official acceptance of cultural differences and support for pluralism would provide a better guarantee of the civic involvement and integration of immigrants and of non-discrimination toward them. Unlike a "melting-pot," these discussions advanced the idea of a cultural mosaic in which distinct parties form a unified, organic whole.

These discussions, among others, were taken into consideration in the Commission's recommendations, which were designed to acknowledge the importance of cultural diversity for Canadian identity and to encourage institutions to reflect this pluralism in their policies and programs. The multiculturalism policy, unveiled in 1971, declared French and English to be the two official languages of Canada. The policy emphasized the idea that ethnic pluralism was a characteristic of Canadian society that deserved to be promoted and preserved.

Political philosopher Will Kymlicka has provided a good definition of the multicultural state: "A state is multicultural if its members either belong to different nations (a multinational state), or have emigrated from different nations (a polyethnic state), and if this fact is an important aspect of *personal identity* and *political life*" (1995, 18). This definition conjoins two seemingly incompatible elements: acknowledgement of individual identity and participation in political life. According to American sociologist Kevin J. Christiano, we can say that "American culture aspires to overcome difference, while Canada strives in politics to guide its passage and in law to control its effects. The Canadian system ingests diversity without really digesting it" (2000, 74).

During the decade following the adoption of the multiculturalism policy, it was observed that if the goal was to prevent discrimination against ethnic minorities in the areas of job access, housing, and education, it would not be enough to simply emphasize pluralism. Consequently, government programs began to focus increasingly on issues of racism and discrimination.

Legal Aspects. Constitutional and legal guarantees have a relatively greater impact than a general policy of pluralism in determining the influence of multiculturalism on political governance and social practice. First, on the constitutional level, Article 27 of the Canadian Charter of Rights and Freedoms is worded as follows: "This Charter shall be interpreted in a manner consistent with the preservation and enhancement of the multicultural heritage of Canadians." In addition, the Charter gives the individual as the subject of law (not the community) prime consideration when it comes to legal interpretation. It guarantees the equality of citizens, whom it protects from discriminatory treatment on many explicitly inadmissible grounds:

> Article 15. (1) Every individual is equal before and under the law and has the right to the equal protection and equal benefit of the law without discrimination and, in particular, without discrimination based on race, national or ethnic origin, colour, religion, sex, age or mental or physical disability.

This list is not closed: the judges of the Supreme Court have interpreted that homosexuality is also a component of personal identity for some people and, as such, gays and lesbians have to be protected against discrimination.

Second, the *Canadian Multiculturalism Act*, which was adopted in 1988, is the official statement of the multiculturalism policy formulated in 1971.[9] It sets out a long list of obligations that are incumbent on the state and public institutions. According to the Act, the Canadian government is committed to the following:

> (a) recognize and promote the understanding that multiculturalism reflects the cultural and racial diversity of Canadian society and acknowledges the freedom of all members of Canadian society to preserve, enhance and share their cultural heritage. . . .

> (c) promote the full and equitable participation of individuals and communities of all origins in the continuing evolution and shaping of all aspects of Canadian society and assist them in the elimination of any barrier to that participation. . . .

> (h) foster the recognition and appreciation of the diverse cultures of Canadian society and promote the reflection and the evolving expressions of those cultures.[10]

The political vocabulary of recognition recurs in these passages. As such, the legal interpretation of the multiculturalism policy in Canada is linked to a type of recognition that places great importance on individual choice (in accordance with the Charter of Rights and Freedoms). In my view, the *Multiculturalism Act* provides safeguards against pressures to conform (either vis-à-vis the majority group or within minority groups) and regards the integration of diversity within the public sphere as a positive value. I agree with philosopher Jocelyn Maclure's normative definition of multiculturalism: "An ethic of recognition of minority cultures is a *justice requisite*, a condition of social justice in liberal democracies whose cultural fabric is diversified" (2007, 65, translation). In other words, as an instrument of social justice, multiculturalism must try to find an equilibrium between respect for cultural pluralism and national integration.

How does this formal recognition translate into the treatment of demands formulated on a religious basis?

The Legal Obligation to Accommodate as a Corollary to the Right to Equality

National legislation necessarily and legitimately bears the imprint of the dominant religious heritage of those who have built the nation; it also reflects the values and habits of those founders. As a result, and as many chapters in this book indicate, ostensibly secular laws and regulations may infringe upon the fundamental principle of equality for all, even in a state that is officially secular. Examples would include the national calendar in which the vast majority of official holidays match the Christian calendar, and marriage laws that are based on Christian— and consequently heterosexual—concepts.

In daily life, neutral laws or rules that apply to everyone in the same way can have an unintentional discriminatory effect on a single group of individuals if the latter are subject to restrictive obligations or conditions not imposed on other members of the population. This is *indirect* discrimination, which may involve age, sex, or physical disability; however, it may also apply to religious beliefs and practices, especially to those of minority groups.

There are numerous examples of indirect discrimination; here I offer only a few. For instance, in public institutions such as the Royal Canadian Mounted Police, rules related to mandatory working uniforms might make it difficult for believers to observe their religion's dress code. As well, the general prohibition on bearing a weapon—a prohibition for which there is wide public acceptance—might contradict the Sikh tradition of wearing a kirpan. Moreover, in many workplaces, religious employees must negotiate with their employers to find a way to fulfill their obligations regarding the times and frequency of worship. In these cases, the regulations governing the establishment of a general norm are not a priori intended to explicitly discriminate on the basis of religion. However, these regulations indirectly and unintentionally discriminate against certain groups and, by extension, against certain individuals.

In Canada, the Supreme Court defined a mandatory legal mechanism to correct this form of discrimination: reasonable accommodation. This is a legal mechanism—applied only in certain instances but also intended to establish a general principle—to force the state, institutions, and companies to modify general norms, practices, and policies so that the (reasonable) particular needs of individuals can be accommodated. Courts are free to compel or promote reasonable accommodation for any of the grounds of discrimination prohibited by Article 15 of the Charter.[11] A number of voluntary adaptations and adjustments can be carried out in institutions, or among individuals, without having to resort to the courts to compel accommodation. In fact, most reasonable accommodation in public institutions and workplaces is implemented without using any adjudicative process.

Both legal doctrine and jurisprudence recognized from the start that reasonable accommodation is both a *logical consequence* and an essential *element* of freedom of religion (see Bosset 2005; Woehrling 1998). In this legal perspective, it is not enough to give voice to rights in theoretical terms. It is necessary to be free to express such rights in actions. In addition, state institutions must adapt their operations while preserving their position of neutrality with regard to religion. While a similar openness to accommodation within the legal and political systems of some other countries is apparent, to my knowledge Canada is the only country in which the concept has acquired the status of legal obligation.

Requests for reasonable accommodation are examined on a case-by-case basis (for example, the wearing of a kirpan by Sikhs can be authorized in certain circumstances and not in others: it has been accepted in schools but not on planes or in courts). Reasonable accommodation is an inherently progressive and additive device, and one that is primarily pragmatic rather than theoretical. That said, clear references are gradually being laid down to determine the reasonableness of requests. Among the criteria that guide the courts' application of reasonable accommodation, the following are noteworthy: the reasonableness of a particular custom or rule; the employer's or institution's efforts to arrive at an accommodation with the applicant; the excessive character of the constraint that the accommodation imposes on the employer or institution; and the degree to which the rights of others are infringed. The courts interpret these criteria in a very liberal way. That is, social acceptance does not always concord with juridical solutions. In fact, the question of what is reasonable arises, particularly in Quebec, because many people think that religion is a private affair.[12]

It is important to note that reasonable accommodation does not involve a privilege accorded to an individual—and even less to a community. It is, rather, a special provision allowing society to counter, as effectively as possible, the indirect discriminatory effects of laws or regulations designed for the majority by adapting them, for religious or other purposes, to individual needs. Thus, the primary objective of reasonable accommodation is not the integration of particular groups of immigrants or even of immigrants in general. Rather, the primary objective is the rational application to all Canadians of the principles articulated in the Constitution, the Charter, and other key documents. However, the principle of reasonable accommodation certainly does contribute to immigrant integration by virtue of the fact that an individual who might be, or feel, excluded from certain institutions due to personal obligations of a religious nature (attire or food, for example) can have access to the same institutions as the population as a whole. So far, the practice of reasonable accommodation has had several positive consequences, including a wider recognition of diverse identities, a more favourable reception of these identities in public institutions, and the opening up of dialogue among the various parties.

However, in recent years there has been growing criticism of multiculturalism, religious accommodation, and decisions of the Supreme Court of Canada in these areas. People have begun to wonder whether accommodation might encourage individuals to withdraw to, or stay within, their communities. As well, one often hears anxieties expressed in public discourse about whether multiculturalism might constitute a danger to social cohesion.

Critiques Concerning Public Recognition of Religious Diversity

There is no doubt that the attacks in the United States of 11 September 2001, the Madrid bombings of 11 March 2004, and the London bombings of 7 July 2005 have been partially responsible for the emergence, in many countries, of a strong criticism of multiculturalism (principle and policy) and the accommodation of minority religious demands. The attacks in Britain were particularly significant because these were acts committed not by foreigners but by (Muslim) British citizens. These events greatly affected people's outlook—not only that of the general population but also of liberal intellectuals, especially in Canada.

In reality, Canadian multiculturalism has been subject to criticism since its conception in 1971. Certain Québécois saw in the policy a tactic to curtail their nationalistic aspirations. According to Kymlicka (1995, 17),

> French Canadians have opposed the multiculturalism policy because they think it reduces their claims of nationhood to the level of immigrant ethnicity. Others feared the opposite: that the policy was intended to treat immigrant groups as nations, and hence support the development of institutionally complete cultures alongside those of the French and English.

English Canadians feared that the policy would weaken their heritage or saw it as an attack on Canadian unity. Empirically, these fears were never realized; nevertheless, within the arena of public discourse, this apprehension has had a significant impact on the extent to which the new form of religious diversity has been accepted. This is especially true in Quebec where there is a growing ambivalence about the religious diversity associated with the new phase of Canadian immigration history. These concerns are focused particularly on Muslim requests for the accommodation of their religious prescriptions in the public sphere.

Increased immigration to Canada has been accompanied not only by a greater number of religious groups in the country but also by a rapid expansion in the minority religious traditions already in existence in the late 1960s, when the immigration patterns began to change dramatically. One important manifestation of these changes is the increased public visibility of these traditions (especially those of Muslims and Sikhs). In fact, only a minority of adherents within these groups are more visible in their attire or embrace an orthodox way of life. However, faced with the growing numbers of visibly different newcomers who sometimes make demands for accommodation on the larger society, some members of the majority group and the intelligentsia have questioned the prevailing model of relations between religions and the Canadian state.

The Canadian model of integration and multiculturalism is rooted in a sense of tolerance and in a relatively liberal, cosmopolitan, outward-looking attitude toward the expression of diversity. However, some individuals overrate the deleterious effects of this juridical-political model. Members of the public have expressed—in blunt and sometimes xenophobic terms—their concerns regarding the actual desire of religious minorities to integrate. People also fear the erosion of democratic values (especially gender equality) if Canada continues to embrace a greater expression of religious affiliation. Moreover, they worry that the new religious visibility could constitute a threat to institutional laicity. In their view, several criticisms may be levelled at multiculturalism and the culture of individual rights resulting from the Charter.

While these fears are legitimate, they are not well founded. In particular, many people overestimate the power of religious factors in the construction of believers' identities, and more often than not, the fears about incompatibility between religious identity and social integration are not substantiated by the facts. In modernity, religious affiliation is seen as only a part of an individual's identity. Most believers select what accords with their way of life from their own traditions; moreover, they share the same democratic values (liberty, autonomy, pluralism) as the secular majority (Hervieu-Léger 1999). Also, while certain groups of believers would like to see their religious standards exert greater influence on public standards and morality (an attitude also common among Canadian-born fundamentalist Christians), they do not have sufficient social capital or democratic power to reverse the process of increasing laicity and liberalization. Nonetheless, let us examine the tensions that have arisen in connection with the changing nature of religious diversity.

Recognition of Religious Diversity and Social Integration

Much theoretical work has been carried out in Canada on multiculturalism and its impact on political affiliation. The importance of the national question in Quebec may account for much of this. There are divergent opinions on the impact of multiculturalism and the Charter on social integration. The harshest criticism, articulated by Bissoondath (1994) and others, is that multiculturalism leads to ghettoization and may thus destroy citizenship. However, this criticism is not based on any study or sociologically demonstrated empirical data. Kymlicka cites a range of indicators that refute Bissoondath's critique of multiculturalism. In *Finding Our Way: Rethinking Ethnocultural Relations in Canada*, Kymlicka (1998) says that in areas such as intermarriage, language acquisition, and naturalization, immigrants to Canada "out-integrate" immigrants to the United States and other places that do not have a multiculturalism policy. Sociological authors including Bramadat (2005), Breton et al. (1990), and Eid (2007), as well as the *Ethnic Diversity Survey* conducted by Statistics Canada (2002), show that there is no correlation between religious identification and geographical segregation and alienation, or at least that what correlations do exist suggest that the alienation and marginalization are related to racial discrimination rather than to religious identity or ghettoization.

By contrast, one could easily claim that the principal aim of recognizing diversity is to avoid making homogeneity a necessary condition for social participation. The purpose of recognition is to allow individuals to feel more comfortable in public institutions and to facilitate their integration. For example, some Sikhs have requested the right to wear a turban as members of the Royal Canadian Mounted Police, while some Muslim women have asked to wear their veils at work. By asking institutions to accommodate relatively minor religious dress requirements, these adherents demonstrate their desire to integrate into, and participate fully in, public institutions.

Norman (2000, 93-110) explores the conceptual and normative connections between justice and political stability to see whether there are reasonable grounds for adherence to an ideology of multicultural citizenship in pluralistic multinational states. In his view, multiculturalism recognizes not only that immigrants must adapt to the social and political norms of the country but also that the country must adapt to the immigrants; in Canada, this dynamic is described as the "two-way street" approach to integration. What is important is to avoid treating an individual's or a community's religious identity—or almost any other facet of identity, for that matter—as a static feature. Identity is fluid and changing (a young Muslim woman may decide for certain reasons to wear a veil for a few years and then, for other reasons, decide to abandon it; the process might unfold in the opposite direction, too). The dual objective of justice and citizenship can then be fulfilled if we follow the idea advanced by Kymlicka (1995): foster a form of multiculturalism that always allows the terms of integration to be renegotiated.

From a sociological standpoint, it is crucial to note that recognition based on religious reasons continues to be an obstacle, even for liberal thinkers. According to McLaren (2006, 155), "Canada as a liberal democratic state continues to have problems in dealing with legal constraints on religious belief and practice. This is especially true in those instances when a religious minority is claiming state accommodation for its beliefs in the context of law or activities thought to be secular in nature." Certain authors think that Quebec has more difficulties in dealing with religious diversity: "The exuberant ethnic and religious variety characterizing Toronto seems not a problem, whereas major increases of minorities in the heartland of Québécois nationalism and semi-monopoly Catholicism might well become so" (Martin 2000, 30). This observation is partly true, but not for nationalistic or religious reasons. In Quebec, the Francophone majority (which represents a minority in Canada) fears that their cultural identity will be diluted if other distinct identities take up a lot of space in the public sphere. In addition, some Québécois (especially members of the intelligentsia) have a closer relationship with the ideas and values associated with France and thus tend to idealize the model of integration found in the French Republic, in which religious affiliation is relegated to the private sphere.

As McLaren (2006, 155-73) has observed, special requests based on normative but non-religious factors are easier to accept than requests based on religious norms. For example, for many people, it seems far more acceptable for a man in the Royal Canadian Mounted Police to request permission to wear a beard due to a skin condition that makes shaving painful than it would be for him to make a similar request based instead on a religious (Sikh) prohibition against shaving. This fact alone reveals a great deal about secular society's relationship with religion. In liberal democracies, there are in fact very few religious minorities (such as the Hassidic Jews and Amish Christians) who prefer to live entirely separate from the broader society in order to protect their community against secularization and modern values. Laicity did not make religiosity and spirituality disappear; as Taylor (2007) has noted in his book, *A Secular Age*, for a great many people, religion is experienced individually and autonomously, rather than strictly within the context of a traditional religious institution. Increasingly, research suggests that many believers—especially younger ones—no longer affiliate themselves in a predictable manner with an external authority (see Beyer 2006; Bibby 2004; Statistics Canada 2001). This deinstitutionalization is increasingly characteristic even of adherents who embrace a relatively orthodox approach to religiosity.

Believers who profess unwavering loyalty to a single institution and to a single religious tradition are often framed by the dominant discourse as renouncing the virtues of autonomy and rejecting the liberal values of modern society. The majority may stigmatize or treat with condescension religious individuals or groups whose approach to religious affiliation is deemed not yet to approximate the mature, critical awareness characteristic of liberal democratic societies. There is, in other words, a subtle hegemonic form of liberalism that tends to naturalize a cosmopolitan and idiosyncratic form of religious identity and, by necessity, to marginalize—as archaic—all other forms of religiosity. The wearing of the veil by Muslim women constitutes a case of this phenomenon, and I will explore this issue shortly.

One commonly heard criticism of the Charter of Rights and Freedoms is that it has increased the litigious nature of social relationships and generated a quest for recognition to the detriment of the articulation and promulgation of common values. Many believe that the Charter, like multiculturalism, favours communalism. Of course, some individuals will prefer to live almost exclusively within the sphere of a single religious or cultural community rather than within the shared realm of the general population. However, there is no evidence to suggest that a causal link exists between the growing strength of minority religions and an increase in antisocial communalism, and thus with a disinclination to adopt or adapt to values assumed to be common. The fact that this anxiety endures in the public arena despite the lack of evidence demonstrates not only that the vulgar form of the secularization hypothesis is alive and well but also that some members of society's majority still view religion as a dominant indicator in a person's identity. This latter view has proved erroneous as research shows that the identity of every individual, even that of orthodox believers, is complex, dynamic, and multifaceted (see Bramadat and Seljak 2005). Nevertheless, it is remarkable that religious identities displayed in public can be so strongly associated with a threat to national identity. In Quebec, more than in other regions of Canada, religion—which dominated the lives of many residents prior to the Quiet Revolution of the 1960s (see Lemieux and Montminy 2000)—has become an indicator of a twofold alienation when practiced by others: obedience to an external authority and, as a result, an inability to participate in public life based on an ideal of rational autonomy.

The criticism that social relationships in Canada have become increasingly litigious is, I believe, exaggerated. On the contrary, in a liberal democracy it is highly appropriate for courts to serve as a forum in which the problems of minority groups can be debated and protected from what Tocqueville has referred to as "the tyranny of the majority." According to Eisenberg,

> Canadians have seen the growth and development of a deliberative culture largely primed by the Charter's entrenchment, though engaged by issues that go well beyond Charter concerns. The Canadian public, or different "publics," is more involved now in shaping the basic principles of democratic governance and coexistence than ever before. (2006, 4)

Furthermore, as the Canadian philosopher James Tully (2006, 26) observes, "A norm of mutual recognition is thus never final, but questionable. It follows that in a free and open society, existing norms of mutual recognition should be open to public questioning so that these reasons can be heard and considered."

Gender Equality and the Fear of Religious Diversity

Within a multicultural society such as Canada, does the official recognition of religious particularity become unfair or unjust when it permits religious groups to violate the individual rights of their own members, especially women? Many of the criticisms advanced against Canada's main way of governing religious diversity—its multiculturalism policy—revolve around this question and so we should address it directly.

The promotion of any particular culture is not within the purview of either the multiculturalism policy or the legal and discursive traditions that have emerged out of the Charter of Rights and Freedoms. Moreover, under no circumstances may the policy allow violations of human rights, even within groups whose rights have been accommodated in formal or informal ways. There is a distinction between (a) individual and group rights protected by multiculturalism and (b) similar rights prohibited by the state.

An example of this distinction is the response of the Government of Ontario to a demand made by an imam to create a tribunal to settle family disputes. The tribunal was to be based on Islamic law and was to have a real effect. Moreover, the proposed tribunal was consistent with Ontario's laws on civil arbitration; that is, the existing laws on arbitration already allowed for religious tribunals (such as those that operate within the Jewish community) to make binding rulings on family law issues. A government report (Boyd 2004) recommended allowing religious courts. The recommendations were based on a set of considerations that included (a) respect for the rights of minority groups who wished to abide by values different from those contained in Ontario civil law; (b) an effort to improve access to justice; (c) an effort to facilitate monitoring by the state of prevailing practices; and (d) a provision to allow the state to determine whether individual rights are being respected. The report elicited many strong reactions.[13] The Canadian Council of Muslim Women fiercely opposed this tribunal and rejected the Boyd report, arguing that Shari'ah law would discriminate against women. After assessing the report and hearing the arguments of the various stakeholders, Dalton McGuinty, the premier of Ontario, announced in 2005 that he intended to change the legislation so that in the future, no religious court of any kind would be allowed in the province, since the practice constituted a threat to "our common terrain."[14] In other words, in order to prevent Muslims from establishing Shari'ah tribunals, and to avoid explicitly discriminating against the Muslim community (by denying Muslim tribunals only), the Ontario government decided that it had to rescind the previously granted right of Jews and Christians to maintain parallel religious systems for resolving matters of family law.

I should note that the original request to establish this tribunal was not linked directly to multicultural policy but to Ontario's laws on arbitration (including family matters such as marriage). Nevertheless, there was obvious confusion in public opinion. Kymlicka commented that to accept these kinds of courts would be to tolerate a form of multiculturalism that had "gone mad."[15] Indeed, one of the fundamental principles of this policy is to take into account the impact on the most vulnerable members of minority groups of any law or institutional mechanism associated with the needs of minorities. To follow Kymlicka's argument, allowing Muslims to create so-called Shari'ah tribunals would have violated this basic principle because many immigrant women are subject to strong internal pressures from their communities and extended families and therefore would not be better served by such a tribunal than they would be by the existing ostensibly secular system of family law.

Nevertheless, for many feminists, and for many people who are highly suspicious of the incursion of religion into the public arena, the principle of gender equality should take precedence over freedom of conscience and religion. However, from both a legal and a social standpoint, this position is very problematic. First, legal theory and jurisprudence establish a balance, rather than a hierarchy, among fundamental rights when there is no unlawful interference with the person and no disturbance of the public peace.

Second, from a sociological standpoint, equality can be expressed in different ways, as long as the methods employed to ensure its implementation do not affect citizens' equality of status, equality of means to manage their lives, and equality of opportunities to access education, work, justice, and health services. To ensure the equality of all, the state is responsible for protecting individuals from two pressures to conform that may be brought to bear on those belonging to a minority group: (a) the pressure applied by the majority group, which often displays more or less explicit expectations that diversity be expressed in the public sphere according to a Christian or even a secular frame of reference; and (b) the internal pressure exercised in minority communities, which often represent the principal social and affective networks of recent immigrants.

There can be no doubt that the right to equality is one of the rights that citizens demand the most. However, the interpretation of equality rights varies significantly. Of course, even in a multicultural society, the geometry of legal equality cannot vary according to religious or philosophical views. Nonetheless, different conceptions of equality can exist side by side in society, as illustrated by the headscarf issue: the interpretation provided by young women in Quebec who wear it teaches us that, for them, it is not necessarily a symbol of inequality between men and women. We need to take into account the fact that while the desire to protect women in minority groups is laudable, it often conceals a paternalism that renders invisible the creativity and fluidity women often demonstrate with regard to issues such as the hijab. One might argue that in such contexts, little net benefit is realized if we simply substitute the state's paternalism for (alleged) community-based paternalism (see Alvi, Hoodfar, and McDonough 2003; Van Praagh 2006).

For some, the hijab appears to contradict values of sexual or gender equality that many citizens believe are entrenched in Canada's liberal democracy. However, a more careful interpretation of the way Muslim women view this religious norm fits the criteria of moral and religious pluralism in a society that does not view citizenship as homogeneous. First, not everyone in a given society is obliged to share the same view of the way sexual equality affects his or her life. In addition, the wearing of a hijab implies nothing about the actual lives of those who do not subscribe to the beliefs underlying this act. Opponents of the veil see it as a symbol of the total submission of women to non-democratic principles. However, as Tully (2006, 18) observes, "individuals are usually subject to many and overlapping norms of mutual recognition and corresponding identities" and, as such, one must be cautious about drawing rigid conclusions about the meaning of a given symbol in the life of an individual or in the community of which she is a member.

Indeed, no law can totally prevent internal—and even rights-denying—pressures that might be applied within religious groups. The law of the state does not eradicate all the sociological mechanisms of real-life situations that can infringe upon gender equality. That said, we cannot allow treatment that is incompatible with a person's physical or psychological integrity, or with human dignity (such as female circumcision, slavery, or rape). In other words, the accommodation

of religious practices that permit or condone a conservative, theocratic, or even an authoritarian patriarchal worldview generally pose
a problem. However, as the jurist José Woehrling stated with regard
to the hijab,

> While it is true that there is no legal obligation to wear a veil, the fact that
> it is allowed in schools allows families to put moral and social pressure
> on the girls to force them to wear it against their will. However, ... when
> all is said and done it is preferable for young Muslims to attend public
> schools while wearing their veil than to be stuck at home or sent to a
> private religious school. If a minority community fears losing its identity,
> there is a greater risk that it will succumb to fundamentalism to defend
> itself against what it views as pressure to assimilate. It is probably better
> to accept traditional pressures—at least those that pose no danger to
> people's physical or psychological integrity—while hoping that these will
> allow members of minority groups to begin their integration into the wider
> community of the host society while continuing to maintain the support
> of their original community. (1998, 400-1)

In addition, requests for accommodation by minority groups are formulated in terms that invoke individual and universal rights, such as
the right to equality and freedom of religion.

The Tensions between Laicity and Religious Diversity

While residents of Quebec seem to be more involved in debates on the
balance between religious diversity and laicity,[16] the rest of Canada also
discusses the topic.[17] In Quebec (especially among the intelligentsia),
laicity is generally perceived as a bastion against the purportedly harm-
ful effects of religiously based affirmations of identity. Thus, laicity is
exploited to regulate diversity, not by the state but by three very different population groups. First, a number of nationalists opposed to Canadian multiculturalism favour a radical laicity that would eliminate
religious particularities from the public sphere by favouring "collective national values" (allowing these nationalists to avoid appearing to
be promoters of an exclusive French-Canadian "ethnic" citizenship).
Second, there are a number of individuals who are mostly cultural
Catholics, who consider cultural diversity as an affront to the Catholic
heritage and its historical prerogatives: they associate laicity (in a loose
sense) with the shared values that would include the secularized Catholic heritage. Third, certain feminist groups argue that religions convey
patriarchal norms opposed to women's rights and invoke laicity to justify—among other things—prohibitions against the hijab.[18] In all three
cases, there is some confusion about the principles of laicity, which I

will examine shortly. However, first let us examine the roots of this confusion and the exploitation of laicity to oppose diversity.

The greatest confusion has been between the secularization of political structures and individual freedom of expression. The institutional or political secularization that has been evident throughout Canada in the past several decades has led to significant changes within the mechanisms of public institutions. This form of secularization has also had the effect of ensuring that broadly influential social norms have become increasingly differentiated from the oversight of religious organizations such as the Catholic Church. Suddenly, segments of the population, the intelligentsia, and even some politicians assumed that this form of institutional laicity must also encompass individuals and that signs of religious affiliation had no place in public institutions. However, in matters of equality, secularization in liberal democracies has been based, among other factors, on the adjustment required to allow for the growing moral and religious diversity of the population. The public discourse in response to these changes has revealed that some individuals have had trouble relating to the new religious diversity, especially when it has been visible. In fact, the explicit desire to "laicize" the public sphere in many countries has often concealed an implicit expectation that the public expression of religious affiliation would be tolerated only when it approximated the way the majority of community members expressed their religiosity.

Laicity as a political principle—and again, there is a distinction between what I have called laicity on the one hand and the republican model of integration in France (or *laïcité*) on the other hand—does not denote ridding the public sphere of every expression of religious affiliation. Religious expressions can have a legitimate place in the city without necessarily compromising neutrality or collective values. Still, the idea that deeply held convictions belong in the private sphere while the public sphere serves only as a context in which to manifest collective values and principles is unsatisfactory. Individuals act, identify themselves socially, and adopt political stances based on their values and convictions, be they philosophical or religious.

Thus, state neutrality does not exclude taking into account the need to accommodate religious expressions (such as requests for alternate holiday schedules, for the right to wear religious dress in public institutions, and so forth) in order to actualize freedom of conscience and religion, although these kinds of discussions must be open-minded as to the methods and accommodation that will be established to ensure this liberty. It cannot be denied that there is resistance to laicization or to liberalization of morality in, for example, the desire of certain religious groups to exercise control within their communities based on internal collective standards. These groups claim the competence to determine the civil rights of their members through exercising jurisdiction in certain areas (as we have seen with the attempt in Ontario to introduce Shari'ah tribunals to adjudicate some areas of family law), through expressing religious standards in the context of public debates (such as in the opposition of many religious groups to the same-sex marriage legislation passed in 2005), or even through making requests—in the name of freedom of religion—for exemptions to certain laws (such as the requests we have seen in the past ten years to allow baptized Sikhs to wear a kirpan in public places). In fact, whether one affirms or rejects the way the courts and other social agencies have responded to these challenges, the relatively pacific debates around these matters remind us of the importance of public deliberation for determining conditions that favour shared and engaged democratic citizenship. Utilizing laicity as an instrument for denying or assimilating differences is to twist its very meaning.

Laicity must remain legally and politically independent of the moral and religious norms of a particular group. It is not meant to eliminate individual religious expression; indeed, it is its guarantor and means of protection. Furthermore, the public components of political justice currently provide the best legitimization of the secular principles of neutrality and tolerance with regard to diversity.

Conclusion

If we accept that citizens must live together despite their moral and religious differences, then it is appropriate to ask how we might foster peaceful relations among them and encourage their participation in all areas of society. In this regard, it is important to take advantage of every forum and opportunity for joint deliberation among individuals who have different beliefs and to do so within shared institutions. At the turn of the twentieth century, the German sociologist Max Weber clearly foresaw the future of modern society: a permanent struggle of values that are based solely on the convictions of those who defend them. Metaphorically, he referred to this as a society with a "polytheism of values" (1965, 427). Here, values are constantly clashing because their underlying beliefs are seen as absolute. In Weber's view, fundamental values coexist only through "compromise," which is not the same as reconciling ideas but is, rather, a modus vivendi that is pragmatic, dynamic, and fluid. As Tully (2006) observes, the norms of mutual recognition never completely crystallize: these norms can constantly be questioned and renegotiated—even by those who benefit from them. Inevitably, the power structure must come to terms with this new situation. The sociological, political, and legal challenge is to draw on each national tradition with its own trajectory, values, religious sensibilities, and habits in order to establish new links between religious identities and the political sphere—or between religious identities *in* the political sphere. The goal, in other words, is to nurture a more inclusive, common sphere of citizenship and the ability to live together.

Notes

1.   I will employ the neologism *laicity* (rather than "secularism"), which refers to a specific political concept: the neutrality of the state toward religion. The distinction between secularization and laicization is helpful in understanding two different processes, the first one at the social level and the second one at the political level (see Baubérot 2007). A broader discussion of secularization can be found in the first and third parts of this book. See also the *Sociology of Religion* special issue on secularization (Swatos 1999), and the *Social Compass* (2000) issue on laicity 47(3).
2.   See my article (Milot 2006, 81-84).
3.   For an excellent explanation of the role of the church (Anglican and Catholic) in this period, see Bramadat and Seljak (2008).
4.   *Chaput v. Romain*, Supreme Court of Canada [1955], (SCC), 834, 840.
5.   *O'Sullivan c. M.R.N.*, [1992]; *Baquial c. Canada (M.E.I.)* [1995] 28 C.R.R. (2d) D-4.
6.   Between 1991 and 2001, the Muslim community increased by 129 percent, the Buddhist community by 84 percent, and the Sikh and Hindu communities each grew by 89 percent. Interestingly, the "no religion" category increased by 44 percent.
7.   However, it should be noted that the provinces of Manitoba, Alberta, Ontario, and Saskatchewan are home to very conservative Christian communities such as the Amish and the Hutterites. As these groups generally live in a closed environment, their "visibility" is probably less disconcerting than that of other immigrants, who circulate in the same institutions as the rest of the population.
8.   I present these principles in my article (Milot 2008).
9.   http://www.pch.gc.ca/progs/multi/what-multi_f.cfm
10. http://laws.justice.gc.ca/en/c-18.7/226879.html
11. Grounds of discrimination include race, national or ethnic origin, colour, religion, sex, age, or mental or physical disability.
12. In the survey "SOM-La Presse," published in *La Presse* on 9 October 2007, a majority of the Quebec population, particularly Francophones and older people, said it is not reasonable to wear a kirpan in school or a turban in the Royal Canadian Mounted Police.
13. Demonstrations were held in several Canadian and European cities on 8 September 2005 and 11 September 2005.

14. *Le Devoir*, 12 September 2005 (translation).
15. Comment cited by Robitaille (2005, translation).
16. To take stock of the debates on reasonable accommodation, the government of Quebec set up an advisory board in March 2007 on accommodation practices linked to cultural differences. Two great intellectuals were co-chairs: Charles Taylor and Gérard Bouchard. The advisory board was created after a number of issues related to religious minority integration were highlighted in the media. At that time, Quebec was in the midst of an electoral campaign, and so the board's creation was interpreted by some people as a way for politicians to avoid dealing with questions about the integration of religious communities during the campaign.
17. In the rest of Canada, the issues centre around the putatively conservative stances of many religious minorities to questions of sexual morality. Two judgments of the Supreme Court of Canada reflect these questions: *Chamberlain v. Surrey School District No. 36*, [2002], (SCC), 86 and *Trinity Western University c. British Columbia College of Teachers*, [2001] 1 R.C.S. 772.
18. That is particularly clear in *Right to Equality between Women and Men and Freedom of Religion*, Conseil du Statut de la femme, Quebec, November 2007.

References

Alvi, S., H. Hoodfar, and S. McDonough, eds. 2003. *The Muslim Veil in North America*. Toronto: Women's Press.

Baubérot, J. 2007. *Histoire de la Laïcité en France*. Paris: Presses Université de France.

Beyer, P. 2006. *Religion in Global Society*. London: Routledge.

Bibby, R.W. 2004. *Restless Churches: How Canada's Churches Can Contribute to the Emerging Religious Renaissance*. Ottawa: Novalis.

Bissoondath, N. 1994. *Selling Illusions: The Cult of Multiculturalism in Canada*. Toronto: Penguin Books. (Revised and updated edition, 2002.)

Bosset, P. 2005. *Réflexion sur la Portée et les Limites de l'Accommodation Raisonnable en Matière Religieuse*. Montréal: Commission des Droits de la Personne et des Droits de la Jeunesse.

Boyd, M. 2004. *Dispute Resolution in Family Law: Protecting Choice, Promoting Inclusion*. Available at http://www.attorneygeneral.jus.gov.on.ca/english/about/pubs/boyd/

Bramadat, P. 2005. "Beyond Christian Canada: Religion and Ethnicity in a Multicultural Society." In *Religion and Ethnicity in Canada*, ed. P. Bramadat and D. Seljak. Toronto: Pearson Longman.

Bramadat, P. and D. Seljak, eds. 2005. *Religion and Ethnicity in Canada*. Toronto: Pearson Longman.

— 2008. *Christianity and Ethnicity in Canada*. Toronto: University of Toronto Press.

Breton, R., W.I. Wsevolod, E.K. Warren, and J. Reitz, eds. 1990. *Ethnic Identity City: Varieties of Experience in a Canadian City*. Toronto: University of Toronto Press.

Christiano, K.J. 2000. "Church and State in Institutional Flux: Canada and the United States." In *Rethinking Church, State, and Modernity – Canada between Europe and America*, ed. D. Lyon and M. Van Die. Toronto: University of Toronto Press.

Doytcheva, M. 2005. *Le Multiculturalisme*. Paris: La Découverte, Collection Repères.

Eid, P. 2007. *Being Arab: Ethnic and Religious Identity Building among Second-Generation Arab Youth in Montreal*. Montreal: McGill-Queen's University Press.

Eisenberg, A.I. 2006. "Introduction." In *Diversity and Equality: The Changing Framework of Freedom in Canada*, ed. A.I. Eisenberg. Vancouver: UBC Press.

Fraser, N. 2005. *Qu'est-ce que la Justice Sociale? Reconnaissance et Redistribution*. Paris: Éditions La Découverte.

Hervieu-Léger, D. 1999. *Le Pèlerin et le Converti. La Religion en Mouvement*. Paris: Flammarion.

Honneth, A. 2000. *La Lutte pour la Reconnaissance*. Paris: Le Cerf.

Kymlicka, W. 1995. *Multicultural Citizenship – A Liberal Theory of Minority Rights*. Oxford: Clarendon Press.

— 1998. *Finding Our Way. Rethinking Ethnocultural Relations in Canada*. Toronto: Oxford University Press.

Lemieux, R. and J.-P. Montminy. 2000. *Le Catholicisme Québécois*. Quebec: Institut national de la recherche scientifique.

Maclure, J. 2007. "Une Défense du Multiculturalisme Comme Morale Politique." In *La Justice à l'Épreuve de la Diversité Culturelle*, ed. M. Jézéquel. Montreal: Yvon Blais.

Martin, D. 2000. "Canada in Comparative Perspective." In *Rethinking Church, State, and Modernity – Canada between Europe and America*, ed. D. Lyon and M. Van Die. Toronto: University of Toronto Press.

McLaren, J. 2006. "Protecting Confessions of Faith and Securing Equality of Treatment for Religious Minorities in Education." In *Diversity and Equality: The Changing Framework of Freedom in Canada*, ed. A.I. Eisenberg. Vancouver: UBC Press.

Milot, M. 2002. *Laïcité dans le Nouveau Monde. Le Cas du Québec*. Coll. Bibliothèque de l'École des Hautes Études. Turnhout, Belgium: Brepols Publishers.

— 2005. "Les Principes de Laïcité Politique au Québec et au Canada." *Bulletin d'Histoire Politique* 13(3):13-27.

— 2006. "Recognition as a Core Value of the Multicultural Paradigm." *Canadian Diversity* 5(2):81-84.

— 2008. "Canadian Multiculturalism, Laicity and the Recognition of Religious Diversity." In *Different Meanings and Perspectives of Multiculturalism in a Global World*, ed. Barbara Pozzo. Athens and Brussels: Stampfli & Cie AG.

Norman, W. 2000. "Justice and Political Stability in the Multicultural State: Lessons from Theory and Practice in Canada." In *Mondialisation, Citoyenneté et Multiculturalisme*, ed. M. Elbaz and D. Helly. Paris: L'Harmattan et Sainte-Foy: Les Presses de l'Université Laval.

Robitaille, A. 2005. "La Charia en Ontario. Est-ce la Faute au Multiculturalisme?" *Le Devoir*, 10–11 September 2005.

Statistics Canada. 2001. *Religions in Canada, Census (Religion and Age Groups for Population)*. Cat. No. 95F0450XCB2001009, Statistics Canada.

Statistics Canada. 2002. *Ethnic Diversity Survey*. Survey No. 4508, Cat. No. 11-001-X1E, Statistics Canada.

Swatos, W., ed. 1999. *The Power of Religious Publics: Staking Claims in American Society*. Westport, CT: Praeger.

Taylor, C. 1992. *Multiculturalism and the Politics of Recognition*. Princeton, NJ: Princeton University Press.

— 2007. *A Secular Age*. Cambridge, MA: Belknap Press of Harvard University Press.

Tully, J. 2006. "Reconciling Struggles over the Recognition of Minorities: Towards a Dialogical Approach." In *Diversity and Equality: The Changing Framework of Freedom in Canada*, ed. A.I. Eisenberg. Vancouver: UBC Press.

Van Praagh, S. 2006. *Hijab et Kirpan: Une Histoire de Cape et d'Épée*. Québec: Presses de l'Université Laval.

Weber, M. 1965. *Essais sur la Théorie de la Science*. Paris: Plon.

Woehrling, J. 1998. "L'Obligation d'Accommodation Raisonnable et l'Adaptation de la Société à la Diversité Religieuse." *Revue de droit de McGill / McGill Law Journal* 43:325-401.

Chapter 6

In Transition: The Governance of Religious and Ethnic Diversity in Contemporary Australia

DESMOND CAHILL

The management and regulation of permanent or temporary migration and interethnic affairs is an issue for all nation states, not least Australia. The approach to these issues varies greatly across the globe, ranging from policies and ideologies based on aggressive assimilation, to overaccommodating multiculturalism, to determined segregationism. Regarding the governance of religious diversity, the spectrum ranges from an aggressive secularism as in officially atheist countries, to areligious or antireligious nation states, to aggressive majoritarian states where the religious majority dominates, if not persecutes, religious minorities, to nation states where natural interreligious rivalry is carried out in competitive harmony. Then there are the theocratic states where the religious law and practice of one faith has paramount influence.

With the mobility of peoples continuing to be on the rise, the management and regulation of religious diversity has global implications both because of the growing multireligious nature of many societies and because of the transnational networks that exist to support their far-flung faith communities and, in the worst case scenario, to cover for religiously inspired terrorists. If Osama bin Laden's pronouncements about Australia are to be believed, the nation's support for US president George Bush in the wake of 11 September 2001 and its role in East Timor have attracted the attention of terrorists to Australia. Almost half the people killed in the first Bali bombing in October 2002 were Australian, 89 in total, and some more were killed in the second Bali

International Migration and the Governance of Religious Diversity, eds. P. Bramadat and M. Koenig.
Montreal and Kingston: McGill-Queen's University Press, Queen's Policy Studies Series.
© 2009 The School of Policy Studies, Queen's University at Kingston. All rights reserved.

bombing. In April 2008, 13 Muslim men went on trial in Melbourne for alleged terrorist planning in association with alleged fellow conspirators in Sydney; apparently, attack plans had included the detonation of bombs at the 2005 football Grand Final when 100,000 spectators would have been present.

Thomas (2004) has argued that there is a recent resurgence of religion worldwide, as has Bouma (2006) in the Australian context. McGrath (2004) has even argued that atheism is in its twilight after a presumed two hundred year (1789–1989) regnum. How does government in the contemporary context deal with religious resurgence and, more problematically, with religiously inspired terrorism?

The Westphalian solution to religious intolerance and the War of Roses (1550–1650) in Europe led to the development of the modern state, the secularization of politics, and the privatization of religion. However, the rejection of the principle *cuius regio, eius religio* ensured that religious pluralism was taken seriously (Thomas 2004). In the past, the fundamental question about church and state has tended to be phrased simplistically: How should church and state be kept separate? But with the diminishment of Enlightenment secularism, together with the revitalization of religions and the growth of ethnic and religious diasporas in many more countries, the question is preferably rephrased: In a civil society, how should religious diversity be managed and regulated to ensure that majority and minority faith communities can coexist peacefully and contribute positively to national social capital? Or, more succinctly, when does good governance require intervention in religious affairs?

Australia is clearly a migration state with the settlement of immigrants and refugees and the formation of ethnic and religious diasporas at the core of its modern experience: according to the 2006 census, 22 percent of its population was born overseas. Immigrants and their Australian-born sons and daughters comprise an estimated 43 percent of the population. Hollifield (2004) suggests that out of the garrison states that characterized the nineteenth and twentieth centuries has evolved the migration state of the twentieth and twenty-first centuries with the developed nations reacting in different ways to the various types of global population flows involved in this transition. In his view, the migration state strives to fulfil three key functions: (a) to maintain security in the face of any military or other threat; (b) to build trade and investment regimes in the quest for prosperity; and (c) to regulate migration, which is a function both of market forces (demand-pull and supply-push) and kinship networks.

In this chapter, I examine the Australian context and the governance of ethnic and religious diversity through the prism of its historical evolution and the exigencies of the current context. With the sixth change of government since the Second World War, Australia has in 2007–08 reached a turning point in its history with regard both to its First Peoples, who represent 2–3 percent of the total population, and to its immigrant and refugee minorities. After a discussion of relevant Aboriginal issues, this chapter will examine the religion-state interrelationship prior to the Second World War, trace Australia's evolution into a multifaith society, and consider ways that such a diverse society is governed.

Australia in Transition

Late in 2007, on 24 November, Australians stepped up to the ballot box and decisively voted out the conservative government headed by John Howard. His government had ruled Australia for close to 12 years and had overseen continuous economic progress driven by Australia's role as a supplier of energy and minerals to China, India, and other Asian countries as well as by its commercial adaptation to the new, networked world.

A quiet vengeance was in the air as Australians looked for new ideas and a new vision for their nation, not just economic security. The erstwhile prime minister, a canny and cunning political operator, whose "honest John" image had gradually been destroyed as his political capital eroded, lost not only his government but also his own electoral seat— the first time this had happened in almost 80 years. Many, if not most, major political careers are said to end in disaster, and this was certainly true in Howard's case. He had had the opportunity to resign in glory the previous year but in an act of personal hubris, he had determined to fight on, convinced that only he could win the election for his beloved party. The end was utter humiliation.

In Australia, particularly since 11 September 2001, religion has returned to centre stage as it has across the world. Howard had been protective of the core Judaeo-Christian heritage of Australia together with the acceptable elements of the Enlightenment. Raised as a Methodist in a family of business people, Howard has in the last several decades practised Anglicanism in seeming deference to his spouse. Australia's history until the 1970s was characterized by tensions between British Protestantism and Irish Catholicism, and these tensions still resonate. Howard would, with subtle and not so subtle moves, particularly with strategic references to the issue of religious schools, reach out to the Anglo-Irish Catholic cohort, which still contains many swing voters.

Thus, it is appropriate to examine the management and governance of religious diversity in the context of migration up to and including the Howard regnum and to peer briefly into the possible future of

Howard's successor, Kevin Rudd. Rudd's Labor party is officially secularist but is historically rooted in Irish Catholicism and Wesleyan Methodism, among other factors. These origins might explain the significance in the party of concepts such as social justice and commitment to the poor and the disenfranchised. Rudd is able to quote papal encyclicals and his religious hero is Dietrich Bonhoeffer.

Raised in a Catholic family where his sister was, for a while, a religious novice, Rudd now attends his local Anglican church with his spouse, always a practicing Anglican. He has yet to explain publicly his denominational allegiance, although when a senior Canberra journalist asked him privately, he maintained that he is still Catholic but dislikes its views of women and homosexuals. Trained and having worked as a career diplomat, Rudd headed the Queensland public service where he gained a reputation as a strong leader during its reform. He is also fluent in Mandarin.

Rudd has not been slow to reflect on the role of his Christian faith in public life nor on the intersection of religion and state, though not in the context of a multifaith society. He believes that "Christianity, or at least certain Christian social norms, form an important part of our civilization" (Rudd 2006, 2), and that "the churches overall have been a significant force for good in shaping of the Australian nation during the two hundred years of European settlement" (2006, 3). He has also expressed concern about the implications of the decline of Christianity.

One factor in Howard's electoral demise was his attitude toward Australia's Aborigines and Torres Strait Islanders, who are practitioners of the world's longest continuous cultural system stemming back more than 50,000 years. The Howard government stopped the reconciliation process that had been gathering some steam through the 1990s with the landmark Mabo land rights decision in 1992, which had given indigenous peoples some access to crown land when there was a proven unbroken linkage to it by the Aboriginal clans.

The Colonization of Aboriginal Spiritualities

In 1992, Howard's predecessor, Paul Keating, in a historic and brave speech for which he paid a political price, outlined the wrongs committed against the indigenous minority over two centuries. Howard was unsympathetic to such claims, dismissing any such reformulation of Australian history as "the black armband view of history" beloved of the Left. He relied on historians such as Melbourne University's Geoffrey Blainey to laud the so-called Australian Achievement, which dismissed Aboriginal oppression as greatly exaggerated. The massacring, poisoning, and near destruction of Australia's First Peoples has thus been, in this long-held version of Australian history, perceived as but a minor blot on the heroic record of the British settlers. Howard also refused any suggestion that the government might express the sorrow of the nation for the terrible wrongs committed. These two versions of history, summed up in the argument as to whether Australia was invaded or settled, remain in competition.

The British colonization of Australia had a profound impact upon the Aboriginal peoples, who became refugees in their own land. In a classic case of destructive colonialism and cross-cultural miscommunication, the Aborigines and their various complex spiritualities were never recognized by the British or by the later Australian political and religious leadership, even though the Australian Aborigines practise the world's most ancient form of religiosity. Today, little has changed in this dismissive approach, although the platform for change has been largely built.

The British colonial mindset dismissed indigenous religious practices as pagan rituals based on superstitious beliefs. The British had a pragmatic reason for this attitude: they were in the process of stealing Aboriginal land for their own agricultural and pastoral purposes. Much about the Aboriginal spiritualities is secretive, focused on the land and the waters; their sacred sites such as Uluru (formerly Ayer's Rock, the largest rock formation in the world) are places of unusual geological significance where extra-human forces or powers were believed to be concentrated (Flood 2006; Hume 2002). Even today, such sites are often the object of derision by many mainstream Australians whose racism is the underbelly of the Australian body politic.

The Europeans brought their various versions of the Christian faith to Australia, but the Aborigines found them incredulous. Anthropologist Ted Strehlow recorded the appraisal of some western Aranda men living near Alice Springs in the heart of Australia:

> On another occasion the preachers came to them saying, "You, too, should learn (Scripture) like the children." The old men said, "But why should we learn? An abundance of different knowledge is ours—we already have our fill." "You are utter heathens," said the preachers to them, "you are utterly ignorant and can perceive nothing." The old men asked, "What are heathens?" The preacher replied to them, "You are heathens." "We are not heathens. We are Iliara men and not heathens—we are men who have been initiated at Inkura festivals." (cited in Hume 2002, 1)

The Aboriginal worldview is based around a triad/trinity of land, people, and spirituality (Flood 2006; Hume 2002) with an emphasis on the maintenance of the fertility of both people and nature and the continuation of traditional society (Flood 2006). The early anthropologists, in their rationalist empiricism, were ill-equipped to explore these worldviews and alternate forms of consciousness such as mental telepathy (Hume 2002).

Today, there is sympathy for Aborigines and their worldview among many members of Australian society, not least through the popularity of Aboriginal art, the building of Aboriginal cultural centres, and the growth of Aboriginal theology. However, the indigenous worldview is little recognized in public policy. For some time, there has been emerging an intersection of Aboriginal spirituality with Christian thinking—a delicate task, given the uneasy relationship between Australia's indigenous peoples and the churches. Historically, the churches provided both welfare and health services to the Aboriginal communities, and yet simultaneously undermined the Aboriginal spiritual mindset by seeking to "civilize" and "Christianize" them.

The Reconciliation Process

A prominent issue associated with the governance of religious diversity in Australia concerns the inexorable descent of the Aborigines into victimhood and social dereliction through alcoholism, petrol-sniffing, and drug use. The absence of state recognition of the harm inflicted by colonialism is partly to blame. There was no such counterpart to the 1840 Treaty of Waitangi with the Maoris in New Zealand. Nor has there been formal recognition of the many massacre sites—these "places of sickness," to use an Aboriginal phrase, that dot Australia's vast landscape. Only one such site is marked with a memorial, in contrast to the many shrines to the fallen of the wars in which Australians have fought. During the mid-1990s, reconciliation was placed on the national agenda. But the opposition of Prime Minister Howard put the issue on the national backburner for another decade or more.

In the very first parliamentary action of the new government, the incoming Rudd Labor administration made a formal apology in February 2008 to the Stolen Generation. These were the mixed-race Aborigines who, as babies and children, had been taken from their mothers throughout the twentieth century until the 1970s and placed in foster homes or orphanages so as to make them "white." In attendance in Parliament House for the occasion was every living former prime minister except John Howard. In reflecting on the "past mistreatment" of Aborigines, Prime Minister Rudd enunciated the feeling of the nation:

> We reflect in particular on the mistreatment of those who were Stolen Generations—this blemished chapter in our nation's history. The time has now come for the nation to turn a new page in Australia's history by

righting the wrongs of the past and so moving forward with confidence to the future.

We apologize for the laws and policies of successive Parliaments and governments that have inflicted profound grief, suffering and loss on these our fellow Australians. We apologize especially for the removal of Aboriginal and Torres Strait Islander children from their families, their communities, and their country.

For the pain, suffering and hurt of these Stolen Generations, their descendants and for their families left behind, we say sorry.

To the mothers and fathers, the brothers and sisters, for the breaking up of families and communities, we say sorry.

And for the indignity and degradation thus inflicted on a proud people and a proud culture, we say sorry.

The next decade will show whether this symbolic gesture is but the first step in righting the injustices of the past through workable and relevant programs.

Religion and State in the Pre–World War II Context

It is instructive to study the period of Australian history from the beginning of British settlement in 1788 until the Second World War. This was a period of contested religious majoritarianism, with British Protestants clearly dominating the mainly Irish Catholic working-class minority.

The Conflictual Competitiveness of British Protestantism Versus Irish Catholicism

Discussions about post-1788 religion in Australia have revolved around such themes as the transplanting of Christianity from the source countries and the initial difficulties in establishing each faith community in Australia, the positioning of the relationship between religion and state, the establishment of organizational structures, the continuance of transnational links with the religious source centres overseas, the integration of subsequent migration waves, and interreligious tensions (Cahill et al. 2004).

European Australia began as a prison colony for prisoners from the United Kingdom and Ireland. Most prisons contained a chapel where it was hoped conversion from criminal behaviour would take place. It was assumed that religion and civil order operated in unison and that religion had the capacity to rid the early convicts of their criminal inclinations and raise them to "respectability." Often convicts did change their ways, though what part Christianity played in this process is still debated.

The Anglican Church endeavoured to gain status as the established church and, while it did have some official status, the Australian situation was too different from that of the British homeland for such an attempt to be successful. The early Anglican chaplains were evangelical and more supportive of democratic processes than their High Church colleagues in the United Kingdom. They had a strong sense of mission and an inner determination to succeed. During the 1820s, as more nonconformist clergy came to Australia, the belief that all faith communities should be treated equally became widespread. The *Church Act* of 1832 made financial aid available to the Anglicans, Roman Catholics, Presbyterians and, later on, to the Methodists and Baptists (Cahill et al. 2004). These funds assisted in the payment of clergy stipends and in the building of churches. Thus were laid the foundations of Christian religious pluralism in Australia.

Though the Catholics were free to practice their faith, they were to be marginalized for many decades. Many of the convicts in Australia's prisons were Irish, and the British settlers feared that Catholic priests might foment discontent and rebellion. Catholic priests were not formally allowed into the colony of New South Wales until 1820, and the Catholic leadership, as it evolved, was determined that Australia would not become a replica of England or of Ireland.

The government financed numerous small denominational schools. However, in the early 1870s, as a result of the strong pressure from secularist governments, aid to private schools ceased. This defunding would be the crux of the stand-off between the British Protestants and the Irish Catholics for the next hundred years. Accordingly, the church-state relationship throughout the nineteenth century was one of guarded cooperation, but it laid the foundations for the state's role of neutrality.

Globalization and Migration in the Post–World War II Context

In 1945, as part of post–World War II recovery, the Australian Labor government made the critical decision to embark on a massive immigration program. At its conception, Australia's overall policy aim was to grow the Australian population in a very substantial way. One of the objectives was that Australia should remain white, monocultural, and European (Price and Martin 1975).

But there were other objectives. Both during and immediately after the war, the catchcry "populate or perish"—motivated by fear of the Japanese—had encapsulated the thinking of many Australians. Such fear had prevailed since the Japanese naval defeat of Russia in 1908, but had escalated during the Second World War when Australia had been saved from Japanese invasion only by US intervention in the Battle of the Coral Sea. Anxieties over the "yellow peril" can be traced back even further, to the various gold rushes beginning in the 1850s when thousands of Chinese men entered Australia in search of their own fortune. In the aftermath of the war, Australian policy-makers, aware of the thinking that an underpopulated Australian continent might well be filled by "hordes of the vast Asian masses," countered with the introduction of a huge migration program to populate the empty spaces (Price and Martin 1975). This goal was never realized, but vestiges of the program remain in the small, rural immigrant communities; the newly arrived were placed in rural zones where their agricultural skills might be utilized.

As another strategy in increasing national wealth and prosperity, immigrants were brought in to work in the nation's new factories. Immediately following the war, the Australian government had found to its astonishment that more Australian workers were leaving than entering the workforce—a trend that would undermine the vast industrialization process the government had in mind. The birth rate had dropped during the Depression and the number of young people, especially men, entering the workforce had been negatively affected by the number of war deaths and casualties.

Immigration was designed to be 90 percent British in order to retain a monocultural Anglo-Australia, and it is true that politicians maintained this kind of fiction until the late 1960s. The arrival of continental Europeans, beginning with the displaced refugees of World War II who were unable or unwilling to return to their Communist-dominated countries of central and eastern Europe, had begun the process in 1947 that metamorphosed Australia into a genuine multicultural society by the mid-1960s, more than a decade before the term was coined in Canada. As soon as the United Kingdom was well on the way to post-war recovery, Australia became less attractive to British migrants, though they still remain the largest immigrant group in the annual intake.

In the late 1960s, immigrants began arriving from Latin America and the Middle East. In 1968, Australia made a choice to recruit immigrants from Turkey in preference to Mexico because it was felt the Mexicans would be more attracted to the United States than to Australia (Keceli 1998). Some Turkish Cypriots had arrived in the early 1950s, but the first large Muslim wave began after 1968. However, it may have been inevitable that one day Australia would be required to confront its Asian location. The White Australian policy had begun to break down in the mid-1950s with the abrogation of the law forbidding the naturalization of Asians married to Australian citizens (Tavan 2005). In the spirit of the principle of gradualism that has characterized immigrant and community relations policy, all vestiges of the racist policy were not abrogated until January 1973. But already some Anglo-Indians, whose power base and status had been destroyed in 1948 with the departure of the British raj, had arrived by the mid-1960s. The 1970s saw the arrival of the comparatively small numbers of East Timorese refugees who were to be badly treated by successive Australian governments who maintained they were the responsibility of Portugal.

But it was the Vietnamese—beginning with the baby orphans arriving just before the fall of Saigon on 30 April 1975—who really began the transformation of Australia from a European to a Eurasian nation. It has been the historic role of the Vietnamese, together with the Chinese who would begin arriving more than a decade later, to prevent Australia from becoming the little Europe of the South just as a century earlier the Irish had begun the process of stopping Australia from becoming the little Britain of the South (O'Farrell 1987). This process continued after the Second World War with immigrants and refugees arriving from central and eastern Europe, as well as from Italy and Greece. At all stages of the historical process, Australian immigration and refugee policies have had to confront the changes in the external environment.

Australia's Changing Ethnic and Religious Profile

Australia continues to evolve as a culturally and linguistically diverse country, and we are seeing, more so than ever, the emergence of a multifaith country, especially over the last decade. The ethnic, linguistic, and religious data from the 2006 census bring home the impact of recent population flows on Australian society. Comparing this data with the information from 1996 allows us to see more clearly the longer-term trends (see Table 1). According to the 2006 census figures, the top 12 birthplace countries are the United Kingdom (representing 23.50 percent of the total overseas-born), followed by New Zealand (8.82 percent), China (including Hong Kong, 6.30 percent), Italy (4.51 percent), Vietnam (3.62 percent), India (3.33 percent), the Philippines (2.73 percent), Greece (2.49 percent), Germany (2.41 percent), South Africa (2.36 percent), Malaysia (2.09 percent), and the Netherlands (1.79 percent).

An examination of Australia's birthplace profile over the past decade, as shown in Table 1, highlights several key points:

Table 1: Birthplace Profile of Australia: 1996 and 2006

1996 Census			2006 Census			
Country of Birth	Number	% of OSB	Country of Birth	Number	% of OSB	1996–2006 % difference
U.K.	1,072,514	27.44	U.K.	1,038,156	23.51	−3.21
New Zealand	291,388	7.46	New Zealand	389,464	8.82	+33.68
Italy	238,388	6.10	China (inc. Hong Kong)	278,383	6.30	+64.30
China (inc. Hong Kong)	169,439	4.34	Italy	199,132	4.51	−16.47
Vietnam	151,053	3.87	Vietnam	159,854	3.62	+5.83
Greece	126,520	3.24	India	147,101	3.33	+89.76
Germany	110,331	2.82	Philippines	120,533	2.73	+29.68
Philippines	92,949	2.38	Greece	109,988	2.49	−13.07
Netherlands	87,898	2.25	Germany	106,515	2.41	−3.46
India	77,521	1.98	South Africa	104,120	2.36	+86.75
Malaysia	76,255	1.95	Malaysia	92,347	2.09	+21.10
Lebanon	70,224	1.80	Netherlands	78,931	1.79	−10.20
Poland	65,113	1.67	Lebanon	74,858	1.70	+6.60
South Africa	55,755	1.43	Sri Lanka	62,252	1.41	+32.50
Ireland	51,469	1.32	USA	61,715	1.40	+24.61
Malta	50,879	1.30	Korea (South)	52,763	1.19	+75.34
USA	49,528	1.27	Poland	52,256	1.18	−19.75
Sri Lanka	46,984	1.20	Croatia	50,991	1.15	+8.54
Croatia	46,981	1.20	Indonesia	50,974	1.15	+15.39
Indonesia	44,175	1.13	Ireland	50,259	1.14	−2.35

Note: OSB = Overseas-born persons

Source: Author's compilation from census data. Australian Bureau of Statistics (1996, 2006).

- Australia is becoming more diversified culturally, linguistically, and religiously with the entry of immigrant and refugee groups from Africa and, more particularly, from Asia and the Middle East.
- The proportion of those born in the United Kingdom continues to decline slowly, but this trend is offset by the migration of those from New Zealand (+33.68 percent) and the United States (+24.61 percent), and especially by the arrival of South Africans (+86.75 percent).
- The number of immigrants to Australia born in Italy (−16.47 percent), Greece (−13.07 percent), the Netherlands (−10.20 percent), and Poland (−19.75 percent) has declined since 1996.

- The communities whose members come from those countries where English is an associate language (i.e., countries colonized by English-speaking colonial powers) have grown significantly in recent decades. For example, the numbers of newcomers from India (+89.75 percent), the Philippines (+29.68 percent), Malaysia (+21.10 percent), and Sri Lanka (+32.50 percent) have all increased dramatically.
- China has now become the most numerous non-English-speaking source country, after 50 years of dominance by the Italy-born group.
- The China-born growth is complemented by the growth from Asia generally, including from Vietnam (+5.83 percent), but especially from the Republic of Korea (+75.34 percent) and the Middle East. By the next census, Vietnam and India will have surpassed Italy as major source countries.

The birthplace trends are complemented by the 2006 language profile of Australia, which is also showing greater diversification. As presented in Table 2, the clear trends are as follows:

- The use of Arabic (+7.74 percent) has increased notably.
- As in 2001, the number of those speaking and writing the Chinese languages (+45.83 percent), especially Cantonese and Mandarin, when aggregated, has surpassed the number speaking Italian, which for 50 years was Australia's most widely spoken language after English.
- Of the 20 major languages, the biggest growth has occurred with Hindi (+106.02 percent), reflecting the number of Indian immigrants in the last five years, together with Persian (+95.21 percent) and Korean (+82.50 percent).
- The continental European languages continue their decline, using 1996 as a baseline, with the exception of Spanish (+7.38 percent) and Serbian (+41.21 percent).
- There has been strong growth in the languages spoken by Aborigines and Torres Strait Islanders (+26.04 percent) because of their high birth rate.

Australia has become one of the great language laboratories of the world. Its linguistic profile over the past two decades has become more interesting. The figures shown in Table 2 highlight the transformation of Australia underway since 1947 from a British to an Anglo-Celtic to a European to a Eurasian country. The nation is walking down this Eurasian path that is its probable future—it was inevitable that Australia would one day have to confront its Asian destiny. Australia's task now is to merge its Judaeo-Christian heritage with Confucian humanism and a globalized ethic.

Table 2: Language Profile of Australia: 1996 and 2006

1996 Census			2006 Census			
Language	Number	% of LOTES	Language	Number	% of LOTES	1996–2006 % difference
Italian	375,718	11.79	Chinese	500,466	15.91	+45.83
Chinese	343,193	10.76	Italian	316,893	10.07	−15.66
Greek	269,770	8.46	Greek	252,222	8.02	−6.50
Arabic	177,598	5.57	Arabic	243,662	7.74	+37.20
Vietnamese	146,264	4.59	Vietnamese	194,858	6.19	+33.22
German	98,814	3.10	Spanish	97,998	3.11	+7.38
Spanish	91,265	2.86	Tagalog	92,330	2.93	+31.07
Macedonian	71,352	2.24	German	75,634	2.40	−23.46
Tagalog	70,441	2.21	Hindi	70,013	2.23	+106.02
Croatian	69,173	2.17	Macedonian	67,831	2.16	−4.93
Polish	62,798	1.97	Croatian	63,615	2.02	−8.03
Turkish	46,204	1.45	ATSI	55,698	1.77	+26.04
Maltese	45,223	1.42	Korean	54,619	1.74	+82.50
ATSI	44,192	1.39	Turkish	53,858	1.71	+16.57
Dutch	40,782	1.28	Polish	53,390	1.70	−14.98
French	39,940	1.25	Serbian	52,534	1.67	+41.21
Serbian	37,204	1.17	French	43,219	1.37	+8.21
Hindi	33,983	1.07	Indonesian	42,038	1.34	+54.58
Russian	30,999	0.97	Persian	37,155	1.18	+95.21
Korean	29,929	0.94	Maltese	36,517	1.16	−19.25

Notes: Language spoken at home by those aged over five years. LOTE = total number of speakers of languages other than English. ATSI = Aboriginal and Torres Strait Islander languages.

Source: Author's compilation from census data. Australian Bureau of Statistics (1996, 2006).

Australia as a Multifaith Country

The Australian government has statistics regarding religious affiliation dating back to 1851. From the 1860s to 1947, Australia's religious profile remained relatively stable. The Anglicans, Presbyterians, and Methodists, together comprising just over 60 percent of the population, dominated this period of Australian religious life. In 1947, Roman Catholics comprised one-fifth (20.7 percent) of the population at 1.57 million, compared with 2.96 million Anglicans and 1.68 million belonging to the Methodist, Presbyterian, Congregational, and Reformed Churches. Buddhists, Muslims, Hindus, and Sikhs were so small in number that they did not rate on the demographic map. Since 1947, Australia's religious profile has changed profoundly in four ways:

- the decline in mainstream Protestantism and the rise of a secularized Australia;
- the impact of migration intakes on mainstream Christianity;
- the rise of evangelical and charismatic Christianity and New Age movements; and
- the rise of a multifaith Australia.

At the same time, we need to examine two major issues in the context of the management and governance of ethnic and religious diversity: (a) the repositioning of the relationship between religion and state; and (b) the dilemmas of multiculturalism and the aftermath of September 11th.

Let us examine these trends in some detail.

The Decline in Mainstream Protestantism and the Rise of a Secularized Australia

Mainstream Protestantism has been in decline for more than four decades after peaking in the early 1960s and is now almost in freefall, especially the Uniting Church of Australia (–14.94 percent over the past ten years), Presbyterianism (–11.30 percent) and the Church of Christ (–23.12 percent; see Table 3). This is part of a global shift away from a rational and global form of Christianity to a more experiential and feeling-oriented form (Bouma 2003). As Thompson (2002, 137-38) observes,

> Australia was transformed into a post-Christian society. Protestant churches lost their previous political power and in many cases the will which had imposed the quiet Sunday on cities such as Melbourne and Adelaide into the 1960s; which also until that decade banned pictures of naked bodies on film screens and kept hotels closed after 6 o'clock and on Sundays. . . . Religion was no longer part of the political rhetoric as in the Menzies [prime minister 1949–1966] era. Politicians, particularly of the New Right, were appealing to the cult of selfishness. The collapse of the religious moral order was observable in rising crime rates and declining standards of business and public probity.

Those who have drifted away tend to tick the "no religion" box; indeed, the 2006 census indicated that 18.7 percent of Australians—many of them fairly young—chose this description (an increase of 3 percent in five years). A recent study (Mason, Singleton, and Webber 2006) has detailed the religious beliefs of Generation Y, born between 1976 and 1990, from all different family backgrounds. Half claim not to have any

Table 3: Religious Profile of Australia: 1996 and 2006

1996 Census			2006 Census			
Religion	Number	%	Religion	Number	%	1996–2006 % difference
Catholic	4,797,365	26.92	Catholic	5,126,252	25.81	+6.86
Anglican	3,903,323	21.99	Anglican	3,718,252	18.72	−4.74
No religion	2,927,134	16.49	No religion	3,706,555	18.67	+26.63
Not stated	1,550,980	8.73	Not stated	2,223,957	11.18	+43.39
Uniting Church	1,334,915	7.52	Uniting Church	1,135,427	5.72	−14.94
Presbyterian and Reformed	672,660	3.79	Presbyterian and Reformed	596,671	3.01	−11.30
Eastern Orthodox	492,304	2.78	Eastern Orthodox	544,160	2.74	+10.53
Baptist	295,176	1.66	Buddhism	418,756	2.11	+109.56
Lutheran	249,996	1.41	Islam	340,392	1.71	+69.45
Islam	200,886	1.13	Baptist	316,738	1.60	+7.30
Buddhism	199,830	1.13	Christian	313,190	1.57	+72.18
Christian	181,897	1.02	Lutheran	251,107	1.26	+0.44
Pentecostal	164,048	0.92	Pentecostal	219,689	1.11	+33.92
Jehovah's Witnesses	83,411	0.47	Hinduism	148,119	0.75	+120.39
Judaism	79,800	0.45	Judaism	88,831	0.45	+11.31
Salvation Army	74,136	0.42	Jehovah's Witnesses	80,919	0.41	−2.99
Churches of Christ	71,308	0.40	Salvation Army	64,200	0.32	−13.40
Hinduism	67,209	0.38	Other Protestant	56,106	0.28	+221.73
Seventh Day Adventist	52,618	0.30	Seventh Day Adventist	55,251	0.28	+5.00
Church of Latter Day Saints	42,168	0.24	Churches of Christ	54,822	0.28	−23.12

Source: Author's compilation from census data. Australian Bureau of Statistics (1996, 2006).

religious affiliation. However, almost a third (29 percent) have a vague belief in reincarnation while about a quarter believe in astrology and séances, though these beliefs are also strong among their parents. The authors comment, "Belief in reincarnation is more like a folk belief that circulates widely in the culture . . . than a seriously understood article of faith connected to its original Eastern religious heritage" (Mason, Singleton, and Webber 2006, 18; also Hughes 2007).

Australia has become more secularized and, in that sense, can be described as a post-Christian society. But this is only part of the present story. Australia has paradoxically become more religious—yet religious in a different way—with the rise of multifaith Australia.

The Impact of Migration Intakes on Mainstream Christianity

Post-war immigration has influenced mainstream Christianity in unexpected ways, not all of them negative. While mainstream Protestantism is in decline, the churches have nonetheless been strengthened by the arrival of newcomers from diverse backgrounds. But it is Catholicism, much more so than Protestantism, that has benefited from immigration. Catholicism is now the nation's largest faith community and will remain so for some considerable time. Its growth was led by the Italians who arrived as the despised "dagoes" in the 1950s but who have since become mostly successful in many areas of Australian life; they have also remained remarkably loyal to their faith tradition, even if many can be described only as "cultural Catholics" (Cahill 2007). Women from non-English-speaking backgrounds, especially Italian, are Catholicism's best Mass attendees (Noseda 2006; Paganoni 2007).

Since the Second World War, refugees have been very much part of Australian Catholicism, fleeing from Nazism, totalitarian Communism and, recently, Islamic fundamentalism. They came from central, eastern, and southeastern Europe immediately after the war, then from Hungary in 1956 and from Czechoslovakia in 1968. In the early 1970s, it was the Chileans and later other South and Central American groups; in the mid-1970s, it was the East Timorese quickly followed by the Lebanese and the Vietnamese, all affected by the political upheavals in their countries of origin. More recently, those fleeing the Horn of Africa, the Sudan, and other parts of Africa as well as another wave of refugees from the Balkans have found refuge in Australia. Catholicism has also been affected by immigrants belonging to its Eastern Churches, including the Maronite Church, the Ukrainian Church, and the Melkite Church, all with their own bishops, as well as priests and laity from other churches such as the Chaldean (mainly from Iraq), the Coptic (mainly from Egypt), and the Syro-Malabar (mainly from southern India).

Hence, the overall profile of the Catholic Church in Australia has been one of increasing diversification, not only among its members but also among priests and religious. An important fact here in the context of the severe priest shortage is that there are now about 150 Vietnamese priests and other religious working in the Australian Catholic Church. This same trend is apparent in the other main Protestant churches. For example, the Uniting Church in 2002 had 117 ethno-specific congregations, led by the Korean, Tongan, Fijian, Indonesian, Samoan, Tamil,

Hindi, Cook Islander, Chinese, and Sudanese communities. Thus, the mainstream churches, both Catholic and Protestant, have interesting futures that could not have been foretold by their Anglo-Celtic heritages.

In addition, we have witnessed growth in the Orthodox churches, led by the Greeks, Macedonians, Serbians, and Russians. These congregations have each remained very attached to their ethnicity. The Greek Orthodox Church has been greatly helped in the transmission of its faith and culture by the change in government policy toward private schools; public funding now supports seven full-time Greek Orthodox schools across Australia. Previously, the Greek Orthodox Church had relied on many part-time after-hours "ethnic schools," which have been assisted by a small government grant since the early 1980s, to teach mostly the Greek dhimotiki language together with some religious instruction.

The Rise of Evangelical and Charismatic Christianity and
New Age Movements

Over the past decade, the evangelical, Pentecostal, and charismatic churches (+33.92 percent since 1996) as well as those groups belonging to the "other Christian" category (+72.18 percent) have grown significantly. This growth has been part of the religious revitalization in Australia. Another expression of this has been the rise in various forms of privatized eco-spiritualities and the importation of various Earth-based religious groups such as Gaia, Goddess religions, and Witchcraft. These latter groups are small, but the religion section of mainstream bookstores attests to their power to attract.

The Rise of a Multifaith Australia

The 2006 census shows that one person in 18 practises a religion other than Christianity (Table 3). Some comments on this data are appropriate at this point:

- In 2006, Christians comprised about 65 percent of the Australian population, led by the Catholic cohort, which represents just over one-quarter of the overall population. The number of Catholics continues to grow, but in proportional terms the number has dropped. This trend also applies to Orthodox Christians.
- The mainstream Protestant groups continue to decline numerically while evangelical and charismatic groups have grown rapidly over the previous ten years.
- Those affiliated with religious Judaism have increased recently in actual numbers.

- Buddhism is the largest of the non-Christian religious groups, with their numbers doubling in ten years. Among Buddhists, the Australian-born is the largest group followed by the Vietnam-born and the China-born.
- Hinduism has grown even more than Buddhism, especially since 2001, and this is also true of Sikhism.
- Over the ten-year period, Islam has grown by 69.45 percent, with the largest group being Australian-born followed by those born in Lebanon and Turkey.

The Repositioning of the Relationship between Religion and State

From the early 1870s to the early 1970s, a rigid separation of religion and state prevailed. This period can be rightly called the secularist era of Australian history, with the Catholics agitating strongly for the funding of their schools. In the end, the government decided that it was less costly to support private schools than to allow the large Catholic school system to crash. Another likely reason for the decision in favour of government funding was that more and more Catholics, by now the largest religious community in Australia, were upwardly mobile and their votes were needed by the liberal conservative party in their three periods of government (1949–1972; 1975–1983; 1996–2007).

The secularist legacy, however, would last beyond the Second World War. Government policy toward religious communities was largely that of neutrality, though relations between political and religious leaders were generally positive. But this neutrality supported a privatized faith: senior religious leaders were regularly told to keep their noses out of politics and out of the nation's bedrooms, especially when their dictums conflicted with a particular party's policy. There was some cooperation; for example, clerics acted as both religious and state celebrants during marriage ceremonies. Further, the state funded religiously sponsored hospitals and aged-care facilities, as well as religious welfare organizations that fed and housed the homeless and looked after people with disabilities.

The legacy of the strict separation was not sustainable in the context of globalization, the decline of the welfare state, and the rise of religious extremism. Accordingly, in Australia, we have seen a repositioning of the relationship between religion and state over the past 40 years. Central to this shift was the government decision in the 1960s to fund private religious schools. Since 1973, the poorer private, mainly Catholic, schools have received almost total funding according to a formula weighted in favour of schools in economically poor areas with a high density of migrants.

This repositioning of the state with regard to religion has been expressed in many other ways:

- the funding of part-time ethnoreligious schools to teach the language of immigrant and refugee communities. If these schools are sponsored by a faith community, religion will usually be taught as well;
- the funding by the commonwealth government of confessional universities such as the Australian Catholic University;
- the appointment of celebrated religious leaders as a governors general and as state governors;
- the funding of welfare officers for some of the more recently arrived groups such as Muslims;
- the inclusion of religious discrimination within the ambit of racial discrimination and human rights legislation;
- the listing of historic places of worship on the national register, and the allocation of funds for their restoration;
- the utilization of religious leaders for civic occasions such as national celebrations and times of national and international tragedy;
- the successful tendering by religious groups for the delivery of unemployment, health, and welfare services as part of the privatization of government services and the winding back of the welfare state;
- the appointment of many more chaplains to government and private schools;
- the financial support by state and federal governments for interfaith events such as those to take place at the Parliament of the World's Religions in December 2009 in Melbourne; and
- the funding of interfaith projects, including the establishment of the Islamic Institute, through the commonwealth government's Living-in-Harmony program.

As this list makes clear, the government and religion are heavily interlocked. This repositioning has unfolded gradually over the past four decades to the murmurings of the secularist left, although no organized backlash has emerged. This is not to say that it might not emerge. But any serious attempt to lower significantly the funding of private religious schools would be an act of political harakiri as occurred in the 2004 election when an unlamented and failed Labor leader of the opposition attempted to tamper with the funding policy for elite private schools. The political rejoinder of a Howard victory was swift. Howard deliberately followed a policy of encouraging the movement of students from government to private schools, a policy now likely to be modified.

It is sometimes argued that Howard's motivation was economic insofar as it is cheaper on a per capita basis to fund a student in a private school (with the per capita funding topped up by school fees) than in a government school. But the policy was probably driven by other factors as well, not least that for more than two decades, the liberal and conservative forces have been opposed to government schools because of their perceived failure in achieving high standards of education. Also, Howard was probably motivated by a concern to bolster the forces of the Judaeo-Christian ethic around which he believes the Australian nation pivots (Madox 2005).

Ultimately, this gradual repositioning of the religion-state relationship reflects the recognition of the importance of religion in the creation of social capital. Hence, despite what the secularists might argue, the future of private religious schools is strong although their public justification might have to be based on very different arguments in the future.

The Principles of Gradualism and Accommodationism

By most indices, Australia's migration and settlement policies have been successful. Australian policy and its implementation have been underpinned by the twin principles of gradualism and accommodation. If migration policy has been gradualist in the introduction of more culturally and racially different groups from Asia and Africa, it has also been self-centred. For example, Australia did not take refugees from Idi Amin's Uganda because it was felt that these refugees might affect the fragile social consensus that supported the program at the time. In tandem with gradualism has been the accommodation mechanism associated with changes in programs or laws to accommodate a particular custom. For example, cemetery regulations have been changed to accommodate Islamic burial practices, and criminal justice laws have been adjusted to accommodate the wearing of turbans rather than helmets and the carrying of the ritual kirpan or Sikh dagger in contravention of the laws on offensive weapons.

In 1998, the Human Rights and Equal Opportunity Commission published its assessment of Article 18 of the Constitution, on Freedom of Belief. Among the issues of religious expression investigated were indigenous heritage protection, marriage laws, polygamy, burials, autopsies, medical interventions, female genital mutilation, paganism, new religious movements, religious discrimination, and incitement to religious hatred. The commission recommended a Religious Freedom Act to combat religious vilification and job discrimination. The government refused to legislate because opposition came from the mainstream churches who wanted complete control over whom they employed in their agencies, especially in schools, so as to preserve the particular religious ethos. Several high profile cases have allowed religious schools to dismiss personnel whose moral lifestyles did not conform to the religion's values and practices.

The commission also recommended a strengthening of indigenous cultural heritage laws and proposed that more work be done in the area of autopsies, indigenous burials, medical interventions that touch the Jehovah's Witnesses' prohibition against blood transfusions, the introduction in recalcitrant states of laws against female genital mutilation, and the repeal of laws concerning witchcraft, fortune-telling, sorcery, and enchantment. It also suggested that the matter of religious coercion needed further investigation.

Little has been achieved since 1998 as the relationship between the Human Rights and Equal Opportunity Commission and the Howard government was not always happy. The commission has just begun another enquiry into Article 18 that will report in 2010.

The Emergence of Multiculturalism

During the assimilationist period (late 1940s to the mid-1960s) and the following transitional melting-pot period (late 1960s to late 1970s), the management of ethnic and religious diversity was framed in the Anglo-conformity model in which ethnic distinctiveness was not encouraged. However, this policy parameter was not applied to religious diversity for two reasons. First, freedom of religious belief and practice is manifestly enshrined in Article 18 of the Constitution, and so immigrant and refugee groups could construct their own churches and synagogues. Second, religion was seen as a private matter, and religious leaders were supposed to be politically inactive. The latter, of course, was never true, most spectacularly with the Catholic involvement in the splitting of the Labor Party over the issue of Communist infiltration in the mid-1950s, during the Cold War. Nonetheless, church leaders followed the more moderate conventions of the church-state divide, as Australia had not developed the antireligious or areligious *laïcité* policy of France or the structural divide one finds in the United States.

The religion-state repositioning begun in the 1970s coincided with the emergence of a multicultural social policy. But it would not be until the new millennium and 9/11 that the multicultural and interfaith lobbies would begin cooperating in earnest. Throughout the 1980s and up to the present, the disputed assumption that religion is part of culture was not in fact accepted by many ethnic community leaders or by their umbrella bodies. Nor was the freedom of religion part of the rhetoric of official government statements except for fleeting but important references. Within the Italian and the Greek communities, the notion that religion was a core part of culture was resisted despite the protestations of ethnic church leaders. Among the Greeks, the church's claim that religion and ethnicity are indisputably linked was not accepted by the secularists. Italian leaders were less strident even though some were imbued with a healthy dose of anti-clericalism, because the Italians saw themselves as part of the broader Roman Catholic Church (Paganoni 2007).

During the height of the multicultural period of the 1980s and 1990s, the expression of the management of ethnic and religious diversity was evident within mainstream churches. For example, within the Catholic Church, more than 150 migrant chaplains played a critical role in defusing the ancient and less ancient hatreds between Australian Croats and Serbs. Another stratagem was also important: since the late 1970s, politicians and senior bureaucrats have been assiduous in attending ethnic and ethnoreligious functions. In more recent times (since 9/11) in some states, the police have begun this practice as part of a community policing policy.

Three other strategies in the management of ethnic and religious diversity were also critical. First, the government provided funding so that ethnic and religious welfare organizations could hire their own workers. Second, the government funded an ethnic radio station, known as SBS Radio (Special Broadcasting Service), and is now partially funding SBS Television. SBS Radio describes itself as "the many voices of one Australia" and broadcasts each week in 68 languages. Third, the government has supported ethnic and ethnoreligious full-time schools. While there are no Baha'i, Buddhist, Hindu, or Sikh schools, the Armenian Orthodox, Coptic Orthodox, Greek Orthodox, Lutheran, and Maronite schools all receive government funding. As well, there are now 30 Muslim schools supported by government funds, and these schools have played a key role in the integration of Muslims into Australia. The provision of this financial support has been an antidote to the racism and Islamophobia they have experienced.

The Aftermath of 9/11 and the Muslim Crisis

It has become common in international political discourse to assume that discussions about the governance of religious diversity are in fact discussions about Islam. Of course, this is not the case. Other religions (especially Christianity, Hinduism, Judaism, and Sikhism) have also been the subjects of heated debates over the past four decades. Nonetheless, since Islam is presently the focal point for most international debates (and national ones as well) about the governance of religious diversity, it is important to note that, in the aftermath of 9/11, there have been five positive outcomes in Australia. Firstly, Muslim communities have come out of their cocoons to interact much more with mainstream Australia, opening their mosques and schools to the general public and initiating and participating in various interactive programs. Ultimately, the task of Islamic leaders, as of all religious leaders, has been to support religious moderation in a struggle that goes to the very heart of global Islam.

The second outcome since 9/11 is that we have seen multicultural and interfaith movements in Australia acting in support of each other. The main expression of this cooperation has been the formation in 2003 of the Australian Partnership for Religious Organizations (APRO) as the primary national interfaith body. Thirdly, as one part of the repositioning of the relationship between religion and state, the Australian and state governments have become involved—in fact, have had to become involved—in the interfaith agenda, especially through the Living-in-Harmony program of the Department of Immigration and Citizenship. The support of the program for APRO has been significant and one can hope that APRO will evolve into an Australian Multifaith Council with a well-funded secretariat. The fourth outcome from 9/11 has been the emergence of local multifaith networks across Australia, particularly in Melbourne. These networks are supported by the Australian chapter of the World Conference of Religions for Peace, the interfaith community body with the biggest coverage across Australia.

As the last outcome, Australia's links with the two major and complementary international interfaith organizations, namely, Religions for Peace International (formerly World Conference of Religions and Peace) and the Parliament of the World's Religions, have been immeasurably strengthened since 9/11. Religions for Peace International, which is headquartered in the UN Plaza in New York, includes its partner organization, the Asian Conference of Religions for Peace, headquartered in Seoul, Korea. These links have culminated in Melbourne being chosen over Delhi and Singapore as the city to stage the Parliament of the World's Religions in December 2009—the most important (though not the biggest) religious and interreligious event ever held in Australia. This event is already heavily supported by commonwealth and state governments.

Through its many activities, almost all at the grassroots level, the interfaith movement is gaining legitimacy in many parts of Australia, especially where there are Islamic community concentrations. Interfaith activity has mushroomed, especially in the larger cities. And the commonwealth and state governments have been very supportive, if not with as many resources as organizations would prefer. Yet, it has to be accepted that presently in Australia, the interfaith movement is organizationally weak though on the ground there are many enthusiasts.

In the aftermath of the Bali, London, and Madrid bombings, with the overhanging threat of homegrown terrorism, and especially after some of the less wise and more extreme imams had been goaded by the press into making statements that exposed their lack of understanding of how pluralist societies operate, the government decided to engage with Islamic leaders. Public opinion at the time had become even more uneasy, heightened by a series of horrific rapes of young Australian women by a gang of Lebanese Muslim youths in Sydney. Their trials reinforced the public's Islamophobia and Islam's alleged denigration of women.

The formation of the Muslim Community Reference Group led eventually to an interim report in April 2006 to which the government responded several months later with *Building on Social Cohesion, Harmony and Security: An Action Plan* (Department of Immigration and Multicultural Affairs 2006). The government adopted the recommendations, committing AUD$37 million for implementation. The report recognized the importance of helping young Muslim youths, whose lack of employment opportunities was built on problematic schooling, in mitigating the threat of so-called homegrown terrorism. Hence, much of the funding was directed toward employment programs in Sydney's southwest. Other strategies addressed radicalization by countering discrimination, reinforcing Muslim identity, counteracting "rigid thinking," and preparing crisis management plans in the event of a terrorist attack and any possible violent backlash. "Better Connections" workshops were held to connect the Muslim communities with wider community networks, particularly in job finding.

National action was taken to link Muslim schools with other schools, and efforts were made to educate and further professionalize the imams themselves. Cahill et al. (2004) had drawn attention to the lack of appropriate training among religious personnel (not just imams) for the Australian context in their report, *Religion, Cultural Diversity and Safeguarding Australia*. One initiative was a successful pilot program for multifaith orientation of incoming religious leaders such as Catholic priests, Buddhist monks, and Muslim imams (Bouma et al. 2007), but it has not been followed up. However, as part of the national action plan, the government funded a national Islamic institute centred at Melbourne University to address education and training issues within the Australian Muslim communities. The institute aims to ensure that imams are trained in Australia and that Islamic lay people become more knowledgeable about their own faith and the society in which they now live.

Another initiative has been the state and territorial Muslim youth summits conducted under the auspices of the Australian Multicultural Foundation between April 2006 and May 2007. The aims were to forge links between young Muslims, build leadership capacity, identify issues of concern, and achieve an ongoing collaboration with the government. These objectives have been more or less achieved, although many of the young people admitted that they did not feel like they belonged in Australia; many also articulated the need for positive role models and mentoring and a desire to do more volunteering (Department of Immigration and Citizenship 2008).

In multifaith Australia, the challenge is to create a climate in which religious extremism cannot thrive and where incoming or homegrown religious terrorists do not have the social oxygen to carry out their deadly work. Or, if they do carry out their deadly work and there is a provocative terrorist event, then there will be sufficient accumulated social capital to defuse any equally deadly reaction and backlash.

The Management of Australia's Religious Diversity

All countries are at different points along the path of development and democratization, and this is also true in respect to faith traditions, their attitudes and their institutions. Mechanisms for managing global, regional, and local ethnic and religious diversity depend on broadening understanding about the functional equality of all persons and all faiths and on building common foundational norms. The separation of religion and state, as we have already seen, does not require a rigid, secularist stance toward religion. Australia has sought historically to espouse what Laycock (1990) has called "a substantive neutrality." While this has described the Australian approach, especially during the secularist period between the 1870s and the 1970s, since then, and especially since 9/11, the stance might be better described as "a brokering and monitoring neutrality." The intention of the state is to create a culture of tolerance, acceptance, and reconciliation through its legislative, judicial, and policing agencies and to prevent the development of religious extremism or a religiously supported ethnonationalism.

According to this perspective, the state's responsibilities are to guarantee an open religious market that prevents the emergence and growth of ultra-fundamentalist religious movements, and to facilitate harmony and contact between the different faith communities. So, in this sense, the state has begun to play more of an active brokering role with regard to religion. It has a monitoring role as well, inasmuch as the state now seeks to detect, at the earliest possible moment, the causes of difference and tensions between religious groups so that such conflicts do not escalate into violence. As we have seen with regard to the Muslim communities since 9/11, this role has not been well handled.

In the creation of a "civic ethos" or "a culture of reconciliation and cooperation," the regulation of religious diversity is an ongoing process that in Australia has had the following features:

1. The state through its constitutional, legislative, judicial, and policing processes officially treats all faith and non-faith traditions on the basis of equality and neutrality.
2. The state establishes the appropriate legislation to regulate the place of religion in civil society and administers the laws in a fair and timely fashion.
3. The leaders of faith communities show how they contribute to the nation's social capital through their teachings and activities.
4. The state does not recognize any statute of religious law, though religious elements (e.g., as in religious marriages) may be incorporated into civil law.
5. The faith communities have the political, economic, and educational space to safeguard, develop, and transmit their traditions; they are able to worship and meditate, own property, form associations, and establish educational facilities freely but within an intercultural and interfaith climate.
6. The state puts into place mechanisms to accommodate essential religious practices in conflict with either state legislation or core national values through a process of cultural/religious impact assessment and accommodation.

Conclusion

The resurgence of religion, the increase in ethnic and religious diversification, the increasingly transnational nature of faith communities, and the rise of religiously inspired terrorism suggest that the evolution of praxis needs to keep pace with the realities of daily life. The management and regulation of diversity is an issue for all nation states.

The Australian case is interesting because of its multicultural profile, its various religious and ethnic diasporas, the stability of its democratic system, and the recent re-articulation of the relationship between religion and the state. An analysis of the Australian case study suggests that a moderate position in the separation of religion and state is the appropriate course of action because the encouragement of religious moderation is the key strategy. Aggressive secularism and aggressive majoritarianism, approaches that encourage violent responses, are inimical to such a strategy. The Australian example may be paralleled to the Canadian example with its evolution from the traditions of the *Ancien Régime* to a civic ethos underpinned by a technocratic pluralism (Côté 2004; cf. Milot's and Bramadat's chapters in this book).

The Australian example contrasts with the French model of *laïcité* and its "strongly positive commitment to exclude religion from state institutions and, in its place, to inculcate principles of nonreligious rationality and morality" (Beckford 2004, 32; cf. Cesari's chapter in this book). Signs are emerging that the new French president may wish to shift the French model to a more moderate position. The Australian model also contrasts with the American one with its strict separation of religion and state (cf. Levitt's chapter in this book), a posture that has possibly strengthened Christian fundamentalism in the United States, with repercussions in the political sphere—as we have seen with the Bush presidency—and in the religious sphere.

The importance of a strong state is also evidenced by the Australian case study. The contrasting case of India (characterized by Hindu majoritarianism) highlights this point. There, a relatively weak state has abrogated its responsibility, leaving the courts to make critical decisions. The inconsistent verdicts have reinforced either the cause of secularism or the cause of Hindu nationalism. The courts have tried on several occasions to determine the essentials of Hinduism (Rao 2004); however, they have not clarified what is "secular" and what is "unsecular."

The management and regulation of ethnic and religious diversity has clearly taken on a new urgency; faith communities and the state must be committed to the process as it unfolds in the context of new exigencies. Scholars and policy-makers may find the story told in these pages to be a useful introduction to the dynamic relationship still emerging between religions and the Australian state.

References

Australia. Department of Immigration and Citizenship. 2008. *Muslim Youth Summits: 2007 Report.* Canberra: Department of Immigration and Citizenship.

Australia. Department of Immigration and Multicultural Affairs. 2006. *Building on Social Cohesion, Harmony and Security: An Action Plan.* Canberra: Department of Immigration and Multicultural Affairs.

Australian Bureau of Statistics (ABS). 1996. Available on the ABS website at http://www.abs.gov.au/websitedbs/D3310114.nsf/Home/Census+Data

— 2006. Available on the ABS website at http://www.abs.gov.au/websitedbs/D3310114.nsf/Home/Census+Data

Beckford, J.A. 2004. "'Laicite,' 'Dystopia' and the Reaction to New Religious Movements in France." In *Regulating Religion: Case Studies from Around the Globe*, ed. J.T. Richardson. New York: Kluwer Academic/Plenum Publishers.

Bouma, G.D. 2003. "Globalization, Social Capital and Challenge to Harmony of Recent Changes in Australia's Religious and Spiritual Demography." *Australian Religious Studies Review* 16(2):55-68.

— 2006. *Australian Soul: Religion and Spirituality in the 21ˢᵗ Century.* Melbourne: Cambridge University Press.

Bouma, G.D., S. Pickering, H. Dellal, and A. Halafoff. 2007. *Introducing Australia: A Course for Clergy New to Australia.* Canberra: Department of Immigration and Multicultural and Indigenous Affairs.

Cahill, D. 2007. "From Dagoes to Doers: Accommodating Australia's Italian Migrants by Church and State." In *The Pastoral Care of Italians in Australia. Memory and Prophecy,* ed. A. Paganoni. Victoria, Australia: Connor Court Publishing.

Cahill, D., G. Bouma, H. Dellal, and M. Leahy. 2004. *Religion, Cultural Diversity and Safeguarding Australia.* Canberra: Department of Immigration and Multicultural and Indigenous Affairs and the Australian Multicultural Foundation (AMF). Available on the AMF website at http://amf.net.au/library/file/Religion_Cultural_Diversity_Main_Report.pdf

Côté, P. 2004. "Public Management of Religious Diversity in Canada: Development of Technocratic Pluralism." In *Religion in International Relations: The Return from Exile,* ed. F. Petito and P. Hatzopoulos. New York: Palgrave Macmillan.

Flood, J. 2006. *The Original Australians: Story of the Aboriginal People.* Sydney: Allen and Unwin.

Hollifield, J. 2004. "The Emerging Migration State." *International Migration Review* 38(3):885-912.

Hughes, P. 2007. *Putting Life Together: Findings from Australian Youth Spirituality Research.* Victoria, Australia: Fairfield Press.

Hume, L. 2002. *Ancestral Power: The Dreaming, Consciousness and Aboriginal Australians.* Melbourne: Melbourne University Press.

Keceli, B. 1998. "Boundary Within, Boundary Without." Ph.D. thesis, Faculty of Education, Language and Community Studies, RMIT University, Melbourne.

Laycock, D.H. 1990. *Populism and Democratic Thought in the Canadian Prairies: 1910 to 1945.* Toronto: University of Toronto Press.

Madox, M. 2005. *God under Howard: The Rise of the Religious Right in Australian Politics.* Sydney: Allen and Unwin.

Mason, M., A. Singleton, and R. Webber. 2006. *The Spirit of Generation Y. Final Report of a 3-Year Study.* Melbourne: Australian Catholic University, Monash University, and Christian Research Association.

McGrath, A.E. 2004. *The Twilight of Atheism: The Rise and Fall of Disbelief in the Modern World.* London: Random House.

Muslim Community Reference Group. 2006. *Building on Social Cohesion, Harmony and Security: An Action Plan by the Muslim Community Reference Group.* Accessed 28 October 2008 at http://www.immi.gov.au/living-in-australia/a-diverse-australia/mcrg_report.pdf

Noseda, M. 2006. "Belonging: The Case of Immigrants and the Australian Catholic Church." Ph.D. thesis, Faculty of Arts and Sciences, Australian Catholic University, Melbourne.

O'Farrell, P. 1987. *The Irish in Australia.* Sydney: University of New South Wales Press.

Paganoni, A., ed. 2007. *The Pastoral Care of Italians in Australia: Memory and Prophecy*. Victoria, Australia: Connor Court Publishing.

Price, C.A. and J.I. Martin. 1975. "The Demography of Post-War Immigration." In *Australian Immigration: A Bibliography and Digest*, ed. C.A. Price and J.I. Martin. No. 3, Part 1. Canberra: Department of Demography, Australian National University.

Rao, B. 2004. "Religion, Law and Minorities in India. Problems with Judicial Regulation," In *Regulating Religion: Case Studies from Around the Globe*, ed. J.T. Richardson. New York: Kluwer Academic Plenum Publishers.

Rudd, K. 2006. "Christianity, the Australian Labor Party and Current Challenges in Australian Politics: A Contribution to the National Forum on Australia's Christian Heritage, Parliament House, Canberra." Accessed 16 January 2008 at http://parlinfoweb.aph.gov.au/piweb/Repository1/Media/pressrel?1AHK60.pdf

Tavan, G. 2005. *The Long, Slow Death of White Australia*. Melbourne: Scribe Publications.

Thomas, S.M. 2004. "Taking Religious and Cultural Pluralism Seriously: The Global Resurgence of Religion and the Transformation of International Society." In *Religion in International Relations: The Return from Exile*, ed. F. Petito and P. Hatzopoulos. New York: Palgrave Macmillan.

Thompson, R.C. 2002. *Religion in Australia: A History*. South Melbourne, Victoria: Oxford University Press.

Chapter 7

Religions and Governance in the United Kingdom: Religious Diversity, Established Religion, and Emergent Alternatives

PAUL WELLER

The common theme of the present volume is the governance *of* religion, especially in the context of management by the state of religious diversity occasioned by the phenomenon of migration. In this chapter, I set out to explore the relationship between governance *and* religion in the United Kingdom—in what I call a complex, three-dimensional society in a Four-Nations-State.

In framing the chapter by reference to governance *and* religion, I am proposing a balanced perspective in which the issues involved are to be seen not only in terms of a set of "problems" faced by states and societies but also in terms of a set of questions posed to the religions themselves, to the wider societies in which they are set, and to the state. In addition to recognizing the inevitable connectedness between governance and religion, I also argue that their proper autonomies should be appreciated and, consequently, that the most fruitful interface between the two requires a strongly *relational* approach.

As with the other chapters in this part of the book, this chapter begins with an outline of the (diverse) institutional arrangements of state, national identity, and religion that are found in the United Kingdom. The second section provides a portrait of the current religious diversity in the UK and how this pluralism has been extended through patterns of migration and community development. The third section identifies some of the key social forces that have driven the formation of public

International Migration and the Governance of Religious Diversity, eds. P. Bramadat and M. Koenig.
Montreal and Kingston: McGill-Queen's University Press, Queen's Policy Studies Series.
© 2009 The School of Policy Studies, Queen's University at Kingston. All rights reserved.

policy at the interface between religion and governance. The final section analyzes the resulting approach to integration and religious diversity.

Institutional Arrangements of State, National Identity, and Religion

A Three-Dimensional Society in a Four-Nations-State

In *Time for a Change: Reconfiguring Religion, State and Society* (Weller 2005), I describe the religious landscape of the United Kingdom as "exhibiting contours that are 'Christian, secular and religiously plural'" and, therefore,

> the contemporary socio-religious reality of England and the UK might be described as "three-dimensional" in contrast with a more "one-dimensional" Christian inheritance or the "two-dimensional" religious-secular modifications made to that self-understanding during the course of the nineteenth and early twentieth centuries. (73)

Arguably, one needs to understand each of these dimensions in the context of the other two in order to appreciate the challenges related to the governance of religious diversity in the contemporary United Kingdom. In addition, one must always bear in mind that the United Kingdom is not a unitary state but a multinational union, or what I have called a "four-nations-state" (73). In this context, the national traditions and religious distinctiveness of England, Scotland, Wales, and Northern Ireland mean that there are significant differences between them in matters of religion and governance.

In fact, in recent years, these contexts have become even more distinctively national, regional, and local. Such developments have been accelerated by the reconstitution of the Scottish Parliament, which deals with some matters of devolved governance in relation to the Scottish Executive (the devolved government for Scotland), including significant aspects of law and social policy. In Wales, a new National Assembly for Wales and the Welsh Assembly Government have been created, while in Northern Ireland (as part of the peace process following the Good Friday/Belfast Agreement of 1998), the Northern Ireland Assembly has been restored and the devolved government of the Northern Ireland Executive has replaced what had been a period of direct rule from London.

In England, there is no English Parliament, and governance structures and traditions are complex and in flux. There are assemblies for the English regions, which are intended to inform the work of the business-led Regional Development Agencies. However, only one of these assemblies (London Assembly) is elected. The other regional assemblies will be abolished in 2010; their executive powers will be transferred to the Regional Development Agencies, and local authorities will be given a greater role in the scrutiny of regional strategies. In some areas, the local authorities are county councils, whether metropolitan or non-metropolitan. Together with metropolitan or non-metropolitan districts, these councils share the responsibility for providing services, as appropriate. Other areas have so-called unitary authorities. At the local level in rural areas there are also civil parishes. Greater London is composed of the London Boroughs and the City of London.

In the UK, as in other European countries, a substantial historical inheritance shapes the interface between religion(s) and governance. This arises from the distinctive history of the different Christian confessions in each of the four national traditions found within the United Kingdom. It is to that inheritance that this chapter now turns, before considering the impact upon it of migration.

The Established Church of England and Its "Special Relationship"

In contrast with the national churches of some other European countries, the Church of England is not, strictly speaking, a "state church" (in the same way, for example, as the Lutheran Church in Norway is a state church), nor is it in general directly funded by the state. The precise position of the Church of England as an established church does not fit easily into the kinds of typologies that have been created to illuminate the varied patterns of relationship between religion and the state. For example, Madeley and Enyedi (2003) have described the Church of England under the headings "indirect state aid, no control" (13) and "limited state subsidies to churches" (16). However, such categorizations are misleading. While the Church of England does, today, have a significant degree of self-rule through the operation of its General Synod, the existence and empowerment of that Synod has its origin in the parliamentary control of the Church of England. Moreover, parliamentary process and Royal Assent continue to be required for major legislative developments in the Church of England, such as in the case of its decision to ordain women to the priesthood.

The Church of England has a constitutional position that distinguishes it from other religious traditions, groups, and organizations—including other Christian churches. At the time of writing, this "special relationship" is given particular expression by the presence of its two archbishops and twenty-four bishops who sit as "Lords Spiritual" in the Westminster Parliament's non-elected second chamber, the House of Lords. This chamber of Parliament has an important scrutinizing and revising function in relation to legislation that first passes through the elected House of Commons and that therefore generally reflects the policy and the will of the governing political party. While the House of Lords also contains political nominees, the independence from party politics of the Lords Spiritual, and also the Law Lords, means that, on occasion, legislation passed by the Commons can be delayed by the Lords and returned to the Commons for further consideration. While religious figures from other Christian traditions, as well as from other religions, have also become members of the House of Lords, they were appointed on the basis of their personal role and contribution to the UK, rather than as Lords Spiritual by virtue of their religious office in the established Church of England.

Since the new Labour Government has been in power, reform of the House of Lords has been on the government agenda. As part of an over-all process of reform, the Royal Commission on the Reform of the House of Lords (2000), otherwise known as the Wakeham Commission, previously made proposals to widen the basis of representation for "organized religions" in the second chamber. The ensuing government White Paper of 2001 envisaged retaining a smaller number of Church of England bishops, together with representative members from other religions, among the appointed section of a reformed second chamber. Most recently, in February 2007, the government also proposed a "hybrid" House, partly elected and partly appointed, that would include continued representation of the Church of England. However, the House of Commons voted in favour of a wholly elected second chamber and, at the time of writing, it is unclear what the way forward might be or if and when further debate and change might take place.

When, in 2007, Gordon Brown became prime minister, a government Green Paper was issued on *The Governance of Britain* that raised a range of matters where modernization of the arrangements for governance were proposed, including the process for the appointment of Church of England bishops in which the prime minister's office currently plays a role. At present, the prime minister is able to choose which bishop to appoint on the basis of two names presented to him following soundings taken among key stakeholders in church and society. A former prime minister, James Callaghan, defended this power as appropriate on the grounds that the place of Church of England bishops in the House of Lords gave them a role in the legislature.

However, while the prime minister's power to choose between two names is now being questioned, *The Governance of Britain* (2007, 25) includes a clear statement to the effect that "the Church of England is by law established as the Church in England, and the Monarch is its Supreme Governor. The Government remains committed to this position."

At the same time, such commitment does not preclude further changes to the future place and role of bishops in the second chamber of Parliament. But pending such change, as in other matters relating to religion and governance, there is a range of different arrangements that define the relationships between religious bodies, the state, and society within the constituent nations of the United Kingdom.

Religion, State, and Society

England. In England, the Church of England's special relationship with the state is embodied in its role as the form of religion "by law established," while other Christian denominations do not have the same formal status (Hastings 1991). The history of this special relationship is closely linked with the fortunes of the monarchy, and in its present form it can be traced back to the rupture between King Henry VIII and Rome. The Church of England's relationship with the state is also linked with the Restoration of the monarchy following the dramatic seventeenth-century upheavals of the English Civil War, Commonwealth, and Protectorate (Hill 1975). It was then further adapted by the events of the so-called Glorious Revolution in which William of Orange took the throne in a move understood by supporters at the time to be a defence of Protestantism against the perceived threat of Roman Catholic forces. This event underlines the strong strand of anti-Catholicism that has informed many of the mechanisms concerned with religion and governance in the United Kingdom, especially in English religious history (Marotti 2005).

In the inherited arrangements, the reigning monarch is seen as the Supreme Governor (and not, as is sometimes popularly but incorrectly stated, the "Head") of the Church of England. The older title "Defender of the Faith" predates the Reformation, having been given by the Pope to King Henry VIII. However, not only in relation to Christian plurality but also in the context of the development of the UK as a more religiously plural society, the Prince of Wales has suggested that the term Defender of the Faith might appropriately be adapted and extended to the more inclusive title and general role of Defender of Faith (Ipgrave 2003).

The Church of England continues to have a special role in public ceremonies and national occasions, such as the prayers at the cenotaph on Remembrance Day. Its clergy have particular rights of presence as chaplains in the Prison Service (Beckford and Gilliat 1998) and in the Armed Forces in ways that are distinct from those of other religious groups, including other Christian churches. Its established position also means that the ecclesiastical law of the Church of England is treated as a part of the public law of England (Robilliard 1984), being passed through parliamentary processes and then receiving Royal Assent. In addition, the ecclesiastical courts of the Church of England continue to have legal power in matters over which (under Parliament) they retain jurisdiction, as in relation to the discipline of the clergy and a range of matters to do with the fabric and grounds of parish churches and cemeteries.

Scotland. Through having a shared monarch since the 1603 accession of James VI of Scotland to the English crown as James I, and followed by the 1707 union of the parliaments, Scotland has had close links with England and Wales. However, it also remains distinct in many ways, both in matters of religion and in its systems, especially of law and education. The 1999 re-establishment of the Scottish Parliament has further reinforced this distinctiveness.

The established church in Scotland is not the Anglican tradition's Episcopal Church of Scotland but the Church of Scotland, which is Presbyterian and has often been understood in Scotland as the "national church." Indeed, even as late as the 1980s, it could still be asserted that "to be a Scot is to be a Presbyterian, even though that designation may say more of cultural identity than of religious persuasion" (Bisset 1986, 3). Indeed, until the recent devolution of powers to the Scottish Parliament and Scottish Executive, what is known in Scotland as "the Kirk" was frequently seen as a kind of surrogate Scottish parliament, with a system of governance composed of a hierarchy of elected clerical and lay Kirk sessions, presbyteries, and a general assembly.

Unlike the Church of England, the relatively "weak" form of establishment of the Church of Scotland does not entail limitations in its self-government. For example, neither the British prime minister, nor the secretary of state for Scotland, nor the first minister of the Scottish Executive has any role in appointing the Church of Scotland's leadership. Nevertheless, despite the status and prominent role in Scottish history of the Church of Scotland, its leaders, in contrast to those of the Church of England, do not have seats in the Westminster Parliament's House of Lords.[1]

Wales. The Anglican Church in Wales was disestablished in 1920. In contrast to the position in Scotland, there has not been a single denominational tradition that has acted as an alternative religious focus for national identity. The absorption of Wales into the English crown had taken place earlier than the 1603 union of crowns with Scotland, with the result that Wales retained comparatively little constitutional or legal distinctiveness in relation to England.

However, in such a context, language and culture assumed more prominence. In particular, the Free Churches in Wales played a significant role in preserving the social and cultural life of the country, including the promotion of the use of the Welsh language that, following the 1960s campaigns of Cymdeithas yr Iaith Gymraeg (Welsh Language Society), was more generally revived. As a result, the Welsh language is more widely used and is also recognized in the public sector.

Northern Ireland (and the Republic). The levels of religious identification, belief, and participation are much higher in Northern Ireland than in England, Wales, and Scotland. But like the Republic of Ireland, Northern Ireland has no officially established form of religion. The Church of Ireland (an episcopal church that is part of the global Anglican Communion) was disestablished in 1871. And following the establishment of the Irish Free State, and then the six-county state of Northern Ireland, the 1920 *Governance of Ireland Act* specifically proscribed the establishment of any particular religion or religious tradition.

In the Republic of Ireland, the 1937 constitution originally gave a "special position" to the Roman Catholic Church, which reflected the fact that the overwhelming majority of the population was Catholic. Subsequently, Catholic teaching exerted a strong influence on legislation related to social and sexual behaviour. However, this clause was abolished in 1972.

In Northern Ireland, the population with a Roman Catholic background is the largest single grouping, although the combined number of people of Protestant backgrounds is larger. Until the emergence of the civil rights movement in the 1960s, the Northern Ireland state had what has often been described as a "Protestant ascendancy" built into many of its social and political institutions. In particular, the electoral qualification criteria prevented many Catholics from being able to vote for members of the Northern Irish Parliament at Stormont. This inheritance was seen by the civil rights movement as entrenched and systematic discrimination.

Communal identity related to religion has been a significant dimension of the national conflict that became generally known as "The Troubles" (Barnes 2002; McSweeney 1989) and which, following British military intervention into the deteriorating situation in the wake of the civil rights movement protests and the reactions to those protests, developed into the violent campaign against British rule by the Irish Republican Army (IRA) and the Provisional IRA (PIRA). These campaigns, together with the violence of a range of Loyalist paramilitary organizations, resulted in a substantial loss of life and personal injury in both Northern Ireland and "mainland" Britain until the ceasefire declared by paramilitary organizations in the context of the 1998 Good Friday/Belfast Agreement.

During the conflict, the Roman Catholic community in the North was identified with broadly nationalist, and often Republican, aspirations, while Protestants were generally identified with a unionist, and sometimes Loyalist, perspective (Bruce 1986). Nevertheless, it is important to realize that despite the history of national conflict and the ongoing existence of the political border between Northern Ireland and the Republic of Ireland, nearly all of the Christian churches are organized on a cross-border, all-Ireland basis.

Migrants and Patterns of Religious Identity and Community Formation

Inheritance and Change

The new and more extended cultural and religious plurality, derived largely from the substantive New Commonwealth migrations of the 1950s through to the 1980s, has created new issues and opportunities with regard to the relationships between religion and governance in the UK. The following section outlines the emergent religious diversity of the UK and the history of migration that has contributed to this.

UK Populations and Religions

Until the last decade, with the exception of Northern Ireland (where a religion question has been asked in the census since the inception of the Northern Ireland state), there was in the UK a relative dearth of statistical information on religion, other than that derived from sample surveys. This changed with the inclusion, for the first time, of voluntary questions on religion in the 2001 decennial Census for England, Wales, and Scotland as well as for Northern Ireland (UK Office for National Statistics 2001).

There is considerable debate (Weller 2004) about how these statistics should be interpreted, bearing in mind that both the form of the questions and the options for response in England and Wales were different from those in Scotland and Northern Ireland. Nevertheless, as Table 1 indicates, around three-quarters of the population of the UK continue to identify with a religion (45,162,895 people or 76.8 percent of the population).

Across the UK, respondents self-identifying as Christian remain by far the largest group, although Voas (2003) and Voas and Bruce (2004) suggest that, especially in England, the response of "Christian" may in many cases say as much, if not more, about ethnicity as about religion. And this may be especially the case given the form of the religion question in England and Wales which, unlike that in Scotland and in Northern Ireland, did not ask about religious belonging in a more denominationally aligned way.[2] This debate has resonance with the

Table 1: Religious Self-Identification in the 2001 Census by Country, United Kingdom

Religion	England	Scotland	Wales	Northern Ireland	UK Total	UK (%)
Buddhist	139,046	6,830	5,407	533	151,816	0.3
Christian	35,251,244	3,294,545	2,087,242	1,446,386	42,079,417	71.6
Hindu	546,982	5,564	5,439	825	558,810	1.0
Jewish	257,671	6,448	2,256	365	266,740	0.5
Muslim	1,524,887	42,557	21,739	1,943	1,591,126	2.7
Sikh	327,343	6,572	2,015	219	336,149	0.6
Other religion	143,811	26,974	6,909	1,143	178,837	0.3
Total	38,190,984	3,389,490	2,131,007	1,451,414	45,162,895	76.8
No religion	7,171,332	1,394,460	537,935	*	9,103,727	15.5
Not stated	3,776,515	278,061	234,143	*	4,288,719	7.3
Total no religion/ not stated	10,947,847	1,672,521	772,078	233,853	13,626,299	23.2

Notes: Due to rounding, percentages may not total 100 percent. *In Northern Ireland, separate statistics for those of "no religion" and "not stated" are not available.

Source: Table reproduced from Inter Faith Network for the United Kingdom (2003a, 3).

broader theoretical debate that has developed around Grace Davie's (1990a) conceptualization of the religion of many people consisting of believing in the "ordinary God" of Christianity and "believing without belonging" (Davie 1990b), and in relation to which I have elsewhere suggested the possibility of reverse salience of the concept of "belonging without believing" (Weller 2007, 36).

After Christian, the next largest group of respondents in the 2001 census across the UK were Muslim; then Hindu and Sikh; then Jewish; then Buddhist; and then Jain, Bahá'í, and Zoroastrian. Yet at the same time, in religious identification, as in many other aspects of life in the UK, there are significant differences among the constituent nations. England has the greatest variety and largest number of people from minority religious traditions. In England, Muslims are followed by Hindus, and then by Sikhs, Jews, other religions, and Buddhists. In Scotland, Wales, and Northern Ireland, respondents who used the "write-in" option of "other religions" were the next largest group after Muslims. Buddhists, Jews, Sikhs, and Hindus follow in different proportions according to the country concerned. In Northern Ireland, although religious diversity exists (Ryan 1996), it is much less pronounced than in other parts of the UK.

In addition to these differences between the countries of the UK, because of the differing patterns of migration and settlement some geographical areas within each country are characterized by a more pronounced religious diversity. In relation to the UK as a whole, the cosmopolitan nature of London means that religious as well as ethnic and linguistic diversity is at its broadest there (Peach 2006), with only three-fifths of London's population recording their religion as Christian. The greatest concentration of people from minority religious traditions is to be found in London,[3] with the exception of Sikhs, whose regional population share is at its greatest in the West Midlands.

Such concentrations of minority religious populations underline the fact that religious diversity is still primarily an urban phenomenon and that, in each country, the greatest religious diversity is found in cities, metropolitan boroughs, and some towns. These urban areas include places that were settled early on by small groups of traders, seamen, and others (Fisher, Lahiri, and Thandi 2007; Visram 1986). Thus seaports such as Liverpool, Cardiff, and London generally have longer-established minority communities. In addition, many old industrial towns and cities of the English Midlands and the North, such as Leicester and Bradford, have communities of South Asian origin that were established as a result of migration from particular areas of commonwealth countries in response to the post–Second World War labour shortages in Britain (Ballard 1994; Coward, Hinnells, and Brady 2000; Jacobsen and Kumar 2004; Knott 1996).

Therefore, contrary to many popular perceptions, religious diversity beyond the varieties of Christianity is not only a twentieth-century phenomenon. At least in "seed" form, incipient elements of the current religious diversity in the UK can be traced to the nineteenth century and, in some cases, even earlier. It is to these origins, as well as to the migrant and refugee population movements of the twentieth century, that the chapter now turns.

Hidden Histories of Migration and Diversity

The roots of today's wider religious diversity can be found in the expansion of the British Empire, especially in relation to the Indian subcontinent. The title of Rosina Visram's (1986) book, *Ayahs, Lascars and Princes*, highlights the categories of migrants who were among the first South Asian visitors to, and settlers in, Britain. Ayahs were nannies or maids, often brought back by families returning from colonial service in India. Lascars were members of maritime labour-gangs, the majority of whom were Muslims from Bengal. Princes and maharajahs were part of the emergent imperial system and visited England for formal occasions. The development of Western education in nineteenth-century India also led to the arrival in Britain of Indian students of law, medicine, and other professions, while Indian merchants came to set up trading links.

However, at this stage in the development of the religious and cultural diversity rooted in migration, the migrant presence was primarily one of collections of individuals and families more than one of strongly organized communities. As Visram writes in her incisive evaluation of this period (1986, 75), "Whatever their profession and their contribution to British society, and despite their small numbers, their experiences of British society were in one important respect similar. Racial prejudice, indifference or at times grudging acceptance characterized their presence."

Profiles, Religious Community Formation, and Organizations

Christians. Visram's assessment of the treatment of early migrants whose religion was other than Christian could also, in fact, characterize the treatment of Christian minorities of non-European background. For example, the first African prose writer to be published in English, Ignatius Sancho (who was born on a slave ship and christened on the coast of Colombia), noted that few English churchgoers had "charity enough to admit dark faces into the fellowship of Christians" (Sancho 1782, I, 200).

However, over the centuries, groups of Christian migrants brought their own distinctive traditions with them. In the earlier period, these groups included the French Reformed Huguenots; then in the nineteenth and twentieth centuries, Irish Roman Catholics; and in the twentieth century, Greek, Russian, and other Eastern Orthodox Christians as well as members of the Pentecostal, Holiness, and Spiritual churches and Sabbatarian churches of mainly African-Caribbean membership (Gerloff 1992). Some of these churches have become a significant part of the contemporary religious landscape of the United Kingdom.

In addition to the emergence in the UK of churches developed from Caribbean and American ecclesiological traditions as well as from African indigenous forms of Christianity, the historic churches of the UK have experienced diversification through the arrival of migrants of various ethnic backgrounds, including people from the Caribbean, Africa, Asia, and Latin America. Most recently, the expansion of the European Union to include Poland has prompted the arrival of a substantial number of Roman Catholic Poles.

Data from the 2001 census show that a vast majority of respondents in Great Britain (i.e., excluding Northern Ireland) who self-identified as Christians were born in the UK (38,579,528 or 94.06 percent of the total), while 1.03 percent (420,700) were born in Africa and 1.76 percent (721,148) were born in the rest of Europe (other than the Republic of Ireland). However, the ethnic composition of Christianity in the UK—and certainly of its active community membership—has been subject to quite substantial change during the last quarter of the twentieth century and the beginning of the twenty-first century. Significant numbers of Christians are of minority ethnic background. Most recently, there has been a growth in African indigenous Christian traditions (Ter Haar 1998), linked partly with migration and partly with refugee movements of people from the conflicts of Africa. This growth is reflected in the relatively high overall numbers of Christians who the 2001 census indicates were born in Africa, although this would also include African Christians belonging to the historic Christian traditions of the UK.

In terms of community membership, and based on Christian Research estimates for the year 2000 (Brierley 2004, Table 2.2.3), out of the total UK population of 41 million, 67.5 percent (28,300,000 people) were Anglicans, 13.8 percent (5,800,000) were Catholics, and the remainder were Christians of Presbyterian, traditional Free Church, Pentecostal, and other traditions.[4] However, if one interprets church membership to signify only adult members and adherents, Christian Research estimates for 2001 indicate that Roman Catholics formed 29.6 percent and Anglicans 28.3 percent of the total number of 5,903,267 church members in the UK (Brierley 2004, Tables 2.22.2–2.22.7).[5]

In contrast to the former British Council of Churches (which was essentially an organization of Anglican and historic Protestant churches), the so-called ecumenical instruments (often known as "Churches Together") now embrace not only the Roman Catholic and Eastern Orthodox traditions but also many Protestant churches of predominantly black membership and leadership. Churches Together represents Christianity at UK, national, regional, and local levels.

Muslims. Today, Muslims form the largest religious minority in the UK (see Table 2). The Muslim presence began in the nineteenth century—although there were Muslim individuals and small groups in the UK before that—when the Indian lascars and other seamen, who were recruited through Aden (Halliday 1992) and from other parts of the Middle East as well as Africa (in particular from Yemen and Somalia after the opening of the Suez Canal in 1869), came into dock. Some settled in the seaports (Adams 1987), leading to incipient Muslim communities forming in Liverpool, South Shields, and to the east of London in England; and in Cardiff in Wales.

But the Muslim community as it is today grew mostly out of the migration of significant numbers of South Asian Muslims between the 1950s and 1970s. At the time of the decennial 2001 census, just under half of the Muslim population in the UK had been born there. Of those born outside the UK, a substantial majority were of Asian (and especially South Asian) background. However, the African Muslim presence has been growing with refugee arrivals and, by now, may well be

Table 2: Distribution of Religious Minorities in the United Kingdom

Religious Group	England		Wales		Scotland		Northern Ireland		Total UK	
	No.	%	No.	%	No.	%	No.	%	No.	%
Muslims	1,524,887	3.1	21,739	0.8	42,557	0.8	1,943	0.10	1,591,126	2.7
Hindus	546,982	1.1	5,439	0.2	5,564	0.1	825	0.10	558,810	1.0
Sikhs	327,343	0.7	2,015	0.1	6,572	0.1	219	0.01	336,149	0.6
Buddhists	139,046	0.3	5,407	0.2	6,830	0.1	533	0.03	151,816	0.3
Jews	257,671	0.5	2,256	0.1	6,448	0.1	365	0.02	266,740	0.5

Source: UK Office for National Statistics, 2001 Census.

a larger proportion of the whole Muslim population of the UK than at the time of the 2001 census.

Because the Muslim population is predominantly of South Asian origin, the Barelwi, Deobandi, and Tablighi Jamaat movements (of Indo-Pakistani subcontinental origin) are numerically strong and socially significant (Raza 1992; Robinson 1988).[6] Sufi orders are also active in most UK towns and cities that have a substantial Muslim presence.

Federations and councils of Islamic organizations have been established at national, regional, and local levels and often have a degree of overlap in terms of membership.[7] Over the years, a range of national organizations have emerged including the Imams and Mosques Council, the Union of Muslim Organizations, the Muslim Parliament of Britain, and the British Muslim Forum.[8] In 1997, the Muslim Council of Britain (MCB) was formally launched and has sought to represent the Muslim community as a whole in its contact with government, public bodies, and the media. The MCB has evidenced organizational stability and some representational breadth of membership. However, especially since the bombings of the London Transport system in 2005, questions have been raised about whether or not this body fully represents the broader Muslim community; in response, other bodies (such as the Sufi Muslim Council) have emerged.

Hindus. Hindus are the second largest religious minority in the UK. Small numbers of Hindus visited and worked in England in earlier centuries, but the main migration took place between the 1950s and 1970s. Initially, men arrived seeking employment and, later, their families joined them (Knott 2000). Also in the latter part of this period, some came as refugees from the Africanization policies of some newly independent African states, bringing with them experience of being diasporic religious minorities.

The 2001 census indicates that a smaller proportion of Hindus than Muslims were born in the UK. Together with the Asian (and especially South Asian) origins of the majority of Hindus in Britain, the relatively later East African migratory origins of a substantial group can still be seen in the country-of-birth data in the 2001 census results. Since 2001, the proportion of Hindus from Sri Lanka is likely to have grown in view of the number of (largely Hindu) Tamils fleeing the war on that island.

The first Hindu organizations in the UK were established in the late 1950s.[9] The oldest Hindu organizations operating at a national level include the Hindu Swayamsevak Sangh, established in 1965, and the Vishwa Hindu Parishad UK, established in 1966. Another national organization, the National Council of Hindu Temples, played a significant role in the formation of the Hindu Council of the UK. More recently, the Hindu Forum of Britain has been established. It has 275 affiliated organizations and aspires to play a role in the Hindu community analogous to that among Muslims of the Muslim Council of Britain.

Especially among Gujarati Hindus, caste or *jati* groups remain a significant social, cultural, and economic factor.[10] There is also a range of *sampradaya* or spiritual movements which include, for example, the various Swaminarayan groups.[11] Other groups include the Pushtimargis, the International Society for Krishna Consciousness (ISKCON)—popularly known as the Hare Krishnas, the Arya Samajis, and the Ramakrishna Mission.

Sikhs. As shown in Table 2, Sikhs form the third largest religious minority in the UK. The relationship of Sikhs with the UK has been strongly influenced by their position within colonial history; in particular, many Sikhs played an important role in the British imperial forces fighting, for example, in both the First and Second World Wars. One of the first Sikhs to live in England was a 15-year-old prince, Dalip Singh, the son of the maharaja Ranjit Singh. He arrived in England as an exile in 1854 after having embraced Christianity a year earlier.

However, as with Hindus, it was only following the migrations from India from the 1950s to 1970s that the contours of an organized community began to emerge. While Sikh teachings do not recognize any religious significance in caste, caste-related social groupings continue to play a role within the Sikh community. In the early years, most of the Sikhs in Britain were Bhats who worked as peddlers or traders, and they pursued these traditional occupations as itinerant door-to-door salespeople (Ballard 1994, 93).

The 2001 census indicates that, in contrast with both Muslims and Hindus, a majority of Sikhs living in Britain were born in the UK. A Sikh organization was first established in London in 1908 and the first gurdwara was opened in Shepherd's Bush, in London, in 1911. By the time of the Second World War, the Bhat pioneers had been joined by Jat (rural land-owning) men, making "several hundred" in all (Ballard 2000, 128).

A range of organizations exist at the national level, such as the Sikh Missionary Society, while a relatively new Network of Sikh Organizations is aspiring to facilitate cooperation among Sikhs in the UK and is developing as a representative umbrella body, with more than 90 member groups.[12]

Buddhists. One of the somewhat unexpected features of the 2001 census was that there turned out to be a larger number of Buddhists than many (probably on the basis of ethnically related projections) had imagined. In contrast with the other religious communities referred to so far, the roots of Buddhism in nineteenth-century Britain began with its academic study by Western scholars (Almond 1988). Thus, for example, in 1881 T.W. Rhys founded the Pali Text Society and in 1898, an Englishman, Alan Bennett, went to study Buddhism in Sri Lanka. In 1901, while in Burma, Bennett was ordained as a monk, taking the name Ananda Metteyya, and in 1907 a Buddhist Society of Great Britain and Ireland was formed to receive a Buddhist mission to be led by him.

In 1893, 1896, and again in 1904, the Sinhalese Buddhist Anagarika Dharmapala visited Britain on a mission. Subsequently, a branch of the Maha Bodhi Society was founded in London, followed in 1928 by the first monastery for Sinhalese monks. In 1924, Christmas Humphreys founded the Buddhist Centre of the Theosophical Society which in 1926 became first the Buddhist Lodge of the Theosophical Society and then, in 1943, an independent organization known as the Buddhist Society (Humphreys 1968).

In the 1960s, individuals and small groups of migrants of Buddhist background also arrived from Sri Lanka, Thailand, and Burma. Indian (mostly Ambedkarite) Buddhists and the Hong Kong Chinese came mainly with the New Commonwealth migrations of the 1950s to 1970s. The number of Buddhists in the UK further expanded with the arrival of refugees, including Tibetans following the Dalai Lama's 1959 flight from Tibet; Vietnamese Buddhists, who arrived in the late 1960s and early 1970s; and more recently, those fleeing the Sri Lankan civil war. Buddhist monasteries, centres, and groups were established in patterns that reflected the diverse migrant and indigenous origins of those associated with the various Buddhist traditions and movements.[13]

Buddhists associated with the Theravada tradition include significant groups of people with personal or ancestral roots in the traditional Theravada countries such as Sri Lanka, Burma, and Thailand, together with the Indian Ambedkarites. Among Tibetan Buddhists, the Kagyupa and Gelugpa schools are numerically the strongest. In 1967 the first Tibetan Buddhist Centre in the West was founded at Johnstone House in Dumfriesshire and was later, in 1988, opened as the Samye Ling Buddhist monastery. The New Kadampa tradition, which has controversial relations with the Dalai Lama, emerged from the Gelugpa school and has centres and groups throughout the UK.

Both the Rinzai and Soto Zen Buddhist Schools can be found in the UK together with the Korean Son, the Vietnamese Thien, and the Chinese Ch'an. Shin Buddhism has been the most influential form of Pure Land Buddhism in the UK, with the Shin Buddhist Association of Great Britain having been founded in 1976 and the Pure Land Buddhist Fellowship in 1977. There is also a range of Japanese-related groups such as Soka Gakkai International, founded as a lay Buddhist association in alignment with the Nichiren Shoshu sect.

Followers of all the Buddhist traditions in the UK include substantial numbers of white converts. The Friends of the Western Buddhist Order attempts to develop Buddhism in forms that are more culturally familiar to indigenous people who are attracted to Buddhism. In addition, there are a number of non-aligned Buddhist groups.

On a national level, the Buddhist Society is the oldest Buddhist organization in Europe. In 1992, the Network of Buddhist Organizations was formed, and it links around 35 member bodies and groups, with a further 10 in associate membership. A range of other Buddhist national organizations also exist, including the Network of Engaged Buddhists.

Jews. Although recent years have seen a demographic decline, for decades Jews were the largest religious minority in the United Kingdom (Roth 1978). The first recorded Jewish settlers came after the conquest by the Normans. However, in 1290 they were expelled by King Edward I on the basis of a "blood libel" allegation made against them. After the English Civil War, Menasseh ben Israel of Amsterdam successfully campaigned for their readmission. Sephardic Jews (those with origins in Spain, Portugal, and the Middle East) have the longest continuous communal history in the UK, having had organizations since the mid-seventeenth century. However, the majority of Jews in the UK today are descendants of two waves of immigration by Ashkenazi Jews (of central and east European origins) who migrated to England for economic reasons or fled from persecution from 1881–1914 under the Russian Empire and, from 1933 onward, under the Nazis.

Reaction to the arrival of approximately 120,000 Jewish people in the 1890s led to popular agitation that resulted, in 1901, in the formation of the British Brothers' League (in many ways a prototype of later populist racist groups). A Royal Commission on Alien Immigration, set up in 1902, contradicted most of the myths surrounding Jewish immigration.

However, it did propose immigration controls and, in 1905, an *Aliens' Act* was passed which brought into being the first immigration controls of the modern British state and thus became the precursor for all the later legislative measures taken to control the free movement of people from outside of the UK. Today, the Jewish community is the minority religious group with the largest proportion of its population born in the UK, reflecting its relatively well-established community presence and profile.

In major local and regional areas of Jewish population, Jewish Representative Councils have been formed to represent the community at its interface with local governance. At the national level, the principal representative organization has been the Board of Deputies of British Jews, founded in 1760, to which every synagogue and national communal organization in the UK is entitled to elect delegates.

In relation to synagogue groupings, the largest of the Orthodox ones is the United Synagogue, which was established in 1870, but other groupings include the smaller Federation of Synagogues and the Union of Orthodox Hebrew Congregations. The best-known Hasidic group in the UK is part of a world movement known as Lubavich (also known as Chabad).

There are also Progressive Jewish traditions, including Reform and Liberal Judaism, which were once distinct but are now very close. The Movement for Reform Judaism was originally organized nationally as the Reform Synagogues of Great Britain, while the Liberal movement (now known as Liberal Judaism) began in the UK with the foundation of the Jewish Religious Union in 1902; its national representative organization has been known since 1944 as the Union of Liberal and Progressive Synagogues. The Assembly of Masorti Synagogues is a relatively small grouping that was founded in 1985, seeking to support a conservative, but modern and open, form of Jewish practice. There are also a number of independent synagogues.[14]

Zoroastrians/Parsis. Zoroastrians are numerically a very small minority in the UK.[15] However, they are mentioned here because they—and especially Parsis, those Zoroastrians with migratory origins in the Indian subcontinent—have arguably had a disproportionate role in the development of the UK as a multicultural society (Hinnells 2000).

The first Indian company to be established in the UK was opened in 1855 by Parsi owners, while the first three Indian members of the Westminster Parliament were Parsis.[16] The Parsis were also the religious minority group with South Asian origins to form significant community organizations in the UK; a Parsi Association was established in 1861, and at that time it was agreed to set up six "Religious Funds of Zoroastrians of Europe." The continuing Zoroastrian Trust Funds of

Europe (Incorporated) and the World Zoroastrian Organization operate at a national level in the UK.[17]

Other Religions. There is, of course, a range of other religious groups present and active in the UK, many of which have been associated at different periods with the migration of people into the country, including Jains,[18] Bahá'ís, and others. Space precludes a full exploration of them here. There are also religious groups and movements that are more indigenous in origin, such as Pagans, who the 2001 census indicates are more numerous in the UK than, for example, Zoroastrians, Jains or Bahá'ís; indeed, there are almost as many Pagans as Buddhists.

Social Forces Driving Public Policy Related to Religious Diversity

Three-Dimensional Policy-Making

The descriptions of religious groups and their communities set out in the previous section provides the raw data which indicates that a balanced understanding of the contemporary religious landscape of the UK needs to take account of its "Christian, secular and religiously plural" nature (Weller 2005, 73). Each of these three dimensions reflects and embodies social forces that have a bearing upon policy-making in matters that relate to religion and governance, in ways explored further in the following subsections.

The Christianity Dimension

As I have indicated above, a high proportion of the UK population continues to self-identify in some way with Christianity; indeed, 92.3 percent of those who report any religion at all identify with Christianity. Christianity also has a social presence and significance that goes beyond the actual numbers of those who identify with it. As a result of both its inheritance and its continuing numerical strength and geographically widespread presence, Christianity is extensively woven into much of the fabric of the historical, artistic, cultural, legal, and other aspects of the heritage of the UK and its constituent parts. The same intimate relationship does not exist between the culture and public institutions of the UK and any other religion.

The established forms of Christianity, and especially the Church of England, are concomitant with the wider, more generalized and day-to-day experiences of religious prejudice, direct and indirect religious discrimination, religious hatred, and institutional Christian hegemony experienced (especially) by Muslims, Hindus, and Sikhs (Weller et al.

2001). At the same time, there are those, including members of minority groups themselves, who argue that having an established church is beneficial as it ensures a space for religion in public life (Modood 1997).

During the nineteenth century, non-established Christian groups secured greater social, political, and participatory space for themselves as the UK state and society began to accommodate a wider degree of religious plurality than had hitherto been the case. An insightful analysis in relation to this process was provided by the legal scholar, St. John Robilliard (1984, ix), who in his book *Religion and the Law: Religious Liberty in Modern English Law* summarized the early modern period in England: "The early story of the struggle for religious liberty is one of sects establishing an identity of their own, with their members being freed from the obligation of supporting a faith they did not hold. From the struggle for existence we pass to the struggle for equality. . . ."

The Religious Plurality Dimension

Arguably, the process that Robilliard outlined with regard to the internal diversification of the Christian dimension of UK society might also, at least in some measure, be paradigmatic for the recent development of religion in the UK. Those associated with minority religious traditions have, during the twentieth and early twenty-first centuries, become an ever-greater proportion of the population and, in the process, what began as a struggle for existence among migrant groups who were initially preoccupied with establishing an identity of their own is now starting to become a struggle for equality. In contrast to some other European countries (for example, Germany), this process is facilitated by the fact that the majority of those in minority religious groups are also citizens of the UK and therefore have a legal and material position within the society from which they can seek an appropriately equitable position.

In the 1960s and early 1970s, newcomers in their early struggle for existence had to focus on meeting their basic economic needs—establishing a sufficient foothold within UK society to find a place to live and work and make financial remittances in support of families back home. Migrant organizations founded in this period were often based on groupings—such as Pakistani Associations—established according to national belonging. Then, with the impact of the tightening of immigration law and rules, male migrant workers were joined by their families. As this happened, individuals and groups started to become more concerned about heritage and identity and, in this context, culture and religion came to play an increasingly important role.

However, social scientists, policy-makers, and politicians paid little attention in the 1970s and early 1980s to the religious characteristics of migrants; the politics of identity and diversity were cast primarily in terms of "race" and "ethnicity." An exception to this was the prescient insight of a Church of England bishop, John Taylor. In an intervention during a 1977 Church of England General Synod debate on the British Council of Churches' (1976) report, *The New Black Presence in Britain,* Taylor (quoted in Wolffe 1993, 193) argued that "the existence of religious minorities presents us with both problems and opportunities which are distinct from those that arise in the presence of racial and cultural minorities, and should not be lost sight of or evaded."

Indeed, it has been in the context of the growing plurality of society—a plurality that has sprung from the growth of communities of faith rooted in migrant populations—that issues related to religious identity and discrimination have again arisen in the public and political agenda of the UK (Weller et al. 2000, 2001). Of course, in Northern Ireland these issues had never left the agenda.

Whereas in the 1960s and 1970s, minority ethnic groups with migratory origins had emphasized either national belonging or a common political "Blackness," first ethnicity and then religion began to re-emerge as markers of individual and community identity. This shift in self-identification then began to be reflected in the work of scholars such as Tariq Modood (1994) and others, initially by highlighting religion as one dimension of ethnicity, but increasingly also looking at religion in its own right.

Moreover, evidence from the Home Office Citizenship survey of 2001 indicates that, especially among ethnic and religious minorities with predominantly migratory origins, the significance of religion is generally higher than is the case among those self-identifying as Christian. Thus, when asked to rank the importance of religion in their lives, the UK population as a whole ranked it ninth, whereas British Asians ranked it second, after family (O'Beirne 2004, 18-19).

The Secular Dimension

The concept of secularization has been commonplace in both academic and popular writing for around 40 years. However, the meanings associated with the concept, as well as the extent of the social reality that it attempts to describe and to interpret, are varied and contested (Barker, Beckford, and Dobbelaere 1993; Bruce 1992; Dobbelaere 1981, 1984; Martin 1978).

Nevertheless, it is clear that alongside the re-emergence of religion in the public sphere, the secularizing trends and alternatives that began to emerge in earnest during the nineteenth century have also continued and, arguably, have accelerated into the twentieth and twenty-first centuries. Therefore, in the 2001 census, 9,103,727 people in the UK (15.5

percent of the population) declared themselves to be of "no religion." Another 4,228,719 people (7.3 percent) did not answer the voluntary question on religion. While the meaning and significance of a non-response is contested, it is clear that this group is likely also to include significant numbers of those who do not align themselves with any particular religion or with religion in general.

In addition, when one takes into account the results of other surveys that asked about religious practice and belief (in contrast to the census question on religious identification), the overall significance of religion in the general population turns out to be lower than might be expected from the census results alone. For example, in the last European Values Survey in 1999–2000 (Halman 2001), 33 percent of respondents in Great Britain (Northern Ireland was surveyed separately) stated that religion was "not important" and 29.7 percent stated it was "not at all important." Similarly, in the British Social Attitudes Survey for 2001 (Office for National Statistics 2003, 226), as many as 41 percent of respondents said they belonged to "no religion," while just over half of the population (54 percent) of Great Britain indicated that they regarded themselves as Christian. Only 4 percent said they belonged to another religion, although it should be noted that these results are based on a small sample size compared with the census results.

The governance of religion initially took place against the backdrop of the first dimension: the diversity of Christian communities. Then, in the nineteenth and much of the twentieth centuries, public actors focused on the real or perceived tension between religion and the second dimension of secularity. Today, because of the increase in the numbers of migrants of other than Christian background, the debate also focuses particularly on the question of the third dimension of religious plurality.

The secularity of those who belong to the "no religion" category is not necessarily rooted in a philosophical or ideological disagreement with religion that one might associate with other European secular traditions, such as Marxism. Nor is it necessarily rooted in an anticlerical tradition of the kind associated with the tradition of *laïcité* in France. At the same time, among those who do not identify with any religion, there are often deeply felt concerns about allowing a privileged or too prominent a role for religion in public life. Religious rights and claims are perceived to be at least potentially antithetical to liberal democratic rights and claims associated, for example, with gender and sexual orientation.

In terms of organized campaigning, these concerns are expressed by the National Secular Society. Similar concerns may be held by Humanists (among whom the British Humanist Association offers a value system, philosophical beliefs, and rites of passage, while nevertheless seeing itself as non-religious) as well as by non-religious members of the general public who may identify themselves explicitly as either Humanists or Secularists. In the 1999–2000 European Values Survey, in response to the question of whether respondents agree or disagree with the statement that "religious leaders should not influence government decisions," 20.3 percent of respondents from Great Britain indicated that they "agree strongly" and 44.9 percent that they "agree," while 19.1 percent said they "neither agree nor disagree." On the other hand, 12.1 percent indicated that they "disagree" and 36 percent that they "disagree strongly" (Halman 2001).

However, such concerns are likely to be considerably more widespread than what has been indicated by committed or "signed up" Secularists or Humanists, especially in the wake of the 11 September 2001 attacks in the United States and the 7 July 2005 bombings in the UK, which have led to the development of anxieties and concerns about the perceived influence of religious "extremism" associated with these atrocities.

Resulting Approaches to the Integration of Religious Minorities

Religion and Social Policy

Thus far, I have introduced an approach to the nature of religious diversity in which I argue that, at least with regard to the United Kingdom, is most appropriately understood as having three dimensions—the Christian, the secular, and the religiously plural—and that addressing each of these dimensions is important for a balanced approach to contemporary social policy. I have also argued more generally that, in approaching the question of the governance of religious diversity, it is important to take account of the relationship between religion and governance.

In the UK of the nineteenth century, the struggle was centred on extending and accommodating a variety of Christian confessional traditions, rather than (as in many other European countries) defining the relationship between two roughly equal Christian blocs or between one majority and one minority Christian tradition. In the UK of the twenty-first century, commentators are concerned with extending and accommodating a wider variety of religious plurality than in those countries where Muslims form the only visible and numerically significant minority that is other than Christian.

Against this background and approach, in this closing section I would like to highlight two concurrent, and in some ways contrasting, approaches to the integration of religious minorities and the governance of religious diversity that, in the last decade, have emerged in the United Kingdom.

The first approach acknowledges the fact that religious groups are bearers of significant social capital. As such, religions have increasingly been factored into government policy for the delivery of services. This represents a shift from the position of a secular society in which religions (other than the established Churches of England and of Scotland) had been excluded from many aspects of public life. A context has now emerged in which religious groups are seen as valuable social partners.

The second approach surfaced after *The Satanic Verses* controversy, and especially after the 7 July 2005 attacks in the UK. At this point, religions became associated in government thinking with the dangers of radicalization, with religious extremism, and with terror. As a result, the government has developed a new emphasis on integration and on what it posits as being the shared values of "Britishness." In this, it is arguable that the effective meaning of integration has shifted from the multiculturalism that undergirded UK social policy in these areas for the past four decades to a contemporary social and political agenda associated with assimilation—one that previously had been rejected in favour of integration.

Religion, Social Capital, and Civil Society

In recent decades, governments of all political positions have become more modest and skeptical about what the state can achieve. As a consequence, governments have increasingly looked for partners in civil society in the development of appropriate social policy and in the implementation of public services. Given that religions involve substantially more people than any other sector of civil society, religious groups and organizations have also, increasingly, become involved in such provision (Smith 2002, 2003, 2004).

This pragmatic approach has been informed by the concept of social capital drawn from the work of American political scientist Robert Putnam (1995, 2000). For Putnam, religious groups can produce both bonding social capital (the kind of energies that create solidarity within a particular group) and bridging social capital (the kind of energies that link groups to the broader society) that can benefit the wider society (Furbey et al. 2006).

In terms of the concrete implementation of this kind of thinking, one of the earliest developments was the formation, in 1992, of the Inner Cities Religious Council (ICRC). The ICRC was created as part of the then Tory government's response to the issues raised by a Church of England report, *Faith in the City* (Archbishop's Commission on Urban Priority Areas 1985). The work of the Council (Beales 1994) stimulated the wider engagement of religious groups in urban regeneration (Ahmed, Finneron, and Singh 2004; Farnell et al. 2003).

At the local level, in fact, quite an extensive range of structures and initiatives have emerged that are concerned with facilitating interaction between the Christian, secular, and religiously plural dimensions of the UK religious landscape. Religious groups and public authorities are increasingly collaborating at regional (Northwest Development Agency 2003), county (Bates and Collishaw 2006) and local city/town levels (Ravat 2004) to document the contributions of religious groups to the wider society. At the same time, City Partnership arrangements and Regional Assemblies (both of which engage local authorities, businesses, and the voluntary and community sectors) have gradually become more religiously inclusive; generally, they no longer liaise with the churches alone but seek to involve a wider range of religious groups in their work.

Consequently, a series of "good practice" guides have been produced in which national and local government units have worked together with the Inter Faith Network, the Inner Cities Religious Council, and also the Faith Based Regeneration Network. Guides of this kind include the Inter Faith Network for the UK and Inner Cities Religious Council's (1999) *Local Inter Faith Guide: Faith Community Co-operation in Action*; the Local Government Association's (2002) *Faith and Community: A Good Practice Guide for Local Authorities*; and the Inter Faith Network's (2003b) *Partnership for the Common Good*.[19]

Religion, "Extremism," Conflict, and Terror

Since the mid-1960s, the social policy and political consensus in the UK that has underlain the equality and diversity policies of central and local governments and other significant social institutions, and which has been shaping the development of law in this field, has been predicated on the promotion of multiculturalism (Parekh 2000; Rex 1985).

The content of such multiculturalism was classically and perhaps most clearly articulated by the former Labour government Home Secretary, Roy (now Lord) Jenkins, who was the architect of the UK's 1968 *Race Relations Act*. Jenkins (1967, 269) argued, "I do not think that we need in this country a melting-pot, which will turn everybody out in a common mould, as one of a series of someone's misplaced vision of the stereotyped Englishman." Rather, he clarified that the aim of government policy was to support integration—understood in those days as the opposite of assimilation. He defined integration as "equal opportunity, coupled with cultural diversity, in an atmosphere of mutual tolerance."

During the 1990s, this vision of multiculturalism came under strain with questions increasingly being raised about whether it could engage with and adequately address emergent developments and realities. An early sign of this was seen in the controversy that surrounded

Salman Rushdie's (1988) book, *The Satanic Verses*. In response to this even Jenkins (1989, 89) was recorded as saying, "In retrospect, we might have been more cautious about allowing the creation in the 1950s of substantial Muslim communities here." The writer Fay Weldon (1989, 31) put it even more starkly: "Our attempt at multiculturalism has failed. The Rushdie Affair demonstrates it."

However, while the controversy did provoke threats of violence against the author and his publishers and some actual violence in the UK (elsewhere it elicited much more actual violence), the conflict over *The Satanic Verses* was conducted primarily in the sphere of culture— although the book-burning and demonstrations associated with it indicated an increasing radicalization of Muslim concerns and demands. But it was following the disturbances in the summer of 2001 in some northern mill towns, and then the seismic global shock of 11 September, that policy development informed by the notion of social cohesion became very much a part of the agenda of national and local governments.

Some of the issues involved were explored in the Denham (2001) report on *Cohesive Communities* and in the Cantle (2001) report on *Community Cohesion*. The emphasis on social cohesion in many ways contrasted sharply with a vision of the UK—advocated earlier by the independent Parekh report of the Commission on the Future of Multi-Ethnic Britain (2000), commissioned by the Runnymede Trust—as a "community of communities." This new emphasis gathered pace and intensity following the Madrid train bombing of March 2004 and, much closer to home, the London Transport bombings of 7 July 2005 (sometimes known, by analogy with 9/11, as 7/7), which resulted in the death of 52 people and the injury of 700 others.

This event in London, followed two weeks later by a failed attempt, resulted in what I have elsewhere described as a "social policy shock" (Weller 2008, 195). The 7/7 suicide bombings were the first to have occurred in Europe and were carried out by young men brought up in the UK who were, to all outward appearances, integrated members of British society. Instead of asking about the degree to which any experience of religious discrimination or Islamophobia—coupled with issues related to foreign policy in Bosnia, Chechnya, Palestine/Israel, Afghanistan, and Iraq—might have set the stage for (though, of course, not excused) the actions of the bombers, the spotlight of public discourse was shone immediately on concerns about religious "extremism" and religious "radicalism," supplemented by a wish to identify the shared values of what, increasingly, people called "Britishness."

The change of approach in both attitude and social policy that accompanied a general sense of alarm following the attacks in London was highlighted in a statement released by the chair of the (former) Commission for Racial Equality, Trevor Phillips, on 22 September 2005.

Phillips (2005) argued that "the aftermath [of the bombing of July 2005] forces us to assess where we are. And here is where I think we are: we are sleepwalking our way to segregation. We are becoming strangers to each other, and we are leaving communities to be marooned outside the mainstream."

At the government level, following a 2006 Cabinet reshuffle, the new emphasis on cohesion led to the establishment of a Race, Cohesion and Faiths Directorate in what became the newly created Department for Communities and Local Government. The Directorate has continued the work initiated by the former Faith Communities Unit in the Home Office, but it is also engaged with the wider agendas of race and cohesion. Significantly, along with promoting interfaith activity in England and Wales and engaging with faith communities to ensure that government policies and services are delivered in appropriate and equitable ways, the new Directorate was also made responsible for tackling racism, extremism, and hate.

In 2006, against the background of the growing concerns around cohesion, the Department for Communities and Local Government set up a Commission on Integration and Cohesion that published a report in 2007 entitled *Our Shared Future*. While the report approaches the concept of cohesion in a more sophisticated way than many politicians do, it nevertheless clearly emphasizes the importance of integration and cohesion. But in the way in which many policy-makers are now seeking to implement cohesion, the question could be posed as to whether, after 40 years, social policy might be coming almost full circle so that integration has come to mean roughly what used to be meant by assimilation.

The Challenge of "Rebalancing" Religion and Governance

In closing, it would seem that something of the *significance* of religion in the lives of individuals and groups is now better understood—at national, regional, and local levels—while, for a variety of reasons, the state has become more attuned to the social resources that religious groups can deploy on the basis of their significant presence and role in civil society. At the same time, there has been an increasing consciousness of the challenges that religious claims and communities can pose to secular presuppositions, as well as of the potentiality that exists within religions for conflict and illiberalism.

What is common to both approaches at the start of the twenty-first century, and in contrast to the position in the 1970s and early 1980s, is that the salience of religion in the lives of individuals and communities is now quite clear. But there is also considerable tension between these two concurrent and contrasting strands of social policy. How a partnership with religions in the provision of social capital will play out in relation to the fear of extremism and emphasis on social cohesion in the UK, and which approach will predominate as we enter the second decade of the new millennium, has yet to be seen.

When one sets these issues within a wider context than that of the UK alone, the complexity and challenges become even more apparent. One wider context is, of course, that of the European Union in its continuing process of social, political, and economic integration. However, beyond that are also issues arising from the relationship between religion and governance across the whole of the Eurasian geopolitical landmass. And, in a globalizing world, no country is an island.

Notes

1. At the same time, the Church of Scotland's formal link with the Crown is symbolized by the Lord High Commissioner's presence at its annual General Assembly.

2. Thus, in England and Wales, the form of the census question on religion was "What is your religion?" Christian respondents were offered the response of "Christian," which included Church of England, Catholic, Protestant, and all other Christian denominations. By contrast, in Scotland, there were two questions: "What religion, religious body or denomination do you belong to?" and "What religion, religious body or denomination were you brought up in?", with the subcategories of "Church of Scotland," "Roman Catholic," and "Other Christian, please write in" offered to respondents. In Northern Ireland, for the question "What religion, religious body or denomination do you belong to?", the Christian-related pre-set responses offered were "Roman Catholic," "Presbyterian Church in Ireland," "Church of Ireland," "Methodist Church in Ireland," and "Other Christian, please write in" (Weller 2004).

3. As a proportion of the total population in local authority areas, the 2001 census shows that in England the greatest concentration of respondents identifying themselves as Muslims is to be found in the London Boroughs of Tower Hamlets (36.4 percent) and Newham (24.3 percent), Blackburn and Darwen (19.4 percent), Bradford (16.1 percent), and in the London Borough of Waltham Forest (15.1 percent). Among Sikhs, it is to be found in the London Boroughs of Slough (9.1 percent), Hounslow (8.6 percent), and Ealing (8.5 percent); and in Wolverhampton (7.6 percent) and Sandwell (6.9 percent). Among Hindus, the London Boroughs of Harrow (19.6 percent) and Brent (17.2 percent), Leicester (14.7 percent), and the London Boroughs of Redbridge (7.8 percent) and Ealing (7.8 percent) have the greatest concentration of respondents. Among Jews, concentrations can be found in the London Borough of Barnet (14.8 percent); Hertsmere (11.3 percent); and the London Boroughs of Harrow (6.3 percent), Redbridge (6.2 percent), and Camden (5.6 percent). Among Buddhists, concentrations are found in

the London Boroughs of Westminster (1.3 percent), Camden (1.3 percent), Kensington and Chelsea (1.1 percent), and Hackney (1.1 percent); and in the Ribble Valley (1.1 percent).

4. A total of 6.9 percent (2,900,000) were Presbyterian; 3.3 percent (1,400,000) were "All Other Churches"; 3.1 percent (1,300,000) were Methodist; 1.2 percent (500,000) were Baptist; 1.2 percent (500,000) were Orthodox; 1.0 percent (400,000) were Independent; 1.0 percent (400,000) were New Churches; and 1.0 percent (400,000) were Pentecostal.

5. With Presbyterians at 16.2 percent (958,268); Methodists at 5.2 percent (343,696); Orthodox at 4.3 percent (255,308); Pentecostal at 4.3 percent (253,722); Baptists at 3.6 percent (215,062); Independents at 3.2 percent (187,497); Other Churches (including, for example, Christian Brethren, Congregationalists, Lutherans, Moravians, and Salvationists) at 2.4 percent (139,983); and New Churches at 2.3 percent (136,054).

6. These include Barelwi organizations such as the Jamaat Ahl-e-Sunnat and the World Islamic Mission, Deobandi groups such as the Jamiat-e-Ulama of Britain, and the Tablighi Jamaat movement (which is linked closely with the Deobandi). The Ahl-e-Hadith and Jamaat-i-Islami movement (linked closely with the UK Islamic Mission) are also present, while Bengali Muslims have established Dawatul-Islam.

7. There are roughly 715 Muslim places of worship in the UK, of which approximately 656 are in England, 24 in Scotland, 24 in Wales, and 1 in Northern Ireland (Weller 2007). There are also an estimated 125 Muslim organizations that operate on a UK basis and at least 2 that operate on a Welsh level. Finally, there are approximately 1,153 local Muslim organizations, of which approximately 1,074 are in England, 36 in Wales, and 43 in Scotland.

8. There are, of course, also what often have been seen as more controversial and less "mainstream" Muslim groups, such as Al-Muhajiroun and Hizb-ut-Tahrir. These groups have been activist in style and oriented toward issues of justice for Muslims and the establishment of a global Muslim caliphate.

9. There are roughly 100 Hindu places of worship in the UK, of which around 92 are in England, 4 in Scotland, 2 in Wales, and 2 in Northern Ireland (Weller 2007). There are also approximately 75 Hindu organizations with a UK scope, together with around 15 organizations working at a regional level in England, 2 in Scotland, and 1 in Wales. Finally, there are approximately 702 local Hindu organizations (including around 683 in England, 9 in Wales, 5 in Scotland, and 5 in Northern Ireland).

10. Examples of national *jati* associations include the Gujarati Federation of Anavil Samaj, the National Association of Patidar Samaj, and the Shri Kutch Leva Patel Samaj.

11. The largest Swaminaryan group in the UK is the Akshar Purushottam Sanstha (the Swaminarayan Hindu Mission), with its headquarters in the purpose-built and classically constructed temple in Neasden, London.

12. There are roughly 194 gurdwaras in the UK: 179 in England, 9 in Scotland, 4 in Wales, and 2 in Northern Ireland (Weller 2007). Moreover, approximately 28 Sikh organizations operate at a UK level. At the regional level, there are some 4 Sikh organizations in England, 1 in Scotland, and 1 in Northern Ireland. At the local level, approximately 280 Sikh organizations exist in the UK: 264 in England, 9 in Scotland, 4 in Wales, and 3 in Northern Ireland.

13. There are around 94 Buddhist centres, monasteries, and places of worship in the UK, of which 84 are in England, 5 in Wales, 3 in Scotland, and 2 in Northern Ireland (Weller 2007). As well, there are roughly 70 Buddhist organizations working at a UK level and 1 Buddhist organization working at each of the English, Scottish, Irish, and Welsh levels. At the local level, there are approximately 422 Buddhist local organizations, including 364 in England, 30 in Wales, 23 in Scotland, and 5 in Northern Ireland.

14. There are roughly 201 synagogues in the UK: 196 in England, 3 in Scotland, and 2 in Wales (Weller 2007). Moreover, approximately 174 Jewish organizations are working at a UK level, 6 at a Scottish level, and 1 at a Welsh level. Six regional-level organizations operate in England, as well as 1 in Northern Ireland and 1 in Scotland. Finally, statistics indicate the existence of around 333 local Jewish organizations, including 327 in England, 4 in Scotland, and 2 in Wales.

15. An analysis of responses to the "other religions" write-in option indicates that there were 3,355 Zoroastrian respondents in England and 383 in Wales. At the same time, the internal records of the Zoroastrian Trust Funds of Europe Incorporated suggest a population of over 5,000 Zoroastrians across the UK as a whole.

16. They included Dadabhoy Naoroji, the Liberal Member of Parliament for Finchley from 1892–1895; Sir Muncherji Bhownagree, a Conservative MP for Bethnal Green North East from 1895–1906; and Shapirji Saklatvala, MP for Battersea from 1922–1929, first for the Labour Party and then becoming the only Communist Party member ever elected to the Westminster Parliament.

17. There are no traditional, formally consecrated, Zoroastrian Fire Temples in the UK. There is, however, a room for Zoroastrian worship at the new Zoroastrian Centre in Harrow, Middlesex, which is now the headquarters of the Zororastrian Trust Funds of Europe and has become the central focal point for Zoroastrian worship and community activity in the UK.

18. The city of Leicester is home to the only purpose-built Jain Temple in Europe.

19. At a UK level, the high watermark of this line of approach could arguably be located in the report produced by the (then) Home Office Faith Communities Unit (2004), *Working Together: Co-operation between Government and Faith Communities.*

References

Adams, C. 1987. *Across Seven Seas and Thirteen Rivers*. London: Tower Hamlets Arts Project.

Ahmed, R., D. Finneron, and H. Singh. 2004. *Tools for Regeneration: A Holistic Approach for Faith Communities*. London: Faith-Based Regeneration Network.

Almond, P.C. 1988. *The British Discovery of Buddhism*. Cambridge: Cambridge University Press.

Archbishop's Commission on Urban Priority Areas. 1985. *Faith in the City: A Call for Action by Church and Nation – The Report of the Archbishop of Canterbury's Commission on Urban Priority Areas*. London: Church House.

Ballard, R., ed. 1994. *Desh Pardesh: The South Asian Presence in Britain*. London: Hurst and Company.

— 2000. "The Growth and Changing Character of the Sikh Presence in Britain." In *The South Asian Religious Diaspora in Britain, Canada and the United States*, ed. H. Coward, J.R. Hinnells, and R. Brady. New York: State University of New York Press.

Barker, E., J.A. Beckford, and K. Dobbelaere, eds. 1993. *Secularisation, Rationalism and Sectarianism*. Oxford: Oxford University Press.

Barnes, L.P. 2002. "Was the Northern Ireland Conflict Religious?" *Journal of Beliefs and Values* 20(1):53-67.

Bates, J. and S. Collishaw. 2006. *Faith in Derbyshire: Working Towards a Better Derbyshire: Faith-Based Contribution*. Derby, UK: Derby Diocesan Council for Social Responsibility.

Beales, C. 1994. "Partnerships for a Change: The Inner Cities Religious Council." *World Faiths Encounter* 8 July: 41-46.

Beckford, J.A. and S. Gilliat. 1998. *Religion in Prison: Equal Rites in a Multi-Faith Society*. Cambridge: Cambridge University Press.

Bisset, P. 1986. *The Kirk and Her Scotland*. Edinburgh: Handsel.

Brierley, P., ed. 2004. *UK Christian Handbook: Religious Trends No. 6, 2003/2004*. London: Christian Research.

British Council of Churches. 1976. *The New Black Presence in Britain: A Christian Scrutiny*. London: British Council of Churches.

Bruce, S. 1986. *God Save Ulster: The Religion and Politics of Paisleyism*. Oxford: Oxford University Press.

— 1992. *Religion and Modernisation: Sociologists and Historians Debate the Secularisation Thesis*. Oxford: Oxford University Press.

Cantle, T. 2001. *Community Cohesion: Report of the Independent Review Team*. Chaired by Ted Cantle. London: Home Office.

Coward, H., J.R. Hinnells, and R. Brady, eds. 2000. *The South Asian Religious Diaspora in Britain, Canada and the United States*. New York: State University of New York Press.

Davie, G. 1990a. "Believing Without Belonging: Is This the Future of Religion in Britain?" *Social Compass* 37:455-69.

— 1990b. "An Ordinary God: The Paradox of Religion in Contemporary Britain." *British Journal of Sociology* 41(3):395-421.

Denham, J. 2001. *Building Cohesive Communities: A Report of the Ministerial Group.* Chaired by John Denham. London: Home Office.

Dobbelaere, K. 1981. "Secularisation: A Multi-Dimensional Concept." *Current Sociology* 29(2):1-216.

— 1984. "Secularisation Theories and Sociological Paradigms: Convergences and Divergences." *Social Compass* 31:199-219.

Farnell, R., R. Furbey, S.S. al-Haqq Hills, M. Macey, and G. Smith. 2003. *"Faith" in Urban Regeneration? Engaging Faith Communities in Urban Regeneration.* Bristol: Policy Press.

Fisher, M.H., S. Lahiri, and S. Thandi, eds. 2007. *A South-Asian History of Britain: Four Centuries of Peoples from the Indian Sub-Continent.* Oxford: Greenwood World Publishing.

Furbey, R., A. Dinham, R. Farnell, D. Finneron, and G. Wilkinson. 2006. *Faith as Social Capital: Connecting or Dividing?* Bristol, UK: Policy Press.

Gerloff, R. 1992. *A Plea for British Black Theologies: The Black Church Movement in Britain in Its Transatlantic Cultural and Theological Interaction, Parts I & II.* Frankfurt, Germany: Peter Lang.

Halliday, F. 1992. *Arabs in Exile: Yemeni Migrants in Urban Britain.* London: I.B. Tauris.

Halman, L. 2001. *The European Values Study: A Third Wave. Sourcebook of 1999/ 2000 European Values Study Survey.* Tilburg, The Netherlands: WORC Tilburg University.

Hastings, A. 1991. *Church and State: The English Experience.* Exeter, UK: Exeter University Press.

Hill, C. 1975. *The World Turned Upside Down: Radical Ideas during the Revolution.* Harmondsworth, UK: Penguin.

Hinnells, J. 2000. "The Zoroastrian Diaspora in Britain, Canada and the United States." In *The South Asian Diaspora in Britain, Canada and the United States,* ed. H. Coward, J.R. Hinnells, and R. Brady. New York: State University of New York Press.

Humphreys, C. 1968. *Sixty Years of Buddhism in England 1907–1967: A History and a Survey.* London: The Buddhist Society.

Inter Faith Network for the UK. 2003a. *Inter Faith Update,* 21 (Spring).

— 2003b. *Partnership for the Common Good: Inter Faith Structures and Local Government.* London: Inter Faith Network for the UK.

Inter Faith Network for the UK and Inner Cities Religious Council. 1999. *The Local Inter Faith Guide: Faith Community Co-operation in Action.* London: Inter Faith Network for the United Kingdom in association with the Inner Cities Religious Council of the Department for the Environment, Transport, and the Regions.

Ipgrave, M. 2003. "Fidei Defensor Revisited: Church and State in a Religiously Plural Society." In *The Challenge of Religious Discrimination at the Dawn of the New Millennium,* ed. N. Ghanea. Leiden, The Netherlands: Martinus Nijhoff.

Jacobsen, K.A. and P.P. Kumar, eds. 2004. *South Asians in the Diaspora: Histories and Religious Traditions*. Leiden, The Netherlands: E.J. Brill.

Jenkins, R. 1967. *Essays and Speeches*. London: Collins.

— 1989. "On Race Relations and the Rushdie Affair." *The Independent Magazine*, 14(3):89.

Knott, K. 1996. "The Religions of South Asian Communities in Britain." In *The New Handbook of Living Religions*, ed. J.R. Hinnells. Oxford: Blackwell.

— 2000. "Hinduism in Britain." In *The South Asian Religious Diaspora in Britain, Canada and the United States*, ed. H. Coward, J.R. Hinnells, and R. Brady. New York: State University of New York Press.

Madeley, J. and Z. Enyedi, eds. 2003. *Church and State in Contemporary Europe: The Chimera of Neutrality*. London: Frank Cass.

Marotti, A.F. 2005. *Religious Ideology and Cultural Fantasy: Catholic and Anti-Catholic Discourses in Early Modern England*. Notre Dame, IN: University of Notre Dame.

Martin, D. 1978. *A General Theory of Secularisation*. Oxford: Blackwell.

McSweeney, B. 1989. "The Religious Dimension of 'The Troubles' in Northern Ireland." In *Religion, State and Society in Modern Britain*, ed. P. Badham. Lampeter, Wales: Edwin Mellen Press.

Modood, T., ed. 1997. *Church, State and Religious Minorities*. London: Policy Studies Institute.

Modood, T., S. Beishon, and S. Virdee. 1994. *Changing Ethnic Identities*. London: Policy Studies Institute.

Northwest Development Agency. 2003. *Faith in England's Northwest: The Contribution Made by Faith Communities to Civic Society in the Region*. Warrington: Northwest Development Agency.

O'Beirne, M. 2004. *Religion in England and Wales: Findings from the 2001 Home Office Citizenship Survey*. Home Office Research Study 274. London: Home Office.

Parekh, B. 2000. *Rethinking Multiculturalism: Cultural Diversity and Political Theory*. Basingstoke, UK: Macmillan.

Peach, C. 2006. "Islam, Ethnicity and South Asian Religions in the London 2001 Census." *Transactions of the Institute of British Geographers* 31:353-70.

Phillips, T. 2005. "After 7/7: Sleepwalking to Segregation." Commission for Racial Equality, 22 September.

Putnam, R.D. 1995. "Bowling Alone: America's Declining Social Capital." *Journal of Democracy* 2:65-78.

— 2000. *Bowling Alone: The Collapse and Revival of American Community*. New York: Simon and Schuster.

Ravat, R. 2004. *Enabling the Present: Planning for the Future – Social Action by the Faith Communities of Leicester*. Leicester, UK: Leicester Faiths Regeneration Project.

Raza, M.S. 1992. *Islam in Britain: Past, Present and Future*. 2nd edition. London: Volcano Press.

Rex, J. 1985. *The Concept of a Multi-Cultural Society.* Coventry, UK: University of Warwick Centre for Research in Ethnic Relations.

Robilliard, St. John A. 1984. *Religion and the Law: Religious Liberty in Modern English Law.* Manchester, UK: Manchester University Press.

Robinson, F. 1988. "Varieties of South Asian Islam." Centre for Research in Ethnic Relations, Research Paper No. 8, University of Warwick, Coventry.

Roth, C. 1978. *A History of the Jews in England.* Oxford: Clarendon.

Rushdie, S. 1988. *The Satanic Verses.* London: Viking Penguin.

Ryan, M. 1996. *Another Ireland: An Introduction to Ireland's Ethno-Religious Minority Communities.* Belfast, Northern Ireland: Stranmillis College.

Sancho, I. 1782. *Letters of the Late Ignatius Sancho, an African.* London: J. Dodsley.

Smith, G. 2002. "Religion and the Rise of Social Capitalism: The Faith Communities in Community Development and Urban Regeneration in England." *Community Development Journal* 37(2):166-77.

— 2003. *Faith in the Voluntary Sector: A Common or Distinctive Experience of Religious Organisations.* Working Papers in Applied Social Research, No. 25, Department of Sociology, University of Manchester.

— 2004. "Faith in Community and Communities of Faith? Government Rhetoric and Religious Identity in Urban Britain." *Journal of Contemporary Religion* 19(2):185-204.

Ter Haar, G. 1998. *Halfway to Paradise: African Christians in Europe.* Cardiff, Wales: Cardiff Academic Press.

The Governance of Britain. 2007. Cm. 7170. London: Stationery Office.

United Kingdom. Commission on Integration and Cohesion. 2007. *Our Shared Future.* London: Department for Communities and Local Government.

United Kingdom. Commission on the Future of Multi-Ethnic Britain. 2000. *The Future of Multi-Ethnic Britain.* London: Profile Books.

United Kingdom. Home Office Faith Communities Unit. 2004. *Working Together: Co-operation between Government and Faith Communities. Recommendations of the Steering Group Reviewing Patterns of Engagement between Government and Faith Communities in England.* London: Faith Communities Unit, Home Office.

United Kingdom. Local Government Association. 2002. *Faith and Community: A Good Practice Guide.* London: Local Government Association Publications.

United Kingdom. Office for National Statistics. 2001 Census. Available at http://www.ons.gov.uk/census/index.html

— 2003. *Classification of Denominations and Production of Annual Statistics for England and Wales on 30th June.* London.

United Kingdom. Royal Commission on the Reform of the House of Lords. 2000. *A House for the Future.* Cmd. 4534. London: Stationery Office.

Visram, R. 1986. *Ayahs, Lascars and Princes: The Story of Indians in Britain, 1700–1947.* London: Pluto Press.

Voas, D. 2003. "Is Britain a Christian Country?" In *Public Faith: The State of Religious Belief and Practice in Britain,* ed. P.D.L. Avis. London: Society for Promoting Christian Knowledge.

Voas, D. and S. Bruce. 2004. "The 2001 Census and Christian Identification in Britain." *Journal of Contemporary Religion* 19(1):23-28.

Weldon, F. 1989. *Sacred Cows: A Portrait of Britain, Post-Rushdie, Pre-Utopia.* London: Chatto and Windus.

Weller, P. 2000. "Equity, Inclusivity and Participation in a Plural Society: Challenging the Establishment of the Church of England." In *Law and Religion in Contemporary Societies: Communities, Individualism and the State,* ed. P.W. Edge and G. Harvey. Aldershot, UK: Ashgate.

— 2004. "Identity Politics and the Future(s) of Religion Questions in the 2001 Decennial Census." *Journal of Contemporary Religion* 19(1):3-21.

— 2005. *Time for a Change: Reconfiguring Religion, State and Society.* London: T. and T. Clark.

— 2007. *Religions in the UK: Directory 2007–10.* Derby, UK: Multi-Faith Centre at the University of Derby in association with the University of Derby.

— 2008. *Religious Diversity in the UK: Contours and Issues.* London: Continuum.

Weller, P., A. Feldman, and K. Purdam, et al. 2000. *Religious Discrimination in England and Wales: Interim Report January 2000.* Derby: University of Derby.

Weller, P., A. Feldman, and K. Purdam, et al. 2001. *Religious Discrimination in England and Wales: Home Office Research Study 220.* London: Home Office Research, Development and Statistics Directorate.

Wolffe, J., ed. 1993. *The Growth of Religious Diversity: Britain from 1945. A Reader.* Sevenoaks: Hodder and Stoughton.

Chapter 8

Islam, Immigration, and France

JOCELYNE CESARI

Since the Second World War, immigration to France has been dominated by Muslims to such an extent that "immigration" and "Islam" are now virtually synonymous terms in both public and academic discourses. For this reason, the question of integrating new religious groups has mainly concerned Muslims even though there is also a growing academic literature on other immigrant religious groups (e.g., Massignon 2000).

The large number of Muslims in France resulted from three migratory movements of the twentieth century. The first occurred between the First and Second World Wars, when Muslim workers from the French colonies were drawn into France to fill a labour gap in the post-war reconstruction boom. These Muslims were not technically immigrants, however. Most of them were French nationals coming from Algeria which, at the time, was a part of France.

Ideologies of the day emphasized ideas of nationalism, anti-imperialism, and socialism, but *not* Islam as a means of mobilizing and giving voice to migrant workers. Moreover, the Muslims in France were an anonymous and largely silent mass of unskilled male labourers working mostly in industry. Most of these workers had left their families behind and intended to earn as much money as possible and then return home. Thus their own views dovetailed with the official outlook of their host and home countries—that this migration was only a temporary one. The second wave from the 1950s to 1974 was an intensification of the first, with one crucial difference: the workers were now nationals of newly independent states.[1]

The 1973 oil crisis signalled the end of this period of French and European economic prosperity, and the process of Muslim immigration entered a third phase. Although European countries closed the doors

International Migration and the Governance of Religious Diversity, eds. P. Bramadat and M. Koenig.
Montreal and Kingston: McGill-Queen's University Press, Queen's Policy Studies Series.
© 2009 The School of Policy Studies, Queen's University at Kingston. All rights reserved.

to unskilled immigrant workers in the 1980s, many earlier immigrants still remained, and family reunification policies now supported the immigration of their wives and children. These newly reunited families moved from the segregated environment of the workers' dormitory to the integrated world of the public housing project, and they increasingly came into contact with representatives of the school system, members of the bureaucracy, and social workers. As Muslim communities came to terms with their status as permanent residents of Europe, prayer rooms began to appear not only in Paris and Marseille but also in London, Bradford, and Berlin. By the end of the 1990s, there were more than a thousand mosques in France, and that number continues to grow.[2] These institutions both reflected and reinforced the growth of Muslim social and religious life, and so gradually Muslims began to demand that mosques receive official recognition and status equal to that of temples, churches, and synagogues. Thus, during this third period of immigration, the visibility of Muslims increased dramatically, crystallizing in 1989 with the beginning of the headscarf crisis. In turn, this visibility raised questions about Muslims' loyalty in the minds of Europeans, who tended to perceive affiliation with Islam as a rejection of mainstream society.

At the same time that French Islam was becoming more visible, Islam was also emerging in the 1980s as a major political force on the international stage and in Muslim-majority countries. This was the decade when Saudi Arabia, Pakistan, and Iran competed (and still do) in efforts to dominate the Muslim world. Long before September 11th, the Muslims of Europe were already quite familiar with perceptions of domestic Islam as a kind of fifth column. The deployment of the Vigipirate plan, the state's new anti-terrorism policy, after the 1995 Paris subway bombings vividly illustrates the long-standing French belief in collusion between the enemy outside and the enemy within. The attack was attributed to the Algerian Armed Islamic Group (GIA), and police responded by targeting French youth from North African backgrounds for extensive surveillance and profiling.

Nevertheless, surveys since the 1980s show that, through the development of Islamic structures and activities, Muslim immigrants have actually come to accept the dominant French culture (Kepel 1994, 1997). Despite this growing acceptance, the French public continues to view Muslims in terms of the colonial and post-colonial aspects of their presence. The public has thus been slow to realize and accept that Islam has become a permanent part of the religious landscape of France. Moreover, because the evolution of Muslims from foreigners to citizens has been a sign of the definitive end of France's universalist and imperialist pretensions, the Muslim presence has often been viewed as a sign of European cultural decline and has therefore met with serious resistance.

The Sociology of French Islam

Islam is today the subject of extensive studies in the sociology of immigration. Oddly enough, religion in general and Islam in particular had long been neglected in studies of immigration, both in Europe and in the United States (Ebaugh and Chafetz 2000; Warner 1998). In the case of France, however, the sociology of Islam was far more developed than in any other Western country. Indeed, when I first began my career as a researcher in the mid-1980s, the existing knowledge about Muslims came primarily from the sociology of immigration (at that point almost all Muslims in Europe were immigrants). This early research (which continues to be relevant) focused on the ways Muslims integrated into French society. In France, as in Europe in general, the key question was to discover whether the integration process for Muslims was similar to that experienced by other immigrants, or if their Muslim identity introduced something new and specific (Buijs and Rath 2003). Sociologists specializing in immigration in France (and in Europe in general) were and are inclined to see the religious identification of immigrants as merely a "given," tangential to the immigration process and thus unworthy of detailed analysis. Other factors such as one's position in the economic marketplace, as well as social and political relationships, continue to be seen as more important than religious identification (Tarrius, Marotel, and Peraldi 1988; Wenden 1988, 1993).

Several reasons may explain this present lack of interest in Islam as a religion in France. First, most French sociologists of immigration have been influenced by a Marxist ideology that interprets religion as a sign of alienation and as an epiphenomenon of the economy. Second, French sociology and anthropology have been dominated by class analysis. Third, as I discuss below in the section on secularism, most of the scholars in question share the assumptions associated with secular nationalism. Finally, as François Dubet (1989, 118-19) has noted,

> The most salient feature of the relationship of the researcher to his research topic is not so much to identify with the studied group but to implicitly try to counter racist or supposedly racist arguments. These silent debates with racism lead to a lack of knowledge because the main goal is not to know what is true but to defend what is just.[3]

In other words, the work of French sociologists took place within the context of intense ideological debate on the legitimacy of immigration to France, colouring the moral assumptions guiding their work.

Despite the relatively superficial scholarly attention paid to Islam as a religious force within the French sociology of immigration, French political scientists have been studying Muslim immigrants since the

1980s and their work has dominated the sociology of French Islam. Scholars like Bruno Etienne, Rémy Leveau, and Gilles Kepel began as experts of Islam in Middle Eastern or North African societies and later redirected their studies toward French Islam (Etienne 1987, 1989; Kepel 1987, 1990; Leveau 1993; Leveau and Kepel 1987). Most of this research was motivated by the desire to counter rising political sentiments within the dominant French society against the integration and recognition of Muslim populations. The political sociology of French Islam thus largely focuses on Muslim organizations and their relationship to mainstream political institutions (the French state, local powers, and political parties). It also looks at political movements such as the Muslim Brotherhood, and Jihadi or Salafi groups that influence or shape the mobilization of French Muslims. Few surveys, however, have been conducted on the religious practices and opinions of Muslims themselves and how they relate to the process of migration. This rich area of scholarship was considered irrelevant by most scholars. It is not surprising that Charnay's pioneering 1977 book on the sociology of Islam was ignored at the time in French academic circles (Charnay 1977).

From the 1990s onward, with the rise of a new generation of scholars, the question of the status of religion in modern society has become more and more central to the research on French Islam. This approach was initiated by Belgian sociologist Félice Dassetto who influenced a significant number of scholars of this new generation by employing the methods of the theorist Thomas Luckmann (1967) in studying Muslim minorities in Europe (Dassetto 1996). This approach concentrated on the use and reconstruction of religious symbols and knowledge by European Muslims (Dassetto 2000). Because of this groundbreaking work, the relationship between the believer and spiritual goods (beliefs, rituals, moral prescriptions), and the importance of individual choice in religious matters, began to achieve prominence in research on French Islam.

A significant amount of work focuses on the individualization of Islamic practices among new generations of Muslims born or educated in France (Babes 1997; Cesari 1998; Khosrokavar 1997). Individualization of religious choice is presented in much of the contemporary scholarship as a democratization of the religious sphere, especially in contrast with the status of Islam in the country of origin. To be Muslim in France means to lose one's relationship to Islam as a cultural and social *fait accompli*, and instead to open it up to questioning and individual choice. This is not to say that such individualism is a characteristic solely of Western Islam: in the Muslim world, people make individual choices and question their relationship to tradition. Nevertheless, the context of such individualism is quite different in the West. In secular democracies, the multiplicity of possible—and sometimes contradictory—choices is not only more noticeable but also more accepted. While first-generation immigrants often live in a state of relative harmony with the religious, social, and national aspects of identity, their children face a tension, if not an outright conflict, between the layers of individual, collective, and national identity. And in a society that is at best indifferent and at worst hostile toward Islam, to be Muslim no longer seems a given.

The individualization of religious practice thus leads to a range of possible Muslim identities that have been explored and classified (Cesari 2004). Some work focuses on female religiosity and its relationship to Islamic prescriptions on dress code (Boubakeur 2004; Venel 2004; Weibel 2000). These scholars note that while the hijab is viewed by many outsiders as a symbol of patriarchal oppression, in fact, many French Muslim women actually voluntarily wear the veil. Nevertheless, scholars do not agree on the overall outcomes of this individualization process. In other words, does it lead to a liberalization of practice and interpretation, or to greater fundamentalism? Some, like Olivier Roy (2002), contend that individualization actually tends to produce a predominance of fundamentalist interpretations because it makes Muslims more vulnerable to strict doctrines insisting on personal responsibility and the duty of believers to follow Islamic prescriptions. Others argue that both liberal and fundamentalist paths are possible and present among French Muslims in particular and Western Muslims in general (Cesari 2004).

Another research focus among scholars of French Islam centres on religious authorities (Bowen 2004; Caeiro 2005, 2006; Frégosi 1998). The common focus in this area of research is the high fragmentation of religious authority in Islam and its accentuation by the French secular environment. Traditionally, religious authority was conferred upon the body of *ulema* (religious experts) in accordance with their theological knowledge and their mastery of the techniques of interpreting the Qur'an and the Hadith (the deeds and words of the Prophet Muhammad). Only those who possessed knowledge that had been passed down through a chain of authorities or a line of recognized masters could claim legitimacy as religious leaders (Eickelman and Anderson 1999; Messick 1993, 135-51). This method of transmitting religious authority was not necessarily a matter of formal education, particularly if the knowledge passed down was esoteric in nature, as in the case of the Sufi masters. For centuries, the ulema class enjoyed a monopoly of interpretation of the Qur'an and the Hadith. They were creators and guardians of Islamic orthodoxy, by means of a huge body of *muftis* (Islamic scholars who issue *fatwas*, or religious decrees), *qadis* (judges), and other religious agents, such as teachers or guardians of *waqfs* (religious endowments). Under colonial rule, and especially as post-colonial states developed systems of secular education, the situation began to change. The ulema were deprived of their monopoly and secular court systems based on foreign legal codes undermined the ulema's judicial status (Taji-Farouki and Nafi 2004, 1-27).

These social and religious changes have enabled the emergence of a Muslim intellectual class who claim to speak on behalf of Islam. The vast majority of the most influential Muslim thinkers of the twentieth and twenty-first centuries are not members of the trained ulema, but rather graduates of secular universities. Established religious figures like the sheikhs of Al-Azhar or Medina, and other prominent imams, are therefore increasingly being supplanted by the engineer, the secular scholar, the student, the businessman, and the autodidact, who mobilize the masses and speak for Islam in arenas, in stadiums, on the radio, or, more and more commonly, on the Internet. The increased availability of communication technology such as magazines, cassette tapes and, most recently, Internet sites aids in this multiplication of Islamic voices. These changes are exacerbated in the Western context where Muslims are a minority and often lack an institutionalized body of imams.

Most studies on Muslim authorities focus on the interactions between clerics/leaders, Islamic organizations, and French institutions and the ways in which they adapt to one another. By contrast, the struggle within the Islamic community itself over the exercise of authority and the ensuing reconfiguration of traditional authority structures have received little attention from contemporary sociologists of Islam. This is undoubtedly another consequence of the pre-eminence of political scientists in the study of Islam in France. Also significant, however, is the influence of the international agenda in shaping what aspects of Islam to focus on. In the French case, this influence did not start with 9/11 but with the long history of political interactions between France and its former colonies as well as with certain political movements in neighbouring Islamic countries—such as the Islamic Salvation Front (FIS) based in Algeria, or the AKP (Justice and Development Party) in Turkey (a reincarnation of the Refah Party, banned in 1998; Said 1997).

Another research focus to take into consideration here is the centrality of what is called Islamophobia. It should be noted that the term *Islamophobia* emerged as early as 1997, during the discussions in Britain on the topic of anti-Muslim discrimination (Runnymede Trust 1997). Its use has since then spread all over Europe and intensified after 9/11, the Madrid bombing in March 2004, and the London bombings in July 2005. The consequence has been that most of the works on Islam published in France are in fact attempts to combat Islamophobia and deconstruct the misrepresentations and false notions that characterize discrimination against Islam and Muslims. A good example of this kind of scholarship is the book *La nouvelle islamophobie* by Geisser and Lorcerie (2003).

Despite these academic efforts, anti-Islamic discourses have grown in France. During the 1990s in France, anti-Islamic statements were almost exclusively the prerogative of the far right. Today, however, intellectuals, journalists, writers, and artists unashamedly express their aversion to Islam (Geisser and Lorcerie 2003). In an interview in the September 2001 issue of the magazine *Lire*, the writer Michel Houellebecq stated: "Islam is definitely the most f...p of all the religions." Oriana Fallaci's *La rage et l'orgueil* (Rage and Pride), which sold more than a million copies in Italy and France (Fallaci 2002), was an incendiary diatribe against Muslims and the Islamic faith that resulted in the author being prosecuted in October 2003 for inciting racial hatred, although she was not ultimately convicted. That same year, on 24 October, the founder of the newspaper *Le Point* declared himself an Islamophobe, calling Islam an "inanity of various archaisms."[4]

It should be noted that the essentialism depicted by Paul Bramadat in the Introduction of this book, and so often decried when it comes to the study of Islam, is not the major flaw of academic research on Islam in France. This essentialism is not so much ethnocentric as it is normative, an approach that characterizes most of the studies on Muslims in other European countries and in North America but which appears in France most of the time only in non-academic essays by journalists or Muslims themselves. In such normatively oriented depictions, Islam is presented as, above all, a set of decontextualized rules; for example, the five pillars of faith, the dietary rules, and the dress code are described as though these rules represent the core or totality of all Muslims' religious lives.[5] Such a rigid presentation of Islam erases the actual diversity of practices and ways of being Muslim that exist alongside the more orthodox perspectives. It also ignores the importance of the society in which Muslims are living and attempting to practice their faith and the extent to which different contexts often demand the reimagining of a living tradition. Muslims, like all religious believers, are constantly renegotiating their relationship to the dogmas and prescriptions of their tradition. The naïve essentialism described by Paul Bramadat can, however, sometimes be found in the French academy when scholars resort to it in order to fight the hostility toward Islam they can sense in the popular press. Under these conditions, academics have had to devote a fair amount of their research to counter pejorative stereotypes and normative generalizations, often leaving them with little time and space for gathering and comparing solid data about Muslims' actual beliefs and practices (not to mention the fact that such an academic posture borders on apologetic).

Islam as a Discursive Tradition

Although the notion of Islam as a discursive tradition has not been sufficiently developed in the French and Western contexts, a few works have some relevance for the research on Western Islam in general. Schirin Amir-Moazami and Armando Salvatore (2003) use Talal Asad's (1993) definition of tradition to advance the idea that Islam is the sum of Islamic discourses, and to relocate the debate on the individualization of religious practice within the larger context of shifting boundaries of Islamic tradition that are being challenged in various ways throughout the Muslim world. Such a perspective is central to understanding the status of the Islamic religion in France and more generally in the West.

To examine Muslim immigration to Europe or North America is to see the foundational moment of a new transcultural space that still remains to be fully analyzed (Cesari 2004). This transcultural moment is taking place within the current period of globalization characterized by the mobility of cultures and religions. Any understanding of the Muslim minority in the West must therefore take the phenomenon of global Islam into account as well. Once again, the risk is of taking Islam out of context and reducing it to a series of essentialized symbols and principles. In order to break through the iron cage of stereotypical Islamic images and representations, then, one must consider discursive practices of religion in general, and of Islam in particular. That is, instead of trying to discover what constitutes the essential nature of Islam, one must examine the social and historical contexts within which Muslims create their discourse on what is important or unimportant in Islam, in *their* Islam.

As Asad (1993) notes, tradition is the conglomeration of discursive practices that allow believers to determine what is correct and meaningful for a given time.[6] To avoid essentializing a cultural tradition means to avoid the assumption that the meaning of that tradition constitutes a unified system, from the international to the national and local level. Islam should be considered as a conglomeration of varied discursive practices, many of which are situated within the democracies of the West. These discursive practices are debates not only about the content of Islamic observance but also about what it means to observe Islam in the first place. The act of going to a mosque to pray, the choice of whether to eat halal, drink wine, wear a hijab or a miniskirt, are as much a part of the continuous discussion about what it means to be Muslim as are books, conferences, and the proliferating and seemingly authoritative websites of Islamic scholars. It is necessary to examine how the production of meaning and cultural symbols intersect among different levels of communication and action—in local, national, and international contexts—and to refuse to define and prioritize these levels a priori.

In order to avoid the trap of essentializing either Islam or Muslims, several considerations must be taken into account. First, it is important to avoid any sort of unilateral approach that confines itself only to the examination of religious or cultural changes among Muslims. That is why this chapter explores the *mutual* transformation of Islamic groups and the Western societies with which they interact. For example, the nationalism and secularism of Western societies are transformed by the Muslim presence, at the same time as these new political and cultural circumstances are transforming Muslims' religious practice into a more private act of faith (Cesari 2004). The secularization of Islam is evident in the transformation of individual religious observance, as well as in the acceptance by the vast silent majority of Muslims (i.e., the ones who do not articulate an Islamic discourse in public or do not belong to any cultural or religious organization) of the separation between public and private space characteristic of each modern society. In some European countries, this secularization has manifested itself in the creation of Islamic organizations designed to represent Islam in the public arena, often under the guidance of the central government, as in Belgium and France. And it is interesting to note that across western Europe, the majority of Muslim leaders and organizations have accepted this idea of a representative and institutionalized Islam within secular states (Cesari 2004).

Nevertheless, Islamic groups continue to be seen largely in terms of culture wars that artificially oppose "enlightened" and "liberal" non-Muslims against "conservative" and "backward" Muslims. This opposition was striking during the debate on the law prohibiting religious signs in public schools, which was adopted in 2004. Its advocates regarded the law as a way to emancipate/enlighten/modernize Muslim students. Most Muslims, however, simply saw it as a blatant attempt to discriminate against their religious practices, an opinion that was held even by those who were not particularly observant.

These interactions and accommodations between Muslims and non-Muslims in the West take place in the broader context of global Islam, referring here to the transnational space of debates and political, religious, and cultural movements that cut across countries, nations, and languages and the political crises that may go along with these movements. Through their words as well as their actions, Muslims in the West contribute to the imaginary of contemporary Islam. As Arjun Appadurai has pointed out, the imagination is now itself a social and cultural force (Appadurai 1996, 27-65). Participation in the Islamic imaginary is given concrete expression in a variety of disparate religious practices and mobilizations. The most visible of these practices has been the formation in France of conservative or proselytizing transnational movements such as Salafi or Wahabi Islam. These groups promote a defensive or reactive identity, sometimes giving rise to a veritable theology of hate. On the opposite end of the spectrum are practices such as the production/consumption of Islam on the Internet, practices that signal an acceptance of Western contexts and that are sometimes, though not always, accompanied by real innovations and new syncretic forms of religion. Perhaps the most significant innovations are the discussions among some Muslims about the role of women in the Islamic tradition (i.e., whether to be more inclusive of women by giving them equality with men in all aspects of worship and social roles) or the status of apostasy (i.e., the creation in recent years of associations of former Muslims in Germany and the Netherlands).

It is also important to examine how the encounter with democratic and secularized culture has intensified certain long-standing crises within the Islamic tradition that used to be limited to the Muslim world—particularly the crisis of religious authority—even while this encounter is encouraging the development of religious innovations. In this regard, some Muslims of the diaspora are in the process of revisiting certain concepts such as democracy, secularization, and human rights; they are questioning many interpretations of Islamic tradition. The situation of contemporary Muslims who live as minorities in democratic and secular societies serves as a practical "case study" of all the theoretical and conceptual debates about democracy that have troubled the Muslim world for centuries. Moreover, the new contexts in which Muslims find themselves have led to adaptations and new debates about the right way to think about ritual practice and theological reflection.

These transformations are especially important as they do not happen in isolation. They also have dramatic consequences for the ideas and concepts being developed in the rest of the Muslim world. The reactions of the Muslim world in 2004 to the French legislation outlawing religious symbols are a perfect example of the phenomenon of global Islam. The 2006 cartoon crisis that started in Denmark and spread all over the world is another case in point. The Europeanization of Islam cannot be dissociated from the space-time of global Islam. In this regard, it would be misleading to consider European or American Muslims only in light of their integration into the West, since most of their issues (women, apostasy, democracy, secularism) are also debated in this transnational space as demonstrated by the Rushdie Affair and the cartoon crisis.

To analyze these transformations and renegotiations of Islamic practices and narratives—in the French context in particular, or in the Western context in general—I propose a framework based on several combined dimensions. On the one side are "origin effects," factors relating to the characteristics of Islam in Muslim countries of origin as well as to the wider deterritorialized and global forms of Islam. On the other side are "destination effects," factors relating to French and European culture, such as the influence of secularism or the influence of social and economic prejudice.[7]

Origin Effects

The first characteristic to take into account is the fact that Muslims in France come from countries where Islam is the religion of the majority and, in fact, the religion of the state. There is no nation-state within the Muslim world that does not claim Islam as a foundational element of national unity. In light of this fact, the state is almost always the primary agent responsible for the authoritative interpretation of tradition. Muslim immigration to Europe and the United States provides release from the "iron grip" of Muslim states on Islamic tradition. This "liberation" is far from simple or ineluctable, and can take a variety of forms, deeply influenced by the different national contexts in which it happens. In order to understand this complex question more thoroughly, it is therefore helpful to analyze the cultural and political principles that shape religious life in Western culture, and the ways in which these principles have influenced Muslims in their adaptation to the secular nations of the West. From such an analysis, several surprising facts emerge. The first is the complex interplay between religion and ethnicity in the identity formation of French Muslims.

Ethnicity Versus Religion

Since the beginning of the major period of Muslim immigration to France after the Second World War, Islam has become an important collective point of reference, and has combined with broader notions of Algerian, Moroccan, or Tunisian national identity to produce a distinctively Muslim ethnicity. Ethnicity in this case refers to a shared system of values and symbols among individuals who consider themselves members of the same group. It should not be seen, however, as a fixed set of cultural attributes but rather as a series of often fluid identifications. These identifications serve to create boundaries between "us" and "them," which can also vary according to different situations and contexts. Thus, the "Islams" of North and sub-Saharan Africa, Turkey, and the Middle East are each characterized by different levels of personal agency, emotion, and sentiment. Collective memories—even the colours and smells of a country—affect the practice of Islam within a group, and each group brings its particular characteristics to the universal brotherhood of Islam. Similarly, common Islamic rituals (fasting during the month of Ramadan, prayers, sacrificial celebrations, etc.) can have a different cultural significance depending on their context. In other words, the divisions between groups of Muslims are deeply coloured by national cultures and identities. The reconstruction and preservation of certain cultural features in Muslim societies (for example, patriarchal order) is thus often effected in the name of Islam by attributing to the Islamic tradition actions or beliefs more cultural than religious.

These ethnonational cultures are usually different from national cultures as defined by the states of origin. In certain situations, identity is indeed based on national ties; usually, however, it is based on regional or even village affiliation. Algerian immigration into Europe, for example, has been heavily Kabyle in character since the 1920s.[8] Thus the expatriate Algerian community in France and Europe includes many aspects of Kabyle culture, an ethnic group that was, in fact, long oppressed by the Algerian state. For the most part, Muslim immigration to France or Europe, especially in the early generations, has been a relocation of village communities. The practice of Islam in France is thus coloured by the specific characteristics of the various cultural systems in place in these original settings: regional traditions such as ancestor worship, veneration of saints (in North Africa), beliefs in magic, and agrarian rites. For Muslims coming from India or Pakistan, it is the belief in *pirs*[9] or the long-standing influence of caste systems.[10] All of these cultural features are reinterpreted through the universal language of religion.

Conventional assimilation theories on immigrant culture maintain that such ethnic identifications eventually disappear in later European-born or educated generations (Roy 1999). Our own observations, however, along with the observations of several other scholars, show that ethnic boundaries, though they may be recomposed and reconstituted, do not disappear, even among second- and third-generation immigrants (Werbner 2002). This is not to say that the common acculturationist or assimilationist assumptions governing academic approaches to Muslim integration in Western society are completely false; clearly, contact with the dominant society, education in that society's schools, and the appropriation of that society's language and manners does happen, but the traditional linear conception of immigrant integration addresses only one aspect of the situation.

We must first of all distinguish between ethnic cultural identity and ethnic belonging (Jacobson 1998). The former has to do with the perpetuation and recreation of linguistic differences, sexual practices, food, eating habits, and so forth associated with a particular group of people. The latter, on the other hand, relates to identification—however loose or distant—with a particular place of origin. Such identification may not even be translated into concrete practice. Ethnic culture and belonging are not synonymous. Many analyses make the mistake of conflating these two types of ethnic identification, and assume that the disappearance or acculturation of certain practices means the end of ethnic identity in general. Admittedly, the newer generations of European-born or European-educated Muslims find it difficult to continue the same kinds of communitarian allegiances or modes of ethnic belonging that are based on regional, village, or ethnic solidarity established by the first migrants (Cesari 1997). Nonetheless, they do often retain at least an emotional attachment to their place of origin. This attachment, at times even taking on a kind of mythological character, contributes to the maintenance of the boundary between "them" and "us."

Family and Women. Family relations and discourse on women in particular are shaped by the ethnic dimensions of Islamic culture. An adherence to family values and habits is the privileged mode of perpetuation of an ethnic group. The categories of generation, age, and sex help to define each person's place in the social fabric, and the relations between them are as much the product of distinct ethnic/regional cultural systems as that of Islam. Polygamy, for instance, is practised much more frequently in sub-Saharan Africa than in the north of the continent. Sub-Saharan family systems are, for the most part, communitarian in nature, structured on a strict differentiation between age groups, which are in turn usually integrated into the political organization of the village (i.e., the pre-eminence of elders in the leadership of the community).

These family systems are generally patrilineal, though matrilineal systems also occur. One noteworthy example of the latter is the Comorians, strict Sunnis who nonetheless manage to preserve a matrilineal system in which inheritance is passed through the women of a family, in contravention of Islamic law. There is thus a bilinearity to the family system in Comorian society, which is also evident in their educational system: girls' education and status are privileged over that of boys. Furthermore, in striking contrast to the situation in North Africa and elsewhere in the Muslim world, most Qur'anic masters in the Comoros and Comorian communities in France are women.

Gender and the Ethos of Honour. Many cultural practices specific to a particular ethnicity or region have been inappropriately attributed to Islam. Among these, one of the most generally misunderstood is the concept of honour.[11] The ethos of honour is defined by at least two principles: the sexual purity of women, which is watched over by the males of the family, and the system of exchange, as expressed in gifts and counter-gifts and the laws of hospitality. Customs regarding exchange come to govern not just the normal process of transacting goods (women among them), but the conditions of social life itself. In societies marked by the dynamics of honour, existing means above all "being for others," that is, submitting to their scrutiny and opinions. The pursuit of honour—and its flip side, the fear of shame—motivate and regulate relations with others. Giving priority to the concept of the group also implies the permanent social control of each individual's behaviour, in order to ensure external cultural conformity. Thus it is that the most frequently observed cultural practices are those with the most strongly marked social character (i.e., those that entail conformity with external behavioural norms). Such culturally mandated practices are, in fact, more frequently observed than the more private customs, such as prayers, which are frequently neglected.

The concept of honour in Muslim communities is particularly associated with competition among families, as well as with the exercise of control over the women in a family. The dynamics of honour are also present in exile. A patriarchal system, in which the head of household is the uncontested authority, is a common feature of Turkish, North African, Pakistani, and Bangladeshi families. Lineage rules these households: this explains, significantly, the preference for marriage between cousins. Intra-familial marriage makes it possible to keep the networks of alliance within the extended family, and reinforces unity by avoiding the dispersion of inheritance. This method of family organization has a variety of names. In Urdu, it is called *biradari* (extended family) and is not always accompanied by the transmission of the family name, as it is in the case of Pakistanis. This social structure has been maintained despite the massive urbanization and waves of migration that, in the past 20 years, have done much to dissipate its power. Indeed, some aspects of this structure have grown stronger or become ossified, for example, the idea that women's purity is the primary means of preserving the integrity and honour of the family name.

Generally speaking, the dynamics of honour entail different requirements for men and women. For girls, the elements of a good reputation reside in the modesty of their dress and in the decorum of their behaviour toward men. Thus Muslim teenagers often express an extreme sensitivity to gossip of a sexual nature, since conflict regarding sexual mores is the primary cause of male violence against women in the Muslim community. The expectations of modesty placed upon Muslim girls result in their near absence from suburban public space: stairwells, streets, shopping areas. Brothers, in turn, are responsible for the honour of the girls in their family. Thus the divergence in attitude regarding family life is strong between the two sexes: whereas girls generally want to manage their sexual life on their own, independent of family tradition, boys feel a social responsibility that often turns into a feeling of disgust at the sight of any girl who achieves a measure of sexual freedom. This divergence can sometimes have dramatic results. In 1993, Nazmyé Likpinar, a 15-year-old Turkish teenager, was killed, with her family's approval, by her brother and her cousin because she had been flirting with a young man of her own age. In her brother's words, Nazmyé was killed for "the sacred honour that is similar everywhere, here and there." It is also in the name of honour that doctors are confronted regularly with requests for hymen reconstruction. Mobile phones have now made it possible for young men to admonish and threaten girls from a distance if their public behaviour does not conform to the criteria of honour (*izzat*).

It is Islam that is consistently used to justify such violence toward women. Thus the control of women, and especially of girls, justified in the name of Islam, has become the principal way in which the dynamics of ethnicity are affirmed. Practices of harassment, physical and verbal attack, the rape of girls seen as "accessible" or "easy" because of the way they dress, restriction of women's freedom of movement, and so forth are common. Nevertheless, these practices are encountering increasing resistance from young women. The movement Neither Whores Nor Slaves was created in 2002 following the murder of a girl named Samira for refusing the advances of a young man in the Paris suburbs. Since the protest march of 8 March 2003, when more than 20,000 people gathered in Paris, the movement has achieved greater visibility, attracting testimonials and support from every suburban community in France. Between 20 and 30 local committees have been created through this movement, and the testimonials posted on their website increase daily.

> Here, if you speak to a boy, they say you gave him a blow job and he brought you to a hotel in Belgium. . . .

> If we don't all dress the same way, people's impressions of you change. I was always a reserved girl, tracksuit. Now that I'm working in a spa, I take more care of myself, so others think I'm a bitch.[12]

The youth of the suburbs are extremely sensitive to the concept of respect. They are deeply afraid of losing face or not having their personal dignity acknowledged. This fear often leads them into confrontations, not only with their peers but also with adults, especially the representatives of institutions and government authority. After the death of a teenager during a police action in Damarie-les-Lys in December 1997, one young man angrily summarized this feeling of unworthiness vis-à-vis authority. In his words, "We are not animals." In this context, the concern over respect takes on an explicitly political dimension. The situation can become particularly volatile when it involves the representatives of the establishment together with young people from the north of Africa, who tend to see anti-Arab racism in any policies or procedures aimed at them.[13]

The sense of honour that has been described above is not exclusively Arab or Muslim as it can be found in other non-Muslim Mediterranean societies. But in Muslim societies, it is always justified in Islamic terms. The conflicts over sexuality and women reflect some of the difficulties associated with the integration of Muslims, especially the tensions between liberal Western values and patriarchal lifestyles.

Global Islam

Islam is a powerful element in identity formation, weaving together solidarity between various groups that are separated by the constraints of very different nations, countries, and cultures. Over the past two decades, two different globalized forms of Islam have attracted more and more followers in different parts of the Muslim world and beyond. One form is embodied in theological and political movements such as the Muslim Brotherhood, the Jamaat-Tabligh, and the Wahabi doctrine, all of which emphasize each Muslim's link to the universal community of believers (*ummah*). Today, the conditions for communication and the free movement of people and ideas make the *ummah* all the more salient, even though national ideologies have declined. Unlike Protestantism, where the diversity in interpretations of religious belief led to the founding of separate communities and the proliferation of sects, the imagined unity of the *ummah* as a constantly renewed community, based on an understanding of a shared fate, has remained strong.

It is important to make a distinction at this point between radicalism and fundamentalism. It is the desire to believe in an Islam based on a direct relationship to the divinely revealed that is often the cause of people's decision to join Salafi or Wahabi movements.[14] They are thus fundamentalists in the sense that they refer back to the sources of the religion, the Qur'an and the Hadith. This return to the source texts can be conservative or puritan as is shown by the growing success of the Jamaat-Tabligh, and by the fact that many in the younger generations find their source for inspiration in schools of thought such as the one built around sheik Al-Albani.[15] However, this return to the divinely revealed sources can also give rise to more open-minded interpretations in touch with the social and political facts and issues of various European contexts, such as the fatwas recognizing Western democracy and citizenship (Cesari 2004).

The other form of global Islam is represented in diasporic networks. In these networks, non-state agents such as religious leaders, immigrants, entrepreneurs, and intellectuals develop bonds and identities that connect at least one national and cultural territory with their place of origin. To achieve diasporic status, a group must possess three main traits: (a) awareness of an ethnic or cultural identity, (b) existence of group organizations across different nations, and (c) development of relations—whether monetary, political, or even imaginary—linking people in different countries.[16]

The forms of so-called virtual Islam are also part of this globalized Islam. "Electronic religiosity" is causing Islam to expand globally via the circulation of audio- and videotapes, the broadcasting of independent television satellite shows and, most significant of all, the creation of websites. In particular, bulletin boards, chat rooms, and discussion forums on the Internet are promoting alternative, even contradictory, understandings of Islam, where only nationally based ones previously existed.[17] In so doing, the various forms of virtual Islam have a major impact on Islamic discourse and have helped to break up the monopoly that traditional religious authorities have had over religious, moral, and political discourse (Mandaville 2000).[18]

Thus, mobility is a key factor for the emergence of transnational social groups. Transnational Muslim networks do not strive to assert themselves as collective participants in a transnational arena; instead, private and personal interests push them into this role. Family reunions, marriage arrangements, and business activities, for example, are usually motivated by individual or family interests, but these activities often involve international mobility. Private decisions affect not only visiting rights, family groupings, and monetary flows but also religious, linguistic, and cultural models, indirectly producing a collective effect on the international scene. The collective and global effects of individual decisions have been studied in depth by some anthropologists (Vertovec and Cohen 1999, 2003).

A glimpse into the complex interaction of local, national, and international groupings characterizing Islam in Europe or in the United States reveals some of the shortfalls of current scholarship on the subject. Because of the importance of transnational networks for the Western Muslim communities, any analysis that stresses Muslims' obligations to the host society, to the exclusion of international influences, fails to provide a balanced view. The adaptation of Islam to the democratic context is a two-dimensional activity, involving both the identification of Muslims with global or transnational forms of Islam and with national cultures in the various "host" countries.

Destination Effects

Secularism

The dominant argument advanced to explain some of the apparent difficulties associated with Muslim integration in the West is the supposed incompatibility of Islam with secular principles. According to this argument, being secular implies that political power is defined by its neutral interactions with religious institutions, bearing in mind that the principle of neutrality with regard to religion that is so central to liberal democracies is not necessarily synonymous with the separation of church and state.[19] In this regard, the French case stands out in Europe because it is the only country with a strict separation of state and religious organizations.[20] Even in this case, however, as in other European countries, secularism does not consist merely in the protection of religious freedoms and the political independence of religious organizations. It is also accompanied by the memory of antagonism between church and state that goes back to the revolutionary period when the Catholic Church was seen as a reactionary force precluding the democratization process of the French state. From 1789 onward, therefore, religion has been synonymous with anti-modern, anti-democratic forces. In contrast to the United States, religion in France is considered a menace to public order rather than a unifying force. Against this background, it is not surprising that many in France, and in Europe generally, see Islam as incompatible with the modern secular order.

The French colonial legacy also continues to exert strong pressure on the contemporary perception and political administration of Islam. Islam has always been considered a "special case" among religions. For example, when the 1905 law was passed separating religious organizations and the state, it was not applied to Islam even though Algeria at the time was part of France. One can argue that the administration of Islam in contemporary France has been a special prerogative of the state since 1989, when the headscarf crisis pushed the growing French Muslim population into the national spotlight. Until that time, Islam had been considered the responsibility of Muslim states like Algeria and Morocco, but the crisis forced the French government to finally take heed of their Muslim citizens. Several interior ministers began an initiative to stimulate dialogue and rapprochement among leading Islamic associations and branches. Because of the influence of the church-state model relationship, there was a political need for a representative body of Islam, akin to the hierarchy of the Catholic Church.[21] After several years of attempting to find a suitable Muslim representative, elections for the establishment of a general assembly finally took place among the Muslim population in April 2003. This assembly, in turn, chose an executive committee on 4 May 2003 with Dalil Boubakeur, rector of the Mosque of Paris, serving as president.

According to the French authorities, the CFCM (Conseil Français du Culte Musulman or "French Council of the Muslim Faith") is expected to function like analogous Catholic, Protestant, and Jewish bodies, serving as the representative of the religion to the state and facilitating dialogue among various Islamic and non-Islamic groups and institutions. However, the credibility of the CFCM is compromised for many French Muslims—and especially for Muslim youth—by its very dependence on the French state. Moreover, the institution has proven unable to solve the problems of social and religious discrimination faced by most French Muslim youth of North African descent. Nevertheless, some optimistically argue that the emergence of Muslim organizations trying to adapt to the pre-existing church-state relations in France signals a positive acceptance of the modern French secular state (Pauly 2004).

The institutional agreements between Islamic organizations and the secular state are only one aspect of the status of religions within Europe. Beyond the differentiation of the political and religious spheres and the notion of neutrality that is so central to so many European liberal democracies, there is an ideological significance to secularism that has its origins in the philosophy of the Enlightenment. Western European countries tend to regard public displays of religiosity as an illegitimate intrusion into civil society. The idea that religion cannot play a role in the general well-being of societies—a mark of the secularized mind—is, in fact, spread relatively evenly throughout Europe, despite the differences in the national contracts between different states and organized religions. Consequently, the various public manifestations of Islam in France are seen as troublesome, or even unacceptable. The hijab controversy leading to the prohibition of all religious signs in schools is a case in point.

As indicated by the great controversy surrounding the headscarf, ideological secularism is most prominent and most institutionalized in France. The philosophy of positivism, which rejects any form of transcendence or metaphysics, exerted a strong influence on the republican founders of modern French secular society. It helped to shape new principles of democratic political action that emphasized individual freedom, equality under the law, and religious neutrality. As a result, French secularism has always been and continues to be extremely rigorous, demanding the exclusion of all signs of religion from the public arena. Religious instruction is banned from state schools, and the display of personal religious symbols has become a cause for controversy. The appearance of the Muslim veil in French state schools was greeted with fierce debate. More than anything, these debates brought into focus the discrepancy between the letter of the 1905 French secularization law and what most French people believe a secular society to be.

First and foremost, French law establishes the separation of religion and state, thereby affirming the official neutrality of governmental administration. Second, the law guarantees freedom of religious expression to all faiths. In accordance with its long tradition as guardian of the law, the Conseil d'État has repeatedly emphasized the importance of respect for religious beliefs. In a decision dated 27 November 1989, the Conseil adopted the position that the law requires only that the officers of public services remain religiously neutral, but that such neutrality is not required of the users of these services. In other words, the Islamic headscarf, as a symbol of individual religious membership, does not contradict legal prescriptions of neutrality in any way. Thus the Conseil d'État has sought to remind people that the "display of a religious sign does not contradict the law of secular society" unless it causes a disturbance in public order.[22]

However—and this is where the shoe pinches—this decision contradicts the common French conception of the place of religion in society. The principle of secularism as it is embodied in law establishes and organizes equal access to the public arena for all religions as institutions and for individual members of all religions while at the same time forbidding state interference in religious matters. Most French citizens, on the other hand, want to see secularism as an apparatus for the delegitimization of religious identity as such.

In 2003, the debate surrounding secularism rose to new heights with the introduction of a bill to ban "ostentatious" religious symbols in public schools. (The bill was ultimately passed in March 2004.) The Stasi Commission, a delegation of scholars and experts created in July 2003 on the initiative of the French president, came out in favour of the law. In a televised speech on 17 December 2003, President Chirac himself endorsed the Commission's decision. The law was an attempt to bridge the gap between the legal and cultural concepts of secularism. Perhaps even more significantly, however, the law reveals an authoritarian conception of secularism that is charged with the protection of individual freedom even against the individual's will. The French state, in other words, declared that only the state knows what true freedom consists of; only the state can emancipate the individual, even against his or her will. Above all, the banning of ostentatious religious symbols imposes a definition of freedom of conscience based on an idealized and homogeneous vision of society—namely, the view that modern citizenship requires the rejection of all public signs of religion. The headscarf ban thus seeks to "liberate" young Muslim women from the oppression of religious symbols (Cesari 2007).

Many Europeans regard the representations of women in contemporary Islam as distasteful or loathsome—hence the debates over Muslim attire that have occurred throughout Europe. These debates often rely upon reified European notions of Muslim civilization in which the veil has come to represent an assault on female dignity. Such interpretations challenge freedom of conscience, as they fail to account for the feelings of those Muslim women who choose to wear the veil.[23] Many educated, integrated French Muslim women wear the veil, undermining the patronizing notion that the veil always signals oppression and subservience.

Emergence of Muslim Congregations

The rapid growth in the number of Islamic centres, including mosques—not to mention the increase in Muslim funeral parlours, halal butcher shops, and Islamic schools—is a striking indication of how well Islam has adapted to its democratic and secularized context. These centres typically assume the traditional North American "congregational" form.

As such, the activities associated with these religious adaptations reflect the principles of (a) voluntarism, (b) management of the congregation by the congregants themselves, and (c) the organization of social and cultural activities as an integral part of the congregation's social function. This model is not utilized in the analysis of religious life by French sociologists, but it may be helpful to understand the building of Islamic institutions in the French context. It should be noted that we are talking here about a de facto congregational model, which means that, while most of the French Islamic centres do not keep rosters, they still can be defined as congregations (Ebaugh and Chafetz 2000).[24]

These three aspects of the congregational model contribute to the changing nature of Islam in France. In Muslim countries, Islam is an official institution of the state. To be Muslim in a Muslim country is an aspect of social and cultural convention. But in Europe and the United States, on the other hand, there is little societal pressure to belong to a religious group of any kind. To belong to or leave a religious group is, therefore, an act of personal choice and a result of the voluntarism that characterizes religious life in contemporary society. Thus the creation of new Islamic centres in France is due, more than anything, to mobilization on the part of the Muslim community itself. That is, the construction, administration, and development of Islamic centres are all the result of voluntarism—the daily involvement of members who donate their time, ability, and money so that such places can exist. By contrast, in Muslim countries, the people are not empowered to run prayer rooms and mosques. These places of worship are public property and are consequently created, run, and maintained by the state. Because this kind of management by state power is largely impossible in Europe, and even less likely in the United States, it is the congregants themselves who take over the management of places of worship.[25]

In addition to religious functions, another important role played by the congregation is organizing social activities. In both Europe and the United States, the mosque is the centre of community life. In other words, the mosque is not just a place one goes to pray but a true "community centre" toward which pre-existing networks of solidarity are redirected. This means that the various activities that set the rhythm of religious life—marriage rites, circumcision, funerals—more and more often take place in the mosque itself. Moreover, Islamic centres now also provide such activities as courses on the Qur'an for children and adults, conference series and seminars, courses for new converts (primarily in the United States), assistance with funeral rites, recreational activities for children and women, social assistance, and even psychological counselling. (In the West, Muslims tend to build Islamic centres, and not simply mosques, that contain a variety of Islamic services including gyms, libraries, meeting halls, and schools.)

Education is by far the mosque's most important function in both Europe and North America. In almost every mosque, adjacent to the prayer room one finds a room reserved for religious training. This training usually consists of lessons on the life of the Prophet, the fundamentals of the Qur'an and the Hadith, and basic Arabic. These educational programs achieve a dual purpose: not only the transmission of religious and cultural tradition, but also the socialization of children in Islamic culture so that they may avoid the "temptations" presented by a Western environment. Islamic education can also take the form of intensive seminars for teenagers and women, conferences, and cultural programs.

In contrast to the simple place of worship—where activities are limited to the observance of ritual practice in which the cleric or religious leader plays the dominant role—the congregation is characterized by the active involvement of its congregants in the creation and administration of the religious space, sometimes even including the direction of religious activity itself (prayers, rituals, religious guidance, and teaching). This model applies not just to Islam but to all religious groups in the United States. It is a striking aspect of American religious life that almost all recent arrivals, including Buddhists and Sikhs, rapidly adapt to the congregational model. Islam's integration into the different societies of Europe also reflects this developing congregationalism, even if the term itself is never really used.

Yang and Ebaugh (2001) note the centrality of the imam's role in the United States as another expression of Islam's adaptation to the mainstream American Protestant model of religion.[26] These structural changes in Islam in the West particularly affect the status of religious leaders. In the West, the imam acquires a centrality unheard of in the Muslim world. We should recall that in countries where Islam is the official state religion, it is organized as a rigid hierarchy with a strict division of religious roles. The principal figures—the qadis and the muftis—have the status of civil servants; that is, they are paid employees of the state. The muftis' role within the religious hierarchy is to provide the community and its adherents with authoritative religious direction through *fatwas* (legal opinions); the qadis are qualified to provide rulings on legal issues such as marriage, divorce, and property. The imams, for their part, are responsible for leading prayer and delivering sermons. They defer to the muftis and the qadis, and sometimes to other specialists in cases where the mosque-goers have a need that is beyond the imam's power to address.

In Europe and in the United States, on the other hand, the imam's sphere of activity is not nearly so circumscribed. The person who leads the prayer service is usually the most highly educated or the most respected member of the community (though this still does not necessarily mean that he has a formal degree in religion). Because there is no true institutional structure, he is simultaneously imam, qadi, mufti, and teacher; he presides over burials, represents the community in official ceremonies, and so on. The list of his roles both within and outside the religious community is potentially endless. The challenge of this kind of expansion of the imam's duties within the community is not merely one of religious competence: it is also and especially one of cultural and psychological skills.

The Prejudice Effect

The nature of the interaction between Muslims and non-Muslims is an important dimension of the way that Muslims define themselves not only vis-à-vis mainstream society but also vis-à-vis their own religious community. In this regard, the marginalized situation of French Muslims heavily influences their identity formation. The socioeconomic condition of French Muslims is one of great fragility. Research produced during the last several years by the Institut National D'Etudes Démographiques shows repeatedly that with equal levels of education, unemployment levels are not only higher than the national average but roughly twice as high for youth from a Muslim immigrant background as for youth from a non-Muslim immigrant background. So if the national unemployment rate in France is 8 percent, the level skyrockets to 20 percent for the age bracket 15–24 years old, in which people of Muslim origin are concentrated (Dassetto, Maréchal, and Nielsen 2001).

This socioeconomic marginality is in most cases accompanied by residential segregation, creating the political problem of the *banlieues* or "suburbs." The often depressed economic and social realities that characterize the *banlieues* have important consequences. For one thing, among some groups there is a strong political temptation to associate Islam with poverty and to assume a causal link between the two. The correlation in public discourse between social problems and Islam has been invoked as one of the reasons for the resurgence of extreme-right political movements, not only in France but also in Belgium, Austria, and the Netherlands. Links between Islam and poverty are used to justify the idea that Islam is incompatible with, and threatening to, Western culture.

A frustrating nexus of poverty, unemployment, and prejudice has led to segregation along racial and religious lines at every level of society, from education and employment to housing and social services. This segregation has intensified since September 11th, the Madrid bombing in March 2004, and the London bombings in July 2005 as the correlation between Islam and terrorism has yielded even more repressive immigration and security policies. These policies are not only compounding the negative feelings of many Western Europeans toward Muslims (Baudrillard 2006; Brighton 2007; Cesari 2005; Fekete 2006;

Jacobs 2005; Leiken 2005; McLaren 2003) but are also reinforcing a tendency for Muslims to use Islam in a defensive or reactive way. Faced with poverty and a lack of equal opportunity, some groups have withdrawn from society, preserving their Muslim identity as a defence against cultural isolation. In other words, we are not looking simply at a question of poverty "causing" religious mobilization, but rather at a much more subtle "collusion" of poverty, prejudice, and pre-existing ethnic, religious, and national forces (Cesari 2004, 21-42). The riots in France in the winter of 2005 were a display of erupting tensions over this situation. It is still too early to measure the full consequences of this conjunction on the religious behaviour of Muslims in France, but it is very likely that it will increase the reactive and defensive use of Islam.

Conclusion

This discussion of Islam in the French context sheds light on the need for a specific methodology for analyzing Muslim immigration to the West. If we accept that the dialectic between Muslim groups and their surroundings is already a key factor in the construction of Islamic identities, then we must avoid, as much as possible, the essentialization of these different surroundings. To this end, a synchronic and diachronic comparison will be necessary; that is, Muslim immigrants must be compared with other contemporary religious immigrants as well as with other immigrants in the history of a specific society. In other words, understanding today's Islamic identities in Europe and the United States means that we must take into account how other immigrant groups associated with religions such as Buddhism, Sikhism, and Hinduism are integrated into given societies. At the same time, we must learn about how immigrant religious groups—such as Jews and Christians—lived through their own integration processes in previous historical periods. Only through such an examination will it become clear to what extent Muslim immigrants occupy a unique place in Western culture.

From this point on, then, only an approach that links the sociology of immigration, the sociology of religion, and the sociology of ethnic groups will allow us to create a more complete picture of this complexity. There is notable work to be done to make sure that religious factors stop being considered irrelevant to the integration process of Muslims in Europe and in the United States.[27]

Notes

1.   During this period, Muslim and European countries signed a number of accords on labour-based immigration. In addition to agreements with

Morocco and Tunisia in 1963, France signed an agreement with Algeria in 1968; Germany signed agreements with Turkey in 1961, with Morocco in 1963, and with Tunisia in 1965.

2. For 2007 estimates on the number of mosques per country, see national profiles in Directorate General (2007, 81ff.).

3. "Le trait le plus constant des chercheurs à leur objet n'est pas tant une identification au groupe étudié que le poids d'un principe d'argumentation adressé à un interlocuteur implicitement supposé raciste ou pour le moins sensible aux clichés et stéréotypes racistes [...] Ces débats silencieux avec le racisme seraient en soi peu gênants s'ils ne conduisaient pas vers des effets de méconnaissance car la question n'est plus de savoir ce qui est vrai ou faux mais ce qui est juste ou pas" (Dubet 1989, 118-19).

4. Debate on La chaîne info, 24 October 2003.

5. One other reason for the lack of essentialist bias in French academic writing is probably related to the fact that very few Islamicists were interested in Islam in France, unlike their German or Dutch counterparts. For an example of the Orientalist bias in the literature on Islam in Europe, see Shadid and van Koningsveld (2002) and Waardenburg (1998).

6. These discursive practices can include the practices themselves (Asad 1993).

7. The terms "origin effect" and "destination effect" are taken from Tubergen (2006). He used them in the context of the debate over integration and immigration, rightly pointing to the necessity of combining characteristics of the country of origin and the country of destination to fully understand the modes of integration possible to immigrants.

8. The Kabyle are a Berber ethnic group located in the northeastern part of Algeria.

9. A *pir* is a sort of saint who possesses esoteric knowledge and has the power to mediate between human beings and God—in contrast to the Sufi, who, in the Tariqa order at least, transmits his knowledge to his disciples.

10. There are three castes for Muslims in South Asia: Ashraf, Zamindar, and Kami. These caste designations determine marriages as well as political alliances.

11. "It is a kind of paradox that honor, a collective attribute of the nuclear family, is also a personal virtue dependent on the individual: individual honor rises from individual control, but is reflected on all those which share the same collective honor with the subject" (Pitt-Rivers 1998, 127).

12. Testimony from the website of the organization, Ni putes ni soumises (Neither Whores Nor Slaves), accessed 6 January 2004 at http://www.macite.net

13. The Pakistani community in England also presents an example of a youth street culture set up according to "district nationalities" and whose violence occasionally reaches the levels of riot. See Ranger, Samad, and Stuart (1996); Werbner (1997).

14. Historically, the Muslim Brothers, founded in 1928, and the Wahabi movement at the founding of the Saudian monarchy were part of the Salafist current. The institutional and political evolution of these two trends have

made the term *Salafist* a synonym for conservatism, or even for "reaction-ary stance," notably within the context of Europe. Let us note that Wahabism is hostile to all forms of intellectualism and religious establish-ment, and even to mysticism. However, this is not true of all Islamic move-ments based on a return to the word of the religious texts. Not all Muslim Brothers, for example, were originally anti-modern or anti-intellectual.

15. A sheikh at the University of Medina, a specialist in Hadiths, who died in 1999.

16. Diaspora is one form of deterritorialized identity that links dispersed peo-ple with their country of origin. In the case of Muslims, even if their bond with their country of origin is strong, it is challenged by a broader solidar-ity with the Muslim world at large. To understand how the term *diaspora* is now used beyond its historical origin to designate transnational identi-ties of immigrants, see Cohen (1997) and Gabi (1996).

17. The *ummah* predates virtual Islam, but the religious discourse since the end of the colonial era has been nationally based and defined.

18. It would be misleading, however, to consider online Islam as an exclusive indicator of a new democratic public space without paying attention to specific social changes within specific Muslim contexts. In other words, to assess accurately what Muslim websites are accomplishing in terms of knowledge, perspective, and affiliation, sociologists must investigate how electronic religiosity is resonating with significant social changes in general.

19. See the Introduction as well as the work of Jürgen Habermas.

20. The other possibilities in Europe are an established state church that ac-knowledges religious minorities (UK), or different forms of recognition of religious organizations (Germany, Belgium, Spain, Italy).

21. In the case of Judaism, the *consistoire* created by Napoleon was also a po-litical effort to unify and centralize the diversity of French Jewish groups.

22. The Fauroux report on Islam in the French Republic, submitted to the Ministry on 14 December 2000, agreed in its conclusions with the Conseil, leading to the resignation of several commission members who were ad-vocates of stricter definitions of secular society.

23. Of course, such failures do not occur only in France. In July 1998, the government of the German *Land* Baden-Württemberg upheld the decision by a Stuttgart school not to recruit a Muslim woman as a teacher because she wore a veil. The government stated that in Islam, the veil was a politi-cal symbol of female submission rather than an actual religious require-ment. Since then, the debate on whether school teachers may wear the hijab has grown ever more heated, as the Federal Constitutional Court turned down the government's decision and some *Länder* introduced leg-islation prohibiting teachers to wear religious signs; see the contribution by Joanna Pfaff-Czarnecka in this volume.

24. In this regard, we do not agree with the reasoning of Peter Beyer (2005) for disregarding the congregational model of immigrant religious communi-ties where member rosters are not kept.

25. There are, of course, exceptions to this rule, such as the aid given by the government of the Netherlands for the construction of mosques during the 1980s.
26. Since the same evolution is occurring in Europe—where the Protestant congregational model is far from the mainstream—we maintain that the so-called Protestant model is more accurately described as an adaptation of religious authority figures to the constraints of postmodern pluralism and relativism.
27. For introductory reflections on the American case, see Casanova and Zolberg (2002).

References

Amir-Moazami, S. and A. Salvatore. 2003. "Gender, Generation, and the Reform of Tradition: From Muslim Majority Societies to Western Europe." In *Muslim Networks and Transnational Community in and across Europe*, ed. S. Allievei and J. Nielsen. Leiden and Boston: Brill.

Appadurai, A. 1996. *Modernity at Large: Cultural Dimensions of Globalization.* Minneapolis: University of Minnesota Press.

Asad, T. 1993. *Genealogies of Religion: Discipline and Reasons of Power in Christianity and Islam.* Baltimore: John Hopkins University.

Babes, L. 1997. *L'Islam Positif.* Lille, France: Ed. de l'Atelier.

Baudrillard, J. 2006. "The Riots of Autumn or the Other Who Will Not Be Mothered." *International Journal of Baudrillard Studies* 3(2). Available at http://www.ubishops.ca/baudrillardstudies/vol3_2/riots.htm

Beyer, P. 2005. "Globalization." In *Handbook of Religion and Social Institutions,* ed. H.R. Ebaugh. New York: Springer.

Boubakeur, A. 2004. *Le Voile de la Mariée. Jeunes Musulmanes, Voile et Projet Matrimonial en France.* Paris: L'Harmattan.

Bowen, J. 2004. "Beyond Migration: Islam as a Transnational Public Space." *Journal of Ethnic and Migration Studies* 30(5):879-94.

Brighton, S. 2007. "British Muslims, Multiculturalism and UK Foreign Policy: 'Integration' and 'Cohesion' in and beyond the State." *International Affairs* 83(1):1-17.

Buijs, F. and J. Rath. 2003. *Muslims in Europe, The State of Research.* New York: Russell Sage Foundation.

Caeiro, A. 2005. "The Muslim Leaders of the French Representative Body: Religious Authorities or Political Actors?" In *European Muslims and the Secular State,* ed. S. McLoughlin and J. Cesari. London: Ashgate.

— 2006. "Transnational Ulama, European Fatwas, and Islamic Authority: A Case Study of the European Council for Fatwa and Research." In *Production and Dissemination of Islamic Knowledge in Western Europe,* ed. M. van Bruinessen and S. Allievi. London: Routledge.

Casanova, J. and A. Zolberg. 2002. "Immigration and Religion in New York City." Working Paper, New School, New York City.

Cesari, J. 1997. *Être Musulman en France Aujourd'hui*. Paris: Hachette.

— 1998. *Musulmans et Républicains: Les Jeunes, L'Islam et la France*. Bruxelles: Editions Complexe.

— 2004. *When Islam and Democracy Meet: Muslims in Europe and the United States*. New York: Palgrave Macmillan.

— 2005. "Ethnicity, Islam, and les Banlieues: Confusing the Issues." Social Science Research Council online forum, 30 November. Available at http:// riotsfrance.ssrc.org/Cesari/

—2007. "The Muslim Presence in France and the United States: Its Consequences for Secularism." *French Politics, Culture and Society* 25(2):34-45.

Charnay, J.P. 1977. *Sociologie Religieuse de l'Islam*. Paris: Sindbad.

Cohen, R. 1997. *Global Diasporas: An Introduction*. Seattle: University of Washington Press.

Dassetto, F. 1996. *La Construction de l'Islam Européen. Approche Socio-anthropologique*. Paris: L'Harmattan.

— ed. 2000. *Paroles d'Islam. Individus, Sociétés et Discours dans l'Islam Européen Contemporain*. Paris: Maisonneuve et Larose.

Dassetto, F., B. Maréchal, and J. Nielsen, eds. 2001. *Convergences Musulmanes: Aspects Contemporains de l'Islam dans l'Europe Élargie*. Louvain-la-Neuve, Belgium: Academica Bruylant.

Directorate General, Internal Policies of the Union. 2007. *Islam in Europe: What's at Stake for the Future?* Brussels: European Parliament, Policy Department Structural and Cohesion Policies. Accessed 10 July 2007 at http://www.euro-islam.info/spip/IMG/Islam_in_Europe_EN.pdf

Dubet, F. 1989. *L'Immigration: Qu'en Savons-Nous? Un Bilan des Conaissances*. Paris: La Documentation Française.

Ebaugh, H.R. and J.S. Chafetz. 2000. *Religion and the New Immigrants: Continuities and Adaptations in Immigrant Communities*. Walnut Creek, CA: AltaMira Press.

Eickelman, D.F. and J.W. Anderson. 1999. *New Media in the Muslim World, the Emerging Public Sphere*. Bloomington: Indiana University Press.

Etienne, B. 1987. *L'Islamisme Radical*. Paris: Hachette.

— 1989. *La France et l'Islam*. Paris: Hachette.

Fallaci, O. 2002. *La Rage et l'Orgueil*. Paris: Plon.

Fekete, L. 2006. "Enlightened Fundamentalism? Immigration, Feminism and the Right." *Race and Class* 48(2):1-22.

Frégosi, F. 1998. *La Formation des Cadres Religieux Musulmans en France: Approches Socio-juridiques*. Paris: L'Harmattan.

Gabi, S. 1996. "Whither the Study of Ethnic Diasporas? Some Theoretical, Definitional, Analytical and Comparative Considerations." In *The Networks of Diasporas*, ed. G. Prévélakis. Paris: L'Harmattan.

Geisser, V. and F. Lorcerie. 2003. *La Nouvelle Islamophobie*. Paris: Editions La Découverte.

Jacobs, D. 2005. "Arab European League (AEL): The Rapid Rise of a Radical Immigrant Movement." *Journal of Muslim Minority Affairs* 25(1): 97-115.

Jacobson, J. 1998. *Islam in Transition: Religion and Identity among British Pakistani Youth.* London: Routledge.

Khosrokavar, F. 1997. *L'Islam des Jeunes.* Paris: Flammarion.

Kepel, G. 1987. *Les Banlieues de l'Islam: Naissance d'une Religion en France.* Paris: Editions du Seuil.

— 1990. *Intellectuels et Militants de l'Islam Contemporain.* Paris: Editions du Seuil.

— 1994. *Exils et Royaumes: Les Appartenances au Monde Arabo-Musulman Aujourd'hui.* Paris: Presses de la Fondation Nationale des Sciences Politiques.

— 1997. *Allah in the West: Islamic Movements in America and Europe.* Stanford, CA: Stanford University Press.

Leiken, R.S. 2005. "Europe's Angry Muslims." *Foreign Affairs* 84(4):120-35.

Leveau, R. 1993. *L'Islam et les Musulmans dans le Monde.* Beirut: Centre culturel Hariri, Recherches et documentation.

Leveau, R. and G. Kepel. 1987. *Les Musulmans dans la Société Française.* Paris: Presses de la Fondation nationale des sciences politiques.

Luckmann, T. 1967. *The Invisible Religion: The Problem of Religion in Modern Society.* New York: Macmillan.

Mandaville, P. 2000. "Information Technology and the Changing Boundaries of European Islam." In *Paroles d'Islam. Individus, Sociétés et Discours dans l'Islam Européen Contemporain*, ed. F. Dassetto. Paris: Maisonneuve et Larose.

Massignon, B. 2000. "Bouddhistes en France." *Social Compass* 47(3):353-66.

McLaren, L.M. 2003. "Anti-Immigrant Prejudice in Europe: Contact, Threat Perception, and Preferences for the Exclusion of Migrants." *Social Forces* 81(3): 909-36.

Messick, B. 1993. *The Calligraphic State: Textual Domination and History in a Muslim Society.* Berkeley and Los Angeles: University of California Press.

Pauly, R.J. 2004. *Islam in Europe: Integration or Marginalization?* Aldershot: Ashgate.

Pitt-Rivers, J. 1998. *Anthropologie de l'Honneur*, trans. Paris: Le Sycomore.

Ranger, T., Y. Samad, and O. Stuart, eds. 1996. *Culture, Identity, and Politics: Ethnic Minorities in Britain.* Brookfield, VT: Averbury.

Roy, O. 1999. *Vers un Islam Européen.* Paris: Esprit.

— 2002. *L'Islam Mondialisé.* Paris: Editions du Seuil.

Runnymede Trust. 1997. *Islamophobia: A Challenge for Us All.* London: Runnymede Trust.

Said, B. 1997. *A Fundamental Fear: Eurocentrism and the Emergence of Islamism.* London: Zed Books.

Shadid, W.A.R. and P.S. van Koningsveld, eds. 2002. *Religious Freedom and the Neutrality of the State: The Position of Islam in the European Union.* Leuven: Peeters.

Taji-Farouki, S. and B.M. Nafi. 2004. *Islamic Thought in the Twentieth Century.* London: St. Martin's Press.

Tarrius, A., G. Marotel, and M. Peraldi. 1988. L'Aménagement à Contre-temps: Nouveaux territoires Immigrés à Marseille et à Tunis. Paris: Editions L'Harmattan.

Van Tubergen, F. 2006. *Immigration Integration: A Cross-National Study.* New York: LFB Scholarly Pub. LLC.

Venel, N. 2004. *Musulmans et Citoyens.* Paris: Presses universitaires de France.

Vertovec, S. and R. Cohen, eds. 1999. *Migration, Diasporas, and Transnationalism.* Cheltenham, UK: Edward Elgar.

— 2003. *Conceiving Cosmopolitanism: Theory, Context, and Practice.* New York: Oxford University Press.

Waardenburg, J.J. 1998. *Islam et Occident Face à Face: Regards de l'Histoire des Religions.* Genève: Labor et Fides.

Warner, R.S. 1998. *Gatherings in Diaspora: Religious Communities and the New Immigration.* Philadelphia, PA: Temple University Press.

Weibel, N. 2000. *Par-delà le Voile: Femmes d'Islam en Europe.* Bruxelles: Complexe.

de Wenden, C. 1988. *Les Immigrés et la Politique. Cent-cinquante Ans d'Évolution.* Paris: Presses de la FNSP.

— 1993. *Les Étrangers dans la Cité. Expériences Européennes* (with Olivier Le Cour Grandmaison). Paris: La Découverte.

Werbner, P. 1997. *The Politics of Multiculturalism in the New Europe: Racism, Identity, and Community.* London and New York: Zed Books.

—2002. *Imagine Diasporas among Manchester Muslims: The Public Performance of Pakistani Transnational Identity Politics.* Oxford: James Currey.

Yang, F. and H.R. Ebaugh. 2001. "Transformations in New Immigrant Religions and Their Global Implications." *American Sociological Review* 66(April):269-88.

Chapter 9

Accommodating Religious Diversity in Switzerland

JOANNA PFAFF-CZARNECKA

Switzerland, a country with an almost equal share of Catholics and Protestants, experienced a prolonged and severe *Kulturkampf* before religious peace was reached and religious freedom was inscribed into the Constitution of 1874.[1] The battle over the place of religion in Swiss society and institutions—in particular in its legislation, governmental structure, and educational institutions—was an integral element in the modernization process (Späni 1999). As a result, Switzerland has continued its venture into institutional secularization, embracing a strong doctrine of state neutrality toward religion and keeping religious expression private.

Throughout the twentieth century, religion seemed to lose its salience in public life, to a large extent. The fact that public holidays follow the Christian calendar and that church bells ring every quarter of an hour around the clock in almost every Swiss town and village went largely unnoticed. Only after Muslim, Hindu, and Buddhist migrants started coming to Switzerland in significant numbers and began claiming the right to express, practice, and spread their religious convictions—described in Switzerland as the right to "outer religious freedom"—was the established institutional order as well as its public understanding called into question. Over the last two decades, non-Christian religions have become noticeable in Switzerland, but they have been less publicly visible than in other Western immigrant societies. Today, the passionate conflicts over the place of "alien" religions in the Swiss state and public realm are perhaps the main feature of their visibility.

International Migration and the Governance of Religious Diversity, eds. P. Bramadat and M. Koenig.
Montreal and Kingston: McGill-Queen's University Press, Queen's Policy Studies Series.
© 2009 The School of Policy Studies, Queen's University at Kingston. All rights reserved.

This chapter narrates the current practices of accommodating religious difference in immigrant Switzerland. It departs from the view that the Swiss religious peace established after the *Kulturkampf* created successful institutional structures for accommodating religious differences within Christianity (as well as for including the Jewish communities that have lived in this country since the Middle Ages).[2] In consequence the state's quest to contain the conflict between Christian adversaries resulted in an institutional pattern that underlies the practices of accommodating religious difference in present-day Switzerland. However, with the influx of Muslim, Hindu, and Buddhist migrants, these institutional solutions as well as public perceptions regarding the place of religion(s) in contemporary Swiss society have been called into question—as the following discussion will reveal.

I interweave two strands of analysis, here. I argue that many concerns of religious minorities do not fit into the established institutional framework geared toward maintaining religious concord among a heterogeneous Christian citizenry. Swiss institutions that for over a century have successfully promoted the peaceful coexistence of people embracing diverse Christian denominations are not necessarily suited for accommodating "new" religions. Some instances of successful accommodation of religious difference in Switzerland will be reported here, but the analysis will also uncover the significant problems facing religious minorities in their everyday religious practice. Public criticism of court decisions supporting the claims of religious minorities, coupled with an increased resentment vis-à-vis Islam since 2001, has negatively affected institutional accommodation, as the ensuing discussion will show.

While immigrants' religious objectives met with some public support during the 1990s—for example, Muslims in Zurich were granted separate burial sites within public cemeteries, and the Supreme Court ruled that students could be exempted from the school curriculum on religious grounds—the first decade of the twenty-first century can already be depicted as a period of "backlash." This trend calls for an explanation. Why is this backlash occurring now? Where are the major obstacles located? In legislation? In the judiciary? In the political parties? In civil society?

One of the most striking features of the recent debates within Swiss society is the intense politicization of religious difference by right-wing political activists. This fact creates the biggest challenge to the successful accommodation of religious difference in Switzerland. The right-wing populist Swiss People's Party (SVP) has managed to cater to public fears associated with migrants in general and with Muslim migrants in particular and, in so doing, has made significant political gains since the beginning of the new millennium. The channelling and mobilizing of post-9/11 attitudes (Imhof and Ettinger 2007) culminated in the substantial gains in terrain in the 2007 election.

This chapter is structured as follows. The first section traces the development of the Swiss understanding of "religious freedom" and "neutrality" within the evolving federalist structure, in which the organization of religion is largely delegated to the cantonal level. This section also describes the major institutional arrangements in the field of religion and identifies the major principles guiding the judiciary in dealing with religious plurality in the context of Basic Law. The second part depicts the religious composition of Swiss society. In the third section, four case studies of negotiations over religious freedom are analyzed to delineate the social forces at work in accommodating religious difference. The final section considers the nature of the current accommodative practices in Switzerland. References to Germany in the third and fourth sections situate the Swiss reality in the context of other central-European societies in which one also sees struggles over the accommodation of religious differences.

Institutional Arrangements of State, National Identity, and Religion

Federal and Cantonal Relationships with Religions

The accommodation of religious difference in contemporary Swiss society occurs within a pre-existing institutional framework that emerged in conjunction with the forging of Swiss identity over the last two centuries. Swiss federalism developed incrementally, evolving from the bottom to the top, from localities via the cantons to the federation. It originated in 1291 when three political units initiated the Swiss confederation through an agreement popularly known as *Rütli-Schwur* (an oath of commitment between the three inner-Swiss cantons of Schwyz, Uri, and Nidwalden). Between the fourteenth and the eighteenth centuries, a number of political units joined the confederation. The League of Thirteen (cantons)[3] was formed in 1513 and thereafter ruled indirectly over conquered territories (comprising the Italian-speaking Ticino, the French-speaking Vaud, as well as the German-speaking Aargau and Turgau). The League also established a coalition with eight Allied Places (*Zugewandte Orte*). The League was the only stable institution of the pre-modern Swiss polity that maintained a permanent assembly of delegates as well as the Diet (*Tagessatzung*), which met regularly to discuss matters of common interest (Wimmer 2002, 225). In the aftermath of the Napoleonic war, this flexible, horizontally organized political system was transformed into an internally complex society within a single federal state (*Bundesstaat*); this arrangement was later sanctioned by the Constitution of 1848.

Swiss federalism therefore came about through centralization and not devolution—which explains the striking diversity in the communal and cantonal politics and administration. The cantons and communes differ in their social and political structures as well as in their cultural foundations, incorporating populations speaking four different languages and innumerable local dialects, and embracing either more urban or more rural patterns of living. Religious legitimacy of the sociopolitical order constituted a significant feature in each and every polity, resulting, once again, in a diversity of patterns. A number of cantons (Fribourg, Luzern, Nidwalden, Ticino, Wallis, Zug) were principally Roman Catholic, while Protestantism (notably in its Zwinglian as much as Calvinist versions) dominated in Zurich, Geneva, Basel, Bern, Waadt, and others, shaping the values and norms in key societal domains. A number of cantons acknowledged early the coexistence of both Christian faiths (Famos 2007).

During the second half of the nineteenth century, such important societal spheres as education, the civil code, and cemeteries—all of which had been governed by the churches—came under the authority of public governmental bodies at the national, cantonal, and communal levels (Raselli 1996; Richner 2006; Späni 1999). Another decisive factor that led to change in legislation was the increased mobility of people. When the law precluding the free movement of persons was abandoned, communities became gradually more religiously diverse; as such, religious differences became a noticeable and sometimes problematic feature of everyday life at the commune, canton, and federal levels.

The role of religion in the Swiss polity had been the major bone of contention between the Catholic and Protestant forces in the early nineteenth century, with the former acting as a hierarchical and largely conservative political and social force, and the latter struggling for a national and liberal outlook of a polity shaped by bourgeois reforms. The prolonged civil war was eventually won by the Protestants. After the final defeat of the Special League formed by the conservatives, the modern Swiss State came into being in 1848. When the state extended its authority over key societal realms formerly controlled by the churches and sanctioned these changes through the total Constitutional Revision process in 1874, potential for overt conflict was significantly reduced. The liberal victory was such that in the subsequent period, most key positions in state administration were in the hands of Protestant forces. The privileges accorded to the Protestant community continued well into the twentieth century, with the distribution of key positions in political and administrative bodies showing a strong Protestant bias:

> In the upper pay classes only 25 per cent of the civil servants or even less, depending on the branch of administration, were Catholic; against 42 per cent of Catholics in the population. The situation is slowly changing. The

overall representation of Catholics in the public service increased from 33 per cent to 43 per cent between 1940 and 1969. (Wimmer 2002, 233)

With the establishment of the Swiss *Bundesstaat* in 1848, religious difference came into conflict with the new doctrine of national unity and the quest for cultural uniformity within state confines. Talking about cultural uniformity may sound strange in the Swiss context, given the country's multicultural nature. Nevertheless, over the course of the Swiss nation-building project, a cultural convergence in civic styles and a rapprochement between diverse Christian faiths became an important feature (Wimmer 2002, 222-68). A rapprochement between persons of different Christian faiths increasingly took place within the realms of party politics, administration, military service, and civic associations. Indeed, Swiss patriotism and the quest to forge a "nation by will" (*Willensnation*)—across linguistic, ethnic, as well as religious boundaries—have largely succeeded, rendering internal tensions as well as the potential for internal boundary-drawing less appealing options. Nevertheless, given the history of tensions as well as exclusionary practices between different forms of Christianity in Switzerland, institutions geared toward maintaining religious peace became all the more important.

Today, Switzerland acknowledges the coexistence of religious law and state law. However, since the foundation of the liberal federal state, the principle of the primacy of state law vis-à-vis religious law has been affirmed.[4] Religious congregations are acknowledged in their autonomy—within confines defined by the state. As communities, they enjoy freedom of religion. But the degree of state recognition of religious communities varies. Public-legal (*öffentlich-rechtliche Anerkennung*) recognition of the Catholic Church in the Canton of Zurich, for example, occurred only in 1963, after Italian and Spanish "guest workers" had decisively increased the number of Catholics in this canton. No Muslim, Hindu, or Buddhist community has attained this status in any of the Swiss cantons, although many immigrant religious communities have private-legal recognition (*privatrechtlich*) as associations.

In Switzerland, religious rights are regulated at both federal and cantonal levels. At the federal level, Article 15 of the Swiss Constitution guarantees the freedom of religion (i.e., the freedom of creed and of conscience) to choose religious allegiance, to associate within religious communities, and to attend religious lessons; it also rules out any compulsion to believe, to associate oneself with a religious community, or to perform religious acts. Religious freedom is accorded to individuals as well as to groups. The state's neutrality vis-à-vis religion is understood positively insofar as it must act with fairness in relation to all religions and must not discriminate on religious grounds. Simultaneously, Article 15 also determines which areas are protected against state interference. Religious freedom obliges the state not only to acknowledge individual religiosity but also to support individuals in this regard. For example, in prisons, religious freedom is understood to compel policy-makers to ensure that prayer is possible for all inmates. In legislation, it is the responsibility of the state to balance the right to religious freedom against other freedoms guaranteed in the Basic Law (Famos 2007, 303-4).

The federal state grants all Swiss cantons the right to define their relationship with religious communities. The 26 cantonal regulations on the relation between the church and the state, which form part of individual cantonal constitutions, stipulate the modalities of public recognition of minority religions within a canton's confines; the striking diversity of these regulations is yet another direct outcome of prolonged political struggles. Still, according to Famos (2007, 306), common patterns come to light particularly in line with specific Christian traditions:

- The Protestant cantons are characterized by a strong link between the cantonal governments and the Protestant churches. Until recently, the cantonal churches (*Landeskirchen*) were extensively integrated into the state at the cantonal level. Hence, the state defined the operating conditions of the churches to a significant degree. Recent cantonal constitutional reforms have brought about important movements toward dissociation (*Entflechtung*). For instance, while the Canton of Zurich previously defined the right of adherents to participate in the democratic governance of their own churches, intra-church voting practices are now regulated by the churches themselves. According to the previous rule (in effect until 2005), the state denied foreign believers residing in the Canton of Zurich the right to vote even in their own churches. In the case of the Roman Catholic Church of Zurich, this meant that one-third of followers—in particular, the many Italians and Spaniards who lived there, but who were not Swiss citizens—did not enjoy the right to vote. The revised Cantonal Constitution gives the church autonomy over regulating the right to vote.
- The Catholic cantons accorded the Roman Catholic Church a significantly greater degree of autonomy. Still, some state interference is demonstrated by the fact that the Catholic Church is characterized by a double organizational structure; besides a church hierarchy, a democratic organization exists in accordance with the law on the church's internal organization (*Staatskirchenrechtliche Organisation*), prescribing some degree of participation among the church members.

- Parity cantons (*Paritätische Kantone*)[5] with a long tradition of coexistence of both major Swiss faiths introduced comparatively early the principle of equal treatment of both confessions.
- Two cantons, Geneva and Neuchatel, follow the principle of separation of church and state. They do not recognize religious communities as public-legal entities (*öffentlich-rechtlich*). All religious collectives are organized (if at all) according to private law. In these two cantons, governmental support for religious institutions is limited; for example, not even the established Christian churches enjoy a judicially sanctioned right to use the state's taxation system to collect fixed financial contributions from their members, as is the case in other cantons.

These patterns have implications for the recognition of immigrant religions, particularly when it comes to equal treatment. These implications are best illustrated by distinguishing three forms of recognition practiced in Switzerland vis-à-vis religious communities (Cattacin et al. 2003).

- Private-legal (*privat-rechtlich*) recognition accorded to associations (*Vereine*) is based upon the freedom to organize. This form of recognition does not entail any privileges but allows political and religious groups to be formed (Cattacin et al. 2003, 12).
- Public-legal (*öffentlich-rechtlich*) recognition endows religious groups with a special status as public-legal organizations (similar to the status granted to public universities in Switzerland). This type of recognition results in the right to collect taxes from the followers as well as the right to state support in tax collection. It entails the right to erect places of worship and, in some cantons, the right to integrate lessons in a given religion into the canton's school curriculum. These rights obviously allow a legally recognized religious community to enjoy a significant advantage in the shaping of social values.
- Recognition as state religion (*Landeskirche*) entails a constitutional recognition of the elevated role of a particular religion. The result of such a designation is significant state involvement in the sense that the state actively supports and represents the religious organization.

While it is comparatively easy to obtain private-legal recognition for a religious community, public-legal recognition is very difficult to acquire. Indeed, one of the most striking similarities revealed by the cantonal regulations is the stipulation of a very high threshold for non-Christian religions (other than Judaism in some cantons) seeking to obtain public-legal recognition. Consequently, with the exception of the Jewish communities that were publicly recognized several decades ago in the cantons of Bern and St. Gallen and in 2005 in Zurich, no other minority religious community has yet been publicly recognized in Switzerland.

The obstacles to public-legal recognition vary from canton to canton, of course. All Swiss cantons foresee the possibility of new religious communities being recognized according to public law, but in a number of cantons formal legal recognition can be conferred only if a constitutional reform takes place. Moreover, these cantons formulate severe conditions that a religious community must meet in order to be considered. As shown in Table 1, the main criteria are the length of time a community has spent in a canton; its compatibility with the dogma of a democratic *Rechtsstaat* (understood as respect for the religious freedom of other communities, respect for law and order, acceptance of cantonal tax regulations, etc.); its charitable orientation; democratic constitution as an organization; and size of membership. Implicitly, the new religious communities are expected to organize themselves according to the model of Christian communities (*Kirchgemeinden*). Not all cantons, however, stipulate the precise conditions under which new communities might be recognized as public-legal bodies.

Table 1: Criteria for Public-Legal Recognition of Religious Minorities

Criterion	Example
Duration	Durability (Solothurn); minimum 20 years (Basel); minimum 30 years (Zurich)
Affirmation of constitutional legality (*Rechtsstaatlichkeit*)	Respect for legal order (*Rechtsordnung* – Basel, Zurich)
Size	More than 3,000 members (Zurich)
Democratic organization	Democratic constitution (Basel and Zurich)

Note: These criteria are defined by a small number of cantons.
Source: Adapted from Cattacin et al. (2003, 25).

A number of Muslim organizations have sought public-legal (*öffentlich-rechtlich*) recognition, but so far without success. Religious representatives of these organizations have repeatedly expressed their concern as well as some degree of frustration. Besides the symbolic value, this type of recognition also brings a series of important prerogatives (note, though, that lack of recognition does not imply that specific prerogatives are denied to a given community, but only that they do not come as a right): the right to establish a theological faculty, to conduct religious service, in prisons and hospitals, to offer religious lessons in schools and to use school premises for religious education, to collect taxes among adherents, and to receive state protection and tax exemptions.

Judicial Principles of Accommodation

Let us now turn to the Swiss legal system, which over the last 15 years has repeatedly been called upon to resolve cases of conflicts related to the Basic Law and has therefore been instrumental in shaping the policy response toward religious diversity. Legal practice needs to strike a balance between diverse interests and diverse principles, privileging more or less either the societal majority or the minorities. Walter Kälin (2000), one of the most prominent legal scholars in the field of Swiss public law (*Öffentliches Recht*) and international human rights law, has formulated five "policies" (*Politiken*) guiding Swiss legal practice.[6] A brief discussion of these principles will shed light on the actual practices of accommodation that have come about through the interplay between adversarial social forces.

Policies of Neutrality. The constitutional guarantee of freedom of religion and freedom of conscience obligated the state to be neutral in relation to religion. The policy of neutrality serves the goal of societal peace. It guarantees individual freedom and is conducive, at least in theory, to identification with the state. Neutrality implies impartiality, but obviously the elevated position of the Christian churches in comparison with other religious communities indicates asymmetries in this relationship. The judicial doctrine distinguishes between two dimensions of this principle. In the negative sense, neutrality means distance, tolerance, and non-interference of the state in the religious sphere. In the positive sense, neutrality demands equal consideration of all. Kälin criticizes the comprehensive nature of this concept, which leaves broad room for interpretation and discretion.

Policies to Protect "Own Identity." Policies designed to maintain the identity of a given polity (or nation) highlight the continuity of majority traditions within national frameworks. In this approach, fundamental laws enjoyed by minorities may be restricted when they seem to threaten the identity of the majority. Although Kälin sees this policy as unsuited to solving conflicts within the Basic Law, he observes that it comes into force when the *ordre public* is threatened. The Swiss praxis foresees, furthermore, the protection of cantonal majorities that are minorities within the national framework; for example, the Romatsch-speakers in the Canton of Graubünden (Kälin 2000, 52-58). Within the Swiss self-understanding, the national political culture is geared strongly toward the affirmation of mutual rights and duties.

The Policy of Minority Protection. This policy, in contrast with the previous one, aims to protect the identity of minorities from discrimination by the majority. Swiss legislation follows this principle in its language politics. At schools, members of religious minorities are protected in that they cannot be forced to identify with other religions or to be judged according to other religions. Kälin (2000, 66) argues that instruments for minority protection are still in the making, and that they are geared toward established members of the majority population rather than toward immigrant minorities. Nevertheless, he accords this principle an important role in highlighting that minority protection entails more than the sum of realizing individual basic and human rights.

The Swiss approach to integration is best demonstrated in Kälin's position (2000, 58-59) that minority protection does not require the recognition of collective rights, which would imply that each minority would be constituted as a legal corporation. In Kalin's view, it is sufficient to accord rights to minorities in such a way as to protect the cultural identity of individual members. The politics of minority protection is realized in Article 27 of the International Pact of Civil and Political Rights, which rules against any attempt to enforce cultural assimilation and protects the right to association and religious freedom. Who decides what counts as cultural assimilation remains an open question. On specific measures of minority protection in Switzerland, see Kälin (2000, 58-66).

Policies of Recognition. These policies focus attention on the importance of cultural identity and the need to protect it. Protection entails equal treatment as well as measures against discrimination. For Charles Taylor (1994), who coined the term "politics of recognition," recognition should be accorded to collectivities in the first place; individuals enjoy recognition through their membership in collectivities. Swiss Basic Law sees the necessity of recognition for the cultural identities of minorities *and* their members. Dissident and weak members of communities need to be protected (see Kymlicka [1991, 1995] on problematizing Taylor's collectivizing approach, which sets boundaries to individual freedom) against the collective pressure of their in-group. Furthermore, collective cultural norms may collide with the ever-changing character of democratic societies (Kälin 2000, 83), which buttress pluralism as well as cultural change. Nevertheless, according to Kälin, the policy of recognition of cultural identities emphasizes the importance of cultural identity and anti-discrimination efforts. This policy can strengthen the claims of weak minorities for protection.

Policies of Multiculturalism. Kälin (2000, 83) uses the highly debated concept of multiculturalism in a restricted sense as an overtly declared and legally sanctioned state policy aimed at the active maintenance and support of cultural diversity, as one finds in Canada and Australia. He sees these policies as especially suited to classic immigrant societies (2000, 87). This vision of equality and coexistence endows all groups of people with the freedom to maintain their own identity and to participate in the polity on equal terms (at least in theory). In European immigrant contexts, this principle challenges homogeneous notions of polities, cultures, and nations. It therefore collides with policies oriented toward protecting the distinctive identity of a particular polity or nation. According to Kälin (2000), the Swiss Basic Law doctrine sees cultural plurality as an important criterion to be considered in legislation, nevertheless. Cultural plurality need not threaten national unity; to the contrary, plurality paired with equal treatment can lead to integration.

As I will discuss below, these five policies partly reinforce each other and partly collide when applied to individual cases. Judicial as well as informal civil society forums are therefore involved in negotiating between the conflicting claims under the given institutional and political opportunity structures. As conflict-laden as these claims may be, their consideration is an important indicator of the scope of Swiss readjustments in the field of Basic Law. The Basic Law becomes an important factor in integration (Kälin 2000, 232-33). According to Kälin, the state's legitimacy in Swiss immigration debates is based on its ability to guarantee equal treatment under the law, to provide equal opportunities for human endeavour, to deepen cohesion and consent, and to counterbalance exclusionary practices. Officially, the Swiss state is averse to assimilatory practices, and cultural and religious diversity are currently understood as conducive to societal progress as well as to individual and collective well-being. However, as several cases discussed in the third section of this chapter will reveal, this position is contested at present.

Patterns of Religious Identity: Community Formation among Migrants

After a long period of emigration throughout the nineteenth and early twentieth centuries, by the mid-twentieth century Switzerland saw the situation reversed.[7] Measured in proportion to population, Switzerland is currently among those countries worldwide with the highest immigration rate. For fifty years now, labour migrants—including "guest workers" from Italy and Spain as well as experts, asylum seekers, and second- and third-generation immigrants—have significantly changed the composition of the Swiss population. In today's Switzerland, more than one-fifth of the resident population (roughly 1.6 million) hold foreign passports.[8]

While labour migration to other European countries brought people adhering to non-Christian religions (in particular, Turkish citizens to Germany, and members of former colonies to France, the United Kingdom, and the Netherlands), the guest workers who came to Switzerland in the decades following World War II were overwhelmingly Roman Catholic. Not only had Switzerland's Jewish population kept a low profile in public affairs for a very long time (Pfaff-Czarnecka 1998), but from the 1950s to 1970s the state had accommodated only a few thousand Buddhist asylum-seekers from Tibet and Cambodia. It was not until the 1990s that the religious composition of Swiss society started to change with the arrival of a number of Muslims from Africa, Asia, and the former Yugoslavia, as well as Hindus from Sri Lanka. Indeed, many Swiss residents started to notice the numbers of non-Christians only toward the end of the 1990s when Muslims began to pursue their right to express their religion publicly.

Table 2 presents the national religious diversity of all residents, including Swiss nationals and non-nationals, based on responses to the 2000 Swiss Census. The table indicates general trends but does not reflect the obvious fact that the non-Christian religious congregations are internally differentiated in many ways. For example, Muslims have established their own organizations and religious structures that reflect their Sunni, Shia, and Sufi communities. Buddhists adhere to Mahayana, Hinayana, as well as Tantric traditions. Further, countries of origin are important identity markers. Switzerland's Muslims originate from roughly one hundred countries including Bosnia, Albania, and Turkey as well as a number of Arab, Asian, and African countries. Swiss Buddhists come from Tibet as well as from Vietnam, Cambodia, China, and Thailand (Bovay 2004, 32). Swiss Hindus, differentiated among themselves by caste, stem mainly from Sri Lanka.

Table 2: Swiss National Religious Diversity, All Residents

Faith	Number	Percentage
Roman Catholic	3,047,887	41.8
Protestant	2,408,049	33.0
Christian Orthodox	131,851	1.8
Muslim	310,807	4.3
Hindu	27,839	0.4
Buddhist	21,305	0.3
Jewish	17,914	0.2
Other religious denominations	358,000	4.9
Non-adherent	809,838	11.1

Note: The numbers do not add up to 100 percent because very small religious groups as well as those who did not reply to the religion question in the 2000 Swiss Census are not included here.

Source: Adapted from Baumann and Stolz (2007, 40).

Non-Christians gravitated toward urban areas, but because of their small numbers, lack of citizen status, and internal divisions, they have yet to form major community organizations or political blocs. Forty-two percent of Swiss Jews live in Zurich and Geneva (Baumann and Stolz 2007, 45). The largest percentages of Muslims are found in Basel (7.4 percent of the total population), Winterthur (7.3 percent), and St. Gallen (6.7 percent). With 20,888 persons, the highest total number of Muslims live in Zurich (5.8 percent; Baumann and Stolz 2007). The greatest concentrations of Hindus are found in Luzern (1.2 percent), Bern (1.1 percent), and Zurich (1 percent; Baumann and Stolz 2007).

According to Humbert (2004), 370 non-Christian organizations have been established in Zurich alone; according to Baumann (2000), a similar number exist in Basel. It is impossible in this chapter to reflect accurately the differentiated field of religious organizations, but some of the most prominent will be mentioned. The Swiss Federation of Jewish Communities, founded in 1904, has its headquarters in Zurich and comprises 18 organizations spread between Zurich and Geneva (with the French part of Switzerland having a comparatively large share of organizations).[9]

Muslims comprise the largest group of Swiss non-Christians, at roughly 5 percent of the overall population. After prolonged preparations, on 30 April 2006 the Federation of Islamic Organisations of Switzerland was formed. This federation is composed of ten Muslim umbrella organizations: the Albanian Islamic Association, the Islamic Community in Ticino, the Organisation of the Islamic Religious Communities of Eastern Switzerland, the Islamic Community of Bosnians, the Swiss League of Muslims, the Swiss Islamic Religious Community, the Union of Muslim Associations of Fribourg, the Union Vaudoise of Muslim Associations, the Aargovian Association of Muslims, and the Association of Islamic Organisations of the Canton Luzern. These organizations represent 130 Muslim organizations and centres in 16 cantons and in all four language regions. It is remarkable but not surprising, given the diversity and organizational patterns of Swiss Muslims, that the Federation of Islamic Organisations of Switzerland still does not represent even one-third of the Muslim organizations in the country.

While the total number of Hindus and Buddhists in Switzerland is small, the Swiss Hindus are represented by over 20 temple organizations. The Swiss Buddhist Union comprises 26 communities distributed quite evenly around Switzerland.

Partnering across religious boundaries is an important characteristic of Swiss religious diversity. Over the last two decades, a number of interreligious forums have been established. Along with numerous individual intermediaries, these forums have played crucial roles in fostering solidarity among members of minority communities, providing information and supporting non-Christian religious groups in their forays into the legal realm, opening up institutional as well as personal links with political and administrative bodies, and engaging in mutual dialogue and rapprochement. Especially influential among these interreligious groups (at both the cantonal and the local levels) are the Inter-religious Working Group of Switzerland, the Commission for Questions of Foreigners, the InfoRel (Information Religion) Basel, the Ecumenical Mission Development, and the Community of Christians and Muslims in Switzerland.

Despite the influence of these organizations, immigrant religions have not been officially recognized by the state. Swiss authorities still have not staged official state-sanctioned events geared toward religious dialogue such as the *Muslimkonferenz* in Germany; nor have interfaith commissions endowed with an official mandate and public funding been established in Switzerland, such as we have witnessed in the United Kingdom. Official politics tends to be reactive, coming into motion *after* specific problems and conflicts have become apparent. Because the Swiss state has not officially engaged in supporting non-Christian organizations, the role of civil society forums and private networks orchestrated by Christian and Jewish organizations is all the more important. These organizations have established stable networks of communication and developed trusted relationships as well as durable forms of support.[10]

So far, neither religious organizations nor forums dedicated to strengthening interreligious dialogue have been subjected to academic scrutiny in Switzerland. Nevertheless, some patterns are evident (Richner 2006, 66-68). Over the last 20 years, immigrants coming to Switzerland initially formed their own organizations. Then, in order to gain access to relevant administrative and political bodies, they sought contacts with organizations oriented toward members of the host society. A number of Muslim-Jewish joint associations were formed. Their rationale was to counter anti-Islamic as well as anti-Semitic tendencies in the broader population and to strive jointly for recognition in the framework of public law (i.e., *öffentlich-rechtlich*).[11] Unlike the Jews, Muslims, and Buddhists, the Hindus coming to Switzerland have been repeatedly impeded by the lack of an organizational structure that would promote their religious objectives. However, along with other religious minorities, Hindus received support from individual Swiss persons and organizations.

Expressing political will proves all the more difficult for the non-Christian religious communities as very few non-Christians (most of whom are immigrants) acquired Swiss citizenship until recently, and only a few communes offer voting rights to foreign nationals on communal issues. To put this in perspective, 92.5 percent of Hindus, 88.3

percent of Muslims, 78.1 percent of Orthodox Christians, and 47.8 percent of Buddhists do not hold a Swiss passport (Baumann and Stolz 2007). The comparatively high Buddhist naturalization rate can be explained by their earlier immigration. These high figures speak volumes about the challenges Switzerland faces with regard to the integration of its religious minorities (most of whom, with the exception of the Jewish community, are newcomers).

In general, non-Christian immigrants are far more likely to experience the challenges of low socioeconomic status. Only the Jewish community includes a substantial cohort of elite professionals. In the field of education, Jews and people describing themselves as non-denominational are the only sections of population with a higher success rate (measured in completed school qualifications) than the majority Christian population. Muslims, Hindus, and Buddhists all fare worse than the majority population (see Bovay 2004 for precise figures). The low level of education is evident in the occupational structure, with many Muslims and Hindus either unemployed or working as unskilled labourers. Such correlations have long-term consequences in that future generations are more likely to experience poverty, barriers to education, and difficult employment circumstances. The comparatively low socioeconomic status of immigrants and their lack of political rights are certainly important factors explaining the problems they face in the present-day negotiations over religious freedom and public recognition.

Social Forces that Drive Public Policy Related to Religious Diversity

Switzerland amply illustrates the fact that accommodative practices of religious diversity occur simultaneously in diverse societal locations as a result of contention and negotiation among diverse social forces. The major "stakeholders" involved in these measures are the political parties; state, cantonal, and municipal executives; the judiciary; the mass media; and civil society actors. This section will analyze four major cases of societal negotiations over the free expression of religious diversity in order to delineate the social forces driving public policy.

The very fact that the cases to be discussed here have been the subject of prolonged and highly contested public debates indicates that Switzerland has yet to acknowledge the increasing religious diversity brought about through the immigration of non-Christians as part and parcel of the Swiss public life. Several provisions considered commonplace by now in Canada or in the United Kingdom—such as the right of non-Christian minorities to erect religious structures and to receive some form of public financial support for religious institutions (e.g., tax exemptions for clergy and religious organizations, direct and indirect funding of private religious schools)—continue to provoke dissent and vehement criticism in Switzerland. Some of the cases will be narrated in more detail than others due to the prolonged nature of specific negotiations. In particular, the recent shifts in public attitudes and the changing political weight of arguments put forward by the stakeholders will be of interest.

Burial Grounds for Muslims in the Canton of Zurich

At the time of writing, only two cemeteries are allotted strictly to Muslims in Switzerland. However, in the 1990s and early 2000s, municipalities in several Swiss cities allowed the creation of special spaces suitable for Muslim burial. Negotiations over the creation of a Muslim cemetery in Zurich go back to 1994 when the city executive acknowledged that the lack of arrangements for burying the dead according to Muslim customs at Zurich's cemeteries could be seen as discriminatory.[12] Zurich (the city with the most Muslim residents in Switzerland) had received several requests over the years from Muslim organizations seeking to establish their own cemetery. These requests were strengthened by claims that adherents were forced to send the bodies of loved ones "home" to their countries of origin (a significant cost and loss to incur in the early days of grieving).

Muslim organizations referred to the existence of Jewish cemeteries as constituting a precedent. Indeed, in the Canton of Zurich, as in some other parts of Switzerland in the second half of the nineteenth century, Jewish communities were granted the right to purchase and administer their own burial grounds (Bloch-Roos 1902; Dreifuss 1983; Guggenheim 1952). Political leaders in Geneva responded to Jewish requests for a private cemetery in a rather unusual way: the entrance to the cemetery they eventually granted the Jews in 1920 sits on Swiss territory (Veyrier), whereas the actual tombs are located in France.[13]

Zurich authorities quickly acknowledged that denying Muslims the right to bury their dead according to their religious prescriptions contravened the principle of ensuring a dignified burial (*schickliche bestattung*) for all (Raselli 1996). As a result, they actively assisted Muslim organizations in their search for a suitable burial site. The policy of minority protection is of importance here. One might ask why Muslim demands could not be accommodated within the existing Swiss context. We must recall that since 1874, public institutions—and not churches—have been responsible for burying the dead and ensuring that everybody can have a place at a public cemetery, that burials are dignified, and that equal treatment is observed for all deceased. The municipal authorities in Zurich have, however, been confronted with particular challenges due to the cantonal ban against the subdivision of cemeteries. Such a rule also exists in Geneva, but not in any other canton. The rule not to subdivide cemeteries has been considered a means of ensuring equal treatment to everyone, and not discriminating through special provisions. Equal treatment in this case meant that the graves were dug in order of registration of the deceased, one after the other in parallel rows. From the point of view of the authorities, the practice of burying the deceased in rows was and is meant to guarantee equality. However, in this case, the principle of equality came into conflict with the principle of religious freedom, since the Muslim prescription that the dead should face Mecca would require a reorientation of the graves.

The historical roots of this regulation are of interest. It was developed shortly after the promulgation of the Swiss Constitution of 1874 in the course of secularization of Swiss society, in which the state took upon itself certain roles that had been previously managed by the churches, including the running of cemeteries. The regulation prohibiting the subdivision of cemeteries was also designed to contain the ongoing *Kulturkampf* between Protestants and Catholics (Stadler 1996). Hence, this Zurich cantonal law has to be seen as a progressive late nineteenth-century provision intended to reduce religious discrimination. It was established in order to counter tendencies to exclude particular individuals (for example, persons who committed suicide, prostitutes) or groups (for example, Jews) and above all to work toward maintaining religious peace between Protestants and Catholics by providing common burial space.

Paradoxically, a rule that was originally designed to accommodate religious minorities based on the principle of equal treatment became discriminatory when immigrant religions required special arrangements. The Muslim wish for accommodation meant reconsidering the original decision—that members of a minority must not be excluded or separated against their will—in light of new demands; specifically, that a particular minority requires separation to maintain its religious practice. Hence, some of the problems Swiss Muslims have confronted did not arise from anti-Muslim laws or sentiments.

In 1996, the municipal executive attempted to resolve this problem by allotting the Muslim community a plot of land adjacent to one of the public cemeteries in Zurich's commune of Altstätten.[14] The authorities formulated a number of conditions, though; in particular, the Muslim organizations were to pay for the land. But this provision—which might be considered to place an unfair burden on Muslims—met with the fierce opposition of the SVP (*Schweizerische Volkspartei* or Swiss People's Party), a right-wing political party. Members of the party alerted the population of Altstätten to the potential of public disturbances occurring during burial processions and circulated erroneous reports that the Muslims would be granted the land for free. Public reaction was strong. In response, the key actors—members of political parties, state officials, members of commissions dealing with immigrant issues, and public figures—time and again organized meetings between Muslim representatives and concerned citizens, creating diverse forums of exchange and disseminating the correct information that the Muslims would not be granted free land.

Nonetheless, the Muslims of Zurich have been unable to raise the approximately US$1.6 million necessary to purchase the land. Initially, Muslim activists were eager to collect private funds for this purpose, but they gave way to the opinion that the cantonal authorities could, and should, amend the legislation to permit the subdivision of public burial grounds. A separate space within the cemetery would allow them to comply with at least some of their religious rules (see Richner 2006), and especially with the most important requirement that the tombs face Mecca. With the support of a number of centre-left politicians, lawyers, and civil society intermediaries, they eventually achieved their goal. The political authorities of the Canton of Zurich ruled on 1 July 2001 that the communes were free to allot separate religious spaces *within* public cemeteries. This ruling adjusted the cantonal burial law insofar as it stated that special fields allotted to a religious community could be established, leaving the implementation at the discretion of the communes (i.e., the communes were not compelled to allot distinct plots of land for minority purposes).

Among the fascinating facets of this case is that at least three options existed in order to render Muslim burials possible in the Canton of Zurich, of which two may be termed "public" and one "private." The public solution finally enforced by the cantonal authorities was to amend the cantonal legislation. A public solution of a different sort would have been to provide public funding to assist the Muslims in buying their own plot of land for a private cemetery. However, this option would have provoked fierce opposition. The Zurich authorities therefore repeatedly made it clear that the land was available, but only if purchased with private funds—which constitutes the third, that is, the "private" option. It is this final option that was embraced by the Jewish community in response to the existing institutional structure.

While Jewish organizations felt compelled *and* able to fund their own cemeteries and most other institutions, they also opted for modes of action away from public scrutiny. The very private way in which Jewish organizations solved their problems without demands constituted a model for other minorities until the end of the 1990s. Consequently, Swiss public institutions were less affected by minority demands than those in many other Western countries. The abolition of the cantonal rule prescribing the subdivision of public cemeteries can be seen—along with the Supreme Court judgments on immigrant religious issues discussed below—as a significant shift in orientation, highlighting the emerging willingness of immigrants to voice their religious demands in public.

Let us draw some preliminary conclusions from this case. That a provision changing the laws governing burials was put into practice in Zurich (though after seven years of negotiations) indicates movement toward some reduction of the obstacles minorities face in their quest to realize their religious freedom within existing institutions. The general reluctance to provide public funds for non-Christian claims is a second important insight one can draw from this case study. Another trend apparent in this example is the emerging political weight of the right-wing SVP in catering to the anti-immigration sentiments and fears instigated by the presence of "alien" religions in Switzerland. As the next case reveals, the SVP managed to significantly expand its popular support during the last decade by engaging in adversarial political activities against Muslim collective objectives.

Minarets

Since settling in Switzerland, non-Christian immigrants have established a number of mosques and Hindu temples (as yet no Sikh gurdwaras have been erected).[15] However, most Swiss immigrant religious structures, in particular houses of worship, are hidden from the public eye—either displaying no visible signs or tucked away in the outskirts and industrial areas. While mosques and temples may be seen in many other Western European landscapes (including Germany), Switzerland lacks almost *any visible* religious structures that are not Christian or Jewish.

Muslim organizations whose members see their identities as being threatened have criticized Swiss restrictions on the public presence of religion in their adopted society. Yet only since the turn of the millennium has the very limited visibility of religious structures become an important item on the agenda of Muslim activists. By 2006, with only three mosques distinguishable as such, Muslim activists had begun to apply for the necessary permits to erect mosques with minarets.

These efforts have met with considerable antagonism. Several conflicts over permits to erect symbolic minarets (e.g., minarets that are so small that they cannot be mounted by a muezzin) were recently brought before Swiss courts. While in Switzerland churches ring their bells every 15 minutes around the clock and are thus more publicly noticeable than in most other Christian countries, even sporadic and merely proposed signs of other religions provoke public outcry.

The SVP has been instrumental in mobilizing public opinion and political opposition, openly criticizing the municipalities' willingness to permit the building of mosques. SVP's anti-Muslim stance culminated in the summer of 2007 in a federal "people's initiative against the building of minarets" (*Volksinitiative Gegen den Bau von Minaretten*), launched together with the EDU (*Eidgenössische Demokratische Union* or Federal Democratic Union). Some 113,540 valid signatures were collected, surpassing the 100,000 signatures necessary to submit the initiative to a popular vote.[16] It is important to note here that the SVP's stance on this issue, coupled with its ongoing critique of immigration as such, led to an expansion of the party's electoral base (D'Amato and Skenderovic 2007).

Yet public reactions to the initiative were mixed. Supporters argued that minarets would strengthen the Muslim presence in Switzerland, while those opposed reasoned that the initiative could instigate Muslim fundamentalism. Umbrella organizations of Swiss evangelical congregations[17] launched a scheme to bring the proponents of the "Against the Building of Minarets" initiative and Muslim representatives to a round-table meeting. In an effort to seek reconciliation, these evangelical groups asked the SVP and EDU to drop the initiative, and also urged the Muslim leaders to voluntarily abandon the project to erect minarets in Switzerland. This latter request was an attempt to maintain religious peace and a plea to Muslims to acknowledge the culture of their host country.[18]

Given how few minarets exist in Switzerland, it is striking to observe the significance of this issue in the mass media over the last three years. One noticeable trend was to link Muslims' request to build mosques (with visible minarets) to the general problematique of Muslim fundamentalism and more specifically to the possibility that the new mosques might promote fundamentalist beliefs and values. Despite the obvious oversimplifications of this common depiction, very few intellectual interventions supporting Muslim requests to build mosques have been voiced publicly.[19] This lack of public response sets Switzerland apart from other European countries, where concerned citizens are involved— on both sides of the debates—in negotiations over religious difference. The relatively homogeneous Swiss approach to this issue differs significantly, for example, from that in Germany or France where similar cases have generated, among intellectuals and other intermediaries, complex debates and both fierce objections to and expressions of intolerance.

The Hijab

The hijab has not generated much public debate in Switzerland. The general public seems to accept that students are allowed to wear the headscarf at schools and universities, whereas teachers, police officers, and other public officials are not permitted to wear this garment. These attitudes reflect the Swiss tendency to draw an explicit line between public and private spheres. Schools are considered public in that teachers are seen as symbolizing the public order. For this reason, Christian symbols have also been banned from school premises in a number of cantons (see Pfaff-Czarnecka 2005). However, within this public space, pupils are allowed to maintain the symbolic expression of their faith. Precluding this expression, according to judgments of the Supreme Court (see below), would put children under stress by possibly creating conflict between the "public" values endorsed by school authorities and the "traditional" values espoused at home.

Compared with Germany, one is struck by the virtual non-existence in the Swiss public arena of debate on the question of teachers' right to wear the hijab. Almost no public criticism was voiced against the Supreme Court ruling in November 1997 that prohibited a teacher who had converted to Islam from wearing a hijab.[20] This ruling was substantiated with the justification that all public displays of religious symbols are banned in order to maintain the religious neutrality prescribed by law in the Canton of Geneva, where the woman was teaching. Right-wing parties have therefore been unable to capitalize on this potentially divisive issue; indeed, not even the few Muslim teachers in Switzerland publicly protested the decision.

School Dispensations

While the restrictions on the hijab elicited little public debate, a significantly more complex picture emerges when we reflect on the example of school dispensations, particularly dispensations from swimming lessons.[21] Among the most striking aspects of this particular case is the rather dramatic turnaround in the Swiss public debate. Although a Supreme Court ruling in 1993 seemed to establish a sufficient basis for dealing with this and future related claims, in late 2006 a reverse trend emerged.

The Supreme Court's ruling on 18 June 1993[22] granted an exemption to a 12-year-old Muslim girl from a Turkish family excusing her from swimming lessons in a co-educational class. This ruling drew an enormous amount of public attention (Hangartner 1994; Kälin 2000, 160-63). The parents' requests for such an exemption had been answered negatively by instances of Zurich cantonal justice in 1991 and 1992. The Justice Department of the Canton of Zurich had maintained that attending school is a civic duty and that attending swimming lessons is an indispensable part of the education of all students. However, the girl's father appealed to the Swiss Supreme Court, which ruled that an exemption from swimming lessons would not seriously affect the girl's education or the performance of her civic duties.

The judges argued that the Swiss Constitution and the European Human Rights Convention both guaranteed religious freedom from state interference. Religious freedom, the judges stated, "combines the inner freedom to believe or not to believe, as well as the outer free-dom—within particular limitations—to express, to practice and to spread religious convictions" (translated by the author). They conceded that sports lessons are prescribed by law, and that religious convictions do not exempt pupils from performing civic duties such as attending school.[23] They also stressed that the Swiss Constitution substantiates the priority of state law over the religious beliefs or the philosophy of any individual person.[24]

However, the judges ruled that civic duties are not to be accorded *absolute* priority. Hence, an area of discretion was allowed. The ques-tion of whether an orderly and efficient academic program could be maintained with this exemption was answered in the affirmative. The Supreme Court also made a point of considering the principle of gen-der equality, and did not see it endangered since the father promised to arrange private swimming lessons (that is, the girl would not be disad-vantaged relative to other girls because of this exemption). The main reason for granting an exemption was framed in terms of ensuring the child's well-being. The judges stressed that they sought to prevent the girl from experiencing any conflict of conscience should she be torn in her loyalty between her school and her home.

On the one hand, the debate over this issue in the media was largely simplistic and one-sided. Critics of the Supreme Court's verdict often resorted to cultural shortcuts, equating this special provision with gen-der segregation and female oppression. The traditional norms embraced by the father were time and again depicted as indicators of fundamen-talism. Most public voices joined in this rather uniform venture of "othering" in which a particular religious minority is framed as "lag-ging behind" the dominant society. Leading Swiss intellectuals pub-licly criticized "alien" religious forms as incompatible with their own country's morals and styles, postulating an unbridgeable cultural dis-tance. That they encountered little opposition in the media from other intellectuals and public figures must be seen as an indicator of a still widespread Swiss self-perception of being a fairly homogeneous, non-immigrant society as well as an indicator of the very recent character of Swiss negotiations over immigrant religions.

On the other hand, the Supreme Court's decision in the case of swim-ming lessons is also an indication of how the Swiss authorities sought to protect immigrants' religious freedom in the 1990s. It is obvious that this ruling proposed a compromise, an attempt by the judges to avoid as far as possible value conflicts between the civic authority at school (and by extension the broader Swiss society) and the parental authority at home. The Supreme Court ruling has special connotations in the Swiss context where few exemptions have been granted. Indeed, for many decades, Jewish pupils travelled from the Canton of Zurich to the Can-ton of Lucerne in order to avoid attending lessons on the Sabbath.

While the Supreme Court's ruling as well as various cantonal regulations conforming to it reflected an open, flexible, pragmatic, and accommodative stance vis-à-vis religious difference, more recently this approach has begun to lose its appeal.

Thus in late 2007, when Pascal Couchepin, the minister responsible for the co-ordination of overall education and research activities (which are regulated mainly at the cantonal level), publicly endorsed dispensations from swimming lessons, his position was sharply criticized not only in the media but also by politicians and by a number of governmental bodies.

This new debate indicates that, by 2006, numerous politicians and their parties had changed their stance on this issue. In the course of 2007, all major political parties voiced criticism of the Supreme Court's 1993 ruling. The centre-left party of Social Democrats (SD) demanded taking—in its understanding—a feminist perspective, that the civic obligation to attend schools must not be diluted by claims emanating from a traditional, patriarchal religious worldview. One SD parliamentarian insisted that the ability to swim must not depend upon one's cultural background. The SVP as well as the liberal FDP (Minister Couchepin's own party) suggested that those who wished to enjoy dispensations or any other special provisions ought to send their children to private schools at their own expense.[25] The general secretary of the CVP (Christian-Democratic Party) insisted furthermore that Minister Couchepin's position creates uncertainty, and demanded that the federal government as well as the cantons develop a joint strategy on this issue. This demand is remarkable given that education is largely managed at the cantonal level and that, so far, the federal structure has resulted in pronounced areas of cantonal discretion in dealing with religious diversity on school premises.

The media focus on religious difference is increasingly carrying cantonal debates to the national level. While the Zurich Ministry of Education had issued guidelines to school authorities and teachers, well before the Supreme Court's 1993 ruling, aimed at enhancing sensitivity toward non-Christian religions (see Pfaff-Czarnecka 2005), the Canton of Basel City has moved in a different direction[26]—one that seems to have garnered more public support nationwide (as revealed in parliamentary debates as well as in the media). In January 2007, Basel integration authorities agreed that all pupils in the canton must partake in swimming lessons in particular and in sports lessons in general. Muslim students may wear special full-body costumes and the schools are expected to make individual shower stalls available. This position does justice to religious requirements to cover the body but rejects exemptions from performing the civic duty of fully partaking in the school's physical education curriculum. In Basel, pupils and their parents are denied the right to appeal to courts for individual exemptions. According to media reports, out of the hundreds of Muslim pupils, only five cases required discussions between school authorities and parents in 2007.[27] Thus in the summer of 2007, Basel authorities claimed that both teachers and parents felt that the issue had been resolved.

Today, the general opinion in the Swiss public sphere is that such resolutions are conducive to integration. The current departure from allowing exemptions can be interpreted as a growing pressure upon immigrants to adjust to the national cultural practice of maintaining civic duties (such as attending school), which underlie the Swiss identity construction (see Kälin 2000). As was the case with the erection of mosques, opponents currently resort to discourses highlighting the Christian foundations of Swiss society.

The Basel case and its public endorsement by Swiss citizens living well beyond its cantonal borders indicate a profound change in Swiss attitudes. Even the Federal Commission against Racism has signalled the possibility that, because of societal change, the 1993 Supreme Court ruling may no longer conform to social values (Thürer 2007). The Court's response to this one case had been widely taken as a legal precedent, and a number of pupils had been exempted from swimming lessons all around the country. The current thrust of argument rejects the rationale put forward by the judges in 1993. The critics highlight the demand that religion and the state must be kept separate and the related demand that religion must not affect school regulations. As such, exemptions from the civic duty of participating in physical activity classes as part and parcel of educational courses are deemed to be unjustified. Clearly, the understanding of "integration" is becoming more restrictive, prescribing more uniformity in lieu of diversity, accommodation, and compromise.

Approaches to the Integration of Religious Minorities

A number of inferences may be drawn from the nature of Swiss accommodative practices vis-à-vis the new religious diversity due to immigration. First, these practices are dynamic. The cases narrated in the previous section indicate the prolonged nature of societal accommodations taking place at the intersections of state, law, politics, and civil society. Stakeholders took their legal claims from lower to higher courts, mobilizing support and occasionally shifting strategies in the course of action. Furthermore, public attitudes toward immigrant religious minorities and their objectives also shifted over time.

Second, accommodative practices in Switzerland, as in other Western societies, are multisited. The well-known *bon mot* "*la Suisse n'existe pas*" is best illustrated by the variety of legal and institutional arrangements observed at the cantonal and communal levels. But "multisitedness" is by no means confined to geographical locations and levels of state organization. It is also evident in the multiplicity of social spaces where rules of coexistence in the Swiss immigrant multireligious society are perennially renegotiated: families, schools, neighbourhoods, courts, mass media, and civil society organizations and forums are important contexts for articulating conflicts and reaching compromises. Accommodative practices are affected by the fragmented nature of this multisited field as much as by the frequent "mutual observations" and ensuing readjustments. It is very likely, for instance, that the changed public attitude toward dispensations from sports lessons was brought forth by the mobilization against minarets. This complexity is magnified by the transnational scope of migrant religious activism (e.g., Levitt 2007), which introduces new role models and frames grievances across national borders.

The multisited character of Swiss accommodative practices tends to be neglected in academic approaches privileging normative or ideal-typical modes of analysis (Koenig 2007). Smend rightly observed as early as 1928 that the state exists only as a permanent expression of the life of actual people; the consent of the people, on which the state rests, must be continuously negotiated.[28] Negotiating consent is an integral part of political life in which normative views intersect with actors' rationalities and perspectives. In particular, as Koenig claims, the judicial system may be regarded as deeply embedded in the political process: "Sustained legal-claims-making is thus conceived as part of broader contestations of state authority and of social power structures" (Koenig 2007, 2).

Third, the right-wing SVP has played a crucial role in orchestrating public opinion, and in politicizing migration in general and Muslim religious objectives in particular. This party was able to capitalize on anti-migration sentiments in Swiss society and the growing fears regarding the increasing influence of Islam outside and inside Swiss borders (D'Amato and Skenderovic 2007). The SVP proved to be immensely successful at galvanizing fears and anxieties with regard to the possible expansion of regulations on naturalization, the growing visibility of immigrant religions, and the Supreme Court's rulings on religiously based exemptions. In doing so, the SVP has influenced the nature of accommodative practices—challenging the migrants' claims for parity and reversing the more accommodative stance initially embraced by Swiss legislation and authorities in granting exemptions to immigrant activists and their organizations.

Besides the growing electoral support for the SVP, the shifting public attitudes have come to light through mass media reporting. As Imhof and Ettinger (2007, 296-97) demonstrate, the major tenor in the Swiss press has changed significantly over the past decade. While immediately after 9/11 newspapers such as the *Neue Zürcher Zeitung* were careful to promote sensitive reporting about Muslims and to limit explicit expressions of Islamophobia, since roughly 2003 the Swiss media has been prone to monolithic depictions of Islam that highlight intrinsic links between this tradition and terrorism as well as the oppression of women.

In combination, the SVP and the media have significantly affected other societal actors who are instrumental in negotiations of religious difference in Switzerland. One of the most prominent Swiss public lawyers, Daniel Thürer (2007), argues that "situative considerations" need to be included in judicial practice in the field of Basic Law—implying that the ebbs and flows in public opinion need to be incorporated into the courts' decision-making process. While the political climate in the mid-1990s allowed for dispensations of Muslim pupils from swimming lessons, societal attitudes have changed so considerably in the last five years, Thürer argues, that new solutions are becoming feasible that are less accommodative to dispensation claims. Koenig's (2007, 4) observation that "if courts diverge too radically from public opinion in the granting of religious claims for recognition, legal claims-making and litigation may even backfire and contribute to more restrictive policy-making" seems to be confirmed by the recent Swiss experience. Furthermore, this significant shift in public perceptions is not counterbalanced by Muslim voices in today's Switzerland. While in several other Western democracies (including Germany), immigrants have managed to acquire sufficient political weight to speak publicly on their own behalf, Swiss Muslims have not yet been able to find, or use, their voice.

It is therefore not surprising that by way of a fourth and final inference, one would have to conclude that the level of accommodation of religious difference in Switzerland is comparatively low. While accommodative practices were once more common in Switzerland than they were in Germany (for a comparative analysis in the educational field, see Pfaff-Czarnecka 2005), this trend has reversed during the last five years. The precise reasons for this turnaround have yet to be established, but it is obvious that in Switzerland, the event of 9/11 instigated fears of terrorism commonly linked to Islam. By 2003, the SVP had become more and more overt in its criticisms of accommodating Islam in Swiss institutions and society; these criticisms catered to fears of Islam within the broader population. Interestingly, public expressions of these fears were not countered by Swiss intellectuals or by Muslims themselves. Hence, the SVP discourse against the public presence of Muslims turned into a highly successful political weapon. According to Kälin (2000, 34-52), the positive meaning of neutrality demands equal consideration for all. However, the actual adverse experience of immigrants is likely to deepen their sense of not belonging to the societal mainstream, with potential detrimental effects.

There are a variety of ways in which non-Christian communities in Switzerland do not experience parity with the Christian majority. Three areas are of particular importance:

1. In a majority of Swiss cantons (even in those cantons where such changes might be allowed in theory), so far not a single immigrant non-Christian religious community has received public-legal recognition.

2. Public funding continues to privilege Christian communities above all other religious communities (Famos 2007, 309-10). This privilege is expressed through various forms of legally sanctioned cooperation between the state and the churches. Communities recognized by public law may enjoy state subsidies for church-sponsored activities such as religious services in hospitals and in prisons; furthermore, the state supports religious—that is, Christian[29]—lessons in public schools.[30] Numerous direct as well as indirect financial privileges result from the historical relations between the state and the church. For instance, the cantons of Bern, Waadt, and Zurich finance Protestant clergy out of state revenue (Famos 2007, 310). Several cantons finance theological faculty who are exclusively Christian.

3. Visible presence in the public domain is largely denied to non-Christian religions. Religious communities also lack symbolic expression in the sense that the government has not established formal commissions and forums geared toward interreligious dialogue, realization of human rights, and anti-discrimination measures. Beyond the practical effects such commissions and forums might produce, their formal character could symbolically indicate state acceptance of minority non-Christian religious traditions (most of which are composed of immigrants) as a permanent feature of Swiss society.

The Swiss accommodation of religious difference centres on issues similar to those negotiated in other Western European societies. However, in comparison to Western societies with a multicultural orientation, Swiss accommodative practices have been quite limited. Religious expression is significantly easier in social spaces considered "private" than in the public realm. The lack of public-legal recognition is mirrored in public attitudes against expressions of non-Christian traditions.[31] This trend has been reinforced since the beginning of the new millennium as revealed in political parties' statements and articles in the mass media (Imhof and Ettinger 2007).

The Swiss negotiations over the modalities of accommodating religious difference are rooted in a publicly felt distinction between the public and the private realm. In Swiss public discourse, religion is typically perceived as private. In this understanding, the Switzerland model resembles the French approach to religion rather than the attitudes prevailing in Germany, where religion is more prominent in the public realm. It goes without saying that in Swiss perceptions, "alien" religious representations are particularly unwelcome. The cases discussed above reveal a disjuncture between Swiss societal dynamics and the self-perceptions voiced in public. Christianity is very clearly the only religion that is state-privileged in Switzerland; all other religions are explicitly and legally (or at least de facto) denied public standing as well as public support (although, as indicated earlier, the relationship between the state and Judaism is complex and ambivalent). Tension arises, therefore, between Swiss discourses about the putatively private nature of religion and the rather explicit practices in Swiss law and tradition that favour Christianity and circumscribe non-Christian religions.

A discussion of immigrant religion in Switzerland cannot be dissociated from Swiss approaches to immigration in general. In order to understand the Swiss integrative pattern vis-à-vis religious minorities, it is important to remember that the thrust of the national "we" group definition is not forged by any notion of cultural uniformity. The Swiss political culture is strongly oriented toward ideals that are commonly deemed republican: what binds the citizens together is a strong sense of mutuality and commonality buttressed by the high value accorded to individual civic rights and duties. Seen in this perspective, the Swiss approach to managing difference is not geared toward a single culture but rather reflects a range of inclusionary practices aimed at individuals. The republican model of common national belonging is not devoid of culturalist overtones, of course. Many citizens would highlight neutrality, work ethic, courage, realism, honesty, reliability, modesty, and inconspicuousness as character traits widely admired in the country.[32] Such common celebrations of Swiss qualities translate into an almost culturalist perception of societal uniqueness. Pride in efficient institutional structures and welfare services is also expressed in exclusivist attitudes toward persons not considered Swiss (Wimmer 2002, 222-68). Under these conditions, immigrants struggle against strong exclusionary practices, and they need to demonstrate—probably more than they would in other Western societies—that they deserve to live and work on Swiss soil.

"Multiple belonging" is therefore an appropriate term to describe the dominant modality apparent in the ways Switzerland integrates religious minorities. Their members are expected to integrate into Swiss society in their individual capacities—*as deserving immigrants eager and able to contribute to the overall success and welfare of Swiss society*. Thus an overt policy of multiculturalism is discouraged, while individual capabilities such as command of the relevant language(s), professional skills, and willingness to engage in "civic commonality" are key criteria in defining one's place and ensuring one's success in Swiss society. Engagement in minority communities is not seen as a contradiction provided that this engagement does not extend to the public domain. While a decade ago it seemed that an overtly exclusionary model of integration that publicly stripped "deserving immigrants" of their culture and religion had been abandoned, recent shifts in mainstream politics indicate that we are witnessing a reversal of this policy.

Notes

1. Article 49. The Constitution of 1874 was the first total revision of the Constitution that had been promulgated in 1848 after the Swiss political form had changed from *Staatenbund* to *Bundesstaat* (i.e., from a "confederation of states" to a "federal state"). The next total revision of the Swiss Constitution was approved by the sovereign on 18 April 1999 and came into force on 1 January 2000. The freedom of religion and the freedom of conscience provisions now form the content of Article 15.
2. See Koenig (2008) for parallel trends in other European countries.
3. Including Zurich, Bern, Basel, and others.
4. "In der Schweiz gilt seit der Gründung des liberalen Bundesstaates grundsätzlich das Primat des staatlichen Rechts" (Famos 2007, 303).
5. Notably Graubünden, St. Gallen, and Aargau.
6. Space does not permit a full discussion of the typologies elaborated by scholars in other countries; however, see Castles (1995) and Bader (2007).
7. Most of the trends described in this section are recorded in more detail in the work of Richner (2006) and Baumann and Stolz (2007).
8. This is not an entirely reliable indicator though, given the comparatively high procedural threshold for those seeking naturalization in Switzerland: adults may apply for citizenship only after having resided in Switzerland for at least 12 years, and the procedure may prove very cumbersome. In addition, in a number of communes, naturalization is granted by popular vote on individual applicant cases—which creates adverse effects for the naturalization of persons who are visibly different, as is the case with women wearing the hijab, for instance.
9. On the history of Jewish organizations in selected Swiss German cantons, see Richner (2006, 38-48).
10. These organizations and their key exponents—Heidi Rudolf, Peter Wittwer, Christoph Peter Baumann, Werner Schatz, Albert Rieger, and others—have

contributed a lot of their knowledge, contacts, and time to creating dense interreligious social fields.

11. However, joint action proved detrimental to the Jews. After Muslim and Jewish organizations engaged in their common quest to gain recognition in public law (*öffentlich-rechtlich*) in the Canton of Zurich, this action was brought to an end in a public vote. Later, in 2005, two of the Jewish organizations achieved an elevated status in Zurich. Formally, they continue as entities of private law but now enjoy a number of prerogatives denied to other communities of private legal status (see http://www.ji.zh.ch/internet/ji/de/aktuelles/staat_und_gesellschaft/kirche_und_staat.html).

12. For a more detailed discussion of this case, see Pfaff-Czarnecka (2004) and Richner (2006). See also Loacker and Hänsli (1998).

13. However, a Jewish cemetery had been established in Carouge in 1800, but it closed after the small area filled with tombs.

14. It is impossible in the space allowed to adequately describe the complexity of political-administrative levels involved in this case. It should be noted, though, that cantonal, municipal, and communal authorities were active here.

15. A number of old synagogues are visible in the urban spaces of Zurich and Geneva.

16. The Swiss sovereign will have to decide on this issue in a national vote. Interestingly, the Swiss federal government (*Bundesrat*) has already stated that it will advise voters to turn down this initiative.

17. Schweizerische Evangelische Allianz; Verband Evangelischer Freikirchen und Gemeinden in der Schweiz. This organization is not to be confounded with the mainstream Swiss Protestant Church and its organizations.

18. By 22 December 2007, Hisham Maizar, Präsident der Föderation Islamischer Dachorganisationen in der Schweiz (FIDS), fasst den Brief «als einen freundlichen, sehr lobenswerten Vorstoss» auf. Ein Dialog könne aber nur Erfolg haben, wenn man bereit sei, «den anderen zu verstehen und seine eigenen Positionen zu verändern» (*Neue Züricher Zeitung*, 23 December 2007).

19. Notable exceptions include a 40-page report on the basic rights of Muslims prepared by the Eidgenössische Kommission gegen Rassismus ("Federal Commission against Racism" 2006) as well as occasional articles published in the *Neue Züricher Zeitung*.

20. BGE 123 I 296.

21. On other school dispensations, see Pfaff-Czarnecka (2005).

22. BGE 119 Ia 178.

23. Swiss legislation requires students to attend school for nine years.

24. See Article 49, paragraph 5, of the old Swiss Constitution (1874–1999): "Die Glaubensansichten entbinden nicht von der Erfüllung der bürgerlichen Pflichten."

25. *Tages Anzeiger*, 28 December 2007, 2.

26. This new direction is also evident in Zurich.
27. *Tages Anzeiger,* 28 December 2007.
28. Der Staat existiert nur als "permantente Lebensäusserung konkreter Menschen" und er beruht nur "auf der immer neuen freiwilligen Zustimmung seiner Angehörigen" (quoted in Kälin 2000, 233).
29. Recently, Jewish communities have also enjoyed this privilege in the Canton of Zurich.
30. These lessons are funded by the state in some cantons and by religious communities in others. In addition, lessons are conducted on school premises in some cantons whereas in others this is not permissible. Patterns also differ with regard to which authorities are in charge of formulating the curriculum. The situation is all the more complicated as religious lessons are considered "school lessons" in some cantons but "confessional" in others. It goes without saying that the rules guiding religious education for non-Christian communities vary as well (Mortanges 2003).
31. Jewish communities are in an ambivalent position, enjoying neither the benefits of the Christian majority nor the obstacles of the Muslim (and other non-Christian) minorities.
32. These characteristics are highlighted in Rolf Lüssy's highly entertaining and accurate film *The Swiss Makers* of 1973, which has not lost its salience.

References

Bader, V. 2007. *Secularism or Democracy? Associational Governance of Religious Diversity.* Amsterdam: Amsterdam University Press.

Baumann, C.P., ed. 2000. *Religionen in Basel-Stadt und Basel Landschaft. Projekt Führer durch das religiöse Basel.* Basel: Manava Verlag.

Baumann, M. and J. Stolz. 2007. *Eine Schweiz – viele Religionen. Risiken und Chancen des Zusammenlebens.* Bielefeld: Transcript Verlag.

Bloch-Roos, S. 1902. *Wie die Israelitische Gemeinde in Basel zu einem eigenen Friedhof gekommen ist. Eine Berichterstattung.* Basel: Basler Handelsdruckerei A. Galliker.

Bovay, C. 2004. *Religionslandschaft in der Schweiz* (Statistik der Schweiz). Neuchatel: Bundesamt für Statistik.

Castles, S. 1995. "How Nation States Respond to Immigration and Ethnic Diversity." *New Community* 21:293-308.

Cattacin, S., C.R. Famos, M. Duttwiler, and H. Mahnig. 2003. *Staat und Religion in der Schweiz – Anerkennungskämpfe, Anerkennungsformen.* Bern: Eidgenössische Kommission gegen Rassismus.

D'Amato, G. and D. Skenderovic. 2007. "Rechtspopulistische Parteien und Migrationspolitik in der Schweiz." Schlussbereicht des Nationalen Forschungsprogramms 40+ "Rechtsextremismus – Ursachen und Gegenmassnahmen" des Schweizer Nationalfonds, Bern.

Dreifuss, E. 1983. *Juden in Bern. Ein Gang durch die Jahrhunderte.* Bern: Verbandsdruckerei Betadruck.

Eidgenössische Kommission gegen Rassismus. 2006. *Mehrheit und muslimische Minderheit in der Schweiz. Stellungnahme der EKR zur aktuellen Entwicklung.* Bern.

Famos, C.R. 2007. "Religiöse Vielfalt und Recht: Von göttlichen und menschlichen Regeln." In *Eine Schweiz – viele Religionen. Risiken und Chancen des Zusammenlebens*, ed. M. Baumann and J. Stolz. Bielefeld: Transcript Verlag.

Guggenheim, G. 1952. "Zur Eröffnung des Friedhofes am obern Friesenberg." In *Erinnerungsschrift zur feierlichen Eröffnung des Friedhofs "Oberer Friesenberg,"* ed. Israelitische Cultusgemeinde Zürich. Zurich: Israelitische Cultusgemeinde Zürich.

Hangartner, Y. 1994. "Dispensation einer muslimischen Primarschülerin vom koedukativen Schwimmunterricht aus religiösen Gründen." *Aktuelle Juristische Praxis* 5:622-26.

Humbert, C.-A. 2004. *Religionsführer Zürich, 370 Kirchen, religiös-spirituelle Gruppierungen, Zentren und weltanschauliche Bewegungen der Stadt Zürich.* Zurich: Orell Füssli.

Imhof, K., and P. Ettinger. 2007. "Religionen in der medienvermittelten Öffentlichkeit der Schweiz." In *Eine Schweiz – viele Religionen. Risiken und Chancen des Zusammenlebens*, ed. M. Baumann and J. Stolz. Bielefeld: Transcript Verlag.

Kälin, W. 2000. *Grundrechte im Kulturkonflikt. Freiheit und Gleichheit in der Einwanderungsgesellschaft.* Zurich: Neue Zürcher Zeitung Verlag.

Koenig, M. 2007. "Religious Claims-Making in the Legal Sphere – Path-Dependence or Motor of Institutional Change." Abstract presented at the conference Accommodating Religious Diversity, St. Petersburg, Russia 26–28 September.

— 2008. "International Human Rights and the Construction of Collective Identities." *International Sociology* 23(1):95-114.

Kymlicka, W. 1991. *Liberalism, Community and Culture.* Oxford: Clarendon Press.

— 1995. *Multicultural Citizenship. A Liberal Theory of Minority Rights.* Oxford: Clarendon Press.

Levitt, P. 2007. *God Needs No Passport. Immigrants and the Changing American Religious Landscape.* New York: New Press.

Loacker, N. and C. Hänsli. 1998. *Wo Zürich zur Ruhe kommt. Die Friedhöfe der Stadt Zürich.* Zürich: Orell Füssli.

de Mortanges, R.P. 2003. "Rechtsfragen zum islamischen Religionsunterricht." *Tangram* 14:19-29.

Pfaff-Czarnecka, J. 1998. "Let Sleeping Dogs Lie! Non-Christian Religious Minorities in Switzerland Today." *Journal of the Anthropological Society of Oxford* 24(1):29-51.

— 2004. "Death, Ri(gh)tes, and Institutions in Immigrant Switzerland." In *Rethinking Non-Discrimination and Minority Rights*, ed. M. Scheinin and R.

Toivanen. Turku: Institute for Human Rights, Abo Akademi University, and Deutsches Institut für Menschenrechte.

— 2005. "School and Religious Difference: Current Negotiations within the Swiss Immigrant Society – A Comparative Perspective." In *Mobile People, Mobile Laws. Expanding Legal Relations in a Contracting World*, ed. F. von Benda-Beckmann, K. von Benda-Beckmann, and A. Griffiths. Aldershot, UK: Ashgate.

Raselli, N. 1996. "Schickliche Beerdigung für 'Andersgläubige.'" *Aktuelle Juristische Praxis* 9:1103-10.

Richner, B. 2006. "Im Tod sind alle gleich." *Die Bestattung nichtchristlicher Menschen in der Schweiz*. Zurich: Chronos Verlag.

Späni, M. 1999. " Die Entkonfessionalisierung der Volksschulen in der Schweiz im 19. Jahrhundert." In *Eine Schule für die Demokratie. Zur Entwicklung der Volksschule in der Schweiz im 19. Jahrhundert*, ed. L. Criblez, C. Jenzer, R. Hofstetter, and C. Magnin. Bern: Peter Lang.

Stadler, P. 1996. *Der Kulturkampf in der Schweiz. Eidgenossenschaft und katholische Kirche im europäischen Umrkeis, 1848–1888*. Frauenfeld: Huber.

Taylor, C. 1994. "The Politics of Recognition." In *Multiculturalism: Examining the Politics of Recognition*, ed. A. Gutmann. Princeton: Princeton University Press.

Thürer, D. 2007. "Religion als Gift – Reaktion durch das Recht. " *Neue Züricher Zeitung*, 14 February, p. 18.

Wimmer, A. 2002. *Nationalist Exclusion and Ethnic Conflict. Shadows of Modernity*. Cambridge: Cambridge University Press.

Chapter 10

Religious Citizenship Versus Policies of Immigrant Integration: The Case of Austria

JULIA MOURÃO PERMOSER AND SIEGLINDE ROSENBERGER

Throughout Europe, concerns over the integration of immigrants have grown in recent years. At the same time, debates over the public display of religious symbols and practices of Muslim immigrants have figured prominently in European public spheres (Klausen 2005; McGoldrick 2006; Saharso 2003a, 2003b; Skjeie 2007). Nevertheless, the relationship between policies of religious accommodation and immigrant integration has not been sufficiently researched. Although both the governance of religious diversity and the socioeconomic integration of immigrants have attracted considerable attention from scholars of political and social sciences (see reviews in Bauböck 2006; Maussen 2007), the two issues are too often studied separately. This chapter attempts to link these two research strands.

We choose to look at Islam as a case study both because it is the third-largest religious denomination in Austria (after Protestantism and Catholicism) and because most Austrian Muslims are immigrants.[1] Moreover, the most controversial issues concerning the accommodation of ethnic and religious diversity in Austria, and in Europe in general, are associated with Muslim communities. As such, this case study allows us to examine the relationship between religious accommodation and migrant integration. Muslim migrants are the object of two highly contrasting (one might even say contradictory) models for dealing with diversity within the population. While the claims of immigrant communities to socioeconomic and political rights are dealt with restrictively and increasingly made conditional on cultural assimilation, a great number of individual and collective rights cutting through the civil,

International Migration and the Governance of Religious Diversity, eds. P. Bramadat and M. Koenig.
Montreal and Kingston: McGill-Queen's University Press, Queen's Policy Studies Series.
© 2009 The School of Policy Studies, Queen's University at Kingston. All rights reserved.

social, and political spheres of life are granted to the same communities on the basis of their religious membership.

Islam is the most important religion among the Austrian immigrant population. According to the 2001 census, approximately 338,988 Muslims live in Austria and constitute 4.2 percent of the total population.[2] In 2001, 71.7 percent of Muslims did not possess Austrian citizenship.[3] There are no reliable data on the number of people belonging to different confessions of Islam, but scholars estimate that between 70 and 90 percent of Muslims living in Austria are Sunni, between 3 and 15 percent are Shia, and about 10 percent are Alevis.[4] Most Muslim immigrants are of Turkish origin and came to Austria in the 1970s as so-called guest workers. These immigrants were brought in with the support of the Austrian state to work in blue-collar jobs for a limited period of time with the expectation that they would return to their home countries sooner or later. Most of these immigrants did not leave, however, and with time they also started to bring their families by way of family reunification. In fact, currently family reunification is the major form of immigration to Austria. The second most important cause of Muslim immigration to Austria was the Yugoslavian War in the 1990s when a great number of Bosnian refugees fled to the country.

In situations in which religious communities are also immigrant communities, the generous policies toward religious minorities could be expected to have a positive influence on the inclusion of migrants into society and on the acceptance of difference resulting from immigration. However, in Austria, this does not seem to be the case. Pluralist policies toward religious minorities coincide with deficient socioeconomic integration and restrictive integration policies for migrants. Thus, this chapter uses Austria as a case study to analyze the tensions that exist between religious rights on the one hand and restrictive immigration and integration policies that create barriers to the acquisition of political and socioeconomic rights by immigrants on the other.

We begin with an account of the different models of the governance of diversity that prevail in Austria in the field of immigrant integration and the accommodation of religious diversity, as well as with an investigation of the institutional framework and historical-path dependencies that have led to the establishment of these models. Whereas Austria can be considered as a typical case of a corporatist church-state regime, it is also a highly specific case within this group because of its early recognition of Islam as an official religion under public law. In the second section, we review the literature on minority rights and develop an improved typology of rights in order to take into account Austrian particularities. Building upon this revised typology, we then describe and classify the religious rights associated with Islam in Austria. In the following part, we argue that the increasing number of rights derived from religious membership amount to a form of "religious citizenship" that transcends nationality and therefore increases the rights of Muslim immigrants. We then proceed to make a preliminary assessment of the relationship between religious citizenship on the one hand and the restrictive integration policies and deficient social and political integration of migrants on the other. Finally, we offer some explanations for these contradictory dynamics.

Contradictory Models of Governance of Diversity

Continuous migration during the last four decades has greatly increased the ethnic and religious diversity of the Austrian population. Interestingly, however, Austrian policies to deal with this diversity do not fit neatly into general classifications. Rather, as we shall see, in Austria two contradictory models of the governance of diversity coexist.

Exclusionary Model of Citizenship

In his discussion of different models of citizenship with regard to the incorporation of immigrants, Castles (1994, 21-23) identifies three ideal types that he terms the "exclusionary model," the "assimilationist inclusionary model," and the "pluralist inclusionary model." He places Austria within the exclusionary model of citizenship and of migrant integration (see also Kraler and Sohler 2005). This model is based on the idea that the nation is a community of birth and descent and therefore citizenship is granted primarily on the basis of *jus sanguinis*. The exclusion of immigrants from formal citizenship due to the rule of *jus sanguinis* correlates with other restrictive and exclusionary policies such as guest-worker systems of labour recruitment, the reluctance to permit family reunion, the refusal to grant secure residence status, and the broad popularity among Austrians of the ideology that their country is not, and cannot be, defined as an immigrant nation.

Access to both formal and substantial citizenship by immigrants in Austria is extremely limited, and the trend is for both citizenship and integration policies to become increasingly restrictive. Since the implementation of the immigration laws (*Fremdenrechtspaket*) of 2002 and 2005, further obstacles have been put in place to limit access to citizenship even more, such as obligatory integration courses, cultural tests, and language proficiency tests (König and Stadler 2003). Although the introduction of coercive "civic integration" policies and the use of restrictive integration criteria to curb immigration can be said to be a European-wide phenomenon (Joppke 2007), Austria's immigration and integration policies rank among the most restrictive of all (Niessen et al. 2007).

Also, the length of residency necessary to become eligible for Austrian citizenship has increased. Most legally resident foreigners are eligible for Austrian citizenship only after ten years. Spouses of Austrian citizens have to wait until they have been married for five years and resident for six years. Children and grandchildren of non-Austrians who are born in the country do not immediately acquire Austrian nationality but must go through a facilitated nationalization process. The regular nationalization process is extremely restrictive and requires applicants to have lived for the past three years without recourse to any welfare benefits, to be fully insured, to have an income above the minimum salary in Austria, and to renounce their previous nationality.

The conditions for acquiring long-term resident status in Austria are the worst in Europe, according to the Migrant Integration Policy Index (Niessen et al. 2007, 23). Immigrants are required to have lived for five years in Austria, and time spent in the country as a student or as an asylum-seeker does not count. In addition, applicants must be in possession of an all-risk health insurance and a stable income that provides enough to survive on without any welfare benefits. Further, they must take 300 hours of integration courses and pass a written and oral test. The whole process takes between nine months and three years, and although it guarantees a number of rights, it does not grant a right to political participation. Long-term residents from non-European Union countries, who make up 7.1 percent of the population, are not allowed to vote in any public elections in Austria. Access to the labour market for foreigners in Austria is also extremely unfavourable. The unemployment rate among non-European Union nationals is 7.5 percent higher than that of Austrian nationals (Niessen et al. 2007).

Moreover, in official governmental discourse and in the general self-understanding of the society, Austria is not considered a country of immigration, despite the fact that, in 2007, 16 percent of the people were either born abroad or did not possess Austrian citizenship despite having been born in the country.[5] In Vienna, the proportion of people with such backgrounds is even higher, reaching over 30 percent. Statistically, this means that Austria has one of the highest proportions of immigrants in Europe. The unfavourable attitude toward immigrants also finds expression in widespread xenophobia among the population. For instance, 29.6 percent of Austrians believe that any legally established third-country national[6] should be deported (Niessen et al. 2007, 25).

Xenophobic sentiments are cleverly mobilized by right-wing political parties, which have a long history of electoral success in Austria. In particular, since the 1990s the nationalistic Austrian Freedom Party (FPÖ) has been running on anti-foreigner and anti-Semitic slogans such as "Stop asylum abuse!" and "Stop foreign infiltration [*Überfremdung*]!" with considerable success. At the height of its popularity in 1999, the FPÖ achieved 27 percent of the vote in the national elections and became a partner in the ruling coalition. Recently, due to internal disagreements, one group split from the FPÖ and created a new right-wing nationalist party, Alliance for the Future of Austria (BZÖ), which ran in the 2006 elections with posters claiming that, if elected, it would promote the "deportation of at least 300,000 foreigners." The party managed to reach the minimum quota for representation in the national parliament.

Inclusionary Model of Religious Diversity

However, where religious diversity is concerned, Austria has very liberal policies. In the normative typology established by Veit Bader (2003, 2007a, 2007b) to evaluate different models of governance of religious diversity, Austria approximates the ideal type of "nonconstitutional pluralism," which Bader considers the most normatively desirable model of all since it "combines dis-establishment or nonestablishment with restricted legal pluralism (e.g., in family law), administrative institutional pluralism (de jure and de facto institutionalization of several organized religions), institutionalized political pluralism, and the religio-cultural pluralization of the nation" (Bader 2003, 271).

If one adopts the classification developed by Castles discussed above, then Austria's church-state relations can be said to follow a "pluralist inclusionary" model of public policy (see also Heine 2005; Kalb, Potz, and Schinkele 2003). This model is usually identified with countries that follow the ideology of multiculturalism, such as Canada, Australia, the United States, and New Zealand. Castles writes that the pluralist inclusionary model "admits immigrants to the political community, while accepting the maintenance of cultural differences" (1994, 22). In Austria, the pluralist inclusionary model of managing religious diversity is characterized by the accreditation of religious communities as public legal entities with a privileged position in the political system and by the granting of several group-differentiated rights both to the community and to individual members of recognized religions. Religious communities and their members have a number of specific rights and privileges that go well beyond the constitutional guarantee of freedom of religion.

This model is largely a product of the Austrian model of church-state relations. As Koenig (2007) points out, although Europeanization is affecting national modes of governance of religion, Europeanization does not always lead to convergence. While significant convergence can be observed at the level of normative and cognitive schemata, where institutional arrangements for the governance of religious diversity are concerned, the historical framework of church-state relations and inherited ideas about the role of religion in public life are still of paramount importance in explaining domestic public policy (Fetzer and Soper 2004; Soper and Fetzer 2007). This is certainly the case in Austria, where the legacy of the way churches have historically related to the state plays a major role in the development of current policies toward Islam.

In general, in Austria there is an institutional separation between church and state in that the state refrains from interference with religious matters and vice versa. Nevertheless, there is no complete separation since the state officially recognizes a number of religious communities and grants them certain legal privileges including large state subsidies (Madeley 2003, 13-16; Potz 1996, 235; Robbers 1996, 324).

Kalb, Potz, and Schinkele (2003, 16) argue that the raison d'être of the Austrian system of religious governance is to provide the necessary legal basis for a pluralistic inclusion of religion in the public sphere. Following this description by Kalb et al., we propose that the Austrian model of church-state relations is one of "pluralistic inclusion" in which the state and several recognized religious organizations cooperate regularly and institutionally without becoming either conflated or formally separated. A major feature of this system is that it gives a prominent role to religious organizations that, as we shall see, exercise an important mediating role. Similar to Germany, Austria can be considered a "state corporatist polity," which means that corporate religious organizations, rather than individuals, are perceived as the main religious actors with whom the state cooperates (Koenig 2005, 224-25).

In Austria, the legal instrument that allows for this institutional cooperation is the Law of Recognition (*Anerkennungsgesetz*) dating from 1874. The Law of Recognition specifies general criteria according to which any religion may acquire the special status of a recognized religious community (*Religionsgemeinschaft*). Of major importance is the fact that the Law of Recognition introduced into Austrian law the principle of the equality of treatment by the state of all officially recognized religions; the law therefore extended to all recognized religions the same level of rights enjoyed until then only by the dominant religion, in this case the Catholic Church (Kalb, Potz, and Schinkele 2003, 72). In other words, the Law of Recognition not only harmonized the rights of different religious traditions, it also did so by "levelling up" the rights of all faiths to the highest standards of the time.

A further relevant point is that the Law of Recognition established that the officially recognized religions were to have a special legal status of "privileged corporations of public law." As Kalb, Potz, and Schinkele (2003, 73) put it: "By this means a great number of 'quasi-state churches' emerged in Austria at that time that were at first equally entrusted with public duties and responsibilities. The inclusion of the Orthodox Church, Judaism and Islam in this way represents an Austrian particularity."[7] Thus, the main hierarchical organization of an officially recognized religious community was recognized as a special public body deemed to be representative of all persons belonging to that religion within the Austrian territory.

This is the case of the *Islamische Glaubensgemeinschaft in Österreich* (Islamic Faith Community Organization in Austria, hereafter referred to by the German acronym IGGiÖ) and its members. Austria is one of the few European countries that recognize Islam as an official religion. Although in several other countries informal arrangements exist that translate into a special status for the Muslim community, Islam has otherwise been recognized as an official religion only in Belgium since 1974 (Kanmaz 2002) and recently in Spain and Croatia, where bilateral agreements were signed by the Islamic communities and the state in 1992 and 2002 respectively (Moreras 2002; US Department of State 2004). As mentioned earlier, this status confers a number of specific rights. Moreover, the fact that Islam is a recognized religion according to the Law of Recognition has influenced the interpretation of the Austrian Constitution. As we shall see, where controversies have arisen with respect to the traditional religious practices of Muslims, the constitutional right to freedom of religion and to public expression of one's religion was interpreted as imposing on the state and citizens a duty to accommodate the Muslim community. In concrete terms, this means that several special governmental decrees have been issued over the years to accommodate Muslim practices and customs. This interpretation of the Constitution reinforces the pluralist inclusionary principle of religious accommodation that forms the basis of the Law of Recognition.

Importantly, however, the official recognition of Islam in Austria is not the product of a policy of multicultural accommodation of ethnic and religious diversity by the modern Austrian state but rather a consequence of historical contingency. The Law of Recognition was enacted by Emperor Franz Joseph I at a time when the Austro-Hungarian Empire had a strongly multiethnic and multireligious character and included a great number of Jews and Orthodox Christians among its subjects. The inclusion of Islam as one of the recognized religious communities dates from 1912 and was the consequence of the annexation of the province of Bosnia-Herzegovina by the Austro-Hungarian Empire. After the end of the monarchy in 1918, when Bosnia ceased to be a province of the Austro-Hungarian Empire and became part of Yugoslavia, these provisions became largely dormant since there was no significant percentage of Muslims among the population in the newly founded Austrian Republic.

It was not until the 1960s that demands for the creation of an Islamic organization started to be voiced by an active group of Muslims. It is important to note that the number of Muslims in Austria was still very low. According to the census of 1971, there were only 22,267 Muslims living in Austria, a figure that represented about 0.3 percent of the population.[8] Despite some legal difficulties that shall not be discussed in detail here, the process of consolidating the legal status of a representative Muslim organization in Austria was comparatively simple (Ferrari 2005, 14) since there was an undeniable legal basis in the form of the law dating from 1912. The question of whether there should be a legal differentiation between different Islamic orientations was discussed, but it was decided in accordance with the wish of the Muslims who were petitioning for recognition that any sectarian differences should be considered as an internal affair and that only one organization would be recognized as representing all Muslims (Schmied 2005, 193). At the time, since there were comparatively very few Muslims in Austria, the question of internal heterogeneity was not so pressing. Today there are tensions within the Muslim community, although the IGGiÖ continues to be the sole organization recognized by the state as the official representative of all Muslims in Austria.

So finally in 1979, the IGGiÖ managed to acquire legal status as a corporation in public law representative of all Muslims living in Austria (Kroissenbrunner 2003; Schmied 2005). The result is that Muslims in Austria, who are mostly immigrants, have a great number of rights because of their religious membership. It is to these rights and privileges that we shall turn now.

Minority Rights – A Revised Typology

In the following, we will review the religious rights that exist both by virtue of national legislation and by virtue of European anti-discrimination and human rights legislation. Nevertheless, before discussing the specific rights possessed by Muslims in Austria, we will outline Kymlicka's typology of rights and expand it in order to take account of Austrian particularities. Although Kymlicka (1995) focuses primarily on the rights of ethnic minorities, we consider that his typology can be adapted to the realm of religious rights. We will therefore establish a revised typology that classifies religious rights as universal rights, group-differentiated rights, or corporate rights. It will be argued that Austria has a particularly generous policy of accommodation of religious diversity based on a combination of the historical legacy of a multiethnic and multireligious empire on the one hand, and a specificity of the modern Austrian political system on the other hand, namely, the tendency toward corporatist forms of representation.

As Kymlicka (1995, 26) points out, virtually all liberal democratic states are multicultural or polyethnic in one way or another and therefore face the challenge of accommodating cultural diversity. The traditional form of accommodating diversity, which forms the core of liberal ideology, is the protection of individual civil and political rights. In particular, in the case of religious diversity, all liberal democracies and international human rights treaties protect the right of individuals to freedom of religion. Moreover, it is increasingly recognized that special measures must be adopted that go beyond individual rights of citizenship. Therefore, Kymlicka (1995) introduces the concept of group-differentiated rights.

Group-differentiated rights are those rights that are granted to a group or to members of a group by virtue of their group membership. Departing from universal rights of citizenship, like the right to freedom of religion, these rights are not available to all citizens but only to those who belong to a certain group. Countries that follow an inclusionary or multicultural policy have conferred group-differentiated rights upon immigrant ethnic communities or religious minorities in order to preserve their ethnic or religious heritage. Special rights might include the right to funding for their activities and the right to be exempt from laws and regulations that disadvantage them. In Kymlicka's (1995, 31) words: "These group-specific rights—which I call 'polyethnic rights'—are intended to help ethnic groups and religious minorities express their cultural particularity and pride without it hampering their success in the economic and political institutions of the dominant society."

For Kymlicka, "group-differentiated rights" is a better term than "collective rights" because the latter is a very broad category that includes more than the kinds of group-differentiated rights related to multiculturalism. Moreover, the notion of collective rights is often associated with the suppression of individual rights, which need not be the case with "group-differentiated citizenship" (Kymlicka 1995, 34-35). As Kymlicka correctly stresses, the defining feature of group-differentiated rights is not who exercises the rights but rather that these rights are accorded on the basis of group membership. In effect, most existing rights aimed at protecting minorities are accorded to individual members of the minority, not to the group as such (Kälin 2000, 44-45).

According to Kymlicka (1995, 38-41), group-differentiated rights can be divided into three categories depending on who possesses the right: individuals, groups, or territories. As an example of an individual group-differentiated right, Kymlicka mentions the right of individual French Canadians to be granted a trial in French even outside of the province of Quebec. This is a group-differentiated right because it is available only to members of one particular group, namely, French Canadians.

Thus a Canadian whose mother tongue is Greek does not have the right to a trial in Greek. Nevertheless, it is an individual right since it is granted to and exercised by individuals, not by the group as such. By contrast, indigenous groups in some countries such as the United States and Canada have rights that are authentic group rights. This is the case of fishing rights granted to Aboriginal tribes, for example. Thus, if one individual Aboriginal is forbidden to fish by the governing body of his people he cannot claim that his right was violated, since the rights are granted to the group, not to individual members of the group. Territorial rights are yet of another kind since they are granted to the administration of a territorial unit where a specific group comprises the majority.

As we shall see, the rights of the Muslim community in Austria are of three kinds. First of all, Austria recognizes the universal right to freedom of religion for all individuals. Secondly, individual Muslims in Austria possess a significant number of rights that can be considered "group-differentiated rights." Also the European non-discrimination Directive 2000/78/EC grants individual members of any religious community (including Islam) the right not to be discriminated against either directly or indirectly on the basis of their religion. We consider this to be a group-differentiated right because, although it is granted to all religious individuals, it is granted only on the basis of their membership in a religious community. Furthermore, Muslims in Austria have a third kind of right that escapes Kymlicka's classification. The Law of Recognition grants the organization representing the Islamic community specific rights that are accorded to the organization itself as representative of all Muslims in Austria. We would therefore like to suggest an enhancement of Kymlicka's typology of individual rights and group-differentiated rights. We propose calling this third category "corporate rights." Having established this revised typology of religious rights, we shall now turn to a detailed analysis of the existing rights enjoyed by Muslims in Austria.

Religious Rights in Austria

Universal Rights

In Austria, the national Constitution provides a guarantee of freedom of religion in general (Article 14 StGG) and also the right to manifest one's religion in private and in public as long as this does not conflict with public order and customs (Article 63 StVSt. Germain). At the European level, the human right to freedom of religion is protected by different instruments, such as the European Convention of Human Rights of the Council of Europe.[9] Moreover, the whole text of the

Convention forms part of the Austrian Constitution. Article 9 of the Convention provides the following:

1. Everyone has the right to freedom of thought, conscience and religion; this right includes freedom to change his religion or belief, and freedom, either alone or in community with others and in public or private, to manifest his religion or belief, in worship, teaching, practice and observance.

2. Freedom to manifest one's religion or beliefs shall be subject only to such limitations as are prescribed by law and are necessary in a democratic society in the interests of public safety, for the protection of public order, health or morals, or the protection of the rights and freedoms of others.

Furthermore, the human right to freedom of religion is reiterated by the European Union Charter of Fundamental Rights.[10] The EU Charter was signed and proclaimed by the presidents of the European Parliament, the Council, and the Commission at the European Council meeting in Nice on 7 December 2000 and shall become legally binding on all EU member states, except the United Kingdom and Poland, if the so-called Reform Treaty is ratified. Article 10(1) of the Charter is a literal copy of Article 9(1) of the European Convention of Human Rights quoted above.

The Group-Differentiated Rights of Muslims

Muslims in Austria are granted a number of group-differentiated rights due to the official recognition of Islam. Moreover, the official recognition of Islam works indirectly to the benefit of immigrants' claims, since the constitutional guarantee of freedom of religion is often interpreted very broadly in light of the Law of Recognition, thus facilitating requests by representatives of the Islamic community for special legal treatment beyond the provisions of the Law of Recognition itself. We will consider the following group-differentiated rights: the right to dress in ways consistent with one's religious community, to religious education about Islam in public schools, to take time off for prayer and religious holidays, and to receive special food in some state institutions. Moreover, the IGGiÖ has several rights as an organization representing a recognized religious community. These rights range from administrative rights to educational, economic, and even political rights.

One of the most important and most contested rights claimed by Muslims throughout Europe is the right to dress according to the traditions of their communities. In particular, the demand of school girls to be able to wear the Islamic headscarf, or hijab, in public schools has led to very heated debates about the proper way to accommodate religious diversity in secular Europe (Benhabib 2004; Motha 2007). In Austria, Muslims are allowed to wear their religiously prescribed dress in public institutions, and there is very little debate in the media about the hijab (Gresch et al. 2008). Nevertheless, in 2004, a controversy did arise over the wearing of headscarves by some students, and so a decree was issued by the Ministry of Education that approved a non-restrictive approach in the state school system.[11] The decree states that the wearing of a headscarf by Muslim students shall be identified as a religious dress code and therefore is to be protected by the constitutional principles enshrined in Article 14 of the Austrian Constitution (*Staatsgrundgesetz*) and by Article 9 of the Human Rights Convention. The right to wear headscarves is thus defined by the state as a religious obligation and hence viewed as guaranteed by constitutional law. Similarly, the right of Muslim students (especially girls) not to participate in mixed swimming and sports classes where this is considered to conflict with the rules of the Islamic faith is also guaranteed by a governmental decree.[12]

Likewise, where discussions have arisen concerning the requests of Muslim employees and students to take time off work or school for prayer or for religious holidays, an inclusive-pluralistic solution was sought. Hence, the *Arbeitsruhegesetz* allows workers to take time off for religious prayer so long as that does not disturb others (Kalb, Potz, and Schinkele 2003, 115-19). A corresponding law ensures the rights of Muslim students not to attend school on two Islamic holidays, the Eid-al-Fitr and the Eid-al-Adha.[13] Although this regulation does not apply to employees, currently negotiations are being conducted between the IGGiÖ and the Austrian Chamber of Commerce regarding the possibility of Muslim employees being granted two days of religious holiday each year (employees would be paid for one of these days). Additionally, special regulations have been adopted to ensure that Muslims serving in the military receive special food and are released from service for the Islamic holidays of Ramadan and Eid-al-Adha.[14]

Further group-differentiated rights are granted to individual Muslims in Austria by European Union legislation. While primary EU law and international treaties to which the European Union and its member states are signatories ensure the individual human right to freedom of faith, EU secondary legislation, notably Council Directive 2000/78/EC (hereafter referred to as the Employment Equality Directive) adopted in 2000, explicitly prohibits employment discrimination on the grounds of religion or belief.[15] The right to non-discrimination established by the Directive is granted to all persons resident in the European Union irrespective of nationality. The Employment Equality Directive goes well beyond a mere guarantee of freedom to choose one's faith to include a prohibition of direct and indirect discrimination, harassment, instructions to discriminate, and victimization. Thus, the Directive grants a group-differentiated right to non-discrimination on the grounds of religion to members of all religious communities. This might be considered a group-differentiated right because it is granted only to religious persons on the basis of their belonging to a religious group. Other kinds of group membership do not have the same protection. For instance, there is no European legislation prohibiting discrimination in employment on the grounds of membership in a political group.

Finally, a very important group-differentiated right granted to individual Muslims in Austria by virtue of the Law of Recognition is the right of Muslim children to religious instruction in Islam. In Austria, religious instruction is a mandatory subject of the normal curriculum of public schools. Thus, all school children are required to attend some kind of religious instruction unless their parents ask for them to be exempted. Religious instruction is confessional, and all legally recognized churches and religious communities have a right to maintain publicly funded religious instruction for students of their faith. This is also the case for Islam. Muslim students have a right to receive religious instruction in Islam in their schools, provided that numbers warrant it. Where the number of students belonging to the Islamic faith is too small to justify a separate class, Muslim students are exempt from attending religious instruction. Currently, the curriculum for Islamic religious instruction in Austrian public schools includes such topics as the meaning of faith, the fundamentals of Islam, how a Muslim has to behave, the biography of the prophet Muhammad, the history of Islam, the values of Islam, fundamentals of Islamic law, and the Islamic social system (Wallner 2005). In the European Union, the right to receive Islamic religious instruction in public schools is unique to Austria and is heralded by the IGGiÖ as a major factor contributing to the integration of Muslims in the country.[16]

Corporate Rights

The right of individual Muslims to religious education is connected to a right granted to the IGGiÖ as the representative organization of the Islamic community to define the curriculum of Islamic religious instruction in schools without interference by the state. Austrian legislation establishes that the content of the confessional religious instruction in schools is to be considered an internal affair of the respective church or officially recognized religious community; the state is responsible only for the organizational and disciplinary aspects of religious instruction (Kalb, Potz, and Schinkele 2003, 355). The only restriction imposed by the legislation is that the content of the religious instruction should not go against the general principles of civic education (Kalb, Potz, and Schinkele 2003, 359). More than that, the IGGiÖ has the right to hire, train, and supervise the religious teachers, even though they then become public servants and are paid by the state (Wieshaider 2004, 32).[17] This right to religious education is very important not only because of the symbolic value of cultural recognition that comes from including a minority's religion in the curriculum of public education but also because it allows the IGGiÖ to intervene directly in the public educational system.

Furthermore, the IGGiÖ shares with all other officially recognized religious groups the right to autonomy and self-determination in internal affairs. Internal affairs include regulations and issues related to religious doctrines, sacraments, and offices; issues related to religious education such as the above-mentioned assignment of teaching posts; and issues related to the organization itself, such as membership duties and rights, and the administration and acquisition of the group's property. Here it is important to note, however, that in order to acquire official recognition by the state, the religious communities must fulfil a number of conditions. In particular, religious organizations must show that they have a positive approach toward society and the state, and they must not encourage their members to engage in any conduct that goes against Austrian law or customs (Kalb, Potz, and Schinkele 2003, 95-102).

In addition, the IGGiÖ has established an important new function in the political arena. Since 2000, the IGGiÖ has been consulted by the government when laws or policies were being negotiated that were deemed to have an impact on religious communities. Although the Catholic and the Protestant churches have always had a privileged position within the political system, for the IGGiÖ this was a major new achievement. Interestingly, the initiative to include the IGGiÖ in important political consultation processes was initiated by a European event (Rosenberger, Mourão Permoser, and Stöckl 2008). In 2000, three experts were appointed to prepare a report on whether the European Union should lift sanctions against Austria that had been levied in the wake of allegations that the Freedom Party (FPÖ), which was then a member of the governing coalition, was xenophobic. When preparing their report, the experts invited not only the Catholic and Protestant churches for official consultations but also representatives of the Jewish community and the IGGiÖ (Ahtisaari, Frowein, and Oreja 2000). Since then, the IGGiÖ and other religious organizations have been involved in several political consultation procedures. For example, the recognized religious organizations were consulted in the Constitutional Convention that took place from June 2003 to January 2005 with the aim of drafting a new constitution for Austria.[18] Similarly, the IGGiÖ was also invited to take part in the recently created *Integrationsplattform*,[19] which was supposed to provide a new integration policy for immigrants in Austria.

These developments fit well with the Austrian traditions of consociational democracy and strong corporatism. The Austrian political system has historically been marked by a particularly strong institutionalization of interest representation in the form of social partnership (Pelinka 1998; Pelinka and Rosenberger 2003). Social partnership refers to the specific form of Austrian corporatism, that is, to the tripartite arrangement between the state, capital, and labour that is marked by "a dense network of interactions between government, state bureaucracy, coalition parties, and highly monopolised, centralised and politically privileged interest organisations, combined to an equally dense bargaining system relating sectoral wage bargaining to centralised coordination of wage policy" (Kittel 2000, 109). Although the rootedness of social partnership in the policy-making process was not formally regulated through the legal system, this did not impede the interactions from achieving an extraordinary degree of institutionalization and legitimacy. In fact, Austrian scholars refer to the informal rules governing the participation of social partners in the political process as belonging to the *"Realverfassung,"* that is, to Austria's real, as opposed to nominal, constitution (Ucakar 2006). Although the role of social partners in the decision-making process in Austria has been waning (see Tálos 2006), this need not be the case of the Austrian tradition of consociational democracy per se. In fact, in the case of representation of religious groups in the political system, the role of religious communities seems to be gaining in importance.

Thus, the IGGiÖ is becoming an increasingly important actor in the policy-making process in Austria in certain policy areas. However, so far only the government has been in the position of determining when the religious organizations are consulted. This gives the political participation of the religious organizations an ad hoc character and leads to inconsistencies. For instance, in the implementation of the anti-discrimination provisions of the Employment Equality Directive, the evidence shows that the government did not follow a policy of consultation with non-governmental and religious organizations (European Commission 2005; Niessen and Chopin 2002). Thus the authors of the Migrant Policy Index write of the field of anti-discrimination in Austria: "The Austrian state does not disseminate information, lead dialogue, introduce positive action measures or oblige public bodies to promote equality" (Niessen et al. 2007, 24).

Nevertheless, despite the weakness of Austria's commitment to employment anti-discrimination measures in general and to including religious communities in the debate on the implementation of EU regulations concerning non-discrimination in particular, the embeddedness of the IGGiÖ in several important policy-making settings definitely represents a major pluralistic and inclusionary feature of the Austrian model of dealing with religious diversity. It also reinforces the notion that religious organizations have the status of public corporations, which is an important aspect of the Austrian religious-rights system.

In conclusion, we see how in Austria, religious rights amount to more than the right to freedom of religion as anchored in the Constitution and in human rights conventions. The right to freedom of religion as inscribed in these documents is based on the traditional liberal ideology of universal individual rights, which does not differentiate between the needs of particular social groups. By contrast, the rights granted by the Recognition Law (and by the specific way in which the Austrian Constitution has been interpreted in the light of the Recognition Law) to individual Muslims in Austria and to the IGGiÖ are best described as "group-differentiated rights" (Kymlicka 1995) and corporate rights, respectively.

Religious Citizenship

Religious rights in Austria are in fact so generous and disconnected from nationality that we would like to argue that they amount to a form of religious citizenship. In this section, we will evaluate this claim by comparing the rights granted to Muslims in Austrian and European legislation with the classic rights of citizenship described by T. H. Marshall. By the term *religious citizenship*, we do not mean, of course, citizenship in the sense of a formal status. As Bauböck points out: "The status of citizenship, by which a state recognizes an individual as its member, is not a formal legal concept lacking any particular content; it implies substantial rights to protection, as well as those against interference, by the state" (1994, 202). It is possible to differentiate between formal citizenship, meaning the legal status that is usually attached to nationality, and substantive citizenship, meaning the complex bundle of rights and responsibilities that are attached to membership in a community (Castles 1994, 3-4).

Formal and substantive citizenship do not always coincide. Thus, substantive rights of citizenship may be possessed by persons who are not legally recognized as citizens. This is usually the case for resident foreigners or "denizens" in modern liberal democracies. In fact, the rights granted to non-nationals in most liberal democracies, and especially in Europe, have significantly increased in recent times, as the discourse of human rights and "universal personhood" enables previously excluded groups to articulate claims to an ever larger number of rights (Soysal 1994). The boundaries of entitlement are shifting in Europe toward a situation in which substantial citizenship is increasingly detached from the possession of formal citizenship.

The rights that constitute substantial citizenship are not all of the same kind. They may themselves be divided into different categories. In his classic analysis of the development of citizenship in the UK, T. H. Marshall (1964) divided the rights of citizenship for analytical purposes into three categories or "elements": civic, political, and social. The civic element of citizenship in Marshall's account was composed of "the rights necessary for individual freedom," including "liberty of the person, freedom of speech, thought and faith, the right to own property and to conclude valid contracts, and the right to justice" (78). The political element, in turn, referred to "the right to participate in the exercise of political power" (78), be it as an elector or as a member of a political body. Finally, the social element in Marshall's view implied "an absolute right to a certain standard of civilization" (103).

Although Marshall did not make this differentiation explicitly, one could say that the social element of citizenship is composed of two dimensions: an economic and a cultural one. On the one hand, social citizenship includes a right to economic sufficiency, that is, the right to a certain level of economic welfare and security (Marshall 1964, 78). On the other hand, it also includes what Marshall called "the right to share to the full in the social heritage and to live the life of a civilized being according to the standards prevailing in the society" (78). By that, he meant principally the right to be treated as an equal and not to be stigmatized due to social class or other group ascriptions (Marshall 1964, 88), and the right to education (89-90), which is a crucial precondition of the former. Thus, we propose to differentiate two categories of social rights for analytical purposes: those relating to economic sufficiency and security and those relating to cultural recognition. A schematic representation of Marshall's concept of citizenship might therefore look like this:

Table 1: Marshall's Three Elements of Citizenship

Civil	Political	Social
Liberty of the person	Right to participate in the exercise of political power	Economic rights: • to a minimum of economic welfare • to security
Freedom of speech		
Freedom of thought		Right to cultural recognition: • to be treated as an equal (without stigma)
Freedom of faith		• to live the life of a civilized being and take part in social heritage – education

Source: Authors' compilation based on Marshall (1964).

We see that religious rights or "freedom of faith" were already included in Marshall's framework, namely, as belonging to the domain of civic citizenship. However, what Marshall meant by freedom of faith is indeed a civil right in all modern democracies; that is to say, freedom of faith is a merely passive right to choose one's own religion. It implies a right to freedom from state interference with one's individual choice of religion or belief, not a positive responsibility by the state to make sure that all religious groups can exercise their religion and fully take part in society on an equal basis despite their religious differences. The rationale behind this non-interventionist right to freedom of religion as described by Marshall is that faith and religious observance are matters of individual choice and belong to the private sphere of life. As with all rights belonging to the civic element, the right to freedom of religion is just a promise without any guarantee of fulfilment (Marshall 1964, 97).

The religious rights that exist in Austria due to the Constitution, the Recognition Law, and the implementation of EU anti-discrimination legislation differ fundamentally from the notion of freedom of faith implied in Marshall's typology. First, religious rights in Austria do not only mean that the state should refrain from interference with each person's choice of religion but also imply a positive duty by the state and by private parties (employers) to accommodate religious diversity and make full participation in society possible for all religious groups. These rights thereby recognize the public aspect of religious observance. Whereas the choice of religion remains a private individual affair, the exercise of religious freedom is recognized as taking place both in the private and in the public spheres of life.

Secondly, in the case of Austria, the religious rights granted to certain groups such as Catholics and Muslims are not individual in nature but actually amount to group-differentiated rights (for instance, Islamic religious education in public schools and Islamic representation in political consultation procedures). Moreover, as we have seen, the rights granted to recognized religious communities are not only civil in nature but rather permeate many spheres of life.

A further particularity of these religious rights is that they are granted independently from the possession of formal citizenship. The IGGiÖ represents all Muslims independent of their citizenship and is consulted in political negotiations in certain areas. Consequently, Muslims who do not have citizenship are nevertheless partially represented in the political system and can sometimes indirectly influence policy-making. This means that in Austria, affiliation with a given religion may at times replace citizenship as a condition for becoming an actor in the political system. Of course, even a relatively inclusive religious citizenship regime does not lead to the same degree of egalitarian political participation and autonomy that might be fostered by an inclusive political citizenship regime. Furthermore, this kind of indirect political participation is only granted on the basis of group representation and religious membership. By contrast, immigrants who are long-term residents in Austria do not have the same right to political representation as religious groups do.

Interestingly, at the level of EU legislation, we can observe a similar pattern. The Employment Equality Directive applies to all persons living in the European Union regardless of citizenship. At the same time, the right to non-discrimination on the grounds of religion is considered to be part and parcel of the distinctive attributes of European citizenship (see Bell 2002).

In this sense, religious citizenship in Austria has roots in Austrian history and in the specificities of the Austrian political system. Nevertheless, it also fits well with the trend toward "a postnational model" as identified by sociologist Yasemin Soysal. She claims that we have entered an era of transnational memberships, a postnational period in which national citizenship is "no longer a significant construction" in the allocation of rights and privileges (1994, 159). In this postnational model, she argues, the dichotomy between national citizens and foreigners has been superseded by forms of transnational membership in which non-nationals are allocated rights that were previously reserved for citizens, thereby undermining the basis of national citizenship (1994, 137). Soysal's main explanation for the erosion of the model of national citizenship is what she calls the "discourse of universal personhood." She contends that in the postnational model, unlike with national citizenship, the source of legitimate claims for equal treatment is no longer a shared nationality but rather the principle of human rights that ascribes a universal status to individuals and their rights. She argues:

> In the classical model, shared nationality is the main source of equal treatment among members. . . . In the postnational model, universal personhood replaces nationhood; and universal human rights replace national rights. The justification for the state's obligations to foreign populations goes beyond the nation-state itself. The rights and claims of individuals are legitimated by ideologies rounded in a transnational community, through international codes, conventions, and laws on human rights, independent of their citizenship in a nation-state. (1994, 142)

In a recent article, Koenig (2008) shows how the spread of a universal discourse of human rights has eroded the importance of the nation and legitimized other forms of collectivities, paradoxically contributing to the proliferation of particularistic rights of sub- and transnational collectivities such as religious and ethnic minorities. Although the establishment of religious citizenship in Austria had other causes, as we have seen, it nevertheless coincides with and is reinforced by a broader trend toward the decoupling of substantial rights of citizenship from nationality caused by the spread of a discourse of human rights that legitimates religious collectivities (as alternatives to the nation) as mediators between the state and individuals in the allocation of rights.

In sum, religious rights as present in Austria go well beyond an individual right to freedom of faith. Rather, they include both individual and group-differentiated rights covering many aspects of life—employment, education, symbols, and so forth—and cutting through all three dimensions of Marshall's concept of citizenship. Moreover, the rights granted by virtue of religious membership break with the traditional conception of citizenship since they are not made conditional on the possession of national citizenship. Therefore, we argue that the increasing number of rights derived from religious membership amount to a form of religious citizenship that transcends the boundaries of traditional nationality-based citizenship. In the next section, we shall discuss the relevance of religious citizenship for policies of immigrant integration.

Contradictory Dynamics

This generous policy of accommodation of religious diversity is not the result of efforts for the multicultural accommodation of immigrants but rather the result of a mixture of opportunity structures based on the historical legacy of a de facto multicultural empire on the one hand, and the specificity of the modern Austrian political system (namely, the tendency toward corporatist forms of interest representation) on the other. This explains, in part, the significant contrast between the generous system of rights granted to Muslims in Austria by virtue of their religious membership and the restrictive, exclusionary integration policies that deny rights to immigrants as residents and members of society.

In fact, as indicated above, Austria has one of the worst integration policies in Europe. According to the Migrant Integration Policy Index (Niessen et al. 2007), Austria ranks 20th out of the 28 countries studied (including the EU-25 plus Canada, Norway, and Switzerland). In specific areas, the picture is even worse. Where the acquisition of nationality is concerned, Austria has the worst policies of all 28 countries studied. Whereas in Canada, for instance, immigrants can naturalize after three years of living in the country and all children born in Canada automatically acquire Canadian citizenship, in Austria most adult immigrants are eligible for citizenship only after ten years, and children and grandchildren born in Austria to immigrant families must also apply for naturalization in order to acquire the nationality of their country of birth. In family reunification policies, Austria ranks second to last among all 28 countries.

In anti-discrimination policies (i.e., policies not related just to religious discrimination), Austria ranks second to last among the EU-15 countries. Whereas Austria has implemented EU legislation prohibiting discrimination in employment, it has not expanded this protection to other areas. Thus in fields such as education, housing, health care, and welfare, victims of discrimination cannot appeal under federal law (Niessen et al. 2007, 24). Moreover, Austria does not strictly enforce its anti-discrimination legislation, and the remuneration granted to victims of discrimination is one of the lowest in Europe. Discrimination on the grounds of nationality is not prohibited (except for EU citizens), and immigrants from outside the EU experience legal discrimination in a number of fields.

Concerning access to the labour market, Austria has extremely restrictive policies. To cite a few examples, the work permit of a labour immigrant is generally coupled to a specific job, so that he or she cannot change jobs without having to apply for a new permit. Moreover, Austria uses the quota system to govern work permits, even after permits have been issued. In other words, the work permit of an immigrant may be revoked, even after several years of legal residence and employment history in the country, in the event that the quota of immigrants in the labour market is reached (Waldrauch 2001, 299-301). Moreover, access to the labour market is blocked for several categories of immigrants such as asylum-seekers and students and only permitted for other categories such as family members brought in through family reunification after a long waiting period.

Long-term resident policies rank third to last among the EU-15. In the areas of labour-market integration and electoral rights, Austria scored a staggering 0 percent in the index's evaluation (Niessen et al. 2007, 21). Besides the fact that long-term residents do not have a right to participate in any public election in Austria, they do not have much security in their status. For reasons of public order, immigrants may be expelled from Austria even after having lived in the country for 20 years. Austria is also the only country in the European Union that requires immigrants to purchase comprehensive health insurance in order to be eligible for long-term residence status. Moreover, applicants must show proof of stable income and must not have received any welfare benefit, despite the fact that access to the Austrian labour market is restricted for immigrants.

These results are shocking for a country where Muslims, 75 percent of whom are immigrants, are considered to be a well-integrated minority. As König and Perchinig (2005, 14-15) put it: "Most advocates trying to advance integration argue that Austrian Muslims are well integrated because of the special legal position of the Islamic faith." In effect, the Austrian model of managing religious diversity, with its official recognition of Islam and the attendant rights that come with it, has been successful in many ways.

On the other hand, the inclusionary regulatory framework does not imply societal acceptance of the religious diversity that comes from immigration. Anti-Islamic sentiments are widespread in Austria and so is discrimination of Muslim immigrants in employment and housing (Niessen and Chopin 2002; RAXEN 2003). This lack of acceptance of the value of religious diversity is also manifested at the level of political discourse, where anti-Islamic sentiments are often instrumentalized by mainstream political actors to win votes or to justify strict immigration and integration policies. The unwillingness to grant third-country nationals resident within the territory comparable rights to national citizens contrasts strongly with the generous policies of religious accommodation directed largely at the same group.

A similarly contradictory dynamic is also at play to some extent at the level of supranational policy-making in the European Union. While the anti-discrimination directives of the year 2000 grant important rights to third-country nationals by virtue of their ethnic or religious membership, policies aimed specifically at the socioeconomic integration of immigrants have failed to achieve such high standards. EU institutions have made repeated rhetorical commitments to achieve equality for legally resident third-country nationals ever since the 1970s. These rhetorical commitments were accompanied by occasional attempts to enact legislation in this area; however, these measures failed to lead to a thorough equalization of the opportunities of third-country nationals because of the lack of agreement among the member states.

The most significant measure to improve the socioeconomic rights of third-country nationals resident in the European Union was the adoption of the so-called Long-Term Residents Directive (LTRD).[20] However, the LTRD does not apply to all third-country nationals, and it permits existing inequalities in the labour market and social assistance schemes to continue. Moreover, the LTRD offers wide discretion to member states to impose mandatory "integration requirements" for immigrants wishing to benefit from its provisions. These integration requirements are not further defined but, in practice, often amount to the imposition of language and civil education tests aimed at assessing whether immigrants have adopted the receiving society's values and morals. In countries that have already adopted such integration tests, including Germany, Austria, the Netherlands, and France, the debate over the "lack of integration" of immigrants is quite prominent. Although the concept of integration has potentially different meanings, in these debates it is used predominantly to refer to the degree of cultural assimilation of immigrants into the national society. Thus, immigrants whose customs do not differ greatly from those of the majority culture are considered to be integrated, whereas those who insist on living their lives according to different cultural traditions (speaking a different language, dressing differently, eating differently) and different value systems are seen as not being integrated.

In Austria, the mandatory civic test for those applying for citizenship requires knowledge of the country's history, geography, and political system. There are no questions specifically aimed at assessing the immigrant's cultural background or value system. The compulsory integration courses for immigrants applying for a residence permit, on the other hand, although mostly focused on providing immigrants with sufficient language proficiency to be able to communicate in German in daily-life situations, are also meant to provide immigrants with a certain degree of knowledge about the "Austrian way of life": the curriculum must include the topic "core values of a democratic European society."[21]

However, in other EU countries such as the Netherlands and some German provinces, these civic integration tests are much more explicitly used as a discriminatory tool, supposedly aimed at assessing the immigrant's commitment to "core liberal values." A case in point is the test that has been applied in the province of Baden-Württemberg since 2006, where applicants for citizenship who come from countries where the population is predominantly Muslim must answer questions such as "What would you do if you found out that your son is gay?" or "In your view were the perpetrators of the September 11th attacks terrorists or freedom fighters?" Similarly, the Dutch government's information DVD sent to applicants for a Dutch visa includes images of naked women and of homosexual couples kissing that are likely specifically targeted at Muslim audiences (Joppke 2007).

Joppke (2007) points out that one very interesting aspect of these new civic integration policies is their obligatory character. The state therefore coerces immigrants into adopting liberal norms and values (or at least into acting as though they have). Obviously such tests become an instrument of the state to manage migration and select immigrants according to their level of education and their capacity or willingness to adopt the general norms and values as well as the language and customs of the hosting society. As Carrera notes, if implemented in a restrictive manner, the application of these provisions would lead to a situation where "the values of a multicultural society and the respect of the fundamental rights of third-country nationals could be seriously undermined. The dividing line between an efficient integration policy and the respect of cultural, ethnic and religious diversity may become dangerously thin" (2005, 19).

In sum, the generous system of accommodation of religious diversity (which over time has been quite beneficial to immigrants, most of whom are Muslim) conflicts strongly with the tendency toward policies of immigrant integration that restrict the political and socioeconomic rights of migrants and make these rights conditional on cultural assimilation into the receiving society. The result of these contradictory rights regimes is that immigrants have their religious identities formally recognized and protected by the state through the Law of Recognition, but they are still excluded from full participation in society as equal members of the polity. In particular, immigrants are often not given an equal chance to improve their economic situation since there are restrictions to labour market participation and to welfare benefits due to their immigrant status. At the same time, it is predominantly their inferior economic status that makes immigrants a target of xenophobic and intolerant arguments. Here Marshall's (1964) insight remains as pertinent as ever, that an adequate level of economic welfare and security is an indispensable element in achieving full social equality. To paraphrase Leonard Besselink (2006, 18), cultural and religious recognition is no substitute for social and economic measures, certainly not if the roots of the problem are mainly social and economic.

Conclusion

It lies beyond the scope of this chapter to give a thorough and definitive explanation for this contradiction between the generous group-differentiated rights offered to third-country nationals on the basis of their religious membership and the restrictive policies of immigrant integration that make a certain degree of acculturation a necessary precondition for the acquisition of socioeconomic rights. Nevertheless, we will attempt to outline a few hypotheses.

As our analysis of the origins of the official recognition of Islam and of the IGGiÖ in Austria has shown, the privileged situation granted today to immigrants on the basis of their religious membership was not due to a conscious effort on the part of the Austrian government to improve the immigrants' lot. Rather, it was the product of a combination of three factors. First, the historical legacy of the multiethnic Austro-Hungarian Empire and its tolerant attitudes toward religious minorities created the legal premises upon which the recognition of Islam was made possible. Second, the existence of a small but very active group of politically engaged Muslims, who saw in this historical legal premise a chance to improve the situation of Muslims in Austria and pressured the government to recognize Islam, was an absolutely crucial factor. Finally, the traditions of consociational democracy and of a highly institutionalized corporatism, which characterize the Austrian political system, have certainly contributed to the IGGiÖ's increasing importance as a political actor.

However, none of these factors implies a true acceptance of the realities of migration and the cultural diversity that comes with it. Had it not been for the clever manipulation of a historical legacy by a group of religious entrepreneurs, it is very unlikely that a similar degree of rights for Muslim immigrants as presently exists would ever have developed. Much to the contrary, xenophobic discourses have been widespread in Austrian politics for a long time (Pelinka and Wodak 2002; Wodak and Reisigl 2000). Moreover, these discourses increasingly have taken an anti-Islamic turn (Rosenberger and Hadj-Abdou forthcoming).

Furthermore, whereas in Europe there is a general acceptance of the liberal idea that people should be free to choose their own conception of the Good and act accordingly, Islam is often viewed as an illiberal religion that does not grant exactly this kind of freedom and autonomy to its members. Thus, attempts are made to "pursue liberal goals with illiberal means" (Joppke 2007, 1) through the creation of stringent integration requirements and so on. Moreover, the fear that liberal policies might nurture and support the illiberal values of certain Muslim communities is manipulated by protectionists who wish to exclude Muslims from national labour markets and welfare systems. In the end, two contradictory systems of dealing with cultural diversity result.

In the case of Austria, we have argued that the reasons for the development of these conflicting rights regimes may be found in the capacity of relevant societal actors to make use of existing institutional frameworks and societal norms. This was not the case with immigrant integration policies, where xenophobic parties and protectionist interests have been largely successful in framing liberal norms as being synonymous with European values and as conflicting with the values of immigrant communities.

At the supranational level, the situation does not markedly differ. As Geddes and Guiraudon (2004) have shown, the passing of the anti-discrimination directives in 2000 was crucially influenced by the fact that a committed group of political entrepreneurs could use the rise of extreme right-wing parties in Europe, especially the Austrian Freedom Party (FPÖ) of Jörg Haider, to frame the new claims to anti-discrimination in the language of contemporary Europe's commitment to countering anti-Semitism and racism. Thus a historical commitment to religious and ethnic pluralism was cleverly instrumentalized by those who wished to improve the situation of immigrant communities in Europe, despite the fact that such a strong commitment to these minorities might not have been present per se among the decision-makers.

By contrast, when it came to the negotiations of the Long-Term Residents Directive in 2003, no such window of opportunity existed. The context was one of ever more restrictive immigration and integration policies in a number of European countries, especially Austria, Germany, and the Netherlands. The European Council was composed of a majority of centre-right parties, and the institutional setting of the negotiations was the Justice and Home Affairs Council—factors that contributed to a framing of the question of immigrant integration as an issue of security and welfare protection, rather than one of fundamental rights. Moreover, we should also remember that the LTRD was signed in the wake of the attacks of 11 September 2001, which contributed to a general securitization of the issue of migration.

In sum, one possible hypothesis to be further explored would be that the success of policies aimed at immigrant integration depend on the capacity of socially progressive actors to frame their claims in terms of existing liberal norms and against those who try to instrumentalize those same norms to justify the exclusion of immigrants from full participation in society. In this chapter, we have argued that this hypothesis holds true for Austria. It will be the task of further studies to show whether it also holds in different national contexts and at the level of the European Union.

Notes

1. See Statistik Austria, table Bevölkerung 2001 nach Religionsbekenntnis und Staatsangehörigkeit, available at http://www.statistik.at/web_de/statistiken/bevoelkerung/volkszaehlungen/bevoelkerung_nach_demographischen_merkmalen/index.html
2. See Statistik Austria, table Bevölkerung 2001 nach Religionsbekenntnis und Staatsangehörigkeit, available at http://www.statistik.at/web_de/statistiken/bevoelkerung/volkszaehlungen/bevoelkerung_nach_demographischen_merkmalen/index.html
3. See Statistik Austria, table Bevölkerung 2001 nach Religionsbekenntnis und Staatsangehörigkeit, available at http://www.statistik.at/web_de/statistiken/bevoelkerung/volkszaehlungen/bevoelkerung_nach_demographischen_merkmalen/index.html
4. Personal communication with Richard Potz. See also *Wiener Zeitung*, 30 November 2006, at http://www.wienerzeitung.at/DesktopDefault.aspx?TabID=3940&Alias=wzo&cob=259469
5. See *Der Standard*, 9 November 2007 (based on data from Statistik Austria), "16,3 Prozent der Österreicher haben Migrationshintergrund," at http://derstandard.at/
6. Third-country nationals are citizens of countries that do not belong to the European Union. Due to European citizenship, citizens of European Union

member states have a number of privileges when living in another member state.

7. Own translation.
8. See Statistik Austria, table Bevölkerung nach dem Religionsbekenntnis und Bundesländern 1951 bis 2001, at http://www.statistik.at/web_de/static/bevoelkerung_nach_dem_religionsbekenntnis_und_bundeslaendern_1951_bis_2001_022885.pdf
9. Signed in Rome, 4 November 1950.
10. OJ of 18.12.2000 No. C364/01.
11. ZI 20.251/3-III/3/2004.
12. ZI 20.251/4-III/4/92.
13. GZ 20.251/2-III/4/87; see also information by the Federal Ministry ZI.21.001/5-Z/10/2003 regarding §9 Abs.6 of the Schulpflichtgesetzes 1985 and §45 Abs. 4 of the Schulunterrichtsgesetzes.
14. GZ 60.900/645-5.1./88.
15. Council Directive 2000/78/EC of 27 November 2000 establishing a general framework for equal treatment in employment and occupation, OJ No. L 300 of 2 December 2000, pp. 16-22. Compliance with the Directive was required of all member states by 2 December 2003.
16. See the website of the IGGiÖ (accessed 9 November 2007) at http://www.derislam.at/islam.php?name=Themen&pa=showpage&pid=154
17. Bundesgesetz vom 13. Juli 1949, BGBl. Nr. 190, betreffend den Religionsunterricht in der Schule.
18. http://www.derislam.at/islam.php?name=Themen&pa=showpage&pid=67
19. "Plattform der großen Erwartungen," *Der Standard*, 21 October 2007. Accessed 9 November 2007 at http://derstandard.at/?url=/?id=3073339
20. Council Directive 2003/109/EC of 25 November 2003 concerning the status of third-country nationals who are long-term residents, OJ No. L 16 of 23 January 2004, pp. 44-53.
21. See Austrian Ministry of Interior at http://www.bmi.gv.at/downloadarea/niederlassung/rechtsgrundlagen/IV-V%20Anlage%20B%20(RC%20D-Integrationskurs).pdf

References

Ahtisaari, M., J. Frowein, M. Oreja. 2000. Report commissioned by the President of the European Court of Human Rights, Paris, 8 September. Accessed 1 January 2009 at http://www.austrosearch.at/pdf/reportwisemenaustria.pdf

Bader, V. 2003. "Religious Diversity and Democratic Institutional Pluralism." *Political Theory* 31(2):265-94.

— 2007a. "The Governance of Islam in Europe: The Perils of Modelling." *Journal of Ethnic and Migration Studies* 33(6):871-86.

— 2007b. *Secularism or Democracy? Associational Governance of Religious Diversity*. Amsterdam: Amsterdam University Press.

Bauböck, R. 1994. "Changing the Boundaries of Citizenship: The Inclusion of Immigrants in Democratic Polities." In *From Aliens to Citizens: Redefining the Status of Immigrants in Europe*, ed. R. Bauböck. Aldershot: Avebury.

— 2006. *Migration and Citizenship: Legal Status, Rights, and Political Participation*. IMISCOE Reports. Amsterdam: Amsterdam University Press.

Bell, M. 2002. *Anti-Discrimination Law and the European Union*. Oxford: Oxford University Press.

Benhabib, S. 2004. *The Rights of Others: Aliens, Residents and Citizens*. Cambridge: Cambridge University Press.

Besselink, L.F.M. 2006. "Unequal Citizenship: Integration Measures and Equality." In *The Nexus between Immigration, Integration and Citizenship in the EU*, ed. S. Carrera. Brussels: Centre for European Policy Studies.

Carrera, S. 2005. "'Integration' as a Process of Inclusion for Migrants? The Case of Long-Term Residents in the EU." Working Document No. 219, Centre for European Policy Studies, Brussels.

Castles, S. 1994. "Democracy and Multicultural Citizenship. Australian Debates and Their Relevance for Western Europe." In *From Aliens to Citizens: Redefining the Status of Immigrants in Europe*, ed. R. Bauböck. Aldershot: Avebury.

European Commission. 2005. *Equality and Non-Discrimination – Annual Report 2005*. Luxembourg. Accessed 24 November 2008 at http://ec.europa.eu/employment_social/fundamental_rights/pdf/pubst/poldoc/annualrep05_en.pdf

Ferrari, S. 2005. "The Secularity of the State and the Shaping of Muslim Representative Organisations in Western Europe." In *European Muslims and the Secular State*, ed. J. Cesari and S. McLoughlin. Aldershot: Ashgate.

Fetzer, J. and C.J. Soper. 2004. *Muslims and the State in Britain, France, and Germany*. Cambridge: Cambridge University Press.

Geddes, A. and V. Guiraudon. 2004. "Britain, France, and EU Anti-Discrimination Policy: The Emergence of an EU Policy Paradigm." *West European Politics* 27(2):335-53.

Gresch, N., L. Hadj-Abdou, S. Rosenberger, and B. Sauer. 2008. "Tu Felix Austria? The Headscarf and the Politics of 'Non-Issues.'" *Social Politics* 15(4):411-32.

Heine, S. 2005. "Islàm in Austria: Between Integration Policies and Persisting Prejudices." In *Religion in Austria*, ed. G. Bischof, A. Pelinka, and H. Denz. New Brunswick and London: Transaction.

Joppke, C. 2007. "Beyond National Models: Civic Integration Policies for Immigrants in Western Europe." *West European Politics* 30(1):1-22.

Kalb, H., R. Potz, and B. Schinkele. 2003. *Religionsrecht*. Vienna: WUV Universitätsverlag.

Kälin, W. 2000. *Grundrechte im Kulturkonflikt: Freiheit und Gleichheit in der Einwanderungsgesellschaft*. Zurich: Neue Zürcher Zeitung.

Kanmaz, M. 2002. "The Recognition and Institutionalization of Islam in Belgium." *The Muslim World* 92(1-2):99-113.

Kittel, B. 2000. "Deaustrification? The Policy-Area-Specific Evolution of Austrian Social Partnership." *West European Politics* 23(1):108-29.

Klausen, J. 2005. *The Islamic Challenge: Politics and Religion in Western Europe.* Oxford: Oxford University Press.

Koenig, M. 2005. "Incorporating Muslim Migrants in Western Nation-States: A Comparison of the United Kingdom, France, and Germany." *Journal of International Migration and Integration* 6(2):219-34.

— 2007. "Europeanising the Governance of Religious Diversity: An Institutionalist Account of Muslim Struggles for Public Recognition." *Journal of Ethnic and Migration Studies* 33(6):911-32.

— 2008. "Institutional Change in the World Polity: International Human Rights and the Construction of Collective Identities." *International Sociology* 23(1):95-114.

König, K. and B. Perchinig. 2005. "Current Immigration Debates in Europe: Austria." In *Current Immigration Debates in Europe*, ed. J. Niessen, Y. Schibel, and C. Thompson. Brussels: Migration Policy Group.

König, K. and B. Stadler. 2003. "Entwicklungstendenzen im Öffentlich-Techtlichen und Demokratiepolitischen Bereich." In *Österreichischer Migrations- und Integrationsbericht*, ed. H. Fassmann and I. Stacher. Vienna: Drava Verlag.

Kraler, A. and K. Sohler. 2005. "Active Civic Participation of Immigrants in Austria: Country Report." European Research Project POLITIS. Available at http://www.uni-oldenburg.de/politis-europe

Kroissenbrunner, S. 2003. "Islam, Migration und Integration: Politische Netzwerke und 'Muslim Leadership.'" In *Österreichischer Migrations- und Integrationsbericht*, ed. H. Fassmann and I. Stacher. Vienna: Drava Verlag.

Kymlicka, W. 1995. *Multicultural Citizenship: A Liberal Theory of Minority Rights.* Oxford: Clarendon Press.

Madeley, J.T.S. 2003. "European Liberal Democracy and the Principle of State Religious Neutrality." In *Church and State in Contemporary Europe*, ed. J.T.S. Madeley and Z. Enyedi. London: Frank Cass.

Marshall, T.H. 1964. "Citizenship and Social Class." In *Class, Citizenship, and Social Development: Essays by T.H. Marshall.* Chicago: University of Chicago Press.

Maussen, M. 2007. "The Governance of Islam in Western Europe: A State of the Art Report." IMISCOE Working Paper 16, Amsterdam.

McGoldrick, D. 2006. *Human Rights and Religion: The Islamic Headscarf Debate in Europe.* Oxford: Hart Publishing.

Moreras, J. 2002. "Muslims in Spain: Between the Historical Heritage and the Minority Construction." *The Muslim World* 92(1-2):129-42.

Motha, S. 2007. "Veiled Women and the Affect of Religion in Democracy." *Journal of Law and Society* 34:139-62.

Niessen, J. and I. Chopin, eds. 2002. "Anti-Discrimination Legislation in EU Member States: A Comparison of National Anti-Discrimination Legislation on the Grounds of Racial or Ethnic Origin, Religion or Belief with the Council Directives." Vienna: European Monitoring Centre on Racism and Xenophobia.

Niessen, J., T. Huddleston, L. Citron, A. Geddes, and D. Jacobs. 2007. Migrant Integration Policy Index. British Council and Migration Policy Group, September. Available at www.integrationindex.eu

Pelinka, A. 1998. *Austria: Out of the Shadow of the Past*. Boulder, CO: Westview Press.

Pelinka, A. and S. Rosenberger. 2003. *Österreichische Politik: Grundlagen, Strukturen, Trends*. Vienna: WUV Universitätsverlag.

Pelinka, A. and R. Wodak, eds. 2002. *'Dreck am Stecken': Politik der Ausgrenzung*. Vienna: Czernin Verlag.

Potz, R. 1996. "State and Church in Austria." In *State and Church in the European Union*, ed. G. Robbers. Baden Baden: Nomos.

RAXEN (National Focal Point for Austria of the Racism and Xenophobia Network). 2003. "National Analytical Study on Housing." European Monitoring Centre for Racism and Xenophobia, Vienna, October.

Robbers, G. 1996. *State and Church in the European Union*. Baden Baden: Nomos.

Rosenberger, S. and L. Hadj-Abdou. Forthcoming. "Islam at Issue: Anti-Islamic Discourse of the Far Right in Austria." In *The Far Right in Contemporary Europe*, ed. B. Jenkins, E. Godin, and A. Mammone. New York: Palgrave Macmillan.

Rosenberger, S., J. Mourão Permoser, and K. Stöckl. 2008. "Religious Organizations as Political Actors in the Context of Migration: From Institutional Partners to Representatives of Migrants?" Paper presented at the ECPR (European Consortium for Political Research) Joint Session of Workshops, University of Rennes, France, 11–16 April.

Saharso, S. 2003a. "Culture, Tolerance and Gender: A Contribution from the Netherlands." *The Journal of Women's Studies* 10(1):7-27.

— 2003b. "Feminist Ethics, Autonomy and the Politics of Multiculturalism." *Feminist Theory* 4(2):199-215.

Schmied, M. 2005. "Islam in Österreich." In *Islam, Islamismus und islamischer Extremismus*, ed. W. Feichtinger and S. Wentker. Vienna: Landesverteidigungsakademie/Institut für Friedenssicherung und Konfliktmanagement.

Skjeie, H. 2007. "Headscarves in Schools. European Comparisons." In *Religious Pluralism and Human Rights in Europe. Where to Draw the Line?* ed. J.E. Goldschmidt and T. Loenen. Antwerp and Oxford: Intersentia.

Soper, C.J. and J. Fetzer. 2007. "Religious Institutions, Church-State History and Muslim Mobilisation in Britain, France and Germany." *Journal of Ethnic and Migration Studies* 33(6):933-44.

Soysal, Y. 1994. *Limits of Citizenship: Migrants and Postnational Membership in Europe*. Chicago: University of Chicago Press.

Tálos, E. 2006. "Sozialpartnerschaft. Austrokorporatismus am Ende?" In *Politik in Österreich: das Handbuch*, ed. H. Dachs, P. Gerlich, H. Gottweis, H. Kramer, V. Lauber, W.C. Müller, and A. Tálos. Vienna: Manz.

Ucakar, K. 2006. "Verfassung: Geschichte und Prinzipien." In *Politik in Österreich: das Handbuch*, ed. H. Dachs, P. Gerlich, H. Gottweis, H. Kramer, V. Lauber, W.C. Müller, and A. Tálos. Vienna: Manz.

US Department of State. 2004. "International Religious Freedom Report 2004: Croatia." Accessed 24 November 2008 at http://www.state.gov/g/drl/rls/irf/2004/35447.htm

Waldrauch, H., ed. 2001. *Die Integration von Einwanderern: ein Index der rechtlichen Diskriminierung*. Frankfurt: Campus Verlag.

Wallner, J. 2005. "Islamic Religious Education in Austrian Schools, Academies and Universities." Paper presented at the conference on Islam at the Universities of Europe – Religious Education and Education about Religion, University of Copenhagen, 8 November.

Wieshaider, W. 2004. "The Legal Status of the Muslim Minority in Austria." In *The Legal Treatment of Islamic Minorities in Europe*, ed. R.B.-P. Aluffi and G. Zincone. Leuven, Belgium: Peeters Publishers.

Wodak, R. and M. Reisigl. 2000. "'Austria First.' A Discourse – Historical Analysis of the Austrian 'Anti-Foreigner-Petition' in 1992 and 1993." In *The Semiotics of Racism: Approaches in Critical Discourse Analysis*, ed. M. Reisigl and R. Wodak. Vienna: Passagen Verlag.

Part III
Comparative and
Global Perspectives

Chapter 11

How Nation-States Respond to Religious Diversity

MATTHIAS KOENIG

For practitioners working in the fields of migration and religious diversity, the most pressing question after reading through volumes such as this is what may be learned about the feasibility and success of various public policy options. What are the "best practices" to ensure that migrants are integrated, their rights of religious freedom are guaranteed, their democratic participation is improved, and the societies in which they settle remain socially cohesive? However, assessing public policy options is a difficult task indeed. Should social scientists attempt to recommend "best practices," they would run the risk of abstracting policy options from the context in which they were initially formulated. They would face the difficulty of reconciling the potentially conflicting policy goals enumerated above. Best practices depend on normative yardsticks which, as even a glimpse at the literature in political philosophical and legal theory demonstrates, are highly contested (see Bader 2007). It is therefore no wonder that social scientists generally prefer to bracket such normative controversies and to avoid prescriptions about particular courses of action. Their more modest aim is to understand and explain the social dynamics of public policies. With respect to the theme of this book, their guiding question may be formulated by rephrasing the title of Stephen Castles's (1995) classical article: How do nation-states respond to religious diversity induced by international or transnational migration?

In fact, answering this question is, upon closer scrutiny, no less difficult than normatively ambitious policy evaluation. Forces such as the mobilization of migrant religious groups affect state responses to religious diversity no less than immigration policies, patterns of church-

International Migration and the Governance of Religious Diversity, eds. P. Bramadat and M. Koenig.
Montreal and Kingston: McGill-Queen's University Press, Queen's Policy Studies Series.
© 2009 The School of Policy Studies, Queen's University at Kingston. All rights reserved.

state relations, and deep-seated constructions of nationhood. Disentangling these various factors and assessing their causal weight has thus become an important research question in the nascent social science literature on the governance of religious diversity. It is this question that shall be addressed in the following chapter in order to put the country cases presented in this volume into broader comparative perspective.

The chapter is organized in three sections. The first section takes up some threads from Paul Bramadat's introduction to this volume and discusses, albeit from a slightly different angle, pitfalls of the concepts of secularization and differentiation, arguing that without their critical revision it is impossible to actually pose, let alone to answer the question of how, in a world of increased international mobility, nation-states do or might respond to religious diversity. Against this background, the second section discusses available analytical tools to comparatively describe and explain state accommodation of religious diversity in immigration countries, old and new. These tools are of great value in systematizing the empirical findings presented in our case studies. Yet, as the third section argues, they fall victim to certain methodological limitations to the extent that they rely on national "modelling." A careful reading of our case studies conveys the necessity of moving toward more process-oriented analyses of negotiating religious diversity across institutional domains and levels. In fact, policy responses to diversity turn out to follow distinctive logics in administrations, parliaments, and courts on local, national, or transnational levels. A concluding section highlights how academic analyses of policy dynamics might ultimately make a modest contribution to context-sensitive reflection upon "best practices" that are so crucial to practitioners.

Secularization Theory and Beyond

The intellectual challenges posed by contemporary religious diversity reflect the strong impact that classical secularization theory for a long time exerted upon almost all subdisciplines within the social sciences, including the study of migration and ethnic relations (see Ebaugh 2002). Of course, it is well known that secularization theory has been subject to various criticisms. Thus, the idea that modernization would inevitably lead to a decline of religion has been questioned for decades in research about what Thomas Luckmann (1967) called "invisible religion" and, later, in research about the global "resurgence" or "revival" of religion (e.g., Sahliyeh 1990). Similar criticism has been mounted against the long-held assumption that the pluralization of modern life-worlds would necessarily undermine the plausibility of religious world views. For instance, proponents of the "new religious economics" have repeatedly argued that religious pluralism and deregulation are in fact conducive to religious vitality (Warner 1993, 1998).[1] And finally, the idea that religion would become privatized in modern society has been confronted with evidence of the continuing and sometimes emergent public and political salience of religion in a number of modern states in the twentieth and twenty-first centuries (Casanova 1994).

In spite of all this criticism, which focused mainly on degrees of religiosity at the individual and communal levels, the paradigmatic core of secularization theory has largely been left intact. This paradigmatic core is the assumption of functional differentiation, according to which political institutions and practices have been progressively separated from religion in the course of modernization (Gorski 2000, 141; see also Tschannen 1991). However, to adequately grasp the contemporary politics of religious diversity it may be necessary to move even further beyond classical secularization theory by relaxing assumptions about the inevitably progressing functional differentiation of modern society. Of course, it would be futile to contest that religious and political authority are indeed often separated in modern societies. Yet, a linear theory of functional differentiation provides unsatisfactory explanations of the politics of religious diversity in all its empirical varieties.

More specifically, the theory of functional differentiation has three analytical deficits. First, it typically lacks systematic attention to *actors* and their interests, as convincingly argued by Mark Chaves (1994). Building on earlier contributions by David Martin (1978) and Karel Dobbelaere (1981), he suggests conceiving of secularization—or "laicisation"—as a variable referring to the relative scope of religious authority in the political arena. Explaining the patterns of (institutional) secularization in any given national (or local) site, then, requires an historical analysis of the relational configurations and the political struggles between religious and political elites over their respective jurisdictional claims—a task that theorists of differentiation have often failed to address.

Second, general theories of functional differentiation between politics and religion also lack attention to the *institutional* environments within which struggles over the scope of religious authority and ensuing processes of differentiation occur. Most importantly, these theories do not problematize, but simply take for granted, the institutional framework of modern nation-statehood, thus falling victim to what has been called the "methodological nationalism" of classical social sciences.[2] As a consequence, theorists have failed to note the elective affinity and, indeed, structural coupling of modern statehood with national identity constructions. Many historians and historical sociologists have noted that with the transition from imperial forms of indirect rule to the direct rule of territorial sovereign states came programs of linguistic and cultural homogenization of entire populations (Anderson 1983; Tilly 1990). Most instructive in this respect is the modern institution of citizenship in which individuals are linked to the territorial state by means of formal membership, rights, and collective identity. It has been argued that idioms of modern nationalism were strongly impregnated with biblical vocabularies and imaginaries. Furthermore, the construction of national identities often drew upon confessional homogeneity that had been achieved in waves of religious cleansing during post-Reformation Europe (Anderson 1983; Greenfeld 1992). And during the nineteenth-century heyday of nationalism, identity formation was strongly interwoven with contestations between secular and religious camps or, in bi-confessional countries, with "culture wars" between Protestants and Catholics (Clark and Kaiser 2003; van der Veer and Lehmann 1999). Capturing different patterns of differentiation and understanding the politics of religious diversity therefore requires careful analysis of historical configurations of state, nation, and religion. Sweeping accounts of modernization often lack such precision.

Thirdly, the theory of functional differentiation has tended to ignore the *cultural* construction of the "secular," a problem that has both a conceptual and a substantive dimension. The conceptual dimension is well articulated in an almost forgotten article by Talcott Parsons (1967, 391), where he argues that differentiation theory cannot adequately capture the sense in which what later becomes differentiated—that is, "religion"—continues to shape orientations in "secular" spheres and society at large:

> The problem then becomes one of analyzing the continuities, not only of the component by the same name in the different stages, e.g., religion, but also of the senses in which the patterns of orientation given in the earlier stages have or have not been fundamentally altered in their significance for the system as a whole, considering the exigencies of the situations in which action takes place and the complex relations of this part to the other parts of the more differentiated system, e.g., the non-religious or secular.

The substantive dimension of this problem is that theories of differentiation do not sufficiently take into account the cultural contexts that define symbolic boundaries between differentiated spheres of action, such as the "secular" and the "religious." As Talal Asad (2003) reminds us, the very meaning of secularism, so often taken as the epitome of modern statehood, depends on how the "secular" is culturally imagined. In the context of Roman Christianity, for instance, the *saeculum*, previously conceived as an interlude between Creation and *eschaton*, was reconceptualized as the unlimited social time-space within which both "religion" and "politics" were situated. A similar argument has been forcefully elaborated by Charles Taylor in his monumental *Secular Age* (2007): his major argument is that modern secularity is a cultural "construal" in its own right, emerging out of the internal transformations of Western Christianity and resulting in an "immanent frame" in which "religions" acquire entirely new meanings. What is important, here, is that the patterns of differentiation we witness in liberal democracies do not unfold according to a universal logic. Rather, they reflect cultural conceptions of nature, society, and the self whose contingent character becomes more obvious today in light of increased globalization and awareness of multiple modernities (Eisenstadt 2003).

To sum up, differentiation theory is ill-equipped to grasp the interplay of actors' interests, institutional environments, and cultural ideas, all of which influence the varying scope of religious authority in given historical settings. To the extent that debates over the religious aspects of migration continue to be impregnated by key assumptions of secularization theory, such debates fail to adequately capture the contemporary politics of religious diversity. Moving beyond this impasse requires discarding the grand narrative of modernization more decidedly and adopting more nuanced explanatory models of secularization. Only recently have there been attempts to move in this direction. José Casanova, for example, quite in contrast to his earlier statement that functional differentiation "remains the valid core of the theory of secularization" (1994, 212), has called for a comparative analysis of variable patterns of differentiation (2006). Similarly, historical sociologists have in this spirit pleaded for an "eschatological agnosticism" that treats differentiation and (institutional) secularization as conceptual variables rather than as long-term developmental trends (Gorski 2005, 174; see also Gorski and Altinordu 2008). Only against the backdrop of these changes in theoretical orientation and analytical focus, which have occurred along with a far-reaching decentralization of Western modernity, has it become possible to meaningfully analyze how different nation-states respond to religious diversity induced by international migration. It is to this question that I now turn.

State Accommodation of Religious Diversity in Comparative Perspective

The question of how nation-states respond to religious diversity has moved up on the research agenda of several subdisciplines. The first important debate in this respect is that on multiculturalism and the politics of recognition within political philosophy and, to some extent, political sociology (Kymlicka 1995; Taylor 1994). In the 1990s, most proponents in this debate implicitly subscribed, by and large, to some

version of secularization theory. Whereas the major normative controversy was about ethnic and cultural identities in liberal democracies,
religion was treated as something to be delegated to the private sphere
(e.g., Joppke 1999; Kymlicka 1995). The more empirical debate concerned
state responses to immigration and ethnic diversity, without paying
much attention to religion, as evinced by Stephen Castles's (1995) own
discussion of differential exclusion (Germany, Japan), assimilation
(France, United Kingdom), and pluralism or multiculturalism (United
States, Australia). A decade later, however, religion seems in these debates to have become an analytically autonomous dimension of diversity in need of more nuanced analysis (see Joppke 2009).

Similar developments may be noted, secondly, in the field of migration studies. Along with the declining plausibility of both secularization
theory and straight-line assimilation theory, migration scholars have
come to acknowledge that religious practices and beliefs play a crucial
role in the formation of migrant identities (notably among the second
and third generation), be it in diaspora communities and transnational
migrant networks (Cadge and Ecklund 2007; Levitt and Jaworsky 2007,
140-42) or in the process of segmented assimilation (Portes and Rumbaut
2006; Warner 2007). As Nancy Foner and Richard Alba (2008) highlight,
there are crucial differences in the way religion has been addressed by
migration scholars on both sides of the Atlantic. While in the United
States there is a long-standing tradition, going back to Will Herberg's
(1960) classical synthesis, that pinpoints the positive aspects of religion
for migrants' psychological well-being, social networks, political participation and, ultimately, for their entrance into the American mainstream, the European literature has typically regarded the religiosity of
post-war immigrants, notably Muslims, as a social problem. European
migration scholars therefore began to address policy responses to religious diversity somewhat earlier than their North American
counterparts.[3]

From a third perspective, responses to religious diversity have been
addressed in the literature on church-state relations. Church-state relations, a topic that had for a very long time been left to historians and
legal scholars, at first received attention within the above-mentioned
sociological debate about secularization. Proponents of the "new religious economics," eager to explain high degrees of religiosity by the
relative autonomy of the religious field, have invested considerable intellectual energy to measure and assess state support for religious monopolies (starting with Finke 1990; see also Fox 2008; Grim and Finke
2006). The same is true of Hugh McLeod's (2000) "socio-political conflict model," which contends that under the conditions of religious
monopolies and state-controlled churches in nineteenth-century Europe,
religious officials, given their interests in maintaining authority, typically

did not ally with oppositional forces of social reform; the unintended consequence was that lay people from the lower strata had to choose between organized religion and social reform. Today, church-state relations, state accommodation of religious minorities, and governance of religious diversity are investigated as macro-phenomena in their own right by political scientists, sociologists, and anthropologists (see Bader 2007; Beckford 2003; Gill 2008; Jelen and Wilcox 2002; Richardson 2004).

In the following, I draw on these literatures with two major aims in mind: to describe how Western immigration countries accommodate religious diversity, and to explore potential causal factors that account for crucial variations in such responses. Before doing so, however, it may be useful to discuss in some greater detail the kinds of political demands arising from religious diversity induced by international migration, as it is to these demands that public policy actually responds.

Migrants' (Religious) Claims for Recognition

Inspired by the philosophical debate about the politics of recognition and drawing on a large body of research about collective mobilization and social movements (e.g., McAdam, Tarrow, and Tilly 2001), social scientists have in recent years made huge steps forward in understanding the contentious politics of citizenship in immigration societies. In light of the exclusionary effects of historically entrenched institutional arrangements of (national) citizenship, the three major components of such arrangements—formal membership rules, rights, and (national) identity—are potentially subject to contestation by migrants. Migrants may demand less restrictive entry, residence, and naturalization laws; they may ask to be granted full civil, political, and social rights independent of their formal citizenship status; and they may thereby call for redefining the symbolic boundaries of the nation. A comprehensive empirical analysis of migrants' claims-making is available in a groundbreaking study by Ruud Koopmans, Paul Statham, and collaborators (Koopmans et al. 2005). They comparatively analyze claims made by migrants themselves or by others on behalf of or against migrants in the Netherlands, Britain, France, Germany, and Switzerland throughout the 1990s. Basing their analysis on a massive coding effort of migration-related speech acts reported in the major newspapers of the five countries, they show that the form and content of migrants' political demands do not simply reflect their factual or perceived disadvantages. Rather, political opportunity structures and publicly available categories of difference (e.g., "race" in Britain or "Ausländer" in Germany) go a long way in explaining the degrees and thematic foci of migrants' collective mobilization. Clearly, then, migrants' contentious politics of citizenship are fundamentally relational. Their claims-making is shaped by nation-states' pre-existing institutional and discursive structures which they, in turn, may alter in the very process of their political struggle.

In times of increased awareness of, if not fixation on, religion, it is important to recognize that explicitly *religious* issues characterize only a very small portion of the entire range of migrants' claims as compared with pre-eminent issues such as residence permits, dual citizenship, and racism or xenophobia (Koopmans et al. 2005, 89). Yet in spite of this, most public controversies and policy responses related to religious diversity are the products of explicitly religious claims-making. To grasp the particular dynamics of migrants' religious claims-making, it is useful to draw on Werner Schiffauer's (2007, 80) ideal-typical analysis of immigrants' religious identification strategies.[4] He distinguishes between first and second generation, and between various strategies of the latter. While first-generation immigrants, considering themselves to be in "exile," use religion to maintain transnational ties with their homeland, second-generation immigrants, even if they see themselves as part of a broader transnational religious community, pursue identification strategies that are related to politics of religious recognition in the recipient society. These strategies may take different forms. A first strategy is the struggle for equality in which immigrants contest individual discrimination based on their religious differences and demand equal access to individual rights—in the educational sector, in the labour market, and the like. When continuing discrimination is experienced, an alternative strategy commends itself—the struggle for the right to difference. Here, immigrants make collective claims to be accepted as full citizens while acknowledging their distinctive religious identities. If both individual and collective claims are denied by the larger society, a third strategy opens up in which immigrants entirely reject the struggle for recognition and engage in ultra-orthodox or radical forms of religion (Schiffauer 2007, 86).

For the contentious politics of religious diversity, Schiffauer's second type of claims-making—the struggle for the right to difference—is of utmost importance. For through this mechanism historical configurations of state, nation, and religion are challenged, institutional varieties of secularism renegotiated, and patterns of differentiation altered. Now, it is important to stress that the collective struggle for the right to difference may in itself take distinctive forms, since religious claims may be aimed at either exemptions or parity (Koenig 2005; see also Amiraux 2005; Koopmans et al. 2005, 159). Legally, exemption claims challenge existing restrictions on religious freedom while parity claims highlight favouritism toward particular religions and, thus, imperfections in the state's religious neutrality. In the following paragraphs, I discuss the symbolic and structural dimensions of both types of collective claims.

Immigrants who for whatever reason turn away from strategies of assimilation and start institutionalizing a hitherto marginalized religion often articulate *claims for exemptions*. To list just a few prominent examples, these claims include demands by some turbaned Sikhs to be exempted from wearing motorcycle helmets; demands by Jews and Muslims for toleration of ritual slaughter practices that would otherwise be prohibited by animal protection laws; and demands by some Muslims and Pentecostals to have their children exempted from co-educatory sports and swimming lessons. All these claims may, first, give rise to substantive controversy because by making publicly visible new religious (or ethnic) identities, they contest the plausibility of prevalent symbolic conceptions of national identity—to the extent that the latter are impregnated, as in many European countries, by confessional cultures. While such contestations are well known from multicultural identity politics more generally, there is a second, structural dimension that is specific to religious exemption claims. It consists in the contestation of secular state authority. In highly centralized states with an expansively defined public sphere, even the least demanding religious exemption claims, such as the claims by school girls to wear their headscarves in public schools, may be perceived as threats to the boundary between the public and the private. More demanding religious exemption claims are highly contested throughout most Western democratic states. Consider religious claims for partial recognition of autonomous legal systems and hence for multireligious jurisdiction, which pose perhaps the strongest challenge to sovereign statehood. While legal pluralism has been quite common in post-colonial states, it seems almost unacceptable in most Western democracies, except for some limited areas in international private law.[5] In fact, most Muslim representatives in Switzerland, France, Austria, Germany, and Belgium would not make such demands for legal autonomy in the first place, instead clearly articulating their full allegiance to the common legal system. Where debates about the incorporation of Islamic legal principles in Western family and inheritance law do occur, as for instance in debates in Canada about whether Muslims should be allowed a degree of autonomous jurisdiction in family law under Ontario's 1991 *Arbitration Act* (see Milot in this volume, p. 120), and related controversies in Great Britain, the intricate problems inherent to multireligious jurisdiction—notably the conflicts between rights to religious autonomy and gender equality— are displayed in sharp profile (see Foblets and Renteln 2009; Shachar 2001). These controversies accentuate the challenge posed by religious exemption claims that require balancing the recognition of religious differences with maintaining a common public sphere.

Parity claims follow a slightly different logic. First and foremost, they are aimed at including new religious actors into the more or less formalized systems of cooperation between the state and churches. Evidently, such claims are less pertinent in countries with strict separation of church and state than in those European countries where the state entertains cooperative relations with religious corporate actors. Here, religious organizations of immigrants may ask to be put on equal footing with established churches in domains such as the religious instruction in public schools or the financial support for private religious schools, or to be recognized as corporations of public law where this legal form for religious organizations exists (Austria, Germany, and several cantons in Switzerland). Even in less corporatist countries, there may be demands for equal recognition within public school curricula. Under the "new constitutionalism" with its emphasis on equality and non-discrimination rights to be enforced by courts that are shielded from democratic majorities, it is hard for liberal states to deny such parity claims. Yet they are no less contested than exemption claims because they may call for a recombination of the central national symbols of identity. Consider national calendars that reflect the pivotal role of Christianity and therefore provoke claims to introduce new holidays from other religious traditions. The recognition of religious diversity in public education is another sharply contested claim, since public schools are considered as major institutions for forming and forging national citizens. Though slightly different in focus, the German headscarf affair can also be cited as an example in this context (see Joppke 2009; Wohlrab-Sahr 2004). At issue was the question of whether a female school teacher, employed as a civil servant, might or might not display her identification with Islam. The Federal Constitutional Court framed the conflict in terms of conflicting constitutional principles (individual religious freedom versus state neutrality) and eventually upheld the claimant's right to religious freedom. However, public and parliamentary debates quickly moved to more substantial questions of national identity. Germany's "Christian-occidental heritage," for instance, was mobilized to counter both secularism and multiculturalism, and led to the adoption of more restrictive legislation in several subfederal states (*Länder*).

By way of conclusion, I wish to highlight that individual non-discrimination claims as well as collective exemption and parity claims by new religious actors form part of the larger politics of citizenship. Both exemption and parity claims, by calling for full and equal incorporation into the cultural and institutional structures of nation-states, show that political institutions and collective identities in modern nation-states are considerably less "secular" and certainly less "neutral" than many members of the majority population assume. The crucial question, of course, remains how nation-states respond to such claims and how patterns of differentiation are thus renegotiated.

Ways of Responding to Religious Diversity

There is now a considerable body of empirical research about state responses to religious diversity in immigration countries, old and new, mostly consisting of single case studies at national or local levels and with a tendency, in Western Europe, to focus on Islam (e.g., Abedin and Sardar 1995; Banchoff 2007; Levey and Modood 2009; Nielsen 1992; Pauly 2004; Vertovec and Peach 1997). However, methodologically rigorous comparisons of state accommodation of religious diversity are still rare. They mainly fall into two types: broad transatlantic comparisons and comparisons of two or three cases within Western Europe. The first approach is perhaps best exemplified by Aristide Zolberg's and Long Litt Woon's (1999) elegant account of why Islam (in Europe) is like Spanish (in the US) in challenging the symbolic boundaries of the nation. This approach also characterizes Jocelyne Cesari's (2004) overview on the situation of Muslims on both sides of the Atlantic as well as José Casanova's (2007) contrast between the relatively smooth incorporation of new religious minorities in the United States with the more contentious politics of religious diversity in Europe (see also Metcalf 1996).

The second approach is exemplified by Jan Rath's research on policies toward Islam in Western Europe, which showed the general situation of Muslims to be most favourable in the Netherlands, with Belgium and Great Britain following suit (Rath et al. 2001, 258). In a similar vein, Joel Fetzer and Christopher Soper have argued that Great Britain is more open to Muslim religious practices than France, with Germany being situated between these poles. To allow for systematic comparison, they attempted to measure accommodation by qualitatively scrutinizing three public policy domains: Muslims' religious practices in public schools, funding for Islamic schools, and the regulation of mosque-building (Fetzer and Soper 2004, 21). An effort to formulate more rigorous "measures" of the state's accommodation of cultural difference is to be found in the work of Koopmans, Statham, and colleagues. Their measures of cultural incorporation include rules related to naturalization, political representation rights, affirmative action, and, what is most important in the present context, two indicators that address the accommodation of minority religions, notably Islam. The first covers allowances for religious practices outside public institutions as indicated by allowances for the ritual slaughtering of animals, for public calls to prayer (*azan*), and for Muslim burials (Koopmans et al. 2005, 55). The second indicator comprises state recognition and funding of Islamic schools, Islamic religious instruction in state schools, the right of female teachers to wear the hijab, public broadcasting programs in immigrant languages, and Islamic religious programs in public broadcasting (Koopmans et al. 2005, 57). While all these indicators change over time, the countries' relative position on the continuum between assimilationist and pluralist policies remains stable, with Switzerland being most restrictive and the Netherlands most open to cultural and religious diversity.

These studies, as well as the transatlantic ones, are extremely helpful means of charting the terrain of nation-states' responses to religious diversity. Yet, there remains ample room for further research, especially as regards the sampling of cases. Comparisons between Europe and the United States in which the former is portrayed as the new and the latter as the old destiny of international migration may be improved by including Canada and Australia as equally time-tested immigration countries with yet distinctive trajectories of state, nation, and religion. And comparisons within Europe may likewise profit from a greater coverage of industrial democracies with large post-war migration. Michael Minkenberg's (2008a) recent study stands out as the most systematic attempt to describe nation-states' responses to cultural diversity. Upon closer scrutiny, his index of cultural integration speaks directly to the issue of religious, notably Muslim, difference. Minkenberg draws directly on Koopmans et al. (2005); in fact, he uses their indicators of religious rights outside and inside public institutions and calculates these indicators for 19 Western democracies, summarizing the average scores for each country into the three categories of low, medium, or high accommodation of cultural (read *religious*) difference (see Table 1).[6]

Table 1: Immigration and Cultural-Religious Integration Policy (1990s)

Immigration Policy	*Cultural Integration*		
	Low	*Medium*	*High*
Restrictive	**Switzerland**	**Austria** Denmark Germany Norway	
Moderate	**France** Ireland Portugal	Belgium **Great Britain** Finland Italy Spain	
Open		**USA**	**Australia** **Canada** Netherlands New Zealand Sweden

Source: Adapted from Minkenberg (2008a, 53); countries covered in the present volume are in bold.

Minkenberg's broader comparative perspective underlines the rationale for case selection in the present volume, which seeks to cover not only both old and new immigration countries but also to consider cases with varying approaches to the accommodation of religious diversity. Next to the old immigration countries of Australia, Canada, and the United States, we therefore include Great Britain, France, Switzerland, and Austria (Germany and the Netherlands also receive some attention). Against the backdrop of the above-mentioned literature, Minkenberg's comparative analysis contains a number of interesting descriptive results that are, by and large, confirmed by the in-depth case analyses in our volume. First, the results of earlier national comparisons within Western Europe are confirmed. Thus, while the Netherlands and Sweden stand out as unusually pluralism-friendly countries, Switzerland and France appear as rather hostile toward cultural and religious diversity. The recent French legislative prohibition of religious signs on public school premises is clearly a case in point. Secondly, there is a relation between a state's openness to immigration and its political acceptance of religious diversity. Typical immigration countries, such as Australia and Canada, which were among the early adopters of multiculturalism policies, display more latitude in accommodating religious diversity than most Western European countries. On the other hand, the contrast between the United States and continental Europe, which many scholars and policy-makers would assume is quite significant, in fact appears much more modest in broader comparative perspective. The following subsection discusses how different nation-states have responded to religious diversity, focusing on possible explanatory accounts of major differences between them.

Crucial Factors Explaining the Accommodation of Religious Diversity

There are a number of potential factors to be taken into account when explaining Western nation-states' accommodation of religious diversity. Foner and Alba (2008), for instance, cite demographic characteristics of recent migration patterns, different levels of secularization, and institutional arrangements of state and religion to explain the variable role of religion in migrant incorporation on both sides of the Atlantic (see also Alba 2005). Fetzer and Soper (2004), situating their work in the social movement literature, discuss resource mobilization, political opportunity structures, codes of national identity, and church-state relations as rivalling causal factors of national differences in how the presence of religious minorities, notably Muslims, is accommodated within Europe. Here I take up these explanatory accounts, linking them to the conceptual analysis of religious claims outlined above by distinguishing three sets of factors: actor-constellations, structural conditions, and cultural contexts.

A *first* set of factors relates to the presence of religious migrant communities as such. Precisely how the composition of the religious field is altered by international migration has crucial implications for religious claims-making and, hence, for the ways in which policy-makers address religious diversity. The simplest issue to be considered is the sheer amount of religious diversity produced by immigration. One might hypothesize that greater religious diversification successively builds up pressure in the receiving societies to adopt more accommodative policies toward new religions. While reliable information for diversification is notoriously hard to obtain, available data on degrees of religious fractionalization may be used as proxy.[7] Beyond the fact that all countries are experiencing an increase in religious diversity, the respective data, as presented in Table 2, give an ambiguous impression. On one hand, it seems that the most accommodative countries (i.e., Canada, the Netherlands, Australia, and the United States) have been characterized by high degrees of religious fractionalization for some time already. On the other hand, the countries that display the greatest increase in religious diversification (i.e., Austria and France) seem to react to the same process rather differently.

It is therefore commendable to look in greater detail at the precise changes in the religious composition of migrant-receiving countries. For instance in Europe, the post-war labour immigration from Islamic countries and the refugee movements in the 1990s from the Balkans have led to an unprecedented presence of Muslims on what for centuries was a largely Christian continent. Of course the patterns vary considerably. Thus, while there have now been decades of migration from Bangladesh and Pakistan to Great Britain and from the Maghreb to France, Muslim immigrants are a more recent phenomenon in Switzerland where "guest workers" were at first recruited overwhelmingly from Catholic Italy and Spain. Even though Muslims are not the only or the largest group of immigrants, Islam and immigration are today inextricably linked in public discourse and policy-making in Europe. By contrast, this is not the case in the old immigration countries. In Australia, substantial immigration from Vietnam first led to an increased number of Catholics, thus altering the historical constellations of a (British) Protestant majority and an (Irish) Catholic minority, and more recently has resulted in a substantial increase in the number of Hindus and Buddhists. Similarly, Hispanic immigration in the United States has increased the number of Catholics, while Muslims constitute less than 1 percent of the American population (see Table 2).

Beyond these patterns of religious diversification, one may also consider how the distribution of resources facilitates or hinders collective mobilization of religious migrant groups. Indeed, it seems that the low socioeconomic profile that has characterized Muslim immigrants in

Table 2: Patterns of Religious Diversity in Nine Western Countries

	Catholics (%)	Protestants (%)	Orthodox (%)	Other Christians (%)	Jews (%)	Muslims (%)	Eastern Religions (%)	Other Religions (%)	No Religion (%)	Religion Not Stated (%)	Religious Diversity ca. 1980*	Religious Diversity ca. 2000*
Canada	43.2	29.2	1.6	2.6	1.1	2.0	2.9	–	16.2	–	0.66	0.70
Netherlands	28.9	24.9	–	–	0.2	2.0	0.3	1.8	41.8	–	0.62	0.72
Australia	25.8	33.3	2.9	1.7	0.4	1.7	2.8	1.2	18.7	11.2	0.74	0.82
USA	24.5	45.1	0.3	6.8	1.4	0.5	1.0	0.9	14.2	5.4	0.88	0.82
Austria	73.7	4.7	2.2	0.9	0.1	4.2	0.2	<0.1	12.0	2.0	0.15	0.41
Great Britain	71.6 (Christians)				0.5	2.7	1.9	0.3	15.5	7.3	0.59	0.69
Germany	31.1	31.0	–	–	–	3.9	–	1.7	32.7	–	0.54	0.66
France	55.9	1.7	0.4	–	0.6	1.2	–	1.4	38.8	–	0.08	0.40
Switzerland	41.8	33.0	1.8	–	0.2	4.3	0.7	4.9	11.1	4.3	0.55	0.61

Note: Countries are ranked by cultural integration index (average 1990–2000) according to Minkenberg (2008a, 63), with Canada being most and Switzerland least accommodative. The table includes all countries covered in this volume plus the Netherlands and Germany, which figure prominently in the comparative literature. Empty cells are due to different census methodologies.

* Religious fractionalization index (0;1), with 1 signifying maximal diversity. Data for 1980 from Chaves and Cann (1992). Data for 2000 from Alesina et al. (2003); see also Minkenberg (2008b, 355-56).

Sources: Canada: census data 2001; Netherlands: International Social Survey Project (ISSP) data 2004; Australia: census data 2006; USA: American Religious Identification Survey 2001; Austria: census data 2001; Great Britain: census data 2001 (United Kingdom total); Germany: extrapolation from census data and church registers; France: International Social Survey Project (ISSP) data 2004; Switzerland: census data 2000.

Western Europe as compared with their counterparts in North America, in combination with the decentralized authority structures of Islam, could explain the general absence of collective mobilization of Muslims to enforce their claims for recognition (Pfaff and Gill 2006). However, as Fetzer and Soper (2004) show, this line of argumentation fails to account adequately for differences between particular European countries such as Britain and France or, as we may add, the Netherlands and Switzerland.

There is a *second*, more structural set of factors potentially affecting how nation-states respond to religious diversity. Some explanations, for instance, highlight opportunity structures that indirectly impinge upon state accommodation of religious minorities. The core argument here is that state accommodation of religious exemption and parity claims, triggered by migrants' collective mobilization, corresponds less to the latter's resources and more to political opportunities, such as laws related to nationality and naturalization, voting rights for foreigners, party coalitions, interest groups, and the like. If we use immigration policy as proxy for political opportunity structure, this argument would go some way to explain differences between old and new immigration countries (see Table 1). It also works well in accounting for some single cases, such as the British one where religious minorities enjoy relatively far-reaching liberties due to the strong bargaining position of Bangladeshi, Pakistani, and other immigrants who as former Commonwealth subjects were granted early access to full civil and political rights. However, the argument does not seem to hold for all cases within Europe equally. Neither the French hostility toward public expressions of Muslim faith by French citizens of Maghrebi origin, nor the far-reaching recognition of Islam in Austria where newcomers face a rather restrictive immigration policy, seems to be explained by reference to opportunity structures associated with these states.

Given these problems, Fetzer and Soper (2004) have prominently argued that historically entrenched church-state relations are a more important institutional factor of nation-states' accommodation of religious minorities than classical political opportunity structures. They aim to show that differences in the accommodation of Muslims in Britain, Germany, and France are explained by the general openness of the public sphere toward religion as expressed in models of established church, state-church cooperation, or full separation (Fetzer and Soper 2004, 18 and 147). Now it is certainly true that church-state relations store institutional templates for governments' interactions with new religious minorities. However, this argument cannot be easily generalized. As Minkenberg (2008a, 57) concludes from his broader comparative analysis of 19 Western democracies, "there is hardly any overall effect of this particular institutional arrangement [i.e., church-state relations] on the degree of cultural integration offered." Consider the cases that are typically classified as separation regimes. France stands out as the only separation regime that opposes the accommodation of religious diversity, while the United States and even more so Australia and Canada are rather accommodative of religious diversity. Likewise, regimes of partial or mixed establishment do not seem to allow per se for better incorporation of new religious minorities, as the comparison between Switzerland and Austria shows.

Yet a problem with both Fetzer/Soper's and Minkenberg's line of argumentation is that upon closer scrutiny the conventional classification of church-state relations upon which they rely may be contested. As Cesari argues in her contribution to the present volume, France corresponds to a model of strict separation of church and state to a lesser degree than is often assumed, since the French state, for historical reasons, grants certain privileges (e.g., subsidies for church buildings) to the Catholic Church and maintains regular consultations with the major religious communities. In light of such obvious discrepancies between official *laïcité* and the actual state of affairs in France and elsewhere, there have been several attempts to develop better measurements of state relations to religion. The most comprehensive measurement is Jonathan Fox's Government Involvement in Religion (GIR) Index, which is a composite measure based on five variables including 62 distinct and individually coded components that capture various aspects of state restrictions, discrimination, or favouritism of religion (Fox 2008, 54; for critical discussion see also Grim and Finke 2006). Table 3 displays GIR data for the seven countries covered in this volume plus Germany and the Netherlands. The contrast between old and new immigration here appears in yet sharper profile. Clearly, the corporatist remnants of former mono-confessional states in Europe contrast with the more denominational religious economy in the former British colonies (see also Casanova 2007).

Finally, there is a *third*, more cultural set of factors that is sometimes cited as influencing state policy toward religious diversity. Historical sociologists following Stein Rokkan and David Martin often argue that confessional legacies and cleavages left their imprint on early state formation, institutionalized church-state relations, as well as discursive repertoires for addressing religion in the public sphere, all of which then strongly influenced the ways relatively new religions such as Islam would be approached.[8] Minkenberg (2008a) draws on this argument and combines it with an analysis of degrees of religiosity. He concludes that there is indeed a denominational effect on integration policies: Protestant countries tend to adopt a more open stance toward religious diversity. Of course, as he also acknowledges, the picture is somewhat more complicated. Of greatest interest—besides the Canadian case with its substantial Catholic population—is perhaps the case of the United States, which is least accommodative of religious difference within the subgroup of old immigration countries. Could this be due to the fact that, of all Western countries, the United States is a highly religious country with almost half of the population attending worship at least once a month (see Table 3)? Peggy Levitt in her chapter hints at the fact that in spite of strict separation of state and church, the Protestant religious imprint on public life continues to be strong; in other words, there is a lack of "cultural separation" between state and religion, which does allow religion to function as a bridge to the American mainstream but also makes it harder for religious minorities to acquire formal recognition.

One should finally also consider public opinion toward migration and migrants. Survey data displayed in Table 3 show a somewhat ambiguous picture. On one hand it seems that greater popular hostility toward Muslims corresponds with less open public policies—almost a fifth of the Swiss population, for example, do not want to have Muslims as neighbours. On the other hand, popular attitudes toward the maintenance of group traditions do not seem to correspond with the ranking of cultural-religious accommodation. Surprisingly, there seems even to be an inverse relation between popular support for minority accommodation and actual government policy.

To conclude, all the factors cited in the literature do explain certain aspects of the complex dynamics of how nation-states respond to religious diversity. In general, low degrees of state regulation of religion seem to be particularly favourable for accommodative policies as do long-standing experiences with immigration and traditions of denominational diversity. However, the single case studies in this volume remind us that we should always be attentive to multicausal constellations that result in specific responses to religious diversity.

Beyond National Models

While comparative analyses greatly enhance our understanding of how religious diversity is governed in contexts of international migration, they suffer from certain limitations. Many of the competing accounts cited above share, in one way or another, a focus on highly stylized national "models" of citizenship or church-state relations. These models often mirror the dominant normative self-understandings of national publics or elites, rather than capture the complicated politics of religious diversity on the ground. The perils of national modelling, which Veit Bader so aptly discusses in his contribution to this volume, are in fact threefold.

Table 3: Factors Affecting State Accommodation of Religious Diversity

	Switzerland	France	Germany (West)	Great Britain	Austria	United States	Australia	Netherlands	Canada
Church-state relations (GIR)[a]	20.5	22.92	19.88	27.67	24.25	0.0	2.50	1.25	3.52
Religiosity (%) Monthly worship attendance[b]	22.3	14.0	26.1	22.5	28.5	48.6	20.8	20.1	41.6
Attitudes toward migrants (%) Muslims not wanted as neighbours[c]	18.5	16.0	9.1	13.6	15.2	10.7	–	11.9	6.5
Maintain group traditions[d]	46.0	26.8	35.8	24.7	27.8	47.4	18.2	29.4	28.9
Help minorities[e]	42.2	19.7	30.2	17.5	35.1	22.9	16.9	20.8	16.6

Notes: Countries are ranked by cultural integration index (average 1990–2000) according to Minkenberg (2008a, 63), with Canada being most and Switzerland least accommodative. The table includes all countries covered in this volume plus the Netherlands and Germany, which figure prominently in the comparative literature.

[a]Government Involvement in Religion (GIR) Index (0; 100); 0 meaning minimum, 100 maximum government involvement in religion (see Fox 2008, 108).

[b]Data from International Social Survey Project (ISSP 2004, v 300, ZA 3950). "Church attendance: How often do you attend religious services?" (sum of "several times a week," "once a week," "2 or 3 times a month," and "once a month").

[c]Data from World Values Survey (1999–2000; 1995–1996 for Switzerland and Australia): "On this list are various groups of people. Could you please sort out any that you would not like to have as neighbors?"

[d]Data from International Social Survey Project (ISSP 2003; 1995 for the Netherlands): "Some people say that it is better for a country if different racial and ethnic groups maintain their distinct customs and traditions. Others say that it is better if these groups adapt and blend into the larger society. Which of these views comes closer to your own?"

[e]Data from International Social Survey Project (ISSP 2003; 1995 for the Netherlands): "Ethnic minorities should be given government assistance to preserve their customs and traditions." Percentage of respondents who agree or agree strongly.

Institutional Change

The first and most important problem is that the fixation on national models does not explain the precise mechanisms of institutional reproduction of arrangements of state, national identity, and religion. How is it that the policy scripts stored in historical church-state relations, for instance, are activated to address new situations of religious diversity? Since much of the literature adopts highly deterministic conceptions of historical path-dependency and institutional inertia, it is ill-equipped to answer this question, let alone to explain institutional change. Yet change there is, as all case studies in this volume amply demonstrate. Perhaps the most noticeable changes have occurred in those new immigration countries of Western Europe where controversies over the incorporation of Muslims have led to strong contestations of existing institutional arrangements. Anglican establishment, French *laïcité*, Austrian (and German) *Staatskirchenrecht*, and Swiss cantonal particularities that were the result of complicated historical trajectories of nation-state formation and "culture wars" (*Kulturkämpfe*) are all currently being renegotiated as a result of the religious diversification associated with international migration.

Proponents of both classical secularization theory and the new religious economics might interpret developments as indicating that European countries have taken a (belated) further step toward full differentiation between politics and religion. However, such an interpretation needs strong qualification. As the case studies in this volume show, strict separation is not quite the direction that institutional changes are taking. This is perhaps most evident in the old immigration countries with long experiences of incorporating newcomers; these countries are currently experimenting with their institutional arrangements of state and religion. For instance, as Desmond Cahill shows in his case study on Australia, the strict separation of church and state—historically an attempt to resolve political tensions between the (British) Protestants and the (Irish) Catholics who ventured to Australia in the late eighteenth century—is untenable if public policy aims to respond to claims of religious freedom and equality. What his analysis rather suggests is that Australia is moving toward what he calls "brokering and monitoring neutrality" (see p. 155). Similarly, Micheline Milot highlights that the concept of "reasonable accommodation" in Canada, a legal innovation that is now a feature of public discourse, has shaped Canadian academic and public debates as well as policy-making. Indeed, the debates occurring under the aegis of reasonable accommodation continue to ensure that some of the most basic foundations of Canadian society are open to ongoing pragmatic negotiation (see pp. 113-14).

Moreover, institutional changes are always reversible, as the backlash against multiculturalism and the return to assimilation policies in many countries demonstrate (Brubaker 2001; Joppke 2004). The British case, discussed by Paul Weller in this volume, is a particularly interesting example, since the successive appraisal of religion as a dimension that has be to added to classical racial relations legislation has gone hand in hand with increasing concerns over threats to social cohesion posed by religious communities that putatively foster segregation and "parallel societies."

Institutional Complexities

Explaining such institutional changes in the governance of religious diversity requires rectifying a second shortcoming in much of the comparative literature, namely, acknowledging the internal contradictions, contestation, multiplicity, and mutability of institutional arrangements. Consider the example of France, the most widely cited case of a seemingly coherent republican policy with a strict separation of church and state. While it is true that its repertoires of governing religion include secularist elements, dating to anti-clericalism in the Third Republic and the 1905 law on the separation of church and state, policy responses also include the interventionist traditions of Gallicanism and Napoleon's *régime des cultes reconnus*. These latent templates of governance were in a sense reactivated by the Ministry of Domestic Affairs in its attempts to organize, in a top-down manner, the central representative body of French Muslims (see p. 212 in this volume; see also Bowen 2006). Or consider Austria where, as Julia Mourão Permoser and Sieglinde Rosenberger show, the Habsburg imperial heritage has allowed for an early accommodation of organized Muslim practices while continuing, at the same time, a rather exclusionary immigration and integration policy. Besides domain specificities, the governance of religious diversity also varies across levels. Noteworthy discrepancies exist between highly ritualized rehearsals of models in national public spheres and the day-to-day practices at municipal levels, where negotiations of religious claims are left to the discretion of local authorities; such discrepancies are especially apparent in times of a neo-liberal devolution of state power from central to local levels or, indeed, to non-state actors (see de Galembert 2005).

The general point should be clear. A more process-oriented mode of analysis requires dissecting and disaggregating "models" so as to understand the potential contradictions of their legitimating ideas, the multiplicity of dormant institutional repertoires, and the differential interests of the major carrier groups.[9] All this provides plenty of opportunities for actors to respond creatively to new situations either by using existing institutions for new aims or by amalgamating them with new institutional elements that have become available through transnational processes.

Transnational Embedding

This brings us to the third and final problem: conventional comparative strategies still seem to assume self-contained units of analysis, thus falling victim to the above-mentioned "methodological nationalism." However, exclusively national frameworks are clearly unrealistic given the importance of transnational, if not global, networks of communication and interaction. As recent works in migration and religious studies have shown, transnationalism is in fact a crucial characteristic of the modes of religious belonging among migrants (Beyer 2006; Ebaugh and Chafetz 2002; Juergensmeyer in this volume; Levitt and Jaworsky 2007; Warner and Wittner 1998). Moreover, political-legal frameworks that have in the twentieth century emerged beyond the nation-state perhaps merit equal attention. In addition to de facto diversity that exists at the local and state levels, a certain normative appraisal of cultural pluralism in these transnational frameworks has transformed classical nation-states and their historically contingent arrangements of politics and religion (see Koenig 2007; Kymlicka 2007). Thus, both the transnational diffusion of ideas of human rights in the post-war period and the institutionalization of rights in governmental and non-governmental organizations have firmly established a charismatic status of "universal personhood" to which rights are, at least in principle, attached independently from formal state membership or nationality (Soysal 1994), which has contributed to the rise of the "new constitutionalism" mentioned above.

Even more importantly, within transnational human rights discourse there has been a proliferation of new rights that clearly go beyond the classical European political tradition. The individual rights to equality and non-discrimination have moved to the centre of human rights discourse and have been successively extended to collective and communal rights. To name just a few documents, the UN Declaration on the Rights of Persons Belonging to National or Ethnic Religious and Linguistic Minorities (1992), the UN Human Rights Committee's General Comment on Article 27 of the International Covenant on Civil and Political Rights (1994), UNESCO's Declaration on Cultural Diversity (2001), and the Convention on the Rights of Migrant Workers and Their Families (1990, entry into force 2003) oblige the signatory states to adopt a proactive approach to promote the identity of ethnic or national, linguistic, and religious minorities—and of migrants—on their territories. As a strong coupling of state membership, individual rights, and national identity loses legitimacy in global discourse, new categories of religious identity are legitimated and sanctioned in putatively secular public spheres. In this broader perspective, the contemporary politics of religious diversity are intimately linked with the transformation of the legitimacy basis of modern statehood.

Not accidentally, almost all contributions in this volume cite the important role played by constitutional courts in negotiating religious exemptions and parity claims. Thus, the Canadian and the American Supreme Courts, the French *Conseil d'État*, and the Swiss *Bundesverfassungsgericht* have considerably strengthened, in a number of cases involving migrants, the equal rights to religious freedom enjoyed by majorities and minorities alike. In Europe, the role of the judiciary is strengthened by international and supranational legal systems under the Council of Europe and the European Union in which religious issues have recently moved up on the policy agenda (Byrnes and Katzenstein 2006; Koenig 2007). In addition to new repertoires of religious claims-making, including forceful anti-discrimination and equality norms, new judicial arenas for claiming rights vis-à-vis majorities and elites have emerged such as the European Court for Human Rights in Strasbourg.

Again, however, it is necessary to conclude this point on a cautious note. As Joanna Pfaff-Czarnecka's discussion of the Swiss case shows, a liberal jurisprudence that departs too strongly from public opinion may, paradoxically, lead to more restrictive and less accommodative legislation in the long run. And the European Court for Human Rights grants states considerable margins of discretion in restricting religious freedom through legislation as long as the legislation can be shown to be, as it were, necessary in a democratic society (see Ulusoy 2007). The precise ramifications of the embedding of human and religious rights discourses (generated in the transnational domain) within nation-states' practices of governance of religious diversity are therefore far from predictable.

Conclusion

In this chapter, I have tried to shed some light on the governance of religious diversity by discussing major factors for policy dynamics in comparative perspective. It should be clear that religious diversity produced by international migration poses challenges for historically rooted arrangements of state, nation, and religion that defy simplistic theories of secularization and differentiation. How nation-states respond to religious diversity and, more particularly, to the claims to non-discrimination, exemption, and parity articulated by immigrants, stems from specific configurations of causal factors and is, moreover, subject to complex dynamics of change.

Responding to religious diversity involves complex policy decisions that bring to the fore a number of paradoxes and tensions. Finding a suitable balance between individual and collective rights, between strict secularism and non-interventionist multiculturalism is a difficult task indeed, and in no state can one find a universal template for such a balance. While individual rights to non-discrimination are in most cases legally, albeit hardly socially, guaranteed in the countries covered in this volume, states' reactions to demands for collective exemption and parity rights vary rather strongly. Another, less obvious tension arises from the organizational models available for collective religious recognition, which tend to presume church-like hierarchies that run counter to contemporary religious individualization—a problem that is particularly salient in European countries with their (more or less) corporatist traditions of church-state relations.

While it may be left to the final chapter by Will Kymlicka to engage in the evaluation of various policy options covered in this volume, I wish to conclude by highlighting a deeper problem raised by the religious claims-making of immigrants. This problem concerns the communicative structure of modern public spheres and, indeed, what Charles Taylor calls the cultural construal of the "secular" itself. To what extent should adherents of secular public reason or representatives of states that officially espouse secular forms of reason be expected to engage in conversations with explicitly religious people about explicitly religious ideas and practices? Or to what extent should religious groups, in turn, have to translate their beliefs into arguments of (secular) public reason? Such are the questions that motivate current debates about "post-secular societies" in which cooperative modes of mutual understanding are said to be required between the religious and the secular sides, if indeed one can even speak of "sides" in such cases (Habermas 2005; Taylor 2007). There are indeed reasons to believe that if churches, mosque associations, and temple communities contribute to a vital civil society, provide social welfare, and sustain human solidarity, their voices may be legitimately heard, though not necessarily followed in the public sphere. Be that as it may, the governance of religious diversity under conditions of international migration does raise the question of how we shall actually conceive of the common public sphere beyond its classical, nation-state format. It is for this reason that the contemporary dynamics of religious diversity are so unsettling and merit sustained scholarly reflection.

Notes

1. Of course, this argument has not gone uncontested on both methodological and empirical grounds; see Norris and Inglehart (2004, 100). For a critical review see also Chaves and Gorski (2001).

2. There are several varieties of "methodological nationalism," of which the most obvious are those theories of social integration that assume

society to be a territorially bounded and culturally homogeneous entity. As Andreas Wimmer and Nina Glick-Schiller (2003) have argued, theories of functional differentiation are a peculiar form of "methodological nationalism" to the extent that they are blind to the constitutive role of national identities for the political form of modern society. If, however, the modern political system specializes in collectively binding decision-making, it by necessity requires a definition of collectivities; nationalism achieves just that. The most balanced account of "methodological nationalism" in the social sciences is offered by Chernilo (2007).

3. There are several strands of this discussion in North America, ranging from evident concerns about security and terrorism to Robert Putnam's recent and highly controversial study about the potentially disruptive effects of diversity for social solidarity within and between groups (see Putnam 2007).

4. Schiffauer's ad hoc model could be reformulated, in a more theoretical mode, by drawing on social psychological distinctions between separation, assimilation, bi-culturalism, and marginalization (esp. Berry 1997), as well as on the recent literature on strategies of boundary maintenance, boundary crossing, blurring, or shifting, and boundary inversion (Alba 2005; Wimmer 2008). For the purposes of my argumentation, however, Schiffauer's model captures essential dynamics of religious claims-making.

5. Under international private law, some Western European courts (e.g., in Germany and France) routinely apply the rules of Islamic family law to adjudicate the marriage and divorce conflicts of non-citizens from Islamic countries of origin; for applications of Islamic law in the shadow of the American legal system see Zaman 2008.

6. Minkenberg's analysis is preferable to Jonathan Fox's coding of restrictions on minorities, since the latter captures state policy toward "sects" more than accommodation of migrant religions; see Fox (2008, 114).

7. The fractionalization index is based on the Herfiendahl formula, which technically gives the sum of squared relative group sizes and is often used as a measure of monopolization in market research. (Religious) fractionalization is calculated as 1 minus the Herfiendahl index and expresses the probability with which two individuals come from different religious groups; see Alesina et al. (2003).

8. This argument has recently been reformulated in debates over multiple modernities. The denominational religious culture of North America is here contrasted with a European culture where, despite the "unchurching" of large segments of the population, religion remains a public utility; see Berger, Davie, and Fokas (2008); Davie (2000).

9. A similar theoretical move is well underway in other fields of research including the literature on varieties of capitalism, welfare state regimes, and types of democracy; for a review see Clemens and Cook (1999).

References

Abedin, Z.S., and Z. Sardar, eds. 1995. *Muslim Minorities in the West*. London: Grey Seal.

Alba, R. 2005. "Bright vs. Blurred Boundaries: Second-Generation Assimilation and Exclusion in France, Germany, and the United States." *Ethnic and Racial Studies* 28:20-49.

Alesina, A., A. Devleeschauwer, W. Easterly, S. Kurlat, and R. Wacziarg. 2003. "Fractionalization." *Journal of Economic Growth* 8:155-94.

Amiraux, V. 2005. "Discrimination and Claims for Equal Rights among Muslims in Europe." In *European Muslims and the Secular State*, ed. J. Cesari and S. MacLoughlin. London: Ashgate.

Anderson, B. 1983. *Imagined Communities. Reflections on the Origin and Spread of Nationalism*. London: Verso.

Asad, T. 2003. *Formations of the Secular: Christianity, Islam, and Modernity*. Stanford: Stanford University Press.

Bader, V. 2007. *Secularism or Democracy? Associational Governance of Religious Diversity*. Amsterdam: Amsterdam University Press.

Banchoff, T., ed. 2007. *Democracy and the New Religious Pluralism*. New York: Oxford University Press.

Beckford, J.A. 2003. *Social Theory and Religion*. Cambridge: Cambridge University Press.

Berger, P.L., G. Davie, and E. Fokas. 2008. *Religious America, Secular Europe? A Theme and Variations*. Aldershot, UK: Ashgate.

Berry, J.W. 1997. "Immigration, Acculturation, and Adaptation." *Applied Psychology: An International Review* 46:5-68.

Beyer, P. 2006. *Religions in Global Society*. New York: Routledge.

Bowen, J.R. 2006. *Why the French Don't Like Headscarves*. Princeton: Princeton University Press.

Brubaker, R. 2001. "The Return of Assimilation? Changing Perspectives on Immigration and Its Sequels in France, Germany, and the United States." *Ethnic and Racial Studies* 24:531-48.

Byrnes, T.A. and P.J. Katzenstein, eds. 2006. *Religion in an Expanding Europe*. Cambridge: Cambridge University Press.

Cadge, W. and E.H. Ecklund. 2007. "Immigration and Religion." *Annual Review of Sociology* 33:359-79.

Casanova, J. 1994. *Public Religion in the Modern World*. Chicago: University of Chicago Press.

— 2006. "Rethinking Secularization: A Global Comparative Perspective." *The Hedgehog Review* 8:7-22.

— 2007. "Immigration and the New Religious Pluralism: A EU/US Comparison." In *Democracy and the New Religious Pluralism*, ed. T. Banchoff. New York: Oxford University Press.

Castles, S. 1995. "How Nation States Respond to Immigration and Ethnic Diversity." *New Community* 21:293-308.

Cesari, J. 2004. *When Islam and Democracy Meet: Muslims in Europe and in the United States*. New York: Palgrave.

Chaves, M. 1994. "Secularization as Declining Religious Authority." *Social Forces* 72:749-74.

Chaves, M. and D.E. Cann. 1992. "Regulation, Pluralism, and Religious Market Structure. Explaining Religion's Vitality." *Rationality and Society* 4:272-90.

Chaves, M. and P.S. Gorski. 2001. "Religious Pluralism and Religious Participation." *Annual Review of Sociology* 27:261-81.

Chernilo, D. 2007. *A Social Theory of the Nation-State: The Political Forms of Modernity beyond Methodological Nationalism*. London: Routledge.

Clark, C. and W. Kaiser, eds. 2003. *Culture Wars. Secular-Catholic Conflict in Nineteenth Century Europe*. Cambridge: Cambridge University Press.

Clemens, E.S. and J.M. Cook. 1999. "Politics and Institutionalism: Explaining Durability and Change." *Annual Review of Sociology* 25:441-66.

Davie, G. 2000. *Religion in Modern Europe. A Memory Mutates*. Oxford: Oxford University Press.

de Galembert, C. 2005. "The City's 'Nod of Approval' for the Mantes-la-Jolie Mosque Project: Mistaken Traces of Recognition." *Journal of Ethnic and Migration Studies* 31:1141-59.

Dobbelaere, K. 1981. *Secularization. A Multi-Dimensional Concept*. London: Sage.

Ebaugh, H.R. 2002. "Return of the Sacred: Reintegrating Religion in the Social Sciences." *Journal for the Scientific Study of Religion* 41:385-95.

Ebaugh, H.R. and J. Chafetz. 2002. *Religion Across Borders: Transnational Religious Networks*. Walnut Creek, CA: AltaMira Press.

Eisenstadt, S.N. 2003. *Comparative Civilizations and Multiple Modernities*. 2 vols. Leiden and Boston: Brill.

Fetzer, J. and J.C. Soper. 2004. *Muslims and the State in Britain, France and Germany*. Cambridge: Cambridge University Press.

Finke, R. 1990. "Religious Deregulation: Origins and Consequences." *Journal of Church and State* 32:609-26.

Foblets, M.-C. and A.D. Renteln. 2009. *Multicultural Jurisprudence: Comparative Perspectives on the Cultural Defense*. Oxford: Hart Publishing.

Foner, N. and R. Alba. 2008. "Immigrant Religion in the U.S. and Western Europe: Bridge or Barrier to Inclusion?" *International Migration Review* 42 (2):360-92.

Fox, J. 2008. *A World Survey of Religion and the State*. Cambridge: Cambridge University Press.

Gill, A. 2008. *The Political Origins of Religious Liberty*. Cambridge: Cambridge University Press.

Gorski, P.S. 2000. "Historicizing the Secularization Debate." *American Sociological Review* 65:138-67.

— 2005. "The Return of the Repressed: Religion and the Political Unconscious of Historical Sociology." In *Remaking Modernity. Politics, History, and Sociology*, ed. J. Adams, E.S. Clemens, and A. Shola Orloff. Durham and London: Duke University Press.

Gorski, P.S. and A. Altinordu. 2008. "After Secularization?" *Annual Review of Sociology* 34:55-85.

Greenfeld, L. 1992. *Nationalism – Five Roads to Modernity*. Cambridge, MA: Harvard University Press.

Grim, B.J. and R. Finke. 2006. "International Religion Indexes: Government Regulation, Government Favoritism, and Social Regulation of Religion." *Interdisciplinary Journal of Research on Religion* 2:1-40.

Habermas, J. 2005. *Zwischen Naturalismus und Religion. Philosophische Aufsätze*. Frankfurt: Suhrkamp.

Herberg, W. 1960. *Protestant, Catholic, Jew*. New York: Anchor Books.

Jelen, T.G. and C. Wilcox, eds. 2002. *Religion and Politics in Comparative Perspective. The One, the Few, and the Many*. Cambridge: Cambridge University Press.

Joppke, C. 1999. *Immigration and the Nation-State. The United States, Germany and Great Britain*. Oxford: Oxford University Press.

— 2004. "The Retreat of Multiculturalism in the Liberal State: Theory and Policy." *British Journal of Sociology* 55:237-57.

— 2009. *Veil: Mirror of Identity*. Cambridge: Polity Press.

Koenig, M. 2005. "Incorporating Muslim Migrants in Western Nation States: A Comparison of the United Kingdom, France, and Germany." *Journal of International Migration and Integration* 6:219-34.

— 2007. "Europeanizing the Governance of Religious Diversity – Islam and the Transnationalization of Law, Politics and Identity." *Journal of Ethnic and Migration Studies* 33 (6):911-32.

Koopmans, R., P. Statham, M. Guigni, and F. Passy. 2005. *Contested Citizenship: Immigration and Cultural Diversity in Europe*. Minneapolis: University of Minnesota Press.

Kymlicka, W. 1995. *Multicultural Citizenship. A Liberal Theory of Minority Rights*. Oxford: Clarendon Press.

— 2007. *Multicultural Odysseys*. Oxford: Oxford University Press.

Levey, G.B. and T. Modood. 2009. *Secularism, Religion and Multicultural Citizenship*. Cambridge: Cambridge University Press.

Levitt, P. and B.N. Jaworsky. 2007. "Transnational Migration Studies: Past Developments and Future Trends." *Annual Review of Sociology* 33:129-56.

Luckmann, T. 1967. *The Invisible Religion*. New York: Macmillan.

Martin, D. 1978. *A General Theory of Secularization*. New York: Harper and Row.

McAdam, D., S. Tarrow, and C. Tilly. 2001. *Dynamics of Contention*. New York: Cambridge University Press.

McLeod, H. 2000. *Secularisation in Western Europe, 1848–1914*. New York: St. Martin's Press.

Metcalf, B., ed. 1996. *Making Muslim Space in North America and Europe*. Berkeley and Los Angeles: University of California Press.

Minkenberg, M. 2008a. "Religious Legacies and the Politics of Multiculturalism: A Comparative Analysis of Integration Policies in Western Democracies." In *The Politics of Immigration and Human Security Post-9/11*, ed. S. Reich and A. Chebel d'Applononia. Pittsburgh: Pittsburgh University Press.

— 2008b. "Religious Legacies, Churches, and the Shaping of Immigration Policies in the Age of Religious Diversity." *Politics and Religion* 1:349-83.

Nielsen, J.S. 1992. *Muslims in Western Europe.* Edinburgh: Edinburgh University Press.

Norris, P. and R. Inglehart. 2004. *Sacred and Secular. Religion and Politics Worldwide.* Cambridge: Cambridge University Press.

Parsons, T. 1967. *Sociological Theory and Modern Society.* New York: Free Press.

Pauly, R. 2004. *Islam in Europe: Integration or Marginalization?* Aldershot, UK: Ashgate Publishing.

Pfaff, S. and A.J. Gill. 2006. "Will a Million Muslims March? Muslim Interest Organizations and Political Integration in Europe." *Comparative Political Studies* 39 (7):803-28.

Portes, A. and R.G. Rumbaut. 2006. *Legacies: The Story of the Immigrant Second Generation.* Berkeley: University of California Press.

Putnam, R. 2007. "E Pluribus Unum: Diversity and Community in the Twenty-first Century." *Scandinavian Political Studies* 30:137-74.

Rath, J., R. Penninx, K. Groenendijk, and A. Meyer. 2001. *Western Europe and Its Islam.* Leiden: Brill.

Richardson, J.T., ed. 2004. *Regulating Religion. Case Studies from Around the Globe.* Berlin: Springer.

Sahliyeh, E., ed. 1990. *Religious Resurgence and Politics in the Contemporary World.* Albany: State of New York University Press.

Schiffauer, W. 2007. "From Exile to Diaspora: The Development of Transnational Islam in Europe." In *Islam in Europe. Diversity, Identity, and Influence*, ed. A. Al-Azmeh and E. Fokas. Cambridge: Cambridge University Press.

Shachar, A. 2001. *Multicultural Jurisdiction. Cultural Differences and Women's Rights.* Cambridge: Cambridge University Press.

Soysal, Y.N. 1994. *Limits of Citizenship. Migrants and Postnational Membership in Europe.* Chicago: Chicago University Press.

Taylor, C. 1994. "The Politics of Recognition." In *Multiculturalism: Examining the Politics of Recognition*, ed. A. Gutmann. Princeton: Princeton University Press.

— 2007. *A Secular Age.* Cambridge, MA: The Belknap Press of Harvard University Press.

Tilly, C. 1990. *Coercion, Capital and European States: AD 990–1992.* Cambridge, MA: Blackwell.

Tschannen, O. 1991. "The Secularization Paradigm: A Systematization." *Journal for the Scientific Study of Religion* 30:395-415.

Ulusoy, A. 2007. "The Islamic Headscarf Problem before Secular Legal Systems: Factual and Legal Developments in Turkish, French and European Human Rights Laws." *European Journal of Migration and Law* 9 (4):419-33.

van der Veer, P. and H. Lehmann, eds. 1999. *Nation and Religion. Perspectives on Europe and Asia.* Princeton: Princeton University Press.

Vertovec, S. and C. Peach. 1997. *Islam in Europe: The Politics of Religion and Community.* London: Macmillan Press.

Warner, R.S. 1993. "Work in Progress towards a New Paradigm for the Sociological Study of Religion in the United States." *American Journal of Sociology* 98:1044-93.

— 1998. "Approaching Religious Diversity: Barriers, Byways, and Beginnings." *Sociology of Religion* 59:193-215.

— 2007. "The Role of Religion in the Process of Segmented Assimilation." *Annals of the American Academy of Political and Social Science* 612:102-15.

Warner, R.S. and J. Wittner. 1998. *Gatherings in Diaspora*. Philadelphia: Temple University Press.

Wimmer, A. 2008. "The Making and Unmaking of Ethnic Boundaries: A Multilevel Process Theory." *American Journal of Sociology* 113:970-1022.

Wimmer, A. and N. Glick-Schiller. 2003. "Methodological Nationalism, the Social Sciences, and the Study of Migration. An Essay in Historical Epistemology." *International Migration Review* 37:576-610.

Wohlrab-Sahr, M. 2004. "Integrating Different Pasts, Avoiding Different Futures? Recent Conflicts about Islamic Religious Practice and Their Judicial Solutions." *Time and Society* 13:51-70.

Zaman, S. 2008. "Amrikan Shari'a. The Reconstruction of Islamic Family Law in the United States." *South Asia Research* 28:185-202.

Zolberg, A.R. and Litt Woon Long. 1999. "Why Islam Is Like Spanish: Cultural Incorporation in Europe and the United States." *Politics & Society* 27 (1):5-38.

Chapter 12

The Governance of Religious Diversity: The Old and the New

WILL KYMLICKA

The essays in this volume provide ample illustration of the enormous variation in how Western countries govern religious diversity, particularly in relation to the faith-based claims of recent immigrants. But what lessons, if any, can we draw from these case studies? Do we have clear evidence that some approaches are more successful than others in terms of avoiding conflict and polarization along religious lines? Or that some approaches are more consistent with underlying values of freedom, democracy, and social justice?

Debates about the governance of religious diversity often take the form of a ritualized opposition between the American model of the rigid separation of church and state and the continental European model that provides legal recognition, financial benefits, and often political representation to particular religious organizations. Within this ritualized debate, defenders of the "secularist" American model typically make two sorts of objections to the "institutional pluralist" or "corporatist" European model:[1]

1. First, critics argue that any public recognition and institutionalization of religion tends to create unintended, perverse effects. Proposals for institutional pluralism are said to exacerbate religious divisions, create hierarchies among different groups, essentialize group identities, empower unrepresentative elites, undermine rational political deliberation, and subordinate the rights of vulnerable individuals within religious groups.

International Migration and the Governance of Religious Diversity, eds. P. Bramadat and M. Koenig.
Montreal and Kingston: McGill-Queen's University Press, Queen's Policy Studies Series.
© 2009 The School of Policy Studies, Queen's University at Kingston. All rights reserved.

2. Second, critics invoke the principle of secularism as a knock-down argument against proposals for institutional pluralism. According to this view, liberal democracy must be secular, and secularism requires a "wall of separation" between church and state, a wall that would be breached by proposals for public funding or political representation of religious groups.

If either of these objections were valid, then the question of how to deal with the new religious diversity brought by immigrants would be a simple one. New religious minorities should be left free to create their own religious denominations—whether churches, mosques, synagogues, shrines, or temples—as required by freedom of conscience and assembly, and they should be protected from discrimination. But they should not ask for or expect public recognition, accommodation, funding, or political representation.

However, the essays in this volume provide strong evidence against both of these objections. The idea that secularism operates as some sort of veto to institutional recognition is clearly misleading, since all Western states are inevitably involved in the process of recognizing religious groups (e.g., for the purposes of tax exemptions) and of accommodating religious belief (e.g., to ensure that believers do not face "undue burdens" in the exercise of their faith). Unfortunately, the myth that secularism entails a rigid separation of church and state blinds us to the often inconsistent and discriminatory ways this is done, and in particular blinds us to the ways that the faith-based claims of immigrants are not accorded the same respect and attention as those of older, more established religious groups.

As Bader suggests in this volume, a better approach, therefore, is to set aside the misleading term *secularism* and instead focus directly on the more basic values that secularism is supposed to serve: values such as individual freedom, equal citizenship, democratic legitimacy, and so on. Proposals for institutional pluralism should be examined for their actual impact on people's lives—for how they enable or inhibit people's ability to exercise agency and participate democratically—rather than be dismissed on the basis of their consistency with this or that abstract model of secularism.

And if we examine the many real-world experiments in institutional pluralism that are described in the various chapters, it is clear that many of them have not had the perverse effects that critics assume. The assumption that institutional recognition inherently conflicts with individual freedom or democratic citizenship is simply not borne out by the facts. On the contrary, there is every reason to suppose that many of these historic practices of recognition and accommodation have helped to strengthen norms of religious freedom and to deepen democracy.

It is important to recall that Western Europe and its colonial settler states were deeply scarred by centuries of religious conflict between Protestants and Catholics. These conflicts often left societies deeply divided between a victorious and hegemonic majority whose religion implicitly or explicitly infused public institutions, and a distrusted and marginalized minority whose religion was either ignored or viewed with suspicion. While this sort of hierarchy can be stable if the minority is small enough (think of Catholics in Britain), it is inconsistent with norms of liberal democratic citizenship. And where the religious minority is larger (think of Catholics in the Netherlands, Switzerland, and Germany), it is inconsistent not only with democratic norms but also with long-term democratic stability.

In these contexts, imaginative and innovative settlements were often required to overcome long-standing patterns of disadvantage, distrust, and exclusion, and to build new relations of equal citizenship. This sometimes involved abandoning the idea of an established church or official state religion—that is, reducing some of the more conspicuous and explicit ways in which the majority religion received privileged recognition in public institutions. But more often, and perhaps more importantly, it involved proactive efforts to enhance the recognition accorded to religious minorities. As the chapters in this book indicate, there is in fact a long and rich history within the West of institutional innovation in this field, including agreements to fund minority religious schools or minority religious education within the public schools, to subsidize the salaries of priests/ministers or the construction of churches, and to ensure that representatives of religious minorities are included on various advisory boards.

There is every reason to believe that these institutional innovations, adopted to deal with intra-Christian religious differences, have contributed to the consolidation and deepening of democracy in the West. In fact, these innovations in governing religious diversity are the origins of the model of "consociational democracy," which many scholars believe provides the only or the best option for deeply divided societies to achieve stable democracy, and which is increasingly promoted by international organizations for democratizing countries around the world.[2] It is difficult to prove the beneficial effects of any specific policy innovation, but it seems clear from the case studies in this volume that these policies have helped to overcome legacies of religious hierarchy and to make religious minorities feel more like full citizens. These innovations have helped to build more inclusive societies, without creating the perverse effects that critics predicted. For example, there is now considerable cross-national evidence about the impact of religious schools in Europe and North America, which provides no support for the claim that separate religious education is inherently corrosive of liberal democratic values. On the contrary, these schools consistently do better than public schools, not just in cognitive results but also in relation to liberal democratic values (Bader 2007, 271-72).

Given this successful track record in using institutional pluralism to accommodate intra-Christian religious differences, it is perhaps surprising, and distressing, that there is so much hesitation and resistance to extend these norms and practices to immigrant groups, particularly to Muslims. The essays in this volume repeatedly show that the inherited systems of governing religious diversity contain rigidities and hierarchies that lock-in privileges for older Christian (and sometimes Jewish) religions, while putting up arbitrary barriers to other religions, particularly those practiced by immigrant groups.

Faced with this inconsistency, it seems only natural, and indeed only fair, to conclude that Western states should be more open to the faith-based claims of new immigrants. If these regimes are to be made more just, they need to provide greater flexibility and lower thresholds for a wider range of religious groups to gain access to public funds and to representation in state councils and boards. This is particularly important in relation to the growing Muslim population in the West, which is the main concern of several of the chapters.

And yet, on further reflection, these essays could also be read as suggesting grounds for caution about this approach. For the status of Muslim immigrants is not just an issue of accommodating religious diversity; it is also, and perhaps more urgently, an issue of integrating newcomers. And these two dimensions of the issue—the fair accommodation of religious diversity and the effective integration of newcomers—may pull in different directions, at least on some matters. Viewed strictly as an issue of governing religious diversity, there is no justification within liberal democratic theory for distinguishing "old" religious minorities from "new" religious minorities in relation to public funding or political representation. For example, if public funds are provided to Catholic schools, they should be provided to Muslim schools. Yet, from the perspective of how to integrate immigrants, there may be legitimate reasons for thinking that newly arrived minorities have specific needs that are not well met by the system of separate religious schools that was set up for old religious minorities. Newcomers need to learn the local language and to learn how the local society operates, both in terms of its formal laws and its informal habits. They also need to build "bridging" social capital, which extends beyond their own co-religionists. It may be the case that immigrants do best on these integration goals when they are encouraged to attend common public schools rather than separate religious schools.

If so, this might be a reason for thinking that a more American-style approach, in which there is little if any public funding for religious schools and no religions are guaranteed representation rights in public bodies, is preferable to European-style corporatist approaches, *at least in terms of its impact on immigrant integration*. (Following Bader, I will call this the "American denominationalism" approach, since it focuses on enabling the formation of self-organized and self-administered religious denominations or congregations within civil society, not on providing public funding or representation). As I noted earlier, we cannot defend the American approach simply by ritualistically invoking secularism as if it were a self-justifying term, or by assuming a priori that public funding and representation of faith-based organizations would have perverse effects. We need to examine the actual record of how different approaches have affected basic liberal-democratic values. Yet my reading of that record is that American denominationalism has been reasonably successful in relation to these values—and most successful precisely in relation to religious groups composed primarily of recent immigrants, including Muslims.

There is considerable evidence that Muslims are doing best in those countries that (broadly) follow the denominational model, such as the United States and Canada. Of course, this may be due to reasons other than the laws governing religious diversity; it may reflect the fact that Muslim immigrants in North America are more likely to be highly skilled than those in Europe, or the fact that the labour market is more open to immigrants. But it is important to note that Muslims in North America are not just doing better than European Muslims in terms of economic indicators, such as income or employment. They also are more likely to express the feeling that their religion and religious freedoms are fully respected, and that they are accepted as citizens. And they are more likely to endorse liberal democratic values and to renounce violence.[3]

From the perspective of immigrant integration, therefore, there is at least provisional evidence for the benefits of denominationalism. Indeed, this is the conclusion of scholars such as José Casanova who has systematically compared the fate of Muslim communities in North America and Europe and has concluded that, empirically, denominationalism is simply working better (Casanova 2007). This is true not just in relation to European countries that have resisted extending corporatist arrangements to Muslims (like Switzerland), but also in relation to those countries that have extended corporatist arrangements (like Austria).[4] Whether corporatism is applied consistently or inconsistently, Casanova argues that it leads either way to less successful immigrant integration than denominationalism.

This raises an apparent paradox. The essays provide clear evidence that corporatist approaches based on institutional pluralism have worked historically for the accommodation of "old" religious diversity, helping to build more peaceful and democratic states, yet there is also suggestive evidence that this approach is not working as well as denominationalist approaches in relation to "new" religious diversity.

Why might this be? Consider again the case of religious schooling, which is perhaps the clearest case of this asymmetry. As noted earlier, there is good evidence that religious schools have worked well in relation to intra-Christian religious diversity, particularly Catholic schools in majority-Protestant countries, and yet there is enormous resistance to the public funding of religious schools for immigrants, particularly Muslims. To critics, this can only be explained as a form of hypocrisy and/or Islamophobia. And clearly this is a large part of the explanation. But it is also possible that studies of the effects of separate schooling for long-established Catholic communities do not provide a good basis for predicting the likely effects of funding religious schools for immigrants today.

This is not, of course, because Islam is somehow intrinsically more illiberal than Catholicism. The point, rather, is that in most European countries, Catholic schools were not intended primarily for immigrants, and so the issue of how separate religious schooling affects the process of immigrant integration did not arise. Take the Dutch case. The Dutch system of separate religious schooling arose historically as part of a broader "pillarization" process creating parallel institutions to deal with the religious and ideological divisions among Catholics, Protestants, and secular liberals. This model undoubtedly worked historically, but this was surely in part due to the fact that Catholics, Protestants, and secular liberals all shared the same national origin, identity, and language—they were all already Dutch in an ethnonational and linguistic sense. As a result, the separate institutions all diffused a common national identity and loyalty, while fairly accommodating their religious and ideological diversity.

This is a success story, but it would be a serious mistake to conclude from the historic success of pillarization in accommodating religious and ideological diversity among Dutch nationals that pillarization is a good way to integrate *immigrants*.[5] Muslim immigrants to Holland have very different needs in relation to public institutions, including schools, than do Dutch Catholics. The former are predominantly recent arrivals from Turkey and Morocco with little or no knowledge of the Dutch language and culture; the latter have been living in Holland for centuries and share the same language and ethnicity as the majority. The challenges of integration and inclusion are simply very different in the two cases, and so there is no reason to assume that what works well for the latter would work well for the former. It is possible, for example, that what immigrants need most is not separate religious schools, but rather a more multicultural approach to education within the common public schools.

Indeed, this is precisely the predicament in which European corporatist regimes find themselves today. They have inherited systems of religious schooling for centuries-old religious minorities that have arguably been a success. But there is grave anxiety about extending this system to immigrant groups. No doubt part of this anxiety reflects racism and Islamophobia, whipped up by sensationalist reports in the media about religious fundamentalism. But it also reflects a plausible judgment that the educational needs of new immigrants differ from those of old religious minorities who share the same language and culture as the majority, and that forms of institutional pluralism that have worked well for the latter may be inappropriate for the former.

The result, as these essays clearly show, is a patchwork of inconsistent rules and hierarchies, with newer immigrants neither fully included nor fully excluded from European corporatist regimes of religious governance.

What, then, is to be done? What is the appropriate route forward? In my view, we should not expect to see Western countries converging on a single model. Since countries differ in their historic patterns of inclusion and exclusion, and since there are competing legitimate goals at stake in governing immigrant religious diversity, Western countries are likely to continue to muddle through in their own idiosyncratic ways. However, at the most general level, I suspect that the broad distinction between (European) corporatist and (North American) denominationalist approaches is likely to persist, since these countries face different challenges that require different responses.

European corporatist regimes face the challenge of overcoming the many inconsistencies and hierarchies discussed earlier. Many commentators argue that, in this context, the only way forward is to extend recognition, funding, and representation to immigrant religious groups. Since there is no realistic chance of removing the historic settlements accorded to old religious minorities—and indeed no reason to do so, since these settlements have been successful in many cases—the only morally acceptable approach is to extend these arrangements to new immigrant groups, despite the risks involved. Pillarization may not be ideal for new immigrant groups, but a liberal democracy can hardly continue to fund Catholic and Anglican schools but not Muslim and Hindu schools.[6] Viewed strictly as an issue of governing religious diversity, we cannot find any justification for distinguishing new from old religious communities.

However, since these legitimate reasons for the even-handed extension of corporatist arrangements to new religious minorities may conflict with the equally legitimate goals of effective immigrant integration, European countries are likely to continue to hedge their bets. They are likely to move partly but not fully toward extending historic intra-

Christian settlements to newer religious communities. With good will and good luck, the resulting hybrid compromises may in fact prove quite successful in navigating the twin requirements of the fair accommodation of religious diversity and the effective integration of immigrants. With bad will and bad luck, the results may prove a failure on both counts, failing to extend full equality to non-Christian religions while also failing to facilitate the integration of newcomers.

In North American societies that have inherited systems of denominationalism, by contrast, I suspect that claims for corporatist arrangements by new religious minorities will continue to be strongly resisted. These traditional "countries of immigration" view the integration of immigrants as pivotal to national development and have powerful national narratives (or myths) about the recipe for successful immigrant integration. These narratives typically emphasize the centrality of common public schools and common political parties as the engines of immigrant integration, both of which fit more comfortably with denominationalist rather than corporatist arrangements for the governance of religious diversity. And while these narratives have their mythical qualities, there is, as noted earlier, some evidence to support the claim that non-Christian minorities are integrating better under North American denominationalism than European corporatism.

In North American countries, the issue of governing new religious diversity is first and foremost an issue of immigrant integration, and immigrant integration is first and foremost about facilitating participation in common public institutions and public spaces. In short, the legitimate goals of effective immigrant integration take priority over putative claims to a fairer accommodation of religious diversity. Moreover, since these countries generally do not accord corporatist rights even to their "old" religious communities, there is less basis for the claim that the fair accommodation of new religious diversity requires public funding or political representation. Under these circumstances, it may be neither unfair nor unwise to deny claims by immigrant-origin faith-based groups for public funding and political representation. In countries where denominationalism is the well-established legal framework for governing religious diversity, and where immigrant integration seems to be working well, shifting to a more corporatist approach would be a dramatic change, with potentially serious risks. It would not only be a change in the way religious diversity is governed but would also, and more importantly, be a dramatic change in the way immigrant integration is governed. And for countries that pride themselves on the historic success of their immigrant integration, such a dramatic change is widely seen as too risky.

To be sure, even in denominationalist regimes, there are many ways in which the historically dominant religion continues to suffuse public life and public institutions, creating (often unintended) disadvantages and barriers for new religious minorities. And so we have ongoing and well-known struggles regarding the "reasonable accommodation" of religious minorities within common public institutions—over school uniforms, school curricula, diet, holidays, prayer spaces, and so on. But these struggles for multicultural accommodations in North America are different from the struggles for, say, the "public legal" recognition of Islam in Switzerland (see Pfaff-Czarnecka's chapter). Both struggles involve exposing double standards and inconsistencies in the governing of religious diversity, and both expose the myth of some inviolable wall of separation between state and church. But there remains a profound difference between denominationalist and corporatist approaches that is unlikely to disappear.

In short, while new religious groups suffer from numerous disadvantages and double standards in all Western democracies, the appropriate remedies are likely to differ from country to country. Neither the inherent logic of liberal democracy, nor the available evidence, suggests that there is only one legitimate way for liberal democracies to govern religious diversity. Different countries can legitimately make different choices in relation to the funding of religious schools or the representation of religious organizations in public bodies. The legitimate resolution of these claims depends in part on the history of previous accommodations, and in part on the way policies of governing religious diversity interact with policies for the integration of immigrants. And both of these factors are likely to vary from country to country.

In saying this, I am presupposing that liberal democratic principles do not inherently require public funding of religious schools. This is not an uncontested claim. Just as many hard-core secularists claim that any public funding of religious schools violates the principle of secularism, so too there are hard-core pluralists who argue that the denial of public funding is a denial of basic human rights such as freedom of conscience or the right of parents to raise their children. I cannot go into those debates here, except to say that in my view, liberal democratic values (and international human rights) neither require nor forbid the funding of religious schools or the provision of guaranteed representation in the political process for faith-based organizations. The guarantees of religious freedom in the Universal Declaration of Human Rights, for example, do not include guarantees of public funding of religious schools or public subsidies of religious organizations.[7] Indeed, I would argue that on the most basic issues of religious freedom for Muslims, American denominationalism has done a very good job—better not only than French laicism but also than the corporatist arrangements in northern Europe. Take, for example, the most basic religious freedom, namely, to establish a house of worship. The interminable battles over building mosques in Europe are virtually unheard of in North America. So too with battles over Muslim cemeteries.[8] The issue between denominationalism and corporatism, therefore, is not whether to respect these basic freedoms, but whether the religious groups whose basic freedoms are respected should be given public funding and political representation. Liberal democratic values alone cannot answer that question. Both denominationalist and corporatist responses are legitimate options, to be judged and evaluated based on the actual impacts of policies on basic liberal and democratic values. Just as secularism should not be seen as a veto against institutional pluralism, so freedom of religion should not be seen as a veto against denominationalism.

In the end, therefore, as so often in these cases, we are left with a plea for complexity and context. Against an overly rigid and indeed mythical secularism that rejects all forms of public recognition and support, we need to emphasize that many forms of institutional pluralism are consistent with liberal democratic values and, moreover, have proven to help deepen and consolidate these values. Yet we must also guard against an overly quick presumption that these historic models of accommodation can or should simply be extended to newcomers. How states respond to new religious diversity must be evaluated not only in relation to pre-existing settlements for established religions but also in relation to the requirements of an effective immigrant integration policy. The appropriate response to these contingencies and trade-offs cannot simply be read off some abstract model of either denominationalism or corporatism.

Notes

1. "Corporatist" is the more common label for the European model, but (following Bader in this volume) I will use "institutional pluralism" instead. The key feature of this model is that the state recognizes specific bodies as the corporate representatives of specific religions, and grants these bodies particular rights and privileges in areas such as education, social services, political representation, anti-discrimination law, and tax status. The term "corporatism" captures this feature but often has the connotation of rigidity and closure, as if corporate recognition were fixed once and for all through a particular historic pact. "Institutional pluralism" leaves open the possibility of a more flexible and revisable conception of which religious groups receive corporate recognition, and of which rights and privileges this entails.

2. The *locus classicus* of the literature on consociationalism is Arend Lijphart's *Democracy in Plural Societies: A Comparative Exploration*. Lijphart developed his consociational model by reflecting, in the first instance, on the "pillarization" adopted to deal with religious diversity in his native Netherlands. For a broader account of how different forms of group-differentiated minority rights can help overcome legacies of ethnic, racial, and

religious hierarchies, and thereby strengthen democratic citizenship, see also Kymlicka (2007).

3.   For some of the relevant evidence, see the series of surveys conducted by the Pew Research Center (pewglobal.org/reports/pdf/DividedWorld2006.pdf) and Environics (www.cbc.ca/news/background/islam/muslim-survey.html), which compare attitudes of (and toward) Muslims in North America and Europe. These surveys are discussed by Adams (2007).

4.   The Austrian case, discussed in the chapter by Mourão Permoser and Rosenberger, is a fascinating illustration of the problem of disconnecting the issue of accommodating religious diversity from the issue of enabling immigrant integration. For contingent historical reasons, Austria has accorded full and equal standing to Islam in its (corporatist) religious governance policies since 1912, but has among the worst policies in Europe regarding immigrant integration. In these circumstances, the potential of the former to promote inclusion is negated by the exclusionary nature of the latter. And developing a more inclusive integration policy may require rethinking aspects of the corporatist religious policy. In any event, the two issues need to be examined in tandem for either to be effective.

5.   I'm assuming here that some level of integration into the language, society, and institutions of the host nation-state is desirable. One could imagine a corporatist model that does not include this aspiration. Arguably, this was the case of the millet system under the Ottoman empire, which provided a kind of pillarization for religious minorities without attempting to promote an overarching common Ottoman/Turkish national identity. But the Ottoman empire was neither liberal nor democratic, and liberal democratic nation-states require some level of linguistic and institutional integration if they are to satisfy principles of equal opportunity, effective political participation, and so on.

6.   As it happens, this is precisely the situation in my province of Ontario, which currently funds Catholic schools but not other religious schools (a provincial exception to Canada's general preference for denominationalism). This is clearly untenable morally, but the correct remedy is less clear. There are credible reasons for thinking that religious schools for immigrants would not replicate the historic success of Catholic schools.

7.   For a helpful overview of current debates about the interpretation of human rights to religious freedom, see Koenig (2008).

8.   For the bizarre hostility toward these basic religious freedoms in much of western Europe, see Klausen (2005).

References

Adams, M. 2007. *Unlikely Utopia: The Surprising Triumph of Canadian Pluralism.* Toronto: Viking.

Bader, V. 2007. *Secularism or Democracy? Associational Governance of Religious Diversity.* Amsterdam: Amsterdam University Press.

Casanova, J. 2007. "Immigration and the New Religious Pluralism: An EU/US Comparison." In *Democracy and the New Religious Pluralism*, ed. T. Banchoff. New York: Oxford University Press.

Klausen, J. 2005. *The Islamic Challenge: Politics and Religion in Western Europe.* Oxford: Oxford University Press.

Koenig, M. 2008. "Institutional Change in the World Polity: International Human Rights and the Construction of Collective Identities." *International Sociology* 23:95-114.

Kymlicka, W. 2007. *Multicultural Odysseys.* Oxford: Oxford University Press.

Lijphart, A. 1977. *Democracy in Plural Societies: A Comparative Exploration.* New Haven, CT: Yale University Press.

Index

Contributors

VEIT BADER, University of Amsterdam, Netherlands

PAUL BRAMADAT, University of Victoria, Canada

DESMOND CAHILL, RMIT University, Australia

JOCELYNE CESARI, Centre National de la Recherche Scientifique, France, and Harvard University, United States

JESSICA HEJTMANEK, Harvard University, United States

MARK JUERGENSMEYER, University of California, Santa Barbara, United States

MATTHIAS KOENIG, University of Göttingen, Germany

WILL KYMLICKA, Queen's University, Canada

PEGGY LEVITT, Wellesley College and Harvard University, United States

MICHELINE MILOT, University of Quebec at Montreal, Canada

JULIA MOURÃO PERMOSER, University of Vienna, Austria

JOANNA PFAFF-CZARNECKA, Bielefeld University, Germany

SIEGLINDE ROSENBERGER, University of Vienna, Austria

PAUL WELLER, University of Derby, United Kingdom

Queen's Policy Studies
Recent Publications

The Queen's Policy Studies Series is dedicated to the exploration of major public policy issues that confront governments and society in Canada and other nations.

Our books are available from good bookstores everywhere, including the Queen's University bookstore (http://www.campusbookstore.com/). McGill-Queen's University Press is the exclusive world representative and distributor of books in the series. A full catalogue and ordering information may be found on their web site (http://mqup.mcgill.ca/).

School of Policy Studies

In Roosevelt's Bright Shadow: A Collection in Honour of the 70th Anniversary of FDR's 1938 Speech at Queen's University and Marking Canada's Special Relationship with America's Presidents 1938 to Present Day, Arthur Milnes (ed.) 2009.
Paper ISBN 978-1-55339-230-9 Cloth ISBN 978-1-55339-231-6

Economic Transitions with Chinese Characteristics: Thirty Years of Reform and Opening Up, Arthur Sweetman and Jun Zhang (eds.), 2009.
Paper 978-1-55339-225-5 ($39.95) Cloth ISBN 978-1-55339-226-2 ($85)

Economic Transitions with Chinese Characteristics: Social Change During Thirty Years of Reform, Arthur Sweetman and Jun Zhang (eds.), 2009.
Paper 978-1-55339-234-7 ($39.95) Cloth ISBN 978-1-55339-235-4 ($85)

Who Goes? Who Stays? What Matters? Accessing and Persisting in Post-Secondary Education in Canada, Ross Finnie, Richard E. Mueller, Arthur Sweetman, and Alex Usher (eds.), 2008. Paper 978-1-55339-221-7 Cloth ISBN 978-1-55339-222-4

Politics of Purpose, 40th Anniversary Edition, Elizabeth McIninch and Arthur Milnes (eds.), 2009. Paper ISBN 978-1-55339-227-9 Cloth ISBN 978-1-55339-224-8

Dear Gladys: Letters from Over There, Gladys Osmond (Gilbert Penney ed.), 2009.
ISBN 978-1-55339-223-1

Bridging the Divide: Religious Dialogue and Universal Ethics, Papers for The InterAction Council, Thomas S. Axworthy (ed.), 2008.
Paper ISBN 978-1-55339-219-4 Cloth ISBN 978-1-55339-220-0

Immigration and Integration in Canada in the Twenty-first Century, John Biles, Meyer Burstein, and James Frideres (eds.), 2008.
Paper ISBN 978-1-55339-216-3 Cloth ISBN 978-1-55339-217-0

Robert Stanfield's Canada, Richard Clippingdale, 2008. Cloth ISBN 978-1-55339-218-7

Exploring Social Insurance: Can a Dose of Europe Cure Canadian Health Care Finance? Colleen Flood, Mark Stabile, and Carolyn Tuohy (eds.), 2008.
Paper ISBN 978-1-55339-136-4 Cloth ISBN 978-1-55339-213-2

Canada in NORAD, 1957–2007: A History, Joseph T. Jockel, 2007.
Paper ISBN 978-1-55339-134-0 Cloth ISBN 978-1-55339-135-7

Canadian Public-Sector Financial Management, Andrew Graham, 2007.
Paper ISBN 978-1-55339-120-3 Cloth ISBN 978-1-55339-121-0

Emerging Approaches to Chronic Disease Management in Primary Health Care,
John Dorland and Mary Ann McColl (eds.), 2007.
Paper ISBN 978-1-55339-130-2 Cloth ISBN 978-1-55339-131-9

Fulfilling Potential, Creating Success: Perspectives on Human Capital Development,
Garnett Picot, Ron Saunders, and Arthur Sweetman (eds.), 2007.
Paper ISBN 978-1-55339-127-2 Cloth ISBN 978-1-55339-128-9

Reinventing Canadian Defence Procurement: A View from the Inside, Alan S. Williams, 2006.
Paper ISBN 0-9781693-0-1 (Published in association with Breakout Educational
Network)

SARS in Context: Memory, History, Policy, Jacalyn Duffin, and Arthur Sweetman (eds.),
2006. Paper ISBN 978-0-7735-3194-9 Cloth ISBN 978-0-7735-3193-2
(Published in association with McGill-Queen's University Press)

Dreamland: How Canada's Pretend Foreign Policy has Undermined Sovereignty, Roy Rempel,
2006. Paper ISBN 1-55339-118-7 Cloth ISBN 1-55339-119-5
(Published in association with Breakout Educational Network)

Canadian and Mexican Security in the New North America: Challenges and Prospects,
Jordi Díez (ed.), 2006. Paper ISBN 978-1-55339-123-4 Cloth ISBN 978-1-55339-122-7

*Global Networks and Local Linkages: The Paradox of Cluster Development in an Open
Economy,* David A. Wolfe and Matthew Lucas (eds.), 2005.
Paper ISBN 1-55339-047-4 Cloth ISBN 1-55339-048-2

Choice of Force: Special Operations for Canada, David Last, and Bernd Horn (eds.), 2005.
Paper ISBN 1-55339-044-X Cloth ISBN 1-55339-045-8

Force of Choice: Perspectives on Special Operations, Bernd Horn, J. Paul de B. Taillon, and
David Last (eds.), 2004. Paper ISBN 1-55339-042-3 Cloth 1-55339-043-1

New Missions, Old Problems, Douglas L. Bland, David Last, Franklin Pinch, and
Alan Okros (eds.), 2004. Paper ISBN 1-55339-034-2 Cloth 1-55339-035-0

*The North American Democratic Peace: Absence of War and Security Institution-Building in
Canada-US Relations, 1867-1958,* Stéphane Roussel, 2004.
Paper ISBN 0-88911-937-6 Cloth 0-88911-932-2

Implementing Primary Care Reform: Barriers and Facilitators, Ruth Wilson, S.E.D. Shortt
and John Dorland (eds.), 2004. Paper ISBN 1-55339-040-7 Cloth 1-55339-041-5

Social and Cultural Change, David Last, Franklin Pinch, Douglas L. Bland, and
Alan Okros (eds.), 2004. Paper ISBN 1-55339-032-6 Cloth 1-55339-033-4

Clusters in a Cold Climate: Innovation Dynamics in a Diverse Economy, David A. Wolfe
and Matthew Lucas (eds.), 2004. Paper ISBN 1-55339-038-5 Cloth 1-55339-039-3

Canada Without Armed Forces? Douglas L. Bland (ed.), 2004.
Paper ISBN 1-55339-036-9 Cloth 1-55339-037-7

Campaigns for International Security: Canada's Defence Policy at the Turn of the Century,
Douglas L. Bland and Sean M. Maloney, 2004.
Paper ISBN 0-88911-962-7 Cloth 0-88911-964-3

Understanding Innovation in Canadian Industry, Fred Gault (ed.), 2003.
Paper ISBN 1-55339-030-X Cloth 1-55339-031-8

Delicate Dances: Public Policy and the Nonprofit Sector, Kathy L. Brock (ed.), 2003.
Paper ISBN 0-88911-953-8 Cloth 0-88911-955-4

Beyond the National Divide: Regional Dimensions of Industrial Relations,
Mark Thompson, Joseph B. Rose and Anthony E. Smith (eds.), 2003.
Paper ISBN 0-88911-963-5 Cloth 0-88911-965-1

The Nonprofit Sector in Interesting Times: Case Studies in a Changing Sector,
Kathy L. Brock and Keith G. Banting (eds.), 2003.
Paper ISBN 0-88911-941-4 Cloth 0-88911-943-0

Clusters Old and New: The Transition to a Knowledge Economy in Canada's Regions,
David A. Wolfe (ed.), 2003. Paper ISBN 0-88911-959-7 Cloth 0-88911-961-9

The e-Connected World: Risks and Opportunities, Stephen Coleman (ed.), 2003.
Paper ISBN 0-88911-945-7 Cloth 0-88911-947-3

Institute of Intergovernmental Relations

*Canada: The State of the Federation 2006/07: Transitions – Fiscal and Political Federalism in
an Era of Change*, vol. 20, John R. Allan, Thomas J. Courchene, and Christian
Leuprecht (eds.), 2009. Paper ISBN 978-1-55339-189-0 Cloth ISBN 978-1-55339-191-3

Comparing Federal Systems, Third Edition, Ronald L. Watts, 2008.
Paper ISBN 978-1-55339-188-3

*Canada: The State of the Federation 2005: Quebec and Canada in the New Century – New
Dynamics, New Opportunities*, vol. 19, Michael Murphy (ed.), 2007.
Paper ISBN 978-1-55339-018-3 Cloth ISBN 978-1-55339-017-6

Spheres of Governance: Comparative Studies of Cities in Multilevel Governance Systems,
Harvey Lazar and Christian Leuprecht (eds.), 2007.
Paper ISBN 978-1-55339-019-0 Cloth ISBN 978-1-55339-129-6

Canada: The State of the Federation 2004, vol. 18, *Municipal-Federal-Provincial Relations
in Canada*, Robert Young and Christian Leuprecht (eds.), 2006.
Paper ISBN 1-55339-015-6 Cloth ISBN 1-55339-016-4

Canadian Fiscal Arrangements: What Works, What Might Work Better, Harvey Lazar
(ed.), 2005. Paper ISBN 1-55339-012-1 Cloth ISBN 1-55339-013-X

Canada: The State of the Federation 2003, vol. 17, *Reconfiguring Aboriginal-State Relations*,
Michael Murphy (ed.), 2005. Paper ISBN 1-55339-010-5 Cloth ISBN 1-55339-011-3

Canada: The State of the Federation 2002, vol. 16, *Reconsidering the Institutions of
Canadian Federalism*, J. Peter Meekison, Hamish Telford and Harvey Lazar (eds.),
2004. Paper ISBN 1-55339-009-1 Cloth ISBN 1-55339-008-3

*Federalism and Labour Market Policy: Comparing Different Governance and Employment
Strategies*, Alain Noël (ed.), 2004. Paper ISBN 1-55339-006-7 Cloth ISBN 1-55339-007-5

The Impact of Global and Regional Integration on Federal Systems: A Comparative Analysis,
Harvey Lazar, Hamish Telford, and Ronald L. Watts (eds.), 2003.
Paper ISBN 1-55339-002-4 Cloth ISBN 1-55339-003-2

John Deutsch Institute for the Study of Economic Policy

The 2006 Federal Budget: Rethinking Fiscal Priorities, Charles M. Beach, Michael Smart and Thomas A. Wilson (eds.), 2007.
Paper ISBN 978-1-55339-125-8 Cloth ISBN 978-1-55339-126-6

Health Services Restructuring in Canada: New Evidence and New Directions,
Charles M. Beach, Richard P. Chaykowksi, Sam Shortt, France St-Hilaire, and Arthur Sweetman (eds.), 2006.
Paper ISBN 978-1-55339-076-3 Cloth ISBN 978-1-55339-075-6

A Challenge for Higher Education in Ontario, Charles M. Beach (ed.), 2005.
Paper ISBN 1-55339-074-1 Cloth ISBN 1-55339-073-3

Current Directions in Financial Regulation, Frank Milne, and Edwin H. Neave (eds.), Policy Forum Series no. 40, 2005. Paper ISBN 1-55339-072-5 Cloth ISBN 1-55339-071-7

Higher Education in Canada, Charles M. Beach, Robin W. Boadway, and
R. Marvin McInnis (eds.), 2005. Paper ISBN 1-55339-070-9 Cloth ISBN 1-55339-069-5

Financial Services and Public Policy, Christopher Waddell (ed.), 2004.
Paper ISBN 1-55339-068-7 Cloth ISBN 1-55339-067-9

The 2003 Federal Budget: Conflicting Tensions, Charles M. Beach, and Thomas A. Wilson (eds.), Policy Forum Series no. 39, 2004.
Paper ISBN 0-88911-958-9 Cloth ISBN 0-88911-956-2

Canadian Immigration Policy for the 21st Century, Charles M. Beach, Alan G. Green, and Jeffrey G. Reitz (eds.), 2003. Paper ISBN 0-88911-954-6 Cloth ISBN 0-88911-952-X

Framing Financial Structure in an Information Environment, Thomas J. Courchene and Edwin H. Neave (eds.), Policy Forum Series no. 38, 2003.
Paper ISBN 0-88911-950-3 Cloth ISBN 0-88911-948-1

Our publications may be purchased at leading bookstores, including the Queen's University Bookstore
(http://www.campusbookstore.com/), or can be ordered online from:
McGill-Queen's University Press, at
http://mqup.mcgill.ca/ordering.php

For more information about new and backlist titles from Queen's Policy Studies, visit the McGill-Queen's
University Press web site at:
http://mqup.mcgill.ca/